Antique Clothing
French Sewing by Machine

Printed by The C. J. Krehbiel Company
Cincinnati, Ohio

Published and Distributed by
Martha Pullen Company, Inc.
518 Madison Street
Huntsville, Alabama 35801
(205) 533-9586

ISBN 1-878048-00-7

Antique Clothing
French Sewing by Machine

by Martha Campbell Pullen, Ph. D.

Illustrations by Angela Cataldo, Cynthia Handy, and Diane Zinser
Photography by Jack Cooper and Di Lewis
Editing and Photography Styling by Amelia Johanson
Book Design by Joia Thompson
Construction/Technical Editing by Kathy McMakin

Dedication

On October 3, 1918, in a small rural house in Jackson County, Alabama, Anna Ruth Dicus Campbell was born. The first child of Belle Baker Dicus and Leonard Houston Dicus came into this world with red hair, a high IQ, and a lot of spunk. These things have never changed. Three years later, her only brother, George Houston Dicus, would arrive. He was one of the greatest joys of her life; his pet name for her was "Sister Fox." Since her heritage included a mother who attended college to become a teacher prior to 1910, it certainly is no surprise that her educational achievements have far surpassed those of most women of her generation. Her Daddy not only farmed several farms at one time, he also built all of the nice houses in Scottsboro. Overachievers certainly lived under one roof. A weekly trip to the library was the highlight of her childhood. Mama, Uncle George, and her first cousins, Billy, Albert, Erskine, David, and Elizabeth (for whom I am named) would travel in the buggy and each check out one book; that was all they were allowed to check out at one time. The whole morning would be spent arguing over which seven books would be chosen. Believe it or not, most of that group of seven children read all seven books each week.

One degree wasn't enough for her; by 1958 she had received her master's and educational specialist's degrees from George Peabody College. For more than 30 years, she served the children and adults of Jackson County as a classroom teacher and later as an administrator of Northeast Alabama Junior College. She was, and presently is, the first woman to be appointed to the Jackson County hospital board; at age 71, she was reappointed for another six-year term. She has served in a volunteer capacity as the teacher's association president of Northeast State Junior College, on the Jackson County Council on Aging, on the board of directors of Jackson County Heritage Center and R.S.V.P. She has served as vice president of the Alabama Retired Teachers Association and the Jackson County Historical Association, on the board of PTA and band boosters. Also, at age 71, she began serving with the Kairos Ministry, which goes into prisons to minister to the inmates. She was elected president of the United Methodist Women at the First United Methodist Church of Scottsboro, Alabama; she has taught Sunday school in this church for approximately 40 years. She is a member of Sigma Tau Delta (English honorary), Kappa Mu Epsilon (mathematics honorary), Delta Kappa Gamma (teacher honorary), Daughters of American Revolution, Alabama Education Association, National Education Association, and American Association Of University Women.

On April 27, 1990, Mama was chosen as Jackson County/Scottsboro Chamber of Commerce's, Citizen of the Year. She was the first woman recipient of this prestigious award. Letters, encouraging the nomination, came from all over Alabama.

This book, the antique illustrations, the French sewing techniques, the beautiful photographs, every last word is devoted to Mama. I guess my sister, Mary, put it best, "Mama's priorities are always in the God-given order — God first, family second, then community and career. Perhaps it is because of these deeply-ingrained values that she has the unusual gift of energy and love to apply to all of these areas."

I have never known anyone who loves Jackson County as much as mother. She has always thought the flowers smelled sweeter, the people were nicer, and the school children just a little smarter in Jackson County. She — and my grandmother before her — has been serving the children and older students of Jackson County with the most fervent desire to offer the best educational opportunities possible.

I think God must have called my mother to the school system of Jackson County as surely as He called her grandson, John, to preach the gospel. Mama has been a teacher all her life, not just directly, as in her 32 years with the Alabama public school system, but also indirectly, through the way she chose to live her life. When I was a child, a week never went by that Mama didn't buy medicine, clothing, underwear, shoes, or other essential items for the less fortunate children in her classrooms. I remember parents arriving at our house at all hours of the night, crying because their children had run away or had gotten themselves into trouble. Mama was always there to cry with them. Today, many of those same children appear on her doorstep to tell her she made a real difference in their lives.

My mother is a champion of the poor. She offers help to anyone in need of a job or better education, if not financially, through caring words and encouragement. Her main purpose in life is to serve the Lord, living by his rules. And, just as she enhances the lives of those in her community, she gives nothing less then her all to a family that adores her. She has never put her needs above her family's needs. She and my father worked hard to provide the best educations for their children. They always offered the kind of guidance God asked them to provide through his teachings.

When I travel around the world, teaching sewing and promoting my books, I'm often asked, "Where do you get the inspiration to do what you do?" God is the giver of all gifts and He blessed me with the perfect mother. I was taught to never be lazy, never quit, and never forget to share what God has given you.

Nearly all of my life, I have seen my mama bake a cake or cook a casserole for a neighbor who had a death in the family. She believes that when people have troubles, you bake them something good to eat and tell them you love them. You also, according to Mama, see if the house needs cleaning, and offer a hand.

When she was nominated for Citizen of the Year, Bruce Patterson, the executive director of the Jackson County Chamber of Commerce, wrote: "We can say that Anna Ruth leaves peace, forgiveness, contentment, flowers of joy, and most of all, love for her fellowman wherever she goes. She leaves a legacy of uplift, encouragement, and inspiration to so many, young and old, in every walk of life. Care, work, alert watchfulness, skill, concern, and self-sacrifice are also traits of Anna Ruth. She never fails to let one know that God is her refuge and strength and that anyone whose faith is as strong as hers is not far from help; this shows through in her personality.

"The people of Scottsboro and Jackson County should say, "thank you" to Anna Ruth for her unselfish contributions."

Mama, I too say "thank you" for your never-ending love and support — I love you with all my heart.

Your daughter,

Martha

Acknowledgements ═══════════════════════════════════════

Psalm 23
A psalm of David.

1 The Lord is my shepherd; I shall not want.
2 He maketh me to lie down in green pastures, he leadeth me beside the still waters.
3 He restoreth my soul; he leadeth me in the paths of righteousness for his name's sake.
4 Yea, though I walk through the valley of the shadow of death, I will fear no evil; for thou art with me; thy rod and thy staff they comfort me.
5 Thou preparest a table before me in the presence of mine enemies; thou anointest my head with oil; my cup runneth over.
6 Surely goodness and mercy shall follow me all the days of my life; and I will dwell in the house of the Lord for ever.

Writing a book this complicated and lengthy requires the help, dedication, and talents of many individuals. I have been very blessed with people who willingly help make my dreams a reality. Although my name appears on the cover of this book, each of these names certainly deserves cover billing also. The encouragement, help, suggestions, inspiration, work, ideas, and love of a number of people always will be a cornerstone for what success I may attain. To the following people, I will be eternally grateful.

My mother and father, Anna Ruth Dicus Campbell and Paul Jones Campbell were my first and greatest teachers. They taught me, among other things, that dreams are not impossible, stars are not unreachable, wrongs are not unrightable, and sorrows are not unbearable. The most important lesson that I learned from my parents was to turn to God first because He is unfailing.

My cousin, Christine Finch Jenkins, spent hours upon hours with me, teaching immature hands to make wonderful things, including Christmas stockings.

My high school home economics teacher, Mrs. Sarah Betty Ingram, instilled the love of sewing even further. She believed that we could sew anything!

My late mother- and father-in-law, Dr. Joyce Buren Pullen and Emma Hodges Pullen contributed hours upon hours of child care, cooking, and encouragement for all of my career ventures. Without their generous gift of time, I doubt that finishing my Ph.D. would have been possible.

My husband's aunt, Anna Mary McDonald, has been more like a mother to Joe and me. She is always there to support us and encourage us in all that we do. She is a very courageous lady who has handled arthritis and all of its problems with grace and dignity.

My friend, Mrs. Lili Jones, has kept my home intact, and has ironed millions of hours on these Swiss batiste clothes for both this book and the magazine.

My late nephew, Alex Walter Jackson, killed by a drunk driver. For all the joy one little, gorgeous, blonde boy could give a family in a short seven years. I would like to thank Mothers Against Drunk Driving for their untiring efforts to get drunk drivers off the highways.

My sister and brother-in-law, Mary and Rick Nixon, for encouraging me in the business, for hours of driving Anna and David to the photo shoots and for squealing over the clothes that I make for the children.

My sister, Dottie, my brothers Cliff and Robin, and their precious families for loving me and for always being proud of my accomplishments.

My son, William Campbell Crocker, for loving me and always putting up with me. Camp's interest in this business, sewing, publishing, people, and selling have earned him a future place in the organizational structure of this business. I have always said that Camp could "sell snowballs in Alaska" because he loves people so much and because he has an uncanny zest and enthusiasm for living. He will be joining the firm upon graduation from Arizona State University with a degree in psychology.

My future daughter-in-law, Laura Welch, for loving Camp and for putting up with him. I am grateful to her for being engaged to Camp, for teaching him about the importance of a college degree and for helping him to obtain his. Her sweet and quiet example for disciplined work before play has changed Camp's life. She is a wonderful Christian who has her values in the proper order: God, family, and work.

My son, John Houston Crocker, for loving me and always putting up with me. John's complete love of the Lord and his unselfish missionary work in Africa continue to thrill me. I have never known any human being who had a more tender and giving heart toward those less fortunate than he. A lot of people will suffer less as a result of John and his wife, Suzanne's, work. I pray that my business will continue to be successful so I can have a financial part in helping them to evangelize, to build churches, and to bring medical clinics to people in Africa for the rest of my lifetime.

My daughter-in-law, Suzanne Laramore Crocker, for loving John and putting up with him. Sometimes you are so blessed from God to have a daughter who thinks only of the Lord's work and of her family. She has treated thousands of people in make-shift medical clinics in Togo. Her unselfishness and her devotion to God's work in Africa and to her family are terribly unusual. Not many wives would love living without electricity, running water, and the necessities of life to follow a husband to Africa to preach.

My son, Mark Edward Pullen, for loving me and always putting up with me. Mark is my great communicator, always counseling and putting things in the proper perspective. Mark's hard work and discipline have almost earned him a dental degree. Mark is not only a competent person but a caring person. It will be a very exciting day for our family when Mark becomes the third generation of Pullen dentists in Huntsville.

Acknowledgements

My daughter-in-law Sherry Ann Green Pullen, for loving Mark and putting up with him. God blessed our family the day that Mark married Sherry Ann. Sherry Ann wrote the book on gentleness, unselfishness, kindness, hard work, consideration, and thoroughly spoiling a husband. When you have your priorities in the correct Christian order, as Sherry Ann does, I shouldn't be too surprised that the Lord would give her these qualities to share with others.

My son, Jeffrey David Pullen, for loving me and always putting up with me. Jeff has the extraordinary ability to love people and help them to understand how special and important they are. Jeff also works harder than anyone I have ever known to do his job and to help others do their jobs as well. My heart almost bursts with pride when Jeff's former employees nearly cry telling me that "Jeff was the most fair and best boss we ever had." We are so proud of the incredible success Jeff has had in two short years in major corporations of this country--Marriott and Hilton.

My future daughter-in-law, Angela Cataldo, for loving Jeff and putting up with him. Our family received one of its greatest blessings the day that God gave us our "Angel." Angela is one of the artists for this book and what an artist she is. She is a wonderful Christian woman who will always put God first, her family second, and her work third. To get such a Godly daughter-in-law and such an outstanding artist in one person is a real blessing.

Joanna Emma Joyce Pullen is the reason I became involved in the French sewing business in the first place. When my little girl was born after four boys, you can just imagine my excitement over my real live doll. All I wanted to do was hold her, tell her how wonderful she was, and dress her up in different dresses and lacy accessories. These clothes are love clothes for Joanna. Joanna is sweet , gentle, quiet, and caring. She loves people, especially children and can't stand to see anyone cry or be lonely. Her volunteer efforts have been phenomenal for a young child; she especially loves volunteering with children and senior citizens. Her talents in dance, gymnastics, drama, singing, and public speaking will take her far in life either professionally or in volunteer work. She is a champion for people less fortunate than she. She is a beautiful Christian, whom I believe God will use mightily in her teen years to influence other teens to stay away from drugs, alcohol, and immorality. She has been a joy every day of her life, and I thank God for entrusting her to us.

Within the heirloom sewing industry there are several people who not only help make this industry what it is today but who have also had a great influence on my life.

Margaret Boyles has always been there for me with her encouragement and creative ideas. She has taught in my schools, written for the magazine, and been one of my number-one supporters.

Elizabeth Travis Johnson can be thanked for being the cornerstone in making this industry what it is today. Without her foundation through the last 40 years, I doubt that smocking and French sewing would have the same flavor and importance in today's international society. I would certainly call her the "Mother Of Heirloom Sewing."

Mildred Turner has been one of my closest friends from that first day she walked by my booth in her lavender ultra-suede suit and told me that she adored heirloom sewing as much as I did. She has written and written for the magazine, taught in my schools, and always been one of my best and most loyal customers.

Eunice Farmer, the mentor to my whole sewing business. She is a beautiful friend and a wonderful inspiration to all who love the sewing world.

I would like to thank each and every teacher who has ever travelled to Huntsville to teach at my School Of Art Fashion during the past six years. Please accept my gratitude for all that they have meant and continue to mean to me.

I would like to thank each and every student of mine, subscriber to *Sew Beautiful* magazine, shop owner who sells Martha Pullen products of any type, and customer of Martha Pullen Co., Inc. Without your loyalty over the years, this book wouldn't have been written because there wouldn't have been any Martha Pullen Company!

No business could be a reality without the talents of many people. This first set of individuals have "run" the business, while the others in the group wrote and produced this book. They are joys in my life and so appreciated for all that they do, day after day, year after year.

Kathy Pearce for loyalty, joy, steadfastness, and competency; Yulanda Brazelton for extra errands, encouragement, and sweet words; Sandra Wilbourn for accuracy, encouragement, and calmness; Westa Chandler for efficiency, counseling with subscribers, and smiling even when two mailbags of envelopes come in the door; Donna King for sweetness, efficiency, and availability when needed.

There are individuals who physically worked on this book in particular. There are not words to express my complete gratitude to them for making this project a reality, not just a dream. I will attempt to thank these vital people for their efforts on this book.

The first people that I would like to thank for their part in this book are my precious models and their mothers. They always wait so patiently and smile so beautifully. They deserve lots of credit for their outstanding performances. I love them, and I thank them. For purposes of child safety, I will list them by first name only: Joanna, Kim, Brooke, Gina, Julie, Misty, Christian, Rebekah, Coulter, Lindsay, Susan, Melissa, Heather, Wilson, Elizabeth, Kathryn, Anna, David, Amelia, Stephanie, Judy, Allison, Warren, Micheryl, Sarah, Lauren, Joseph, Erin, Elizabeth, William, Sarah Marie, John, Adam, Harris, Eleanor, Pam, Kim, Patty, Kay, Cason, Shelley, Leah, Abby, Mirinda, Rachel and Jessica.

The Bethnal Green Museum of Childhood, which is a division of the Victoria and Albert Museum, London, England, has graciously consented to allow us to use the photography that we did several years ago while were visiting and researching part of their costume collection. I would like to personally thank Noreen Marshall, children's costume curator, for her knowledge and her uplifting manner of helping people. She is one of the most delightful people that I have ever met in my life, and the museum is my very favorite.

Acknowledgements

Di Lewis photographed all of the museum clothing while we were on location in London. Her work is of the highest quality, and she is a lovely person to know.

Susan York made some gorgeous garments from our new patterns and loaned us many of her other collection for photography.

Dody Baker made garments, at the last minute, from our patterns so we would have more to show you, using the fabulous patterns in this book.

Kay Becraft brought hundreds of props to my house for the photo shoot and designed some of the settings. She also made garments for the photo shoot.

Lynn Swanson of Lynn Swanson Interiors worked with me one year to reform my house into the Victorian setting for this book.

Jack Cooper photographed all of this book with the exception of the Bethnal Green Museum Of Childhood portion of the photos. His patience with children and his keen eye for making a picture "happen" has been very appreciated for this book.

Louise Baird was the creator of my vision for Richelieu Bars on the collar of the blouse pattern included in the book. I drew what I wanted for a blouse with scallops, stitched bars, and fabric flowers. In her usually talented and precious manner, she mastered those bars, those scallops, and those flowers and then wrote the pattern directions and the machine embroidery instructions for us.

Patty Smith has sewn overtime for years to make all of our publications a success. Her design and sewing skills are known all over the world and she can make more dresses under pressure than anyone in the industry.

Becky Lambert for helping coordinate the photo shoots and other aspects of writing this book. Becky is always willing to help with the whole business in any way possible.

Margaret Taylor for writing pattern directions, sewing garments from the unmarked pattern pieces, helping coordinate the photo shoots, helping write some of the technique sections, and making a million phone calls and writing lots of letters concerning details, details, and more details. I certainly can't forget her typing all of the orders into the computer.

Cynthia Handy for working with me several months to illustrate this book. Cynthia's lace absolutely dances, and her original shadow work embroidery designs are breathtaking.

Diane Zinser for illustrating all of the pattern directions, lots of the book, and for helping write some of the technique instructions. Diane's sewing ability is invaluable since some of the illustrations she simply drew from my writing. Her antique clothing section illustrations are so real they seem to be more than 100 years old.

Angela Cataldo for designing, with her pen and ink, new garments from antique ideas and for illustrating most of the antique garments from my personal collection. She will become Angela Pullen this summer since she will marry my son, Jeff. Just look for more "Pullen and Pullen." Angela's dresses seem to breathe, and the creativity for garment design in her head is almost unbelievable.

Kathy McMakin for designing, writing pattern directions, helping me with lots of the techniques, creating some of the techniques, proofing, sewing some of the garments, and always reminding me not to quit. Kathy has been writing with me for so long, that I cannot ever imagine days when she wasn't helping me do everything. She is a critical and vital link to any of my business endeavors from travelling and teaching to writing.

Scott Wright, who now works with me, took my original attempt (a box of photographs, homemade art, typed manuscript with lots of typos, and pretty color slides) at writing a book back in 1983 and put it together in book form. It became a best seller; I soon hired Scott! He has designed the layout on the color section of this book with his usual talent and creativity.

Amelia Johanson has more journalistic and artistic talent in one finger than most of us ever acquire in a lifetime. I have renamed her "Ms. Magic Words" because her command of the English language is more delightful than any I have ever known. She can edit the most ordinary of words into lovely phrases, which seem to live and breathe. Her work in editing this book delights me.

Joia Thompson's book design was carefully researched and planned before she made her final decisions about the most wonderful and beautiful presentation. She has been working overtime for months executing exactly the right type of creativity for each section and perfectly placing hundreds of illustrations in the correct order, which is no small matter in a sewing/technique book. I love her design and layout of this book. I thank her for hundreds of hours in making this gorgeous book come alive.

There is one person to whom I am especially grateful for not only this book but for the whole business success I have had. My husband, Joe Ross Pullen, has always believed in me more than I believed in myself. He encourages me to "go ahead and try" any publishing or product that I think might be successful. He wants me to be happy in my work, and he has always been willing to pay the bills to keep my business going, through the hard times. He is one of the most wonderful Christian men that I have ever known, and I admire him not only for his local dental work but also for his dental missionary work with our church. He has a heart of gold, which goes out to those less fortunate than he and this book is not long enough to name the thousands of people for whom he has done free dentistry and for whom he has bought food and medical supplies. His love of dentistry and learning has led him all over the world to study implant dentistry and to 15 countries to teach other dentists how to do implants. One of my fondest dreams for the next few years is that I can take over a little more of the bill paying, and that Joe can do a little more horseback riding and farming. He is so faithful to God's work; he is so faithful to his family's needs and desires; and he is so faithful to making sure that I can realize my business dreams, including the publishing of this book. He is my best friend and my partner; I love him and I thank him.

Antique Clothing
French Sewing by Machine

Table of Contents

Foreword

by Pati Palmer, President
Palmer/Pletsch Associates

Martha Pullen is in the center of a world of creativity most of us can only imagine being a part of. Yet, she has inspired hundreds of thousands of you to find your creative essence and helped you develop it.

When Martha and I were both guest speakers in Australia last year, I got to know her personally. It is always a delight to see a positive, fun, and talented person in the fashion sewing industry. My only regret was that she preempted me on Australian television. The previous year I'd appeared on a show similar to our Today Show. This year her wonderful southern accent captured Australia's heart and I say, "More power to her!!" A salute to all of you Southerners. She represented America exceedingly well.

Martha is the only person I know in this industry that could truly produce a "museum quality" book. Her flair, attachment to history, and desire to inspire make her unique in book publishing.

As the Education Committee Chairman of the American Home Economics Association and being very concerned about our youth learning to direct their free time to rewarding experiences such as sewing, I applaud Martha Pullen. She believes in youth and their capabilities, in sewing as a beautiful skill that gives a great sense of self-worth, and in all of our futures.

Read this beautiful book and be inspired. Create an heirloom based on Martha Pullen's inspiration. You will have your own original to value as much as Martha values those in her collection.

I still get goose bumps thinking about the very first French dress I made. Has a decade passed already? What a blessing these 10 years have been. Starting a business centered around heirloom sewing opened up a whole new world for me. My love of "white clothes" has only deepened. Looking back, it seems when I wasn't sewing lace garments, I was rummaging through antique stores and flea markets, hoping to add to the heirloom clothing collection, which would someday be the subject of my first hardback book. I searched the United States, Australia, and England to put together a stunning collection of turn-of-the-century garments. I don't think I've ever gone into an antique store without saying to myself, "I bet a real beauty is waiting for me in here." Now, all of my beauties await you in the pages of this book.

This book has several objectives. First, I wanted to share my antique collection and the techniques used to create these garments. In doing so, I've included advanced lace shaping techniques with easy-to-understand directions and step-by-step drawings. Some people are terrified by the idea of making diamonds, hearts, flip-flopped bows, ovals, and scallops. Yet, with clear directions, lace shapes are a snap. I spent months writing "first-grade easy" instructions. I also updated my original French sewing techniques, adding to them some new ideas. A lot has happened in this field since my last book was published in 1985.

Second, I wanted to encourage you to borrow ideas from antique garments and apply them to clothing that is more suitable for today. I developed a collection of patterns for you to use as as the basis for designing your own garments. Four beautiful and serviceable patterns are included in the pattern envelope. To encourage your creativity, my artists and I redesigned several antique dresses, revising the original lines and details to fit the to-the-waist and middy patterns.

Third, I hoped to feature new and old French sewn clothing through gorgeous color photography, so you could see for yourself these priceless pieces. I first advertised that there would be 16 pages of color in the book; but after reviewing my collection, I knew I'd have to expand the color section. There are now 48 full-color pages for you to enjoy. Also included in this section are a number of photographs courtesy of the Bethnal Green Museum of Childhood, a division of The Victoria and Albert Museum in London, England. Photographer Di Lewis captured some of the Bethnal Green collection on film, and I appreciate the museum's permission to reprint her work.

Fourth, as I have travelled and taught during the last 10 years, many questions have been put to me concerning French sewing basics. Thus, I decided to include question-and-answer sections at the end of the technique chapters, to address these "most asked" questions. Just remember, there is no one way to do "French sewing;" my responses are simply suggestions to get you started.

Fifth, I believe that there are some methods presented in this book that have never been recorded. These techniques were taken from some of the antique garments in my collection. Patterns and instruction books were scarce around the turn of the century; individual sewing skills and personal ingenuity were about the only tools with which a seamstress had to work. In today's heirloom industry, which, by the way, is absolutely taking the world by storm, there are patterns and books in abundance. Heirloom-type outfits worn by the Royal children have had worldwide impact on the revival of this type of clothing. Costume collections are prominently displayed in museums everywhere.

Finally, new magazines, particularly *Victoria* from the Hearst Corporation, reinforce a joyful return to romantic clothing for women and children. I have long loved the classics of Laura Ashley and Ralph Lauren, and now the clothing industry is playing host to a Victorian influence through other designer works.They are feminine, classic, and flattering to a woman.

I started making heirloom clothing as "love clothes" for my daughter, Joanna. That's really what these clothes are, love clothes made for very special children. I'm sure this held true when the antique clothing was being made. Mothers have always loved dressing their children, and these clothes say, "You are the most wonderful child in the world." I am looking forward to the day when I will have grandchildren to dress.

Since French sewing by machine is such easy sewing, it is a pleasure to share its magic. It always gives me a feeling of contentment when I introduce someone to French sewing by machine only to hear them remark, "To be so beautiful, this is so easy!" Before concluding this introduction, I must tell you that it is so much fun to French sew, to have your special child be the center of attention, and for that child to say, "Mommy made it.!" Don't be afraid to tackle anything in this book.I feel sure you can do it! It is the easiest sewing that I have ever done, I promise.

This book has been written with love for you to enjoy!

- **Martha Campbell Pullen**

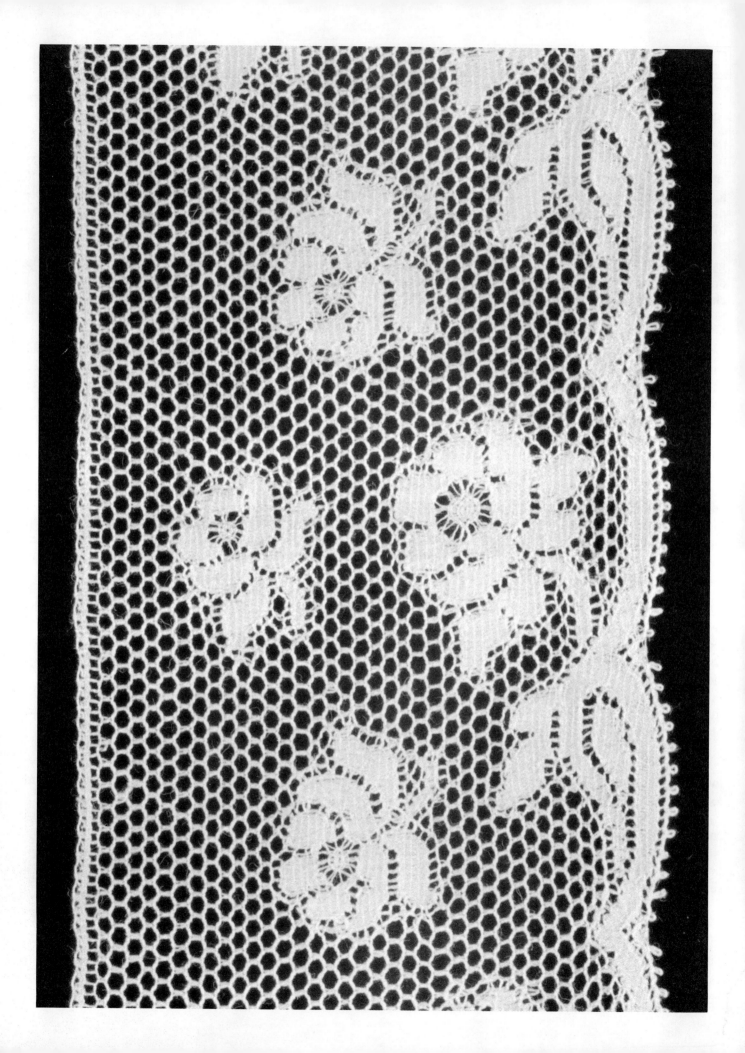

Martha's Collection

Chapter One

Martha's Favorites
Breathtaking style,
stunning techniques.
Elegant, yet simple.

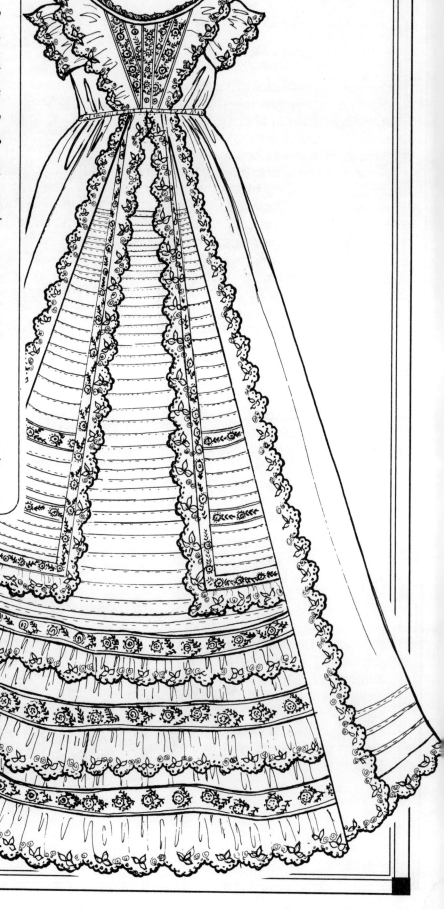

Each time I found an heirloom garment at a flea market or antique store, my mind raced to the book I would one day write. How would this piece fit in? What elements could I reproduce in a modern-day French sewn garment? What techniques did the seamstress use? And how would my readers benefit from seeing this dress?

I bought some dresses for a single feature, a single detail. Others tickled me with simplicity and elegance because they could be re-created easily. There were some with breathtaking style, filled with stunning techniques. And then there were garments I was drawn to for no particular reason, other than their beauty. I can't tell you why I bought each and every piece. I just hope, with all of my heart, that through these descriptions and Angela's and Cynthia's drawings, you enjoy reading about my collection as much as I have enjoyed building it and recording its glory. Enjoy!

Royal Christening Dress

- Australia, circa 1880

Among my collection of Australian garments is this gorgeous christening gown (illustrated on the opposite page). The scooped neckline style leads me to believe it was constructed between 1850 and 1880, however, the machine work, including the eyelet, places the piece closer to 1880. Swiss-manufactured eyelets first began coming out of Switzerland about 1850. They were commonly used in fine, baby garments by 1880. Machine sewing of tucks began to appear around 1870. Before this time, the garments were usually made entirely by hand. A combination of tucks and insertions was used in the 1870s and 1880s. These tucked-front gowns remained very popular until 1900. Another sign that the dress was made closer to 1880 is the triangular panel in the front.

The whole front panel is one piece of fabric, tucked completely across. The front panel measures 34 inches long. It is 9 inches wide at the very top and 18 inches wide at the very bottom. The tucks are 1/8-inch tucks, placed 1/2 inch apart. There are 41 tucks, total, on the christening dress panel. The white-on-white embroidered insertion is 1-1/4 inches wide. Where the tucking panel stops and the straight insertion begins on the panel, the measurement is 14 inches across.

On the bodice, the center panel of embroidered insertion is straight; the others are placed at angles, tucked under this one straight piece of embroidered insertion. The Swiss embroidered edging is 2-1/4 inches wide. It is used around part of the tucks on the tucked panel, underneath the insertion on the bottom portion of the tucked panel, around the bottom of the dress, on the sleeve, on the bodice, and up and down the whole tucked panel on the front. The bias binding at the top of the bodice of the dress is 1/4 inch wide; it is made like a casing, and a string is run through it to adjust the neckline for individual fit for infants.

The dress laps right over left when viewed from behind. There are no buttons or buttonholes; beauty pins were probably used to close the back. There may be some concern as to whether a baby could wear a dress of this style during the cooler months. These short-sleeved, low-necked dresses were indeed worn during the day.

Variation Of Royal Christening Dress

This dress is not in my collection. It is Cynthia Handy's artistic variation of the Royal Christening Dress. This artist's rendition (as shown on the following page) includes the gorgeous "Turn-Of-The-Century Diamond Shaping" technique along with puffing for a completely different christening dress. You can use this skirt idea not only for christening dresses but also for skirts, children's dresses, sleepwear, or aprons. I love the way she has placed the puffing in the center of the unique V shaping on the bodice. Exquisitely-placed lace, shaped around the puffing panel, makes this design a royal treat. The use of both French lace and Swiss eyelet in one dress is one of my all-time favorite ways to make a French garment.

Variation of
Royal Christening Dress

Fabulous Square-Yoke Middy

- Australia, circa 1885-1895

The search for this piece took me down two flights of stairs and through countless booths before I found the one antique clothing dealer rumored to be in this particular store. My roving was well worth it. The Swiss eyelet alone makes this dress a sight to behold. It's one of the most beautiful middy dresses I have ever seen. The square neckline of the dress lends itself to adapting one of the patterns in this book. Notice the mitering of the Swiss insertion with the entredeux on each side. Swiss eyelet travels over the sleeves and down to the slightly-dropped waistline. The lace trim on the front makes a beautiful mitered square about 2 inches down on the eyelet skirt of the dress. The sleeves have six tucks and rows of insertion at the top and bottom of the tucks. The skirt is made of bordered eyelet.

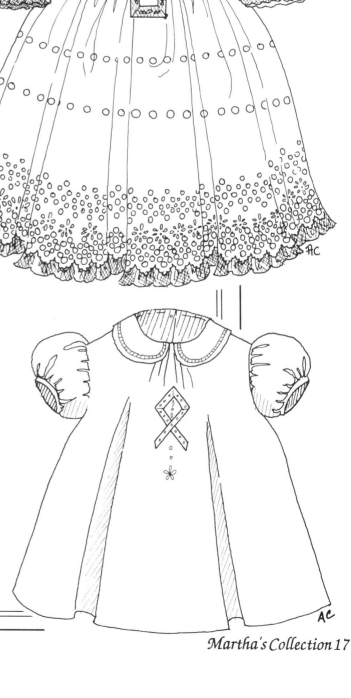

Plain, Sweet, Silk Dress

- America, circa 1935-1945

This New England child's dress is an ecru-on-ecru silk. The extended diamond and delicate embroidery at center front are the only embellishments. It is vintage 1935-1945. Slight gathers at the neckline add fullness to the garment, as do the two large pleats in the front. A plain bias binding fashions a cuff on the puffed sleeve.

Australian Organdy Masterpiece

- Australia, circa 1900

    On my first trip to Australia, I came across a bridal shop, which specializes in bridal garments with antique flair. Dripping with romantic bridal whites, the front room was enchanting. But, it wasn't until I walked into the second room that my heart practically stood still. Displayed on the wall, surrounded by silk flowers, antique shoes, old gloves, and other trousseau trinkets was this organdy antique dress. It would become the most beautiful garment in my collection.

    Hexoganal lace figures, shaped around hand embroidery, enhance the bodice. The lace shaping can be reproduced, using most any button-up-the-front pattern. Those same techniques would flatter the to- the-waist dresses, blouses, or middy patterns included in this book's pattern envelope.

Tucked Puffing Blouse

- America, circa 1900

This garment is the companion blouse to the skirt described below. The bodice has three sets of three tucks, 3/8 inch wide, spaced 1/8 inch apart. The sets of tucks are spaced 1 inch apart. The neckline is finished with a bias binding. The tucks at the top of the sleeves are 3/4 inch wide, gradually decreasing at the bottom of the sleeve to 3/8 inch wide. After straight stitches are run in the sleeve, they are gathered to make puffing. The sleeves of the blouse are lined with a relatively straight sleeve in the shape of the puffed over-sleeve. The waistline of the blouse is 22 inches. The blouse closes with hooks and handmade eyes on the shoulder and down the sleeves and side of the bodice.

Four-Ruffle Skirt

- America, circa 1900

I bought this batiste and lace skirt along with the "Tucked Puffing Blouse" at the Nashville Flea Market. Circa 1900, the skirt measures 45 inches in length and has a 22-inch waistline. Five gores enhance the circle design; the seams are French. Before adding ruffles, the seamstress put in a 10-inch hem, then stitched the four rows of 3-inch ruffles directly to the outside of the skirt. Logic holds that the designer opted for a large hem to reinforce the light batiste fabric and keep it from pulling under the weight of the ruffle rows. The lace-trimmed edge of each ruffle strategically covers the top of the next ruffle, thus hiding the top-stitching. The skirt is finished by turning up two turns on the bottom of each ruffle and straight-stitching the flat lace on top.

Beautifully-Embroidered 1890s Blouse
- America, circa 1890

Fig. 1

Purchased in Nashville, this blouse is typical of the 1890s. The original garment is white-on-white; however the floral embroidery easily accommodates color. Included here is a sketch of the embroidery for you to reproduce on any style blouse or dress. The shoulder details are illustrated in Figure 1. Figure 2 gives you the actual embroidery on the front, the center front, and on the panels, running down the sides of the center bodice.

Fig. 2

Tucks And Swiss Dress

- America, circa 1900

I was tempted to name this dress, "Puritan Dress," because it looks somewhat like the styles worn by our earliest settlers. The most appealing feature on this 1900 garment is the spectacular use of tucks. Tucks are everywhere; on the shoulders, the sleeves, and the skirt. Gathered eyelet trims the neckline, the sleeves, and the armscye. The "To-The-Waist" pattern in this book can be used to reproduce the "Tucks and Swiss Dress." The original is about a size 8; however, the subtle styling is appropriate for sizes up to 14.

Stripes And Curves Middy

- Australia, circa 1890

This dress was purchased from an antique clothing dealer on the outskirts of Sydney. Its charm is graceful simplicity. Using a few easy techniques — tucking on the skirt and zigzagging, Swiss insertion down the front and around the bodice — you can reproduce the antique design.

The trim on the bodice is almost like a bias tube finished with a featherstitch. A bias casing circles the neckline, enclosing a drawstring. This neckline treatment is common in heirloom clothing dated prior to 1910. The adjustable design assures a fit no matter what size the child's neck. It's logical, considering these garments were passed down for generations. The string also takes the place of a top button. Flat buttons, which continue down the front, are covered with batiste.

I am reasonably sure that these buttons are pearl, two-hole buttons. To cover them, a seamstress placed a circle of batiste on the front of the button, then stitched a smaller circle of batiste on the back.

The word "Carter" is written in black ink inside the dress. Additional markings, which read "C-2940," can be found in the neckline. I suspect that this is a commercially-made dress. My guess is that it was made for an exclusive customer by a dressmaker named Carter.

The "Victorian Middy" pattern by Ann Taylor for Martha Pullen would make a lovely reproduction of this design; however, any middy pattern could be adapted, including the two found in this book.

Crossed Tucks Silk Dress

- America, circa 1890

This dress came from a former student of mine who lives in California. The students who come to the Martha Pullen School Of Art Fashion often bring garments to see if I am interested in purchasing them, as was the case with this piece. Cross-tucking is an easy technique resulting in clean geometrical lines on the bodice of this dress.

This particular dress is made of ecru silk. The gathered waistline is relatively high for a middy. Four small tucks embellish the ruffle on the shoulder and the arms. Two large tucks enhance the skirt. Using the middy pattern with the round neckline in this book, you can easily re-create this dress.

High Yoke Slip

- America, circa 1900

This heavy Swiss batiste slip has bias bindings around the neck and the arms. The technique used to apply entredeux to the slip and to the laces is the "Folded Down Seam Allowance Method — 1/4-inch seam allowance." If you would like this style slip underneath your high yoke dresses, simply use the dress pattern, and take off a 5/8-inch seam allowance around the neck and armscye.

Fig. 1

Shadowwork Christening Dress
- America, circa 1915-1920

A friend of mine bought this dress at an auction in Florida, thinking that I might be interested in buying it from her. She was correct. I am entranced by the shadowwork embroidery. It isn't terribly delicate, yet it has become one of my favorite shadow embroidery designs. Because of the relatively large design, it stitches up quickly. The design is included here for you to re-create.

The skirt embroidery features shadowwork flowers, bows, and circles (Fig. 1). The yoke embroidery repeats the same floral/bow arrangement (Fig. 2). The antique version is white on white; however, the choice of color is yours. The back dress length is 31 inches; the circumference of the skirt is 53 inches. The front panel measures 3-1/2 inches at the base of the yoke and 6-1/2 inches at the bottom of the dress. A 3-inch hem is stitched at the top with a straight machine stitch. The dress laps right over left and has no buttonholes or buttons, indicating beauty pins were originally used.

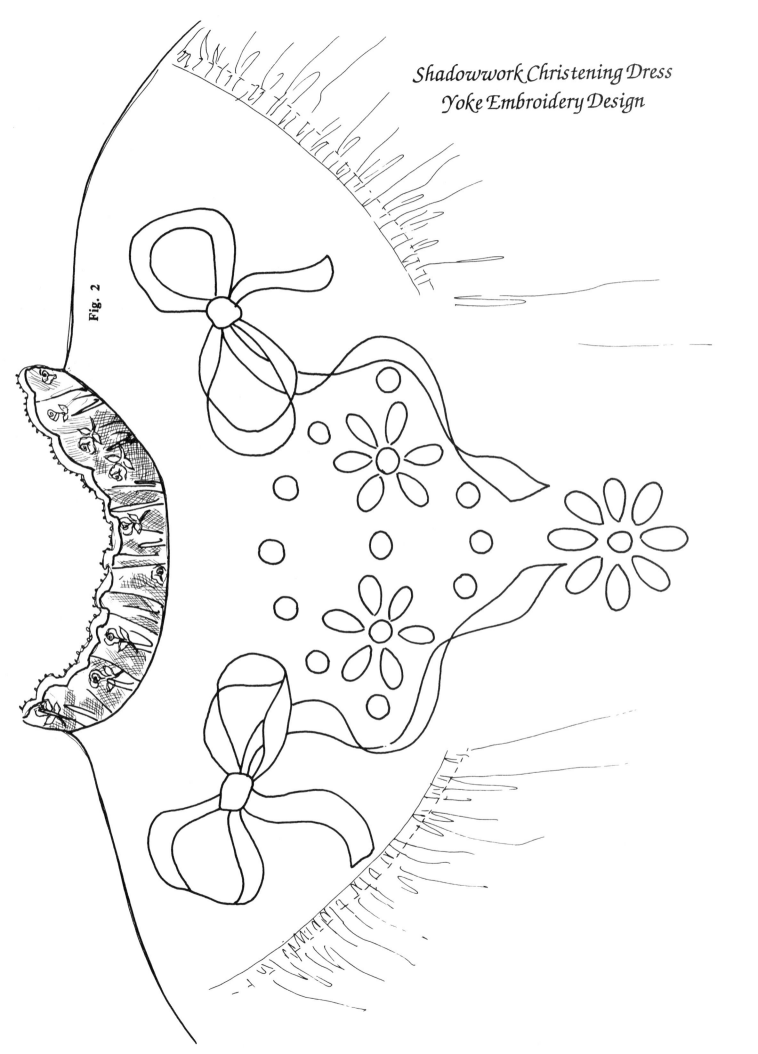

Shadowwork Christening Dress
Yoke Embroidery Design

Fig. 2

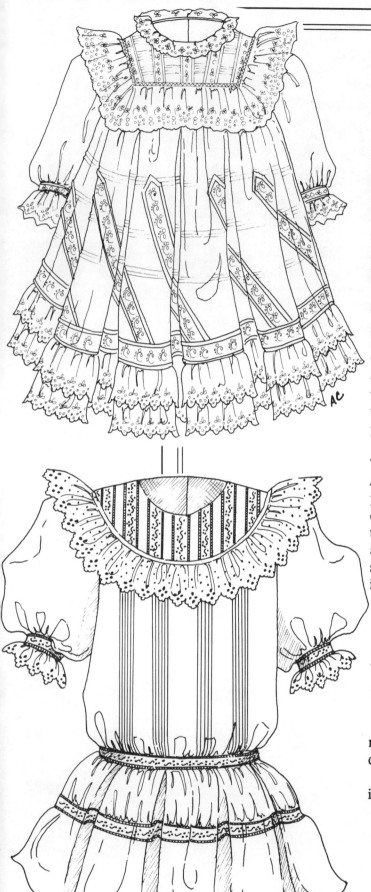

Angled Swiss Insertion Dress
- Australia, circa 1900

I bought this dress during an excursion to Melbourne, Australia. The antique store was a 45-minute cab ride from where I was staying, and when I finally arrived, I found it filled with glassware, furniture, maps, silver, and other collectibles. I had just about decided my trip was in vain when I noticed a flight of stairs. The descent led me to the basement, and in the far end of the room, I spotted a display of "white clothes." My "find" yielded this magnificent heirloom piece.

I'd never seen insertions placed in this manner — on top of tiers of tucks. The double ruffle of Swiss edging is gathered daintily to make one ruffle. Angles are used to some degree in the placement of the insertions over the tucks on the high yoke. As is typical of a turn-of-the-century child's dress, the sleeves are three-quarter length and trimmed with Swiss insertion and gathered Swiss edging trim. The gathered Swiss edging repeats around the high yoke and neckline.

To reproduce this dress, I suggest using the pattern "Heirloom Party Dress" from *French Hand Sewing By Machine, The Second Book*, by Martha Pullen or any high yoke dress. You will have to lengthen the sleeves to three-quarter; the rest of the pattern can be adapted by adding the tucks and insertions. Any Swiss batiste, Swiss insertion, and Swiss edging could combine for stunning results. With silk, opt for French or English laces instead of the Swiss insertions and edgings.

Round-Yoke Middy
- England, circa 1910

The trims on this quietly-elegant dress are Swiss. Four rows of tucks create an elongated silhouette. The extended dropped waistline indicates it was made around 1910.

Silk with Swiss eyelet insertion would blend brilliantly in a reproduction of this design.

Netting And Puffing Dress

- America, circa 1915-1920

I found this dress one Saturday afternoon as I was browsing through an antique mall in Huntsville. It is made of netting with a tiny dot in the fabric. It has no lace, no ribbon (except for the tiny rosette), no trim of any kind. This is truly "French sewing by machine" on a budget. The trim, puffing, and ruffles are made of fabric.

The skirt has four panels; two straight and two puffed. The front and back straight panels measure 14 inches wide. The puffing panels measure 35 inches each. The total circumference of the skirt is 98 inches. Each side skirt has two sets of puffing; one right under the yoke and one down further on the skirt. These sets of puffing are inserted into the straight pieces of the skirt. A single set of puffing on each panel looks as if two rows of puffing are stitched together. On the contrary, it is actually one wide row of puffing (2-1/2 inches wide) with a straight-stitch run down the middle of the puffing before the gathers are made at the top and at the bottom. I call this unusual technique "Fake Double Puffing."

The skirt is attached to the yoke with a double ruffle sandwiched between the stitching. The yoke double-ruffle is a 3/4 inch finished width ruffle. To make this ruffle, cut a 2-1/2-inch piece of netting or batiste, whichever your chosen fabric. Fold it in half. Factor a 1/2-inch seam allowance, leaving a 3/4-inch finished width of ruffle.

The sleeve ruffle is a finished width of 2-1/2 inches. Begin with a 5-1/2-inch piece of netting; fold it in half and press. That leaves room for a 1/4-inch seam allowance into the sleeve. In the middle of this folded piece, make a straight-stitch through both layers of netting. This gives a "matching" effect to the fake puffing in the skirt.

The neck ruffle has a finished width of 2 inches. Begin with a 4-1/2-inch piece of netting; fold it in half and press. In the middle of this folded piece, make another straight-stitch. Gather and stitch into the neckline using a bias binding.

The skirt ruffle has a finished width of 2-1/2 inches. Begin with a 5-inch piece of netting; fold it in half and press. In the middle of this folded piece, make another straight-stitch. Gather and stitch onto the skirt.

Australian Embroidered Dress

- Australia, circa 1910

No matter where my busy schedule takes me, I always factor in time to browse antique stores in hopes of adding to my collection. During my first trip to Melbourne, I hit the jackpot. I found not one, but several Australian heirlooms.

One was this child's, white-on-white, embroidered dress; so elegant and simple. Every stitch is made by hand. Embroidery adorns the skirt and high yoke. Delicate sleeves flaunt tucks and gathered lace insertion. Entredeux outlines the sleeves, the neckline, and the high waist. The total length of the dress is 19 inches. An elegant addition would be the use of buttonholes for ribbon slots, spaced 1-1/8 inches apart around the front and back yokes. The buttonholes are exactly 1 inch high; 1-inch ribbon is slipped through the beading and tied in a bow at the back. Around the neckline, above the entredeux, is 3/8-inch gathered lace edging.

I've included a sketch of the embroidered design for you to copy or adapt to your favorite embroidery stitches. The actual bows are shadowwork; the large flower centers are point de Paris or needlepoint lace. Most of the small flowers are satin-stitched.

If you prefer not to embroider on the dress, choose a Swiss eyelet for the skirt, and work the bordered Swiss fabric into the bodice. Swiss batiste, with either elaborate shadowwork or wide eyelet, would complement this design.

Embroidery Design from Back Yokes

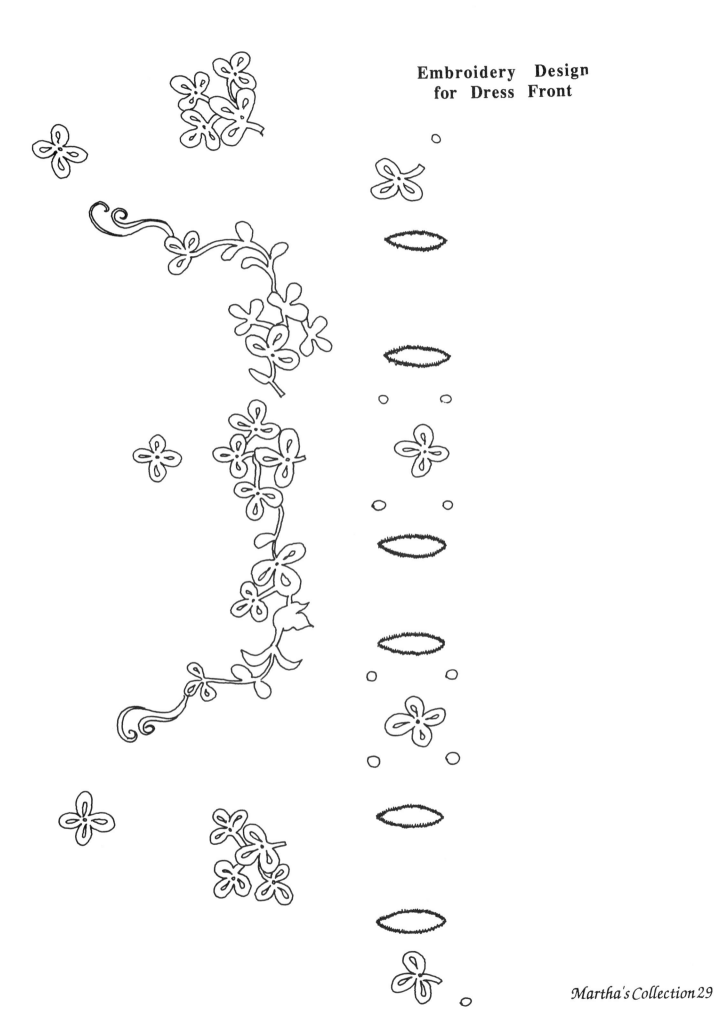

Embroidery Design
for Dress Front

Martha's Collection 29

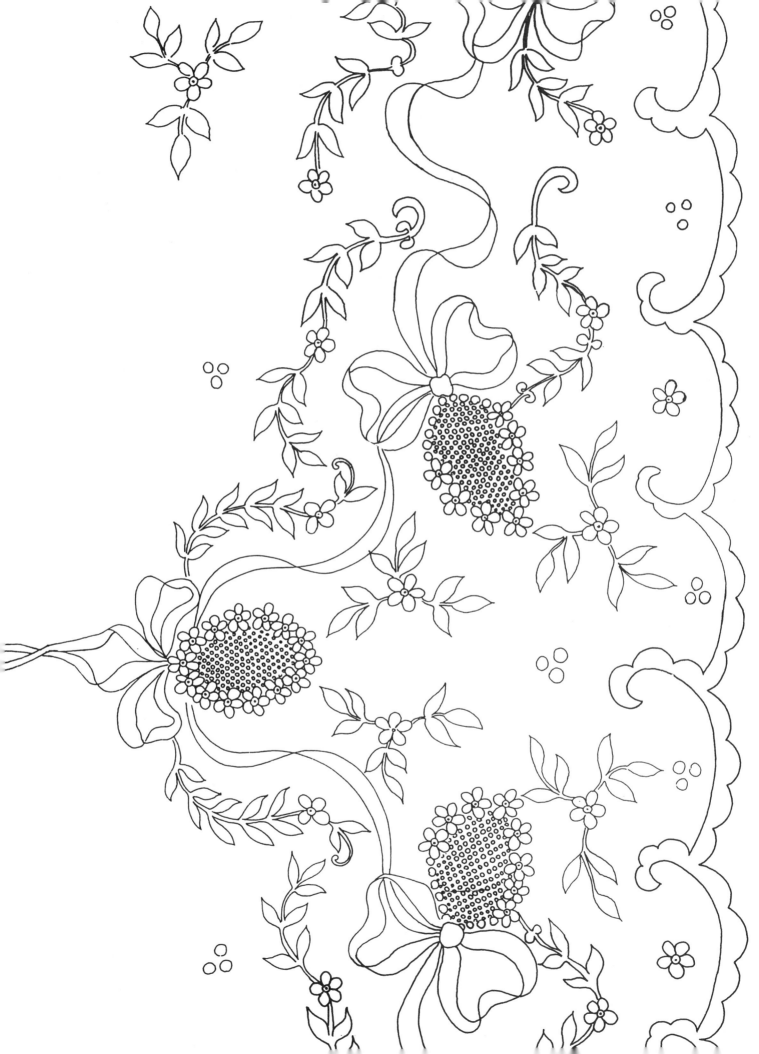

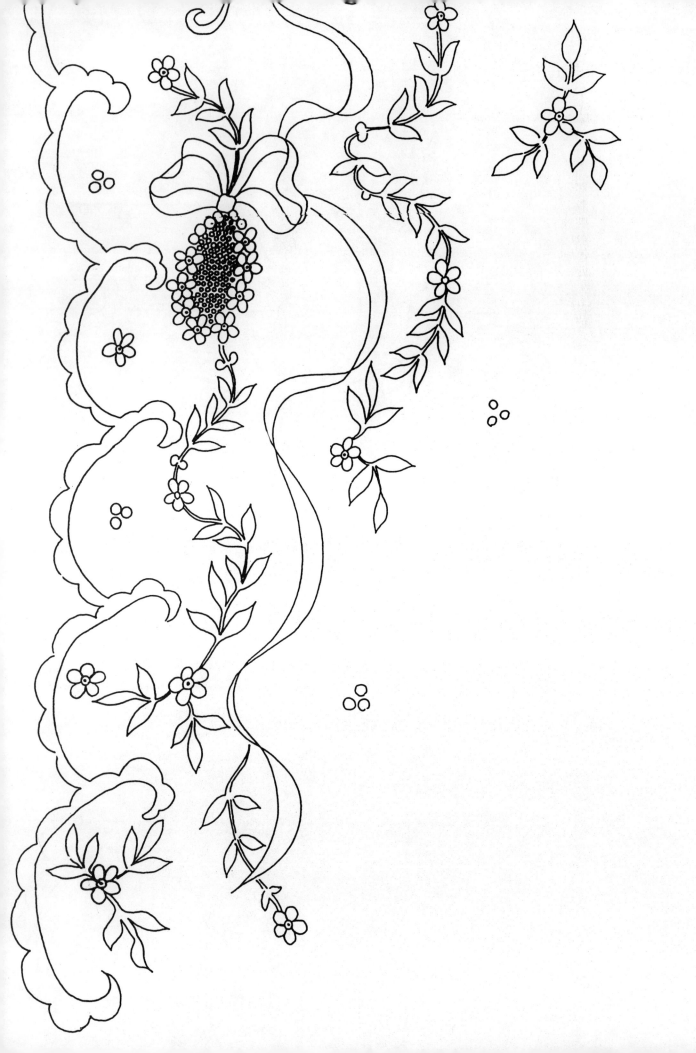

Tucked Eyelet Middy Dress

- England, circa 1890

Although this dress was purchased from an American antique clothing dealer, I suspect it is English in origin. There are several unusual design elements on this middy dress. The first is the tucked, dropped waistband. Using your pintuck foot, you can put five — or 10 tucks for that matter — into any waistband. The four sets of tucks on the front bodice also have five pintucks. French insertion is found at the armhole and at the lower bodice line. The skirt is purchased eyelet; the embroidery on the bodice is hand embroidered. On the back of the dress are two sets of five tucks on either side of the buttoned closing. The straight sleeve has a row of French insertion with a flat row of lace edging to match. Pearl buttons close the back of the dress.

To put the lace insertion into a straight sleeve, as is done on both the armhole of the dress and the armhole of the sleeve on this design, refer to the technique "Lace To Flat Fabric." On the actual antique dress, the lace insertions have been straight-stitched on, and the fabric has been cut away from the back. With the proficiency of today's sewing machines, I would recommend zigzagging the insertion onto the garment, then cutting away the fabric from behind.

The square yoke, antique, middy dress pattern that comes with this book would be ideal for a guideline pattern. Stitch all of your front ideas, then fold the fullness out of the pattern, matching the pattern yoke to the gathers that are in the front, below the yoke. Another appropriate pattern to use as a guideline is "Victorian Middy Dress" by Ann Taylor for Martha Pullen. The sleeve pattern in the "California Antique Dress" is almost identical. It is found in the Fall 1987 issue of *Sew Beautiful* magazine.

Any weight Swiss batiste would make an elegant reproduction. The easiest way to get the embroidered effect on the skirt is to choose Swiss or American eyelet by the yard. Swiss insertion could also be used in place of the embroidery on the long front panels; this would be less time consuming than hand embroidery.

Tucked Eyelet Middy Dress
Construction

1. Make sets of five pintucks in the approximate place the pattern would permit. Draw off your bodice with a water-soluble pen.
2. Mark the places where the lace insertions will be sewn. Do not cut out anything; you are still working with a large square of fabric.
3. Trace your embroidery on the two front panels, and embroider the pattern of your choice.
4. Place your lace insertion on the fabric and zigzag. Trim the fabric away from behind the five pieces of lace insertion.
5. Stay-stitch around the bodice neckline areas. Cut out your bodice.
6. Make your tucked, lowered waistband. The finished width of this band is 1-1/2 inches. The original dress is about a size 4. The lowered waistband can be widened or made narrow, according to size.
7. Notice the mitered corners on the lace insertion and lace edging which square around the neckline. I would attach the edging to the insertion before applying it to the neckline. Miter both the insertion and the edging at the same time. (Refer to the section on mitering square corners for the technique.)

Shoulder Ruffle Dress

- America, circa 1910

This dress, made entirely by hand, was purchased from an estate in Massachusetts. Made of an extremely delicate Swiss batiste, the dress has a high yoke bodice that ends 1 inch below the armhole. The bodice, shoulder ruffle, and fancy band are made with a combination of Swiss eyelet insertion and French insertion and edging (Fig. 1). The fancy band on the sleeve is constructed of entredeux, lace insertion, entredeux, beading, and gathered lace (Fig. 2). The circumference of the skirt — 68 inches — is relatively full for a dress of this era.

The bodice front is made with alternating Swiss insertion and French lace insertion. To accurately reproduce this trim, the Swiss insertion must have a finished edge on either side. The antique Swiss insertion on this dress has a peculiar finish, which looks a lot like the tape used to make Battenberg lace. Such a finish is no longer available. I suggest an entredeux finish on both sides of the Swiss insertion. The beading at the bottom of the bodice is Swiss entredeux beading, since it has entredeux on either side. Ribbon is run through the beading. The back bodice is exactly like the front bodice. The lace is 3/4 inch wide, and the Swiss insertion is 7/8 inch wide. There is no required width of lace or Swiss needed to make the bodice; simply zigzag together enough pieces until you get a desired width.

Making The Bodice And Shoulder Ruffles

1. For the bodice, zigzag the parallel insertions together in the large square (Fig. 3).
2. Trace off the front and back bodice pattern. Stay-stitch around the tracing (Fig. 3).
3. Cut out the front and back bodices.
4. Seam the shoulders together.
5. The shoulder ruffle's finished length is 18 inches long by 3 inches wide at the widest portion of the shoulder. Your ruffle width, before you run your gathering threads, should be about 3-1/4 inches wide; that gives you space for your gathering threads. The total measurement to which this ruffle is gathered on this size 4 dress is 11 inches. This is almost a 2-1 ratio of gathering. For larger sized dresses, make your ruffle longer. The 18-inch ruffle would probably work for dresses as small as size 2.
6. The ruffle is made with lace insertion, Swiss eyelet insertion, lace insertion, and lace edging (applied flat, not gathered) for the outside of the ruffle (Fig. 1).

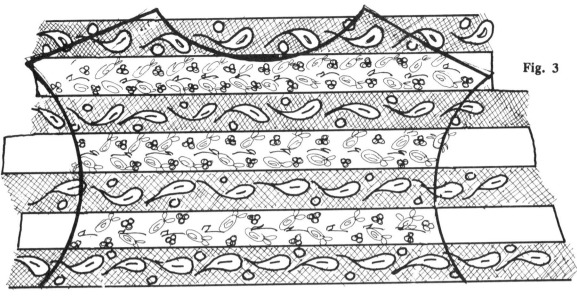

Fig. 3

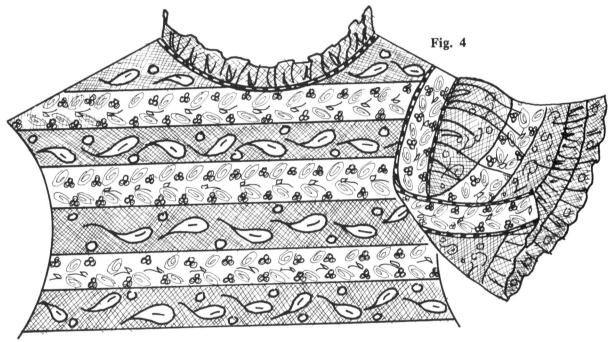

Fig. 4

7. Gather the ruffle, decreasing on the very end, allowing the ruffle to curve in at the bottom. Run two rows of gathering threads. Zigzag the ruffle to the entredeux-finished straight piece of Swiss insertion. You have now finished the ruffle that will be attached to the bodice.

8. Pin and zigzag (Stitch length=2, width=2) the insertion/ruffle onto the bodice, stitching from the front to the back (Fig. 4). If you think another length and width stitch will better suit the entredeux-trimmed Swiss insertion, the option is yours. Press.

Fig. 1

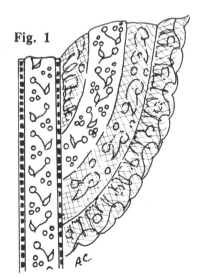

Fig. 2

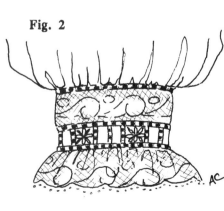

Martha's Collection 35

Swiss Triple-Eyelet Dress

- England, circa 1900

This dress is a product of Merry Old England; I suspect that the mother who made it loved fullness in fabrics and trims as much as I do. Basically, this is a high-yoked dress, tucked across the front and back yokes (Fig. 1). The tucks are 1/4 inch wide and are spaced 3/8 inch apart. Tucks are pressed to the center, which means they face opposite directions. The actual antique dress, comparable to today's size 8 or 10, has 28 tucks.

The gathered strip (middle section) that joins the high yoke with the waistband, is 30 inches wide; it is gathered only in the center section in the front of the dress. This same 15-inch width is on both sides of the back. The back sections are cut on the selvage, which folds back to form a back placket. Piping is inserted in the armhole, at the bottom of the Swiss insertion waistband, and around the neck of the dress. What interesting places for piping in a French dress!

The double Swiss eyelet ruffle around the bottom of the yoke is made from 4-1/2-inch eyelet and 2-1/2-inch eyelet (Fig. 2). If you don't have matching eyelets in these widths, take two strips of 4-1/2-inch eyelet, and cut one of them to fit. The ruffles are gathered together at the top. The length of each eyelet strip is 80 inches; the distance around the yoke is 28 inches. The fullness of these ruffles is almost 3-to-1. The ruffles are gathered together and applied, right sides to right sides, directly on top of the dress. A bias binding is stitched on to cover the seams. This process forms what appears to be a flat felled seam under the ruffles. You could also use a narrow lace insertion to cover this stitching or serge the edges of these ruffles to finish the seam. This would be done after the ruffles are attached. None of these ruffle seam finishes show (Fig. 3).

The skirt on the dress is gathered with pleats. You can accomplish this effect by using a pleater machine. For the pleats in the top of the skirt, run 3/4 inch of rows, using your half spaces. Use quilting thread. The gathering rows are left in when the dress is complete. No smocking is done on the pleats.

The skirt is four panels, with 28 inches of fullness in each panel. The finished skirt measures 112 inches around the bottom. It has a batiste pocket in the right side. In fact, it is the only heirloom dress I have come across with a pocket.

The waistband is Swiss insertion. Don't forget the piping at the bottom of the waistband. When you construct such a waistline, pretend that you are piping a smocked dress at the yoke. The sleeves have this same Swiss insertion plus a gathered ruffle of the Swiss edging; the seams are flat felled. The fabric on the bottom and at the top of the sleeves could be gathered with a pleater.

The neckline has a row of gathered Swiss edging, piping, and a row of gathered French edging above the piping. Close examination of the gathered lace above the piping shows that the gathered lace is attached by hand. A 6-inch hem is put in with the tiniest straight-stitch that any sewing machine could run.

The dress laps right over left and has 12 buttons and buttonholes, spaced 1 inch apart on the back.

Swiss Triple Eyelet Dress

Fig. 1

Fig. 2

Fig. 3

Martha's Collection 37

Cathedral Tatting Dress

- Australia, circa 1918

I call this Australian gem the "Cathedral Tatting and Lace Dress." The trim around the neck and inside the cathedral shapes on the bodice is tatting. French insertion is used for part of the neckline shape and for the trim around each cathedral window of tatting. Ten tucks grace each side of the front bodice; 1/8-inch tucks are spaced 1/4 inch apart.

The total circumference of the skirt is only 45 inches. Tatting trims the three cathedral shapes on the front and back of the skirt. The dress is embroidered between the front two shapes. Edging at the bottom of the dress is the same intricate pattern found on the insides of the cathedral shapes. Lace is mitered, going down onto the skirt from the bodice; however it is flip-flopped to go around the front and also flip-flopped to go around the top of each cathedral shape on the skirt. Entredeux outlines the interest on the bodice back and front; it is also used in the armhole to attach the short sleeve and is used as the first row of finish on the neckline and on the sleeves. Narrow tatting is stitched to the trimmed entredeux.

Viewing the dress from the back, you will notice that the buttonholes are on the right side of the dress; they run horizontally (sideways). Two-hole, pearl buttons close the dress.

Angel-Sleeve Dress

- England, circa 1920

This English dress flaunts Swiss insertion with entredeux edges and French insertion and edging. The edging on the sleeves and the insertion on the bottom of the dress do not match. Tiny beading trims the neckline, encasing a ribbon, which ties at the back of the neck. It is interesting to note that the neckline is bound underneath the beading. Beading and ribbon also finish the bottom of the yokes.

A novel construction technique on this dress is the batiste border on the entredeux edge of the Swiss insertion. The designer of this garment made a tiny "fake" flat felled seam with it. She turned it under once and made two rows of stitching. One is in the ditch of the entredeux; the other is 1/8 inch from the first stitching line. The total seam is 1/8 inch wide. The laces — insertion and edging — are stitched with both of the straight-stitches — the stitch-in-the-ditch and a stitch 1/8 inch over. Those two straight-stitches attach the lace to the little seam of the entredeux. Another noteworthy design element is the bodice, which is lined with netting.

The angel sleeves have a double row of beading (one, right on top of the other) sewn at the bottom of the sleeve. In this type of sleeve the ribbons run through the beading gathering the sleeves.

All of the interior seams of this dress are French, including the sleeve insertion. The circumference of the bottom of this size 3 dress is 62 inches. The buttonholes run vertically (up and down) along the back placket. If you are looking at the back of the dress, the buttonholes are on the right side of the dress. Four-hole, pearl buttons close the dress.

Tucked-To-The-Shoulder Dress

- France, circa 1900

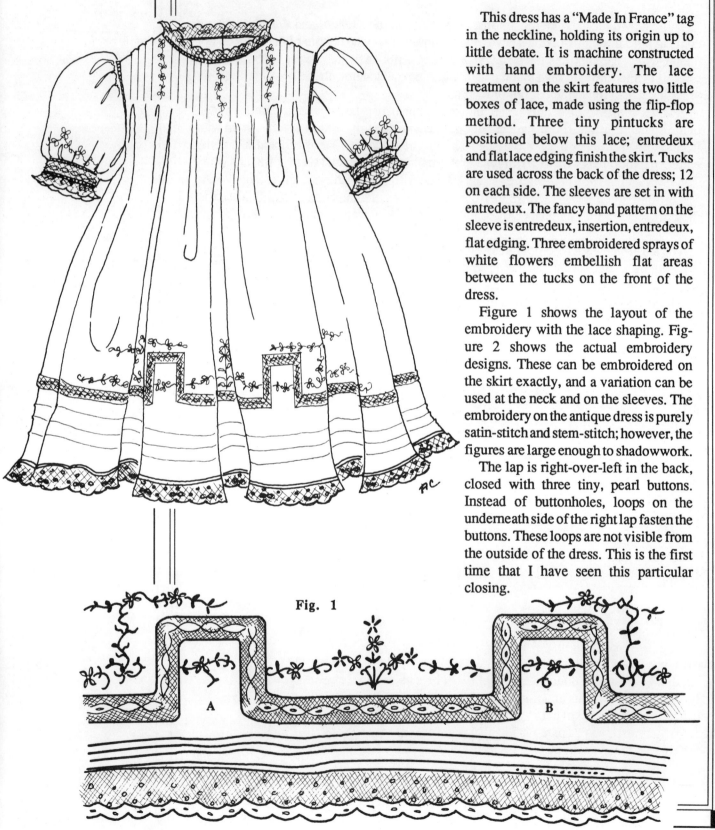

This dress has a "Made In France" tag in the neckline, holding its origin up to little debate. It is machine constructed with hand embroidery. The lace treatment on the skirt features two little boxes of lace, made using the flip-flop method. Three tiny pintucks are positioned below this lace; entredeux and flat lace edging finish the skirt. Tucks are used across the back of the dress; 12 on each side. The sleeves are set in with entredeux. The fancy band pattern on the sleeve is entredeux, insertion, entredeux, flat edging. Three embroidered sprays of white flowers embellish flat areas between the tucks on the front of the dress.

Figure 1 shows the layout of the embroidery with the lace shaping. Figure 2 shows the actual embroidery designs. These can be embroidered on the skirt exactly, and a variation can be used at the neck and on the sleeves. The embroidery on the antique dress is purely satin-stitch and stem-stitch; however, the figures are large enough to shadowwork.

The lap is right-over-left in the back, closed with three tiny, pearl buttons. Instead of buttonholes, loops on the underneath side of the right lap fasten the buttons. These loops are not visible from the outside of the dress. This is the first time that I have seen this particular closing.

Fig. 1

A   B

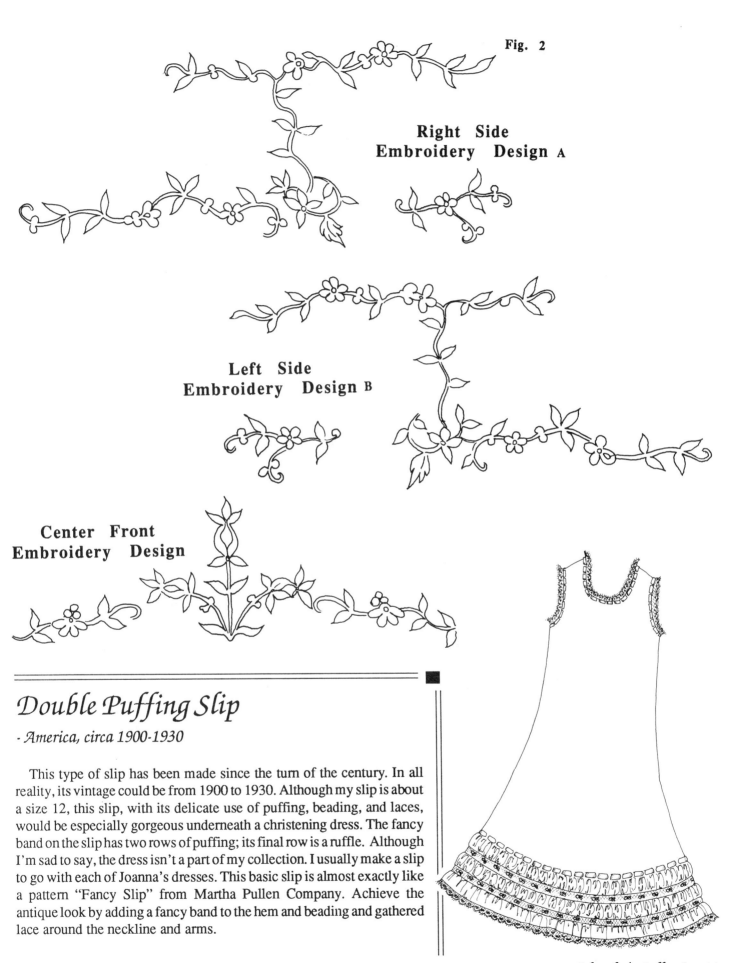

Fig. 2

**Right Side
Embroidery Design A**

**Left Side
Embroidery Design B**

**Center Front
Embroidery Design**

Double Puffing Slip
- America, circa 1900-1930

This type of slip has been made since the turn of the century. In all reality, its vintage could be from 1900 to 1930. Although my slip is about a size 12, this slip, with its delicate use of puffing, beading, and laces, would be especially gorgeous underneath a christening dress. The fancy band on the slip has two rows of puffing; its final row is a ruffle. Although I'm sad to say, the dress isn't a part of my collection. I usually make a slip to go with each of Joanna's dresses. This basic slip is almost exactly like a pattern "Fancy Slip" from Martha Pullen Company. Achieve the antique look by adding a fancy band to the hem and beading and gathered lace around the neckline and arms.

Shoulder Puffing Christening Dress

- England, circa 1890

This hand sewn, English piece is a work of art with near perfect stitching. It is made of a Swiss batiste with Swiss trims. The Swiss trim used is only 1/4 inch wide after the batiste edges have been removed. The beading around the neck is also 1/4 inch wide. The entredeux beading is mitered at the corners in the front and in the back. The square neckline is finished with a 3/8-inch lace edging, which is slightly gathered. The finished width of the puffing over the shoulder is 1-3/8 inches wide. The same Swiss insertion is used at the edge of the puffing attached to the sleeve. All of the seams are French.

Exquisite baby puffing garnishes the sleeves. The same 1/4-inch Swiss insertion is used at the top and the bottom of the sleeve fancy band. The puffing's finished width is only 5/8 inch.

The full width of the dress, which is gathered across the front bodice, is 18 inches. The same fullness is gathered across the back. There is a 7-1/2-inch placket in the back skirt below the waistband. The total back opening from the neckline down to the bottom of the skirt placket is 14 inches. Each side of the back of the skirt, from the puffing band to the back opening, has a bias seam encasing a delicate cord, which looks almost like a very delicate shoestring. This cord pulls in the fullness of the back; the little sash is for decorative purposes. The puffing band at the waistline is 4 -1/2 inches wide and measures 1 inch from top to bottom. The waistline puffing band has 1/4-inch trim on both sides and 1/2-inch puffing in the center. Each side of the sash, which attaches on either side of the waist puffing band, is 26 inches long and 3 inches wide. The sash is hemmed with a 3/4-inch hem. Three-eighths-inch lace edging is butted to the hem and zig-zagged.

The hem is 1-1/4 inches wide with three tucks above it, measuring 1/8 inch each. The total length of the skirt from the waist puffing band is 29 inches. The circumference of the skirt is 66 inches. The buttons to close the back of the dress and the sleeves are batiste-covered, double-eyed buttons. The dress laps right over left, when viewed from the back. A combination of button loops and buttonholes fit the buttons.

Raglan Sleeve Christening Dress

- America, circa 1910

Since I purchased this dress in Huntsville, Alabama from an antique dealer, it is most likely a domestically-made garment. It appears to be a country piece, since the fabrics aren't terribly delicate, the laces are crocheted, and the embroidery is heavy. The cutwork is beautifully done; however, it appears that the seamstress didn't have access to the delicate thread typically used to embroider gowns of this era.

The dress is a handkerchief linen weight, a heavier fabric than most early christening gowns. The bodice is unusual in that it is cut in one piece without shoulder seams. Hand-crocheted beading circles the neckline and sleeves; ribbon is then run through, tying the back together. The dress is completely made by hand, with the exception of the flat felled seams that are used to close the side seams, the underarm seams, and the stitches on the tucks. The embroidery on the bodice and the skirt is cutwork.

The neckline is 11 inches around. The width of the dress across the bodice from sleeve edge to sleeve edge is 22 inches. The length of the dress bodice front, from the shoulder line to the beginning of the crocheted waist insertion, is 6-1/2 inches. The total length of the skirt, from the bottom of the waistline insertion, is 22 inches. Skirt fullness is 60 inches. Crocheted insertion is 1 inch wide. Crocheted edging on the bottom of the dress is 2 inches wide. The tucking band is 2-1/2 inches wide. The tucks are 1/8 inch and, in two sets of three tucks, 3/8 inch apart. The embroidery on the bodice is 11 inches across. The embroidery spray on the skirt is approximately 9 inches long by 5 inches wide. And, the finished sleeve fancy band is 5-3/4 inches around.

The dress laps left over right. The buttons are two-eyed, batiste-covered pearl.

Embroidered Yoke And Skirt Christening Dress

- America, circa 1900 - 1910

This christening dress was purchased at an antique show in Massachusetts. Every stitch is done by hand. Stitched inside is a tiny white tag with the name "E. J. Roberts" woven in red. The design elements lead me to the conclusion that it is dated before 1910.

The bodice of the dress is embroidered, white-on-white, with satin-stitch, French knots, and eyelet daisies. A tiny, open-weave French lace insertion forms a V and a curve on the body of the garment. A fine Swiss trim encircles the neckline, the bottom curve on the bodice, and the waistline of the dress. Three sets (seven tucks per set) of 1/32-inch tucks decorate each back bodice. The neckline measures 10-3/4 inches. The finished circumference of the sleeve is 6 inches.

The skirt measures 35 inches from waist to the bottom of the 3-inch hem. It is hemmed by tiny running stitches, not a slip-stitch. A 1/2-inch lace edging trims the bottom of the sleeves and the neckline of the dress.

You will find the exact embroidery design that runs along the skirt of this dress in the pattern envelope included with this book. The antique embroidery is white-on-white; however, pastel embroidery would complement the design as well. The embroidery design, which could be done by hand or machine, is suitable for any child's dress.

The buttons, viewed from the back of the dress, are on the left side; the buttonholes, which are made on the facing, not through the tucks, are on the right. The dress laps right over left.

This embroidery design is included in the pattern envelope.

44

Swiss Pique Coat

- England, circa 1890-1900

It is common for coats of this era to have two collars — Peter Pan and shawl. Both have the gathered Swiss eyelet trim. The Swiss edging that trims the shawl collar is attached with the "Swiss Pique Coat Entredeux Method" found in the technique section of this book. The hem is 3-1/4 inches deep and is hemmed by a straight-stitch at the top of the hem. The coat is machine made. All interior seams of the coat are bound with a bias seam binding. Piping falls between the gathered Swiss edging and the pique on the Peter Pan collar. The Swiss insertion with the entredeux edge is stitched right on top of the sleeve. The seam allowance is folded back to 1/4 inch and stitched onto the sleeve using two rows of straight-stitching.

Ladies Silk Triple Ruffle Skirt

- America, circa 1900

Purchased from an antique dealer who buys primarily in Massachusetts, this gorgeous skirt is one of my favorites. Twenty one inches around the waist and 42 inches long, the skirt must have been worn by a tall, slim woman. The skirt is machine stitched; the silk ribbon embroidery is by hand. The silk ribbon flowers on the skirt have seven bullion wraps in the center. The stems embroidered on the skirt are stem-stitched.

A triple ruffle dances around the hem of the skirt. The first row of trim below the embroidery is a bias tube, 3/4 inch wide. It is stitched to the skirt with a straight-stitch down the middle of the tubing. The first ruffle is bias, the second is cut on the straight of the grain, and the last ruffle is on the straight of the grain; however, it is made of a stiffer material so it would cause the other two silk ruffles to stand out. The skirt has 12 gores and measures 120 inches around the bottom before the ruffles begin. Directions for making this triple ruffle on the bottom of a skirt are found in the technique section of this book.

Ribbon and Lace Dress

- England, circa 1930-1940

This mid-20th century dress is made entirely of lace insertion and edging straight-stitched to ribbon — no easy task. For techniques on stitching lace insertion to ribbon, refer to the section on "Ribbon To Lace." Gathered lace edging with beading at the top trims the center bodice of the dress. Pink ribbon is run through the gathered trim and a rosette is placed to one side. Although there appears to be two widths of insertions used on the bodice, one is not insertion, but edging used as insertion. The gathered beading/edging trim is used to cover the joining of the edging. The edging is placed over the insertion in a lapped method and simply straight-stitched to join.

The sleeve is not formed like a typical sleeve, but is made of two pieces of ribbon, 1-1/2 inches wide, joined to one piece of insertion, 2 inches wide. The top piece of ribbon is gathered and treated as the sleeve cap. The sleeve is gathered at the bottom with the same beading/edging stitched straight on the bottom of the ribbon. The ribbon, run through the beading, gathers the sleeve. The sleeve is made with two 16-1/2-inch pieces of ribbon and one 16-1/2-inch piece of insertion.

The fullness of the skirt is 62 inches. The ribbon at the top of the skirt is hand gathered; however, the gathering foot on a sewing machine or two rows of long stitches would give the same results. The gathered ribbon skirt is butted to the lace insertion of the bodice and zigzagged together. The skirt is lengthened with an extra fancy band, which has been added below the straight, wide edging. The techniques for this extra lace fancy band can be found under the section "Lace-On-Lace Fancy Band."

Lace insertion is used for both back facings. The right side of the back, onto which the buttonholes are placed, has the insertion facing on the outside of the dress. The technique for this is found under "Double Lace Back Placket."

Tucks and White Braid Dress

- England, circa 1915

The three-quarter-length sleeves on this dress are typical of an early 1900s design. The dress has 33, 1/8-inch tucks across the high yoke bodice and 12 tucks each on the back bodice yokes. The fabric of the unusual collar has a finished width of 1 inch; the lace is 5/8-inch wide and is attached with the technique "Fake Tiny Tuck And Lace Edging Finish." A bias binding finishes the top neckline.

A 3/8-inch white braid and tiny, embroidered flowers curve around the front and back of the dress. This is my first encounter with braid since I began collecting French dresses. The skirt has five 1/8-inch tucks placed 1/8 inch apart. The 3-3/4-inch double hem has hand hemstitching, which is 1/4 inch wide.

The back is closed with three pearl buttons; it laps right over left with horizontal buttonholes on the right of the dress.

Eyelet Fabric Dress

- England, circa 1930

My husband Joe and I gave my mother a trip to England for her 70th birthday. Her assignment, other than to have a wonderful vacation, was to frequent flea markets and antique areas of London in search of something special to go in my new book. When she returned from her trip, she pulled this treasure from a plastic bag.

The dress, dated 1930, has an eyelet skirt and batiste sleeves. The bodice features Swiss trim with entredeux on either side, butted up to a heavy, yet loosely-woven French lace. A beading that looks like a wide entredeux trims the bottom of the bodice where the skirt is attached. The circumference of the dress is 54 inches.

Part of this dress is made by hand, part by machine. The skirt is gathered by hand and whipped to the entredeux at the bottom of the bodice. The dress laps right over left and is closed with three pearl buttons and thread button loops.

Handmade Christening Cape

- England, circa 1900

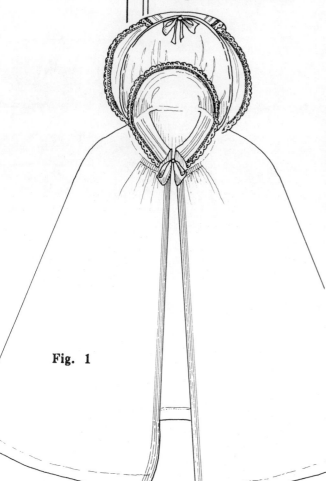

Fig. 1

I've dated this piece between 1890-1915, a period when christening capes were extremely popular. Even the eyelet on this English christening cape is handmade.

The total length of the cape is 24 inches. The front view is shown as if the hood is up and tied to fit the infant (Fig. 1). The back view shows how pretty the collar and the hood are when not pulled up over the infant's head. The ribbon loosens to the point that the hood lies flat around the shoulders of the cape (Fig. 2).

The eyelet trim is attached to the two collars (one is an actual collar and the other makes a hood when it is drawn up) by faggoting. The embroidery on the handmade eyelet is French knots, satin-stitch, and buttonhole-stitch for the scalloped edges (Fig. 3). The back seams are attached with a handmade trim which features French knots down the center and faggoting on either side of the French knots. French knots are on either side of the faggoting, and they hold back the tiny seams (Fig. 4). The neck measurement on the cape measures 13 inches; however, a tiny drawstring, encased at the edge of the hood, serves to draw it up to fit. Four tiny tucks run up and down the front of the cape.

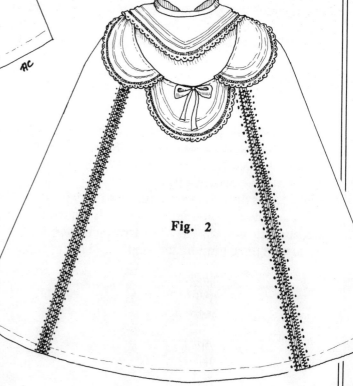

Fig. 2

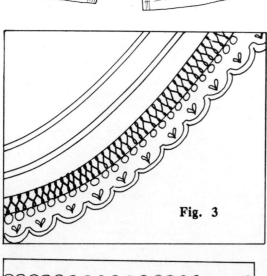

Fig. 3

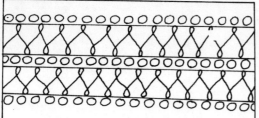

Fig. 4

Silk Charmeuse Button-On Boy's Suit

- America, circa 1920

This elegant boy's suit is made of cream silk charmeuse and lined with a China-weight silk. I purchased it at an estate sale in Huntsville, Alabama; chances are it was made here. The buttonholes are handmade. The trim is crochet; from its sheen it appears to be made from silk thread. The pants button on with 10 heavy pearl buttons; two on the sides, three in the center front, and five on the back. Four buttons embellish the front, double-breasted closure; two for buttonholes and two for decoration. A tiny snap holds the overlap of the shirt into place where the two collars cross.

Angles Of Lace Dress

-England, circa 1890

This dress was purchased by the light of a torch (or flashlight, as we know it) at a flea market in London. An elaborate use of all-over lace limits this rich design to special occasion dressing. Unfortunately, the laces on the original piece are not available today. Because of the creative use of lace angles on this dress, it has been featured in a "Grandmother's Trunk" article in *Sew Beautiful*. Insertion circles the sleeves, the waistline, and the skirt. The front panel is a stairway of angled insertion. The square middy pattern in this book could be adapted to reproduce this design.

Corded Puffing Christening Dress
- England, circa 1850-1880

Fig. 1

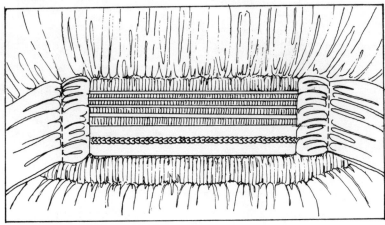

This dress is a short English christening dress, measuring only 18 inches from the shoulder seam. The handmade garment is so short I initially believed it to be a child's dress, not an infant's christening dress. But, the underarm sleeve length of 4 inches indicates it is, indeed, an infant's dress, and a very small one at that.

The semi-heavy Swiss batiste dress features a scooped neckline. Puffing forms a crescent shape at the yoke. There is no puffing on the upper back bodice. Joining the puffing and the waistline treatment is a gathered portion of the lower bodice. The bottom of the puffing is pleated in the tiniest pleats that I have ever seen. To satisfy my curiosity concerning how these tiny pleats are made, I opened the dress to discover minute handmade stitches which pleat the dress almost exactly like a smocking machine pleats fabric. The seamstress must have dotted the fabric by hand and pulled up the pleats.

The pleated area at the waist (Fig. 1) extends for about 1-1/4 inches. The tiny pleats appear to be stitched 3/8 of an inch each for a total of three lines of pleating. Four rows of cording are stitched right on top of the first 1/4 inch of pleating; that's right, four rows of tiny cording are whipped right on top of an area that is only 1/4 inch wide. If I were making this dress today, I would pleat the center area on a smocking pleater and smock a stem-stitch rather than whip on the baby cording. This baby cording is so tiny, it is no thicker than three strands of embroidery floss, pulled together tightly. The solid area underneath the cording is a bias strip, which also serves as the waistband to connect the whole bodice to the skirt. The sash, 3 inches wide by 23 inches long, is gathered and attached on either side of this beautiful waistline treatment.

1-1/4" wide

Simple, Sweet Hand-Embroidered Dress

- America, circa 1930-1940

This dress was purchased at an antique store in Nashville; it is one of the later pieces in my collection, vintage 1930-1940. I've re-created the attractive embroidery on the front yoke for you to copy (Fig. 1) exactly. You can re-create the design on the skirt simply by elongating the leaves from the bodice. The flower is the same. Entredeux circles the neckline, the front bodice, the back bodice, and the sleeves. The skirt is finished with a simple, rolled hem, with gathered lace straight-stitched on top.

Three tiny tucks are stitched vertically on the back bodice. The dress laps right over left when viewed from behind. Two pearl buttons, which fasten with handmade button loops, are on the left-hand side. The embroidery stitches are primarily satin-stitch; however, this design could be shadowwork embroidered easily. The circumference of the skirt is 45 inches.

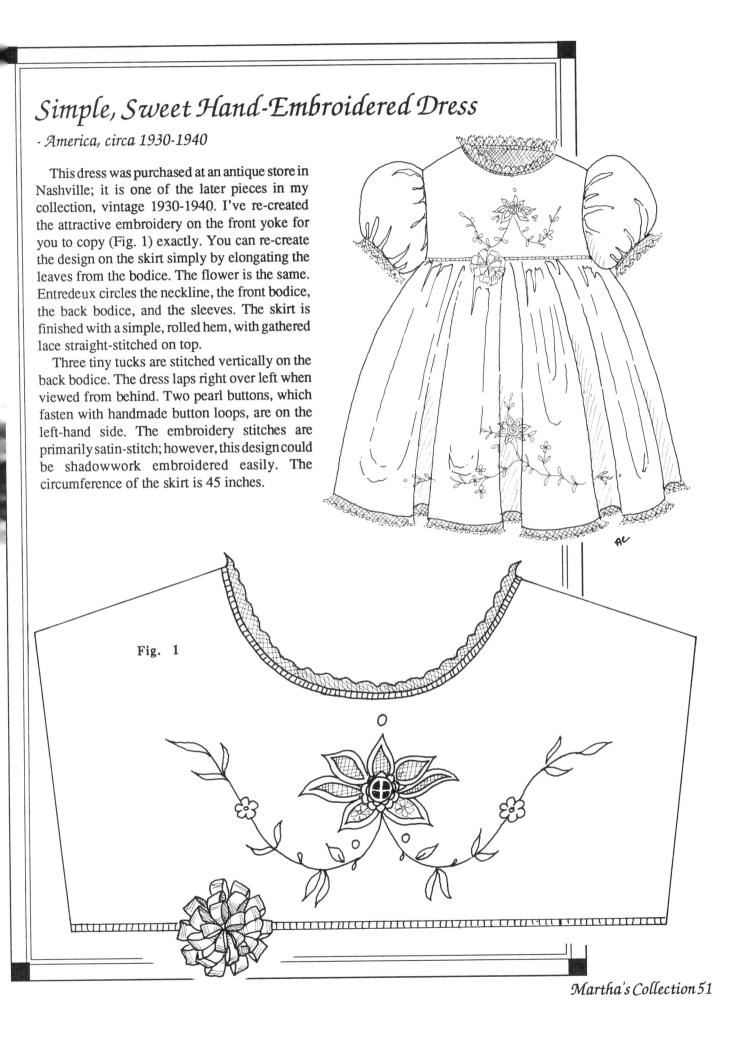

Fig. 1

Middy Embroidered Dress With Raglan Sleeves

- America, circa 1890

This American dress was purchased from an antique clothing dealer in Nashville. The dress is machine made; the embroidery is done by hand. The dropped waist design is laden with techniques worth reproducing. First, the neckline, the skirt bottom, and the sleeves are hand scalloped using a buttonhole-stitch. Gathered lace edging is whipped to the edges of scallops, following the curved shape. There are 18 of these 3-inch scallops on the skirt; nine in the front and nine in the back. Gathered lace edging runs along the yoke line where it joins the gathered, lowered bodice. The band that joins the bodice and the skirt has a finished width of 2 inches. The circumference of the skirt is 54 inches. The edging around the yoke of the dress is 7/8 inch wide; the edging on the bottom of the sleeves is 3/4 inch wide. The two edgings on this dress are completely different patterns.

We have duplicated the front yoke (Fig. 1), sleeve (Fig. 2), and skirt (Fig. 3) embroidery exactly. The circles of embroidery on the sleeves and on the skirt run horizontally or crosswise to the scallops on the bottom of the sleeves and the skirt. Five circles, arranged from large to very small, enhance the skirt. The sleeves boast four circles.

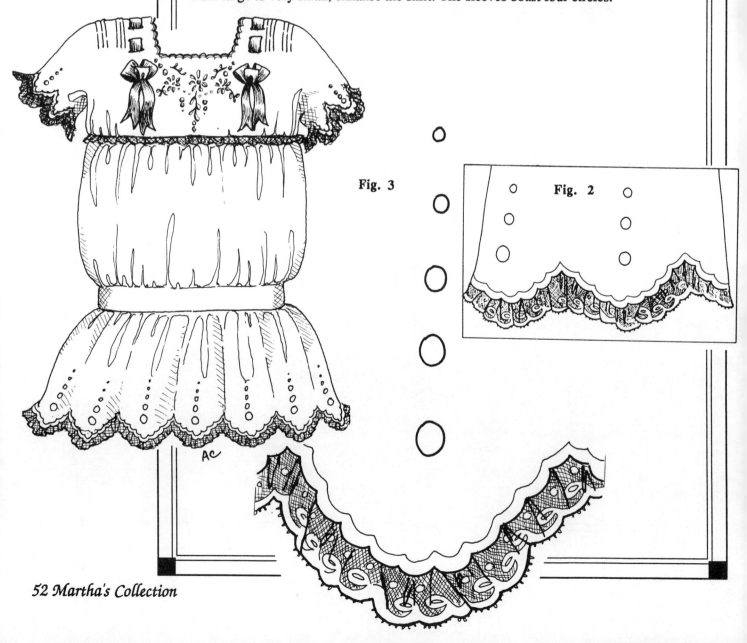

Fig. 3

Fig. 2

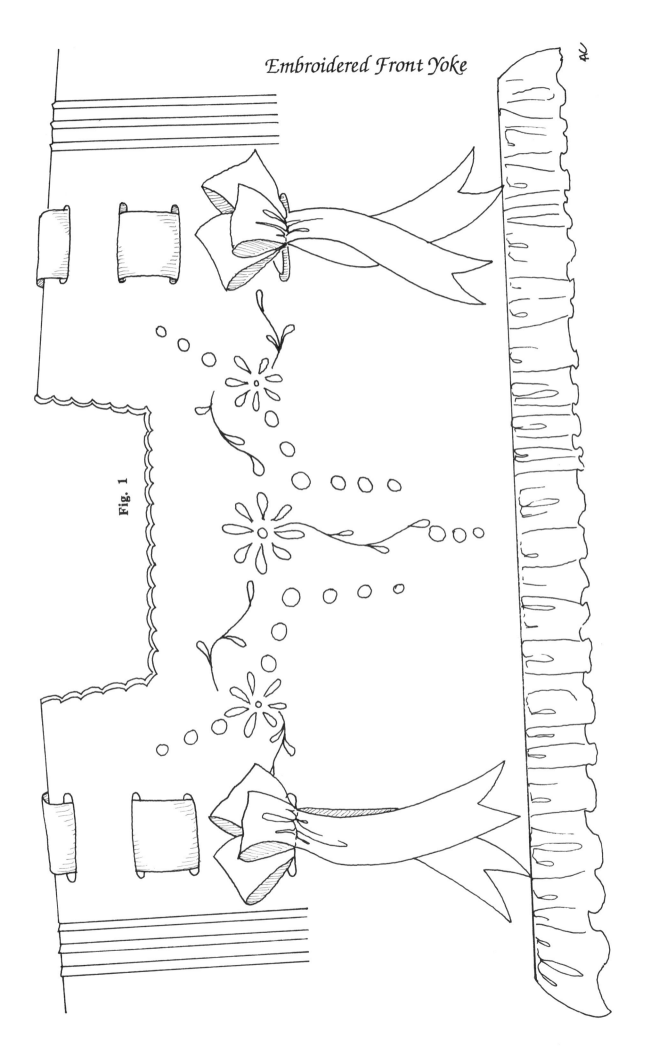

Embroidered Front Yoke

Fig. 1

53

Smocked Puffing "Christening" Dress
- England, circa 1890

This dress is English in origin and is made of a heavy cotton broadcloth. The fabric is the heaviest in my collection. After careful analysis, I have come to the conclusion that is not a christening dress at all but a long, sturdy baby dress, which was durably constructed for daily wear.

The body of the dress is one piece of fabric; there is no separate yoke or waistband. The center front is gathered (about 5-1/4 inches across the front, finished) and smocked with baby waves reversed to form diamonds. The total length of the smocked puffing, from the neckline to the Swiss trim at the waistline, is 4-1/2 inches. The distance between the rows of smocking is 1-1/4 inch. The smocking gives the illusion of puffing. The technique for making this "smocked puffing" is found in the technique section of this book. A Swiss embroidered trim is stitched right on top of the dress at the approximate waistline; a narrow sash is attached to the ends of this Swiss insertion. The sash is only 5/8 inch wide where it attaches to the Swiss insertion, but increases to 2-1/2 inches at the end. Total sash is 24 inches long; the same Swiss edging that trims the sleeve and the neck also trims the bottom of the sash. The finished dress length is 33 inches. The neckline is finished with a casing into which a drawstring is inserted; this is to adjust to a growing baby or to the next generation of babies. All the seams in the dress are flat felled. Part of the dress is made by hand; the straight-stitches in the hem, the sash, and the finished neckline are made by machine; the other stitches, including the armscye seam, are flat felled by hand.

The dress has no buttonholes; it closes in the back with a neckline tie and a sash at the waist. I'm assuming that tiny beauty pins were used to close the section between the neckline and the sash. The hem is a 3/4-inch width and is turned up and straight-stitched with a machine for its finish. Featherstitch, by hand, is found on the neckline casing, which is a relatively wide 3/8 inch. Swiss edging, 1-1/2 inches wide, is gathered around the neckline.

Fig. 1

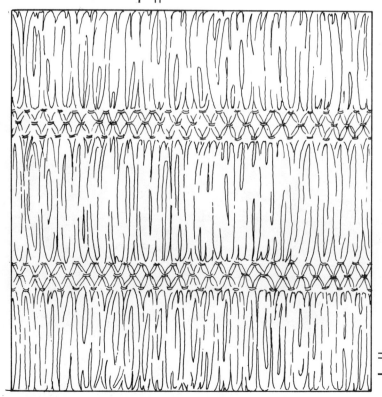

Techniques For Smocked Puffing: (Fig. 1)

1. Pleat the area to be smocked into puffing.
2. Smock two rows of baby diamonds (1/2-space waves); leave 1-1/4 inches, and smock it again. Repeat for as wide as you want your smocked puffing.
3. Pull out the pleating threads for puffing effect.

Smocked Puffing "Christening" Dress

Hem-Stitched/Drawn Work Swiss Batiste Dress
- England, circa 1900

This dress is one of my oldest. Purchased in England, it is of the early 1900s. Three clues indicate this turn-of-the-century dating. (1.) The technique of running the skirt up to the shoulder, framing the set-in yoke panel, is found on many patterns around the turn of the century. (2.) The sleeves are below the elbow or three-quarter-length — a style typical of this time period. (3.) The neckline adjusts with the use of a tiny drawstring run through a casing. I have yet to find this technique used on any dress made later than 1910.

Although the seams on the dress are made by machine, all of the trims are handmade. Hemstitching and drawn work with lovely patterns are the only embellishments. The stitches are flawless.

You can adapt either of the middy patterns found in this book to reproduce the dress. They both have a shoulder treatment that comes over the bodice and then down. You would have to lengthen the middy pattern to make a high yoke dress.

Tucks And Insertion Christening Dress

America, circa 1915-1920

This christening dress was purchased from a New England estate. The tucks are completely handmade; so is the delicate white-on-white embroidery at the neckline of the garment. Notice the lace insertion V below the embroidery and above the 18 tiny tucks on the bodice. The lace insertions are attached by turning under one tiny seam on the fabric of the dress and the fabric on the Swiss insertion, which runs the full length of the dress. The lace insertions are placed on top of this seam and straight-stitched to the garment, leaving a raw seam edge.

Six tiny tucks flatter the shoulders and travel all the way out to the armscye of the gown. Entredeux and gathered lace are used around the neckline and the sleeves. The skirt is especially pretty with its puffing, insertion, and ruffled fancy band.

Released tucks are 1/8-inch tucks, spaced 1/8 inch apart. The total length of the Christening dress is 30 inches; the total circumference, not including the ruffle, is 50 inches. One-sixteenth-inch tucks, spaced 1/8 inch apart, embellish the back. Two sets of five tucks are the only fancy stitches on the back. The dress laps right over left when viewed from behind; the two buttonholes are handmade. The buttonholes are spaced 4 inches apart; which is a bit unusual. Pearl buttons fasten the back. Buttoned, the circumference of the neck is only 9 inches.

Antique Tucked and Shadow Diamond Skirt

- America, circa 1890-1910

This skirt, which may have been a petticoat, is one of the most beautiful and yet one of the simplest garments in my antique collection. It was purchased from an antique dealer in Nashville. The fabric is white Swiss batiste of a medium weight. Every stitch of the 15 tucks and the 58 diamonds is put in by hand. The stitches are so fine I needed a magnifying glass to view them.

The tucks are 5/8 inch wide and are placed 3/4 inch apart. A skirt, with nothing more than these tucks, would be magnificent. Yet, this skirt also features a shadow of diamonds peeking through the hem.

The skirt is very full, with a finished circumference of 132 inches. The finished length is 36 inches. It is made with four skirt widths of 34 inches each. It's not necessary for you to make your reproduction this full; however, it would be more authentic that way. Refer to the technique chapter for complete instructions on making this skirt bottom.

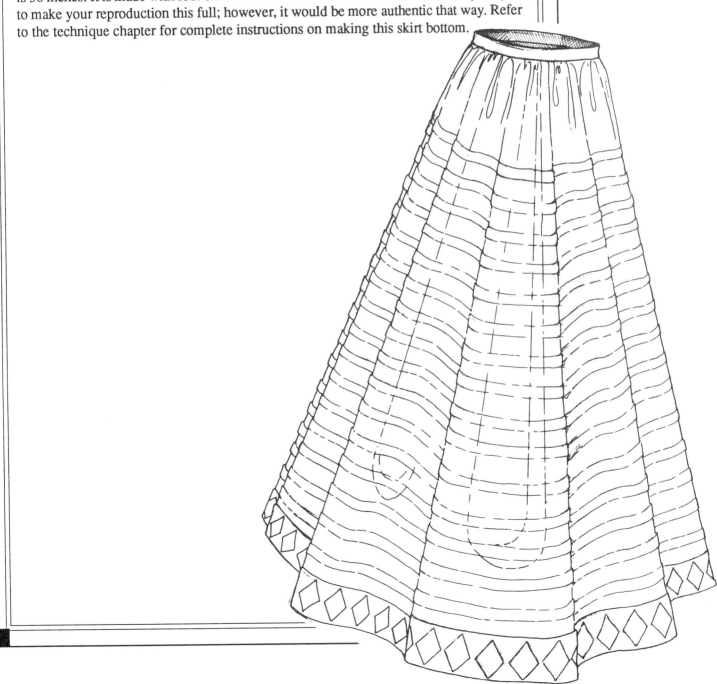

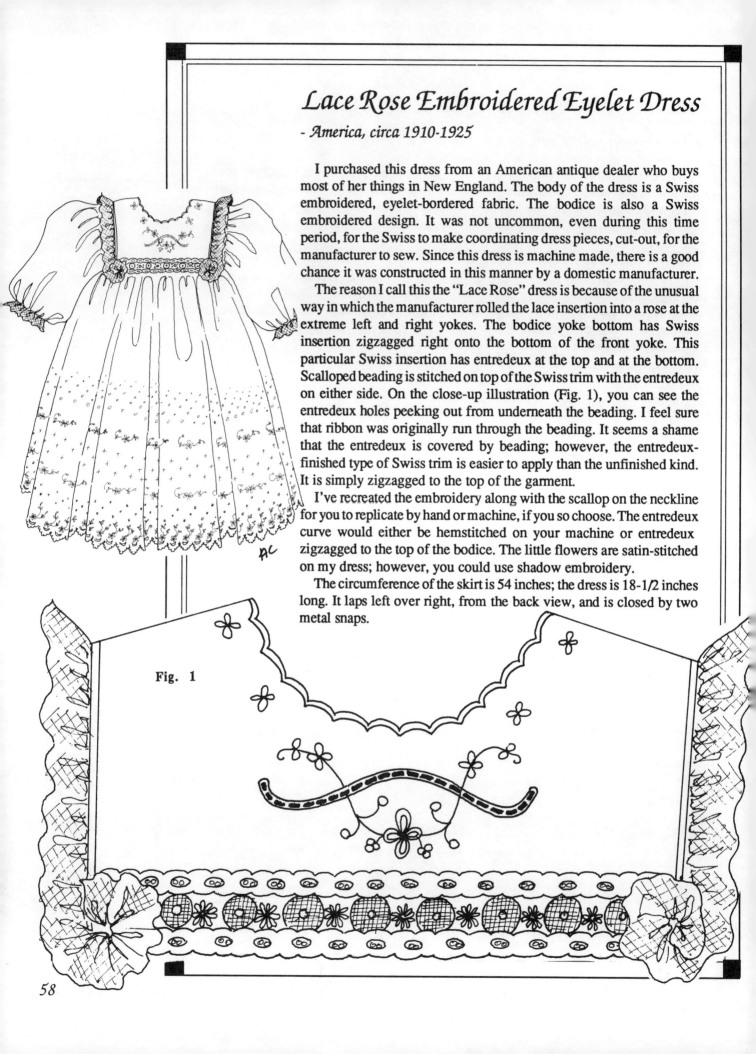

Lace Rose Embroidered Eyelet Dress

- America, circa 1910-1925

I purchased this dress from an American antique dealer who buys most of her things in New England. The body of the dress is a Swiss embroidered, eyelet-bordered fabric. The bodice is also a Swiss embroidered design. It was not uncommon, even during this time period, for the Swiss to make coordinating dress pieces, cut-out, for the manufacturer to sew. Since this dress is machine made, there is a good chance it was constructed in this manner by a domestic manufacturer.

The reason I call this the "Lace Rose" dress is because of the unusual way in which the manufacturer rolled the lace insertion into a rose at the extreme left and right yokes. The bodice yoke bottom has Swiss insertion zigzagged right onto the bottom of the front yoke. This particular Swiss insertion has entredeux at the top and at the bottom. Scalloped beading is stitched on top of the Swiss trim with the entredeux on either side. On the close-up illustration (Fig. 1), you can see the entredeux holes peeking out from underneath the beading. I feel sure that ribbon was originally run through the beading. It seems a shame that the entredeux is covered by beading; however, the entredeux-finished type of Swiss trim is easier to apply than the unfinished kind. It is simply zigzagged to the top of the garment.

I've recreated the embroidery along with the scallop on the neckline for you to replicate by hand or machine, if you so choose. The entredeux curve would either be hemstitched on your machine or entredeux zigzagged to the top of the bodice. The little flowers are satin-stitched on my dress; however, you could use shadow embroidery.

The circumference of the skirt is 54 inches; the dress is 18-1/2 inches long. It laps left over right, from the back view, and is closed by two metal snaps.

Fig. 1

Broadcloth/Eyelet Christening Dress Or Daygown

- England, circa 1850-1880

The heavyweight fabric suggests this garment was used as a daygown rather than a christening gown. It is one of my older pieces, as indicated by the drawstring at the neck. It's a shame this technique is rarely used today; the practical design can adjust to fit generations of babies.

In fact, this particular design would have come in handy when my sister's son, David was recently christened. David was born, weighing an average 7 pounds, 11 ounces. I immediately started planning his christening gown. Although my brother-in-law Rick did agree to let his son wear a gown, he requested that I limit the frills. I found a dark antique lace with a crown motif in Australia and chose a gown style with simple 1-inch tucks in the skirt — masculine enough. The end results pleased both Aunt Martha, Mama Mary, and Daddy Rick. But, by the time the christening date rolled around — three months after David's birth — he had grown to the size of most 12-month-old babies. The dress was a 9 month size, and I had originally feared it would be too big. When I arrived in Albertville for the christening and found David's dress wouldn't button at the top button, I was mortified. Turned out, the christening dress looked gorgeous and only those seated in the front row could have noticed. Still, I might have avoided the problem all together if I had thought to design the gown with an adjustable, antique neckline.

The total length of this dress is 39 inches. The circumference is 80 inches. The skirt fancy band has 4-1/8-inch tucks spaced 1/4 inch apart. A simple row of Swiss insertion and a flat piece of Swiss edging finish the fancy band. The Swiss insertion did not have a finished edge; it is simply stitched to the bottom ruffle and to the top tucking strip like a regular seam (right sides to right sides, stitch), yet the seam is a very narrow 1/8 inch. The seam wasn't pressed open, just left and pressed down. The side seams are regular seams also; however, the selvages are used for finishing the seam. Two rows of Swiss eyelet, 1/2 inch apart, travel over the shoulder from the bottom of the front bodice to the bottom of the back bodice. Three rows of eyelet trim the front of the bodice. Lace edging outlines the center row of eyelet. Gathered lace edging trims the neckline and the sleeves.

So that the sleeves gather to fit the individual child, a 1/4 inch tuck is constructed on the inside. A string runs through this tuck, which is then gathered to fit the child. A flat felled seam finishes the bottom of the sleeve. The flat lace is butted to the bottom of the sleeve and stitched. You could use this technique for an elastic casing. A 5/8-inch casing runs around the waist with a wider string used as a drawstring. The gathers on this dress are like so many of the older dresses that appear to be pleated by machine. The finished pleats lay to one side.

Ladies Split Peplum Blouse

- America, circa 1890-1910

One of the most unusual details of this blouse is the incorporation of lace edging where insertion is traditionally used (Fig. 1). In Figure 1, notice where the lace edging is turned upside down and used like insertion to join the sleeve fancy band with the sleeve. The edging lay on top of the sleeve bottom and is straight-stitched (in a curve to follow the curves of the bottom of the edging) to the raw edge of the blouse. The effect is a scalloped edge. The fancy band on the sleeves runs the length of the sleeve. It consists of two sets of four tucks spaced 1/16 inch apart. One-half inch separates the sets of tucks. Lace insertion is beside both sets of tucks (Fig. 1). As is so typical of the insertion techniques from the turn of the century — before the invention of the zigzag sewing machine — the raw edge of the fabric and tucking strip are folded back (about 1/2 inch), and the lace insertion edge is placed on top and straight-stitched to the garment. The raw edge of the lace insertion (which isn't raw at all) is visible from the top of the garment.

The embroidery design running down the front of this blouse is recreated here for you to copy (Fig. 2). That alone would be exquisite down the front of a dress or blouse. The embroidery in the petals of the flower is Ayrshire, which is a difficult stitch unless you are an advanced embroiderer. If you don't know Ayrshire, shadowwork petals for a similar effect. White- on-white like the original, or pastels would suit the embroidery design.

Fig. 2

Embroidery Design

Fig. 1

Decorative Cording
Christening Dress

Australia circa, 1850

This Australian dress, purchased in Melbourne, is museum quality. Every stitch is put in by hand, including the embroidered eyelets. Because of this, I've dated the dress 1850s to 1860s.

The circumference of the dress is 82 inches. The front panel of elaborately-corded work is 35 inches long. The top of the panel is only 1 inch wide; the bottom measurement is 21 inches across. What appears to be a panel is a fake panel. The elaborately-corded embroidery and eyelets are actually embroidered right onto the dress skirt, which is simply two gathered strips of fabric. The 2-1/2 inch wide embroidered edging is flat felled to the garment at the edge of the embroidery, by hand of course. The cording is made of what appears to be a cotton soutache. It is shaped on the garment and hand-stitched down the center. The eyelet work and buttonhole stitch scallops are absolutely breathtaking. The seams are flat felled on the sides and at the points, joining the handmade eyelet trims. The neckline and the waistline adjust for fitting with a drawstring casing. The neckline casing is 1/4 inch wide and the waistline casing measures 3/8 inch..

The dress laps right over left, when viewed from behind. The strings from the casing appear to be the only method of closing the garment. Beauty pins were probably used in between the casings and at the top and bottom for decoration, as well as for function.

Rouching Baby Dress

- America, circa 1860-1870

Rouching was very popular in the 1850s to the 1870s. Every stitch of this garment is put in by hand. Since the trims are Swiss, my thinking on the date would be between 1860 and 1870. Remember, that the first Swiss machine-made trims left Switzerland around 1850. Rouching or gathering, which appears on the bodice panel, prevailed during this period. This is a separate panel. The gathering (rouching or puffing) is made on a square piece. Cotton soutache is sewn on at sunburst angles, and the panel is cut out to fit into the bodice of the dress. The top of the rouching section measures 4-1/2 inches wide. The bottom of the rouching section measures 1-1/2 inches wide. These measurements do not include the Swiss trim that is attached flat beside the rouching section. The Swiss eyelet edging that is attached right beside the rouching has a finished measurement of 7/8 inch; I am sure that this seamstress started with 1-inch edging. In other words, it looks like puffing, but it isn't. It is gathered fabric with braid stitched down on top of the gathering. In consulting a history book, I found that narrow ribbons stitched down to form the little puffing rows was a common technique.

The neckline has the casing found in most baby dresses from 1850-1900. The casing measures 1/2 inch wide; it is embellished on the top with a 1/2 inch wide Swiss insertion. Tiny strings, which resemble delicate shoestrings, are run through both the neckline casing and the waistline casing. These two string ties are the only visible fastenings on the back of the dress. A 1/4-inch Swiss edging trims the triangular shapes on the top and bottom of the sleeves and the neckline. The same Swiss insertion, which travels around the neckline casing, is used for the cuff on the bottom of the sleeve.

The cap and cuff of the sleeve have tiny, double-triangular fabric trim, edged with the same trim that is around the neck (Fig. 1). Cynthia has drawn an illustration giving the exact size of the triangular shapes on both the bottom of the cuff and on the top of the sleeve (Fig. 2). As you can see, the triangular shapes do not go all the way around the sleeve or the cuffs.

The total dress length is 36 inches. The circumference of the skirt is 74 inches. The skirt has 3-1/2-inch tucks, which are spaced 1/2 inch apart; the hem measures 1-3/8 inch deep. The skirt has the fold-over method of gathering; this is where a bit of fabric (in this case 1/4 inch) is folded down to the back. The skirt is gathered and the folded-down top of the skirt is butted to the finished waistline of the bodice and whipped on by hand.

The waistlines on some of the mid-1800s dresses were pleated, the fullness held in with tiny pleats. My guess is that seamstresses dotted the fabric and gathered the fullness much like a smocking machine would do today. These pleats are so precise, it's hard to believe they weren't set in by machine. The finished pleated edge is butted to the finished top and whipped on, catching a stitch at every pleat. A small placket in the back is folded back and whipped. The back skirt placket is 8 inches long; it is simply a slit in the back of the dress with two tiny fold backs that are whipped in.

Rouching Baby Dress

Fig. 1

Fig. 2

Antique Diamond Blouse

- America, circa 1885

    This ladies blouse and skirt (described below) came from an estate in New England. The design and the antique diamond sewing technique hint that it is of an 1885 vintage. The technique "Turn-Of-The-Century Diamond Shaping" can be found in the technique chapter.

    Gathered fabric flatters the high yoke front. The laces are stitched onto the fabric; the fabric is then cut away from behind. You can use the basic blouse pattern in this book by drawing a high yoke and adding fullness to the bottom of the blouse. The fullness across the bottom of the blouse front is 32 inches. The insertion on the top of the blouse yoke is 2-1/2 inches wide. This type of insertion is hard to find because of its width. You could get the same effect by stitching two rows of insertion together to make a wider insertion. The main portion of the sleeve is embellished with the wide insertion; the bottom of the sleeve has one row of 1-inch insertion plus a piece of 1-1/2 inch edging below that insertion and a piece of 1-inch edging on the bottom. In order to attach the two rows of edging, simply overlap the heading of the bottom piece with the scalloped edge of the middle piece and straight stitch.

    The raw edge at the bottom of the sleeve is folded over two times (1/8 inch each fold) and two rows of running stitches, done by hand, are stitched at the bottom and at the top of this 1/8-inch fold back. These two rows are gathered, leaving a finished edge on the bottom. The lace insertion is butted to this finished, gathered edge and whipped on by hand. If you are stitching by machine, just butt the finished edge and zigzag. Refer to "Fold Back Method For Attaching Gathered Fabric To Lace Insertion."

    The inside arm seam (underarm) is slightly gathered; stay-stitching holds the gathering into place.

Ladies Diamond Puffing Skirt

- America, circa 1885

This skirt was purchased with the Antique Diamond Blouse (opposite page). The front panel extends around the hipline and drops to the bottom of the skirt. Diamond lace shapes are positioned on the tucking. Shirring or "double fake puffing" gathers the skirt. The waist on this skirt is 22 inches. The dropped waistline yoke of this skirt is 7 inches long. The front panel goes from the waist to the floor. The circumference of the skirt is 140 inches. A beautiful 2-inch tuck and a matching 2-inch hem accent the bottom of the skirt. This antique skirt is gored; however, if I were making a modern version, I would avoid the gores and make a full circle. From the top of the large diamond to the bottom, the skirt measures 13 inches. The lace insertion used for the diamonds is 2 inches wide. Since lace insertion that wide is difficult to find, I suggest zigzagging two pieces of insertion together to make a wide insertion.

Directions
Ladies Diamond Puffing Skirt:

The diamonds are made in a unique manner on the hip band and down the skirt front panel. The panels were made separately and then stitched into the skirt.

1. Plan the diamond shapes on the panel.
2. Cut pieces of lace insertion to be placed in diamond shapes from side to side (Fig. 1).
3. Place and pin your lace insertion pieces so that they form diamonds in the center and half diamonds on the sides (Fig. 1).
4. After all of the diamonds are shaped in this manner, straight-stitch down the side of this panel to hold your laces in place (Fig. 1-a).
5. Zigzag the laces to the fabric in the center diamonds first (Fig. 1-b).
6. Next, zigzag your laces to the fabric in the side diamonds (Fig. 1-c). **NOTE:** Do not zigzag over the intersections where the laces cross.
7. Cut away the fabric from behind the laces.
8. Use this newly-created lace diamond panel for the front of the skirt.

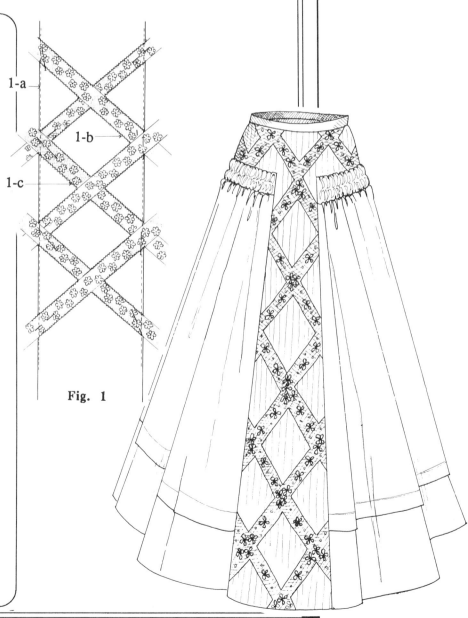

1-a
1-b
1-c

Fig. 1

Triangular Sleeve Christening Dress
- England, circa 1900-1930

This dress was purchased in England. Its unique design effect includes a three-triangle motif over the sleeve and bias tubing trim on the laces. The dress is made by hand, except for the double-stitching of the bias tubing. To reproduce the lace technique on this dress, it is necessary to have a heavy, round thread lace with a large single pattern, which has space between each pattern. Such laces would include large single rose lace or large dot lace. You will have to shop for your lace insertion very carefully to achieve the effect on this dress. But the results will be worth the effort.

The pattern for the three triangles trimming the sleeves is given here. They have a 1/4-inch seam allowance and are trimmed with 1/4-inch lace. A double row of French knots outlines the diamonds, the neckline bias binding, the trim on the bodice of the dress, and around the waistline of the dress.

The bodice of this dress is lace insertion (3/4 inch wide) zigzagged together. Any width insertion can be used in place of the 3/4-inch width. The zigzagged lace piece should measure about 8-1/2 inches by 11 inches in order to be placed at a bias angle into any size christening dress. Bias tubing 1/8 inch wide is double-stitched using a double needle right on top of the zigzagged lines. Refer to the technique section for instructions on making bias tubing. The insert is cut out of this square (Fig. 1).

Fig. 1

Reproducing the Fancy Band

1. Use this same insertion with the large pattern in it.
2. Angle the 1/8-inch bias piping, and double stitch it on top of the insertion.
3. Sew three 1/8-inch tucks, 1/2 inch apart above and below the tubing-trimmed lace. The total distance from the bottom of the lace insertion to the hem of the skirt is 3 inches; the skirt has a 2-inch hem, which is slip-stitched into place. The total length of the christening dress is 42 inches.

Chapter Two

Incorporate
yesterday's
details into today's
to-the-waist
dress.

The purpose of this chapter is to help you successfully incorporate yesterday's construction details into today's French sewn garments. On the pages that follow, artists Angela Cataldo and Cynthia Handy and I present 15 heirloom dresses adapted from original turn-of-the-century patterns.

"How do you look at antique clothing from history or old pattern books and adapt those ideas into clothing you can wear now? What about those funny-looking gored skirts? How do I change the pigeon-breasted blouse to something that I like better? How much or how little of an antique idea do I use on a garment for myself or for my child? What about those high necks that I don't like; how can I get the same idea on a garment without putting that choker neckline on it? What if I like a simple sleeve rather than a 'killer sleeve?'"

Those are some of the questions I have been asked since taking an interest in heirloom sewing. Here, I've described both the historical "idea" garment and the "new" garment, including fabric suggestions. After comparing the two and studying the interpretations, feel free to reproduce exact designs, or create a style all your own.

Antique Pattern Used In Designing
"Railroad Crossing Dress"

Handkerchief Linen And Lace
5614 Tucked Blouse 32 To 40 Bust
5587 Nine Gored Tucked Skirt, 22-32 Waist

Railroad Crossing Dress

The crisscross lace shapes, embellishing the bodice, skirt, and sleeves of this reproduction, resemble the familiar configurations that denote train tracks. This explains why I've decided to call it the "Railroad Crossing Dress." The lace technique is simple. First, tuck a straight piece of fabric in a subtle V fashion; this will become your bodice, so the original fabric piece must be wide enough to tuck and still fit the pattern. After tucking is complete, place your bodice pattern over the tucked piece so that the longest tuck hits the pattern at mid bodice. This will leave a section of untucked fabric to blouse above the waistline. Cut out the bodice.

The lace on this design is placed flat and zigzagged onto the bodice; fold the lace into a point at the end, and zigzag the crisscross shape directly on the dress. Follow the same pattern for the sleeve. Next, trace the design onto the skirt. You can "flip-flop" the lace at each intersection or you can miter it to make the "railroad crossings." Again, point the lace into a V at each cross section, and zigzag it to the dress.

On Angela's version of this design, shaped lace insertion around the neckline dips to a lower point than on the original. Gathered lace edging, which is the preferred neckline for today's French dresses, was used to finish the entredeux neckline at the base of the neck. The gored skirt was eliminated in favor of a gathered skirt. Any gored skirt may be adapted to a gathered skirt with a little creative thinking. The sleeves are to-the-elbow rather than below-the-elbow as seen on so many of the antique dresses. Three-quarter length — between the elbow and the wrist — is still a lovely option. A ruffle placed at the bottom of the dress and a sash at the waist completes the look.

Any pastel batiste, silk, or linen would suit this design. I envision a gray Nelona dress with stark white laces and a pink silk sash or ecru-on-ecru with a wide peach sash. For a more tailored look, you could use pale blue linen with white Swiss trims in place of the French laces.

Handkerchief linen is durable and makes a most charming lingerie gown. This one combines a simple yet attractive blouse with a tucked skirt, giving long and slender lines to the figure. As illustrated, it is trimmed with the German Valenciennes lace that endures laundering better than any other, but any lace or embroidery could be substituted. The gown can be made from any material considered appropriate for lingerie.

Railroad Crossing Dress

Bolero Lace Dress

The "Bolero Lace Dress" is fit for a Spanish senorita. Rounded lace insertion — two rows — and gathered lace edging create the bolero lines on the bodice. Delicate released tucks are centered between the laces.

To make the bodice, sew tucks on a section that just about reaches around the front neckline. Shape laces after the tucking is complete and the bodice is cut.

Two rows of entredeux, insertion, and edging form the neckline. Two rows of entredeux and one row of insertion are fitted at the waistline. This dress has two skirts; one overskirt with the most grand of points and a plain tucked skirt. Notice the tuck, which acts as the hem of the skirt.

Because of the strong Spanish feeling of the garment, I picture it made in heavy green silk with ecru laces. White Nelona Swiss batiste or perhaps white Finissima, which has more body, would do nicely for spring. The dress would be stunning in white with ecru laces and trims. Perhaps the tucks should also be stitched in ecru thread to accentuate their design power. For a romantic flair, you could choose organdy sleeves and an organdy peplum over batiste or silk. A burgundy or black velveteen embellished with shiny trims rather than laces would create a glamorous holiday dress. A wool challis trimmed with braid would make the design appropriate for school. Whatever your preference, this Spanish-inspired design is suitable for a variety of fabrics and trims.

Antique Pattern Used For Designing "Bolero Lace Dress"

5177 Fancy Blouse With Bolero Effect, 32-40 Bust
5105 Fancy Aprons, One Size

This antique drawing from an 1894 May Minton Glove Fitting Pattern Book, really isn't a dress at all, but rather a fancy blouse and apron. Actually the pattern came with two aprons. Lace shaping and gathered lace edging on the body of the garment defines the edge of the "bolero" thus, the name of the blouse, "Fancy Blouse With Bolero Effect." Since the apron resembles a peplum, Angela chose to combine the blouse and apron into a fancy dress.

The antique version has tucks in the middle of the bodice and tucks on the shoulders. As you can see from the back view of the antique drawing, the gathered lace continues around to the back. The triple-tucked skirt makes the perfect underskirt.

Loops Of Joy Dress

Since ice cream is one of my weaknesses, I have to think of this dress as peach sherbet or strawberries and cream. In order to make the bodice with the released tucks below the lace shaping, refer to the blouse chapter. Draft your lace shaping onto the bodice front of fabric, actually shape the laces, and then tuck another piece of fabric. Stitch the tucked bodice fabric to the upper portion, then, finish cutting your bodice.

Gathers and tucks dance across the skirt of this garment; the sleeves are a masterpiece. The double edging on the insertion trims the skirt. More lace and entredeux trim the ruffle at the bottom of the dress.

Since peach sherbet is one of my favorites, why not make this dress in peach fabric with ecru trims. Pink and white would work as well. A Christmas taffeta plaid, trimmed with laces would make the design a festive delight. If silk or linen is your passion, so be it; either would complement this design. Since lace is easier to shape into curves and loops than Swiss trim, I would opt for the former. So many of the ideas on this dress can be adapted to whatever style you prefer. Loop your laces and be ready to receive the compliments.

The joy of lace looping and shaping is certainly in full revival in the heirloom sewing business. Thus, I named this blouse "Loops Of Joy." Angela's inspiration for this dress was the blouse with the fancy looping on it; however, she let her creativity take over. The sleeves are a strong design feature. The tucks on the skirt add interest; so many of the antique skirts had tucks. The skirt is precious and features our beloved ruffle plus other tricks of the trade!

> *Antique Blouses Used For Designing "Loops Of Joy Dress"*
>
> *Blouse I = 5348 Fancy Yoke Blouse, 32-40 Bust*

> *Blouse II = 5102 Tucked Blouse With Yoke, 32-40 Bust*

Touches of pattern 5102 can be found in Angela's "Loops of Joy" design. Tucks circle around a scalloped yoke of looped lace. Loops at the cuff inspired the lace design on our sleeve. Although the skirt wasn't used in this particular dress, notice the tucks, which also curve around the back of the skirt; the front is left untucked. Gathered edging finishes the sleeve, delicately repeating the lace shaping.

Diamond Waterfall Dress

Some of Hawaii's most cherished gifts from nature are the glistening waterfalls framed by tropical greenery. Since I recently returned from a trip to America's tropical paradise, the waterfall image is what first came to mind when I looked at this heirloom dress. Notice the lace diamonds trickling down the front to the pool of ruffles and lace at the hem.

To make this bodice, with its three tiny tucks on either shoulder, first partially trace the bodice pattern onto the fabric around the neckline and out to the shoulders. Then, shape your laces on the fabric and trace almost exactly where the laces will go once you begin your lace shaping. Directly outside the area where your laces stop, mark three tucks. Stitch the tucks. Lay your pattern on your tucked piece, and cut out the bodice. Shape your laces onto the actual bodice and zigzag them to the bodice of the dress.

On the skirt, two rows of insertion are connected by the diamond "waterfall," which has mitered corners. The stitching on the bottom ruffles is hidden by double rows of lace edging, insertion, and entredeux.

Yellow Nelona, silk, or linen would positively light up this design. With the petite embroidery inside each diamond, you could pick up any color of Swiss batiste or silk. Velveteen or taffeta would be smashing for a winter version of this dress. The lace work on bodice and skirt could be shaped from Swiss trims as well as from laces. For a glitzy look, black and gold braid could substitute for laces. Sticking with tradition, this design would make a priceless first communion dress in white-on-white. Whatever the occasion, let your imagination be your guide, and enjoy!

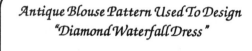

Antique Blouse Pattern Used To Design "Diamond Waterfall Dress"

5304 Tucked Yoke Waist, 32-40 Bust

5315 Blouse Or Shirt Waist, 32-40 Bust

Angela combined ideas from two blouses to re-create this "Diamond Waterfall Dress." If you will examine 5315 carefully, you will notice that the bodice on this design is similar to the "Diamond Waterfall Dress." Yet, lace shaping was also borrowed from 5304. Since she had no skirt to use for ideas, she transferred the shaping and the gradual increasing and decreasing of the diamond shapes to a skirt of her choice. Do you see how you can let your imagination run wild in taking a small detail from one garment and transferring it to another?

Bodice Embroidery

Skirt Embroidery

Roman Ribbons And Lace Dress

This "Ribbons and Lace" dress is indicative of Roman architecture. Notice the columnar silhouette, heavy trims, strong tailoring. Figures on the skirt incorporate three different textures. Pointed English lace — the inside configuration — is outlined by lace insertion finished into points; ribbon, stitched to echo the rectangular design, finishes the motif. This is the perfect place to use your new skills to miter around corners. Ribbon around the sleeves, the armscye, and the neckline adds a decorative touch. A lace inset with curved insertion follows the curves to grace the neckline. The same English edging is repeated around the armscye.

Almost any fabric could be used for this dress. Washable wool, velveteen, corduroy, heavy silk, broadcloth, prints, polished apple, or Viyella would suit a less fancy design. Swiss batiste, linen, or lightweight silk trimmed with pale ribbons would be perfect for special occasion dressing. Consider dusty rose Nelona with deeper shades of dusty rose ribbons and ecru trims. Brass buttons on a heavy fabric such as velveteen would give the dress a military feeling. Self-covered buttons would work on any fabric. Pearl buttons would suit a delicate, pastel dress.

As girls become teens they want a more tailored look in their Easter finery. A variation of the "Roman Ribbons and Lace" design makes for a more sophisticated, French dress. Since nautical is always in, why not reproduce this design in a heavy, white cotton, or linen, trimmed with navy ribbons for the skirt motifs and waist pieces. Try brass, military buttons for the bodice and waist, and run red ribbons through the beading on the sleeves and along the hem of the skirt. White laces could be used throughout. For a severely tailored look, opt for Swiss trims rather than lace.

> *Antique Pattern Used For Designing*
> *"Roman Ribbons And Lace Dress"*
>
> *5481 An Afternoon Gown-*
> *32-40 Bust, 22-30 Waist.*

The afternoon gown that is made with a blouson waist and skirt is an exceedingly important one. It is a bit more dressy than the shirtwaist model, yet simple enough for home wear. The dress is made from champagne-colored lace and linen, with trimming of brown velvet on the skirt, the arm bands, and the chemissette.

Tucks accent the shoulders of the shaped bodice gown. The open, velvet rectangles encompass lace trim; the lace is repeated on the bodice. The shaped trim features self-covered buttons probably out of the same brown velvet. This garment is relatively tailored and would have been suitable for receiving guests at home for 4-o'clock tea.

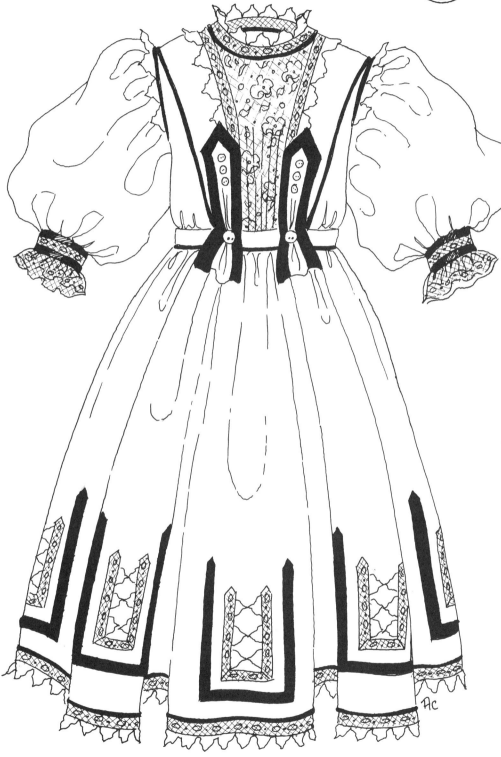

Puffing Peplum Dress

Double or triple puffing is easy to make when you follow the techniques found under "Double Fake Puffing" in this book. This dress boasts double puffing and a double fabric ruffle at the bottom of the sleeve. The peplum can act as a double skirt or can be detachable. The plain collar is treated with a delicate sewing machine scallop for its final edging. The entredeux on the shoulder as well as on the peplum and skirt incorporates the seam allowance of the entredeux as part of the dress.

Pale blue with stark white laces or peach silk with ecru laces would do justice to this frothy creation. For more color, you might try lavender Nelona with white laces and delicate embroidery in pink, yellow, blue, and stem green. If Swiss trims are to be used exclusively, they would especially complement a heavier, Laura Ashley-type Swiss batiste (Finissima). If this dress were to be made of a heavier fabric, such as velveteen, I would eliminate the puffing and place emphasis on the peplum, the shoulder treatment, and the ruffle around the shoulder.

> *Antique House Gown Pattern*
> *Used for Designing*
> *"Puffing Peplum Dress"*
>
> *5265 House Gown*

This house gown is actually a skirt and a breakfast jacket. A wide flounce on the bottom is sometimes called a Spanish flounce. The design appears to have triple puffing with a ruffle at the top. The fake puffing can be made with elastic or with a gathering thread so the look of this glorious house dress can be had today. Peplums are in fashion now as they apparently were in 1894.

Spring Shadow Embroidered Fantasy Dress

Although this dress appears to have a fancy collar, the zigzag of lace shaping that extends from the neckline is actually sewn onto the bodice. But, don't misunderstand me; you could draft a separate collar, if that is your preference. The easiest way, however, to achieve the look is to miter the lace in the shape indicated directly on the bodice. A word to the wise; embroider the floral/bow design on fabric before cutting out the bodice or skirt. Why? Because laces can stretch. I like to mark the lines where the laces will be stitched to the dress and work embroidery before attaching the laces. Again, there are few absolutes in French hand sewing. It is perfectly alright to shape your lace and zigzag it onto the dress before you embroider, as long as you leave plenty of fabric to fit into the embroidery hoop. The "Entredeux and Lace String" technique found in this book will help you achieve the desired effect on the bodice. The sleeve design calls for elastic rather than beading in gathering; sleeves are trimmed with insertion, entredeux, and edging.

Pink, white, or pale green would flatter this design. Delicate embroidery, in spring-like bows and buds encourages a white background with pink, blue, yellow, green, and lavender embroidery. As always, there is no getting around the elegance of white on white or ecru on ecru. We have Margaret Boyles to thank for its popularity. The design would serve as a magnificent Easter portrait dress no matter what your choice of fabrics and trims.

> Antique Dress Pattern Used For Designing
> "Spring Shadow Embroidered Fantasy Dress"
>
> 5601 Child's Dress, 1, 2 and 4 years.

Anyone with an eye for design can borrow the trim techniques from one dress and apply them to another dress to create an entirely different look. Using this turn-of-the-century child's dress, Angela adapted the ideas in her up-to-date, to-the-waist dress for older girls or ladies. Flip-flopping laces can be used for ease in stitching; however, these laces have been mitered. Delicate embroidery embellishes the bodice and skirt. Angela chose to drop the lace-trimmed angel sleeve, shown on the original dress, from the older girl's version.

Spring Shadow Embroidered Fantasy Dress

To-The-Waist 83

Lace Ruffle Overlay Dress

The Lace Ruffle Overlay Dress was adapted from an illustration of an antique wedding dress. This design would call for yards and yards of lace, limiting a reproduction to special occasions — graduation or a debutante's coming out. Since this much lace could be overpowering for a small child, you may want to extend the front tucks all the way around the dress, and reserve lace for the sleeves and hem. The original appears to be made of a lace netting; I would use the same on a reproduction. Refer to the "Netting Ruffle Technique."

Antique Wedding Dress Pattern
Used For Designing
"Lace Ruffle Overlay Dress"

5593 A Wedding Gown Bust 32-40
Waist 22-30

This antique wedding gown is absolutely gorgeous. The short sleeves are accentuated by the wearing of long gloves, kid I would presume. My thinking is that the antique gown has ruffles made of netting, batiste, or silk. Tucks run down the front of the wedding gown and skirt. The wedding veil appears to be of a dotted veiling.

Buttons, Entredeux, and Handloom Dress

A simple skirt from the *1894 May Minton Glove Fitting Pattern Book* inspired this clean-line dress. Swiss handloom with entredeux or faggoting aptly trims the center bodice and skirt. Groups of three buttons march down both sides of the handloom from the neckline to the hem.

A design this plain merits almost any fabric. Batiste would make a dressy version; tailored wool would be elegant for winter. Experiment with your favorite fabrics.

One might assume that this skirt buttoned in the back since the trim runs right down the front and the pleats travel around the skirt. The embroidered trim was probably handmade. A variation of this design would make a lovely reproduction in dark green wool with black velvet ribbon trim.

Antique Skirt Pattern Used For Designing
"Buttons, Entredeux, and Handloom Dress"

5214 Pleated Afternoon Skirt
22-30 Waist

Tucks And Swiss Motif Dress

If you have been wondering how motifs can embellish French sewn garments, take a look at this design. It's begging for motifs; I recommend white-on-white or pastel pink, green, and blue-on-white.

To make the tucked bodice, work with your straight piece of fabric and make your tucks, gradually sinking to mid bodice. After you have tucked the fabric, cut out the bodice. Insert or zigzag a straight piece of Swiss trim on top of both sides of the bodice. Repeat decorative tucks at the hip line, on the bottom of the sleeve, and on the cuff of the sleeve. Decorate the sleeves and skirt with motifs.

Tucks give a tailored look with a minimum of effort. Since motifs don't have to be "handmade" or "machine made" you're practically home free after the tucks are completed.

This dress would be spectacular in many fabrics, but my first choice would be handkerchief linen. Opt for white motifs on white linen or pick up one of the center colors of the motifs. The dress would be pretty in silk with silk motifs, however, silk motifs are difficult to find. Rayon motifs are more readily available and could be adapted to this type of dress; these are generally used in bridal wear.

> *Antique Pattern Used For Designing*
> *"Tucks and Swiss Motif Dress"*
>
> *5351 Tucked Shirt Waist With Star Shaped Yoke,*
> *32-40 Bust*

What we call "motifs" today, the designer of this dress, circa 1904, called "medallions." Much of the original blouse design was incorporated into the reproduction. The motifs form a star shape on the neckline of the bodice. The stair-step tucks found at the shoulder of the the original blouse were used at both the shoulder and hip line on the "Tucks and Swiss Motif Dress." More tucking dances around the hem of the skirt. The three rows of insertion, which encircle the neckline, are a striking way to add neckline interest without borrowing the uncomfortable high neckline from the original design. Notice that in the antique blouse, as well as in Angela's dress, the sleeve fancy band is wide enough to bear a motif.

Tucks and Swiss Motif Dress

Dancing Embroidery Dress

Some of you reading this book may know of my passion for ballet. This dress made me think of "Pavlova," "Swan Lake," little 3-year-olds in pink tutus, and the Sugar Plum Fairy. I adore the laces, tucks, and embroidery that appear to dance around the bodice and hem of the dress. The insertions run vertically to the waist — embroidery is worked between three rows; V's of insertion with tucks below the bottom V enhance the others. Lace edging is inserted around the armscye, at the neckline, at the sleeve bottom, at the skirt ruffle bottom and top, and at the waistline. Two rows of insertion elegantly shape the fitted waistline.

Ballet and pink go hand-in-hand. I'd also wager that most mothers think their baby girls look best in pink. Thus, pink Swiss Nelona is my first choice for this dress with various shades of pastel floss for the delicate embroidery. White lace would enhance the pastels in the embroidered bands. Any pastel shade of batiste or silk would work if you choose to embroider the dress as pictured. Navy linen or other colors with Swiss eyelet on linen produce a tailored version of the dress. Older girls, wanting a glitzy Christmas look, might prefer this design in velveteen with heavy English laces and no embroidery. Organdy worn over different-colored slips or camisoles and half-slips would exude the misted color that enchants the ballet stage.

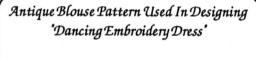

Antique Blouse Pattern Used In Designing
'Dancing Embroidery Dress'

5405 Fancy Lingerie Blouse, 32-40 Bust

Tucks are used in three strategic places on this blouse. Each set of tucks moves into a V shape like the laces that are mitered in the V's on the shoulders and in the center front of the blouse. The sleeves are relatively plain but elegant. The back view shows buttons up the center and tucks down either side.

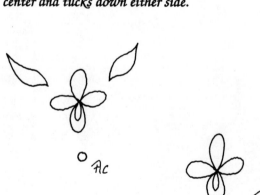

The Fan Dress

Fans are a brand new shape for the heirloom sewing digest. The lace illustrated in the picture almost looks like a string of buttons. Actually, if your fabric were heavy enough, buttons would be a fascinating treatment for shaping. The tucks run horizontally across the bodice with the gathers under the tucks. To make this bodice, tuck your fabric, and trace off your lace shape onto the tucked fabric. Gather the fullness you desire, about 30 inches across, and stitch around the shape you have just drawn. Then, cut away the tucked layer slightly below the stitched line. You are ready to stitch the second time through both layers.

The tucks on the skirt underneath the fan shapes are a unique treatment. Tuck your skirt first; then, shape the fans, zigzagging them onto the skirt. The choice is yours, concerning whether or not to cut away the fabric from behind the lace shaping. It is pretty either way.

I envision this design in velveteen or taffeta for Christmas. If Nelona or silk is your passion, standard white would take on a new appearance with this fan design. Linen with a heavier English lace would suit this dress especially since the tucks make it a little more tailored than some of the other dresses in this series. If this dress were made of velveteen or some other heavy fabric, the shaping could actually be done with buttons, if only on the bodice. Buttons could also accent the ribbon waistband. The tiny puffing between the insertion on the arm fancy band is one of those finishing touches that makes French sewing an art form.

> *Antique Blouse Pattern Used For Designing*
> *"The Fan Dress"*
>
> *5303 Fancy Yoke Waist, 32-40 Bust*

The unique lace shaping is what drew me to this design. I've yet to see fan-shaped lace on a modern-day French sewn garment. Yet it seems like such an obvious expression of lace work. Fans adapt themselves perfectly to this type of sewing. On the antique blouse, three fans embellish the bodice of the dress and a fan is found on each sleeve. This particular blouse has the connecting laces shaped into points; curves are another option.

Lowered Neckline Puffing Dress

Angela designed this dress and the shadow embroidery design. Notice the lowered neckline. By drafting out about 1 inch all the way around the pattern you can have a scooped neckline rather than a jewel neckline. The first step toward making this dress is to stitch your pintucks on your fabric about 1-1/2 inches apart. The shadow embroidery design is about 1 inch wide; that gives you 1/4 inch on both sides of the shadow embroidery before getting to the pintucks.

Next, choose a neckline. Identify the center of the garment, and trace off your neckline, using the pattern as your guide. Trace in your desired neckline. You may opt for the high neckline. After stitching your pintucks and tracing off your neckline, trace off your shadow embroidery designs on the sections between the pintucks. Lengthen or shorten the design, according to the number of flowers you want on the section and to the size of the garment you are making. Stitch your embroidery.

Antique Patterns Used For Designing
"The Lowered Neckline Puffing Dress"

5477 Corset Cover 32-40 Bust
5425 Five Gored Petticoat 22-32 Waist

Stay-stitch the neckline before you cut out the bodice. This will stabilize the neckline before you add your laces at the completion of the garment. By the way, a double row of edging has been stitched together by butting together two rows of edging and gathering them down the middle for the neckline trim. The sleeves of the dress have gathered edging.

Anytime I see gorgeous embroidery, I first think of white Nelona Swiss batiste embroidered with delicate shades of puffing pink, sky blue, spring yellow, robin's egg blue, lilac and stem green. A monocromatic touch can be achieved by embroidering pale pink Nelona in three shades of pink silk embroidery floss.

Puffing this wide is often called Austrian Shade Puffing. On this dress it has a finished width of about 5 inches. You can make yours wider or more narrow, depending on your preference. A wide gathered Swiss trim adds the finishing touch. You could use a fabric ruffle rather than the Swiss trim.

The inspiration for the "Lowered Neckline Puffing Dress" came from a corset cover and a five-gored petticoat pattern. Even yesterday's petticoats and 'drawers' as they were called, were so elegant, they displayed a wealth of design options for today's French sewn dresses. Notice the tiny tucks that flare when the ribbon is tied at the waist. Lace accents the armscye of the corset cover. Thus, lace and entredeux trimmed the armscye on Angela's design, as well. Lace beading with ribbon running through it was used at the waist of the corset cover. Angela placed insertion at the waist of the new dress. The petticoat sports wide Swiss eyelet at the bottom, as does the reproduction. Although in the antique illustration there doesn't appear to be entredeux at the top and bottom of the beading, I would assume it was used. Whether or not it was, Angela chose to add it to her version. When you look through antique clothing books, let your designing eye look for the tiny details, which can enhance other garments. Perhaps you can look for one detail in three or four different garments and completely create your own design.

Baby Puffing V Dress

Five, count them, five garments from the antique pattern books were used as inspiration for this one dress! Puffing is one of the long-lasting treatments in heirloom clothing. It can be as wide or as narrow as you wish it to be. In this design, Angela featured baby puffing throughout. Even the sleeves show two rows of puffing separated by a row of insertion. Straight tucks at the neckline and at the bottom of the the skirt and angled tucks on the bodice are a classic addition that subtly offset the ornate puffing.

The little puffing fancy band on the skirt is approximately 3-4 inches wide. The skirt and hem treatment give the impression of three fancy bands — the delicate puffing one, the set of two tucks, and the entredeux, insertion, and edging at the very bottom. A fabric sash ties at the waistline.

Because of the puffing, this dress almost has to be made of silk or batiste. I envision pink with white laces, perfect for the Easter parade. For fall or holiday, ecru on ecru-or-ecru laces on peach batiste would suffice. Children would adore this dress in lavender with white laces.

Five Antique Patterns Used For "Baby Puffing V Dress"

I can't stress enough that more than one pattern can inspire a single garment, as in the case of the "Baby Puffing V Dress." You will find elements of each in the final design.

> Antique Pattern I-5376
> Seven Gored Shirred Princess Gown,
> 32-40 Bust

This gown is shirred not puffed. Since puffing is a first cousin to shirring, Angela chose to design the gown using puffing instead of shirring. The shirring dips into a peasant neckline and is repeated at the sleeve and waist. This was the main inspiration behind the sleeve fancy band for the "Baby Puffing V Dress." Generally shirring is smaller than puffing, which is why I called this puffing, "baby puffing."

> Antique Pattern II-5243
> Fancy Tucked Blouse,
> 32-40 Bust

Notice the deep V in the front of the bodice with angled tucks trailing from it. The idea for angled tucks and the V front on the reproduction were inspired by this design.

Baby Puffing V Dress

Antique Pattern III-5118
Shirred Waist,
32-40 Bust

Shirring must have been popular in this particular era, just as puffing is a favorite treatment today. The idea from this blouse was to shape puffing in something other than straight rows. Although this shaping is circular, we transposed it into a V-shaped design.

Antique Pattern V-5277
Fancy Yoke Waist With Bertha Collar

It's hard to tell whether gathers on this collar are puffing or shirring; however, it appears to be puffing. The sleeves here are similar to those on pattern 5376. Gathered edging is zigzagged into the elaborately-shaped collar. In this case, I didn't analyze the details of the garment, exactly, but defined what the picture inspired me to do on another garment; shaped puffing was what I noticed.

Antique Pattern IV-5498
Fancy Yoke Waist,
32-40 Bust

The main idea from this pattern is the use of tucks shaped in the yoke of the dress. Although it is used here in an oval shape, it adapted well to a V neck.

To-The-Waist 95

Tailored Tucks and Lace Dress

When standing alone, this dress may or may not be considered a "tailored" garment. However, this design's geometric lines establish a much more tailored appearance than seen in some of the other reproductions we've covered. The laces circle the skirt ending in a point on each side of the tucked center portion. The neckline has all-over lace centered in a point with lace echoing the V. Notice carefully that on the bodice the lace comes up in a point at the center front, covering the miter of the neckline laces. Five released tucks on the either side of the shaped lace add fullness to the bodice. An entredeux and gathered lace neckline finishes the dress. Insertion defines the waist, here, although, a wide sash or a ribbon would be just as pretty.

This dress could easily be made of black velveteen, heavy linen, garnet red corduroy, or emerald green taffeta for the colder months. With the simplicity of the lace treatment, almost any fabric could be used. I can even see it in a calico with Cluny laces for a school dress. Cluny laces also complement dark taffetas and corduroys. Any dress, from the most tailored to the most delicate, is gorgeous in Swiss batiste or sheer silk. Heavier Swiss batiste (Finissima) — I refer to it as J.G. Hook batiste or Laura Ashley batiste — would keep with the tailored lines. With its primarily vertical lace treatment, this is the perfect dress to use Swiss trims, which don't curve as well as other laces.

Antique Skirt Pattern Used For Designing "Tailored Tucks And Lace Dress"

5334 Seven Gored Skirt, 22 to 32 Waist

This example incorporates a gored skirt into another dress, while keeping the design intact. The seven-gored skirt is a strong A-line, emphasized through tucks in the front and back. This particular skirt features lace trim; however, velvet ribbon would offer more color options. Lace ends in a V on both the antique skirt and the dress reproduction.

Cathedral Window Dress

Cathedral window is an appropriate name for this dress, as it would seem a shame not to wear such an exquisite design to a special church function. In all my years in the French sewing industry, I've seen few dresses as breathtaking as this one.

Sensing that the antique shoulder treatment wasn't as up-to-date as that found in today's heirloom garments, Angela altered the tucks on the bodice and sleeves to fit her design. The lace line on the bodice was flipped and exaggerated at the bottom of the skirt. For those of you who love to shadow embroider, this is a dream dress. It is so spectacular that I might make this for Joanna's cotillion dress when she is in the tenth grade. If you want to go completely crazy with embroidery, make four cathedrals on the skirt, and stitch four sets of embroidery!

A white Nelona dress, garnished with white laces and pale pink, rose, yellow, blue, lavender, and green embroidery would be stunning. A striking alternative would be white silk. The subtle beauty of a monochromatic shading could be achieved, using any color Nelona — robin's egg , pale blue, peach, or dusty rose — with the same shade embroidery floss. Laces could be ecru or bridal white. Even the darkest and most antiquated looking laces would complement pastel fabrics. I especially adore a dark, almost brown, lace teamed with paler shades of ecru or bridal white. It's perfectly acceptable to mix and match your laces in one dress.

> *Antique Blouse Pattern Used For Designing*
> *"Cathedral Window Dress"*
>
> *5447 Fancy Tucked Blouse, 32-40 Bust*

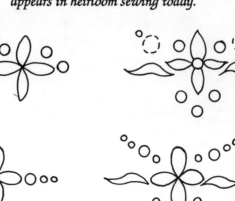

It continues to amaze me that blouses with such intricate detail and handwork were viewed as everyday apparel in 1904. A dress adapted from this design, with all its embroidery, would be treasured by even the most adored little girl. Tucks, curved lace bodice, embroidery, motifs on the tucked sleeve with gathered edging around the motif, insertion and gathered edging at the bottom are the touches that make this an exquisite design. The word "fancy" in the name "Fancy Tucked Blouse" has never been more fitting. The idea of gathering fullness with tucks, often appears in heirloom sewing today.

Buttons And Piping Dress

Who says French sewing has to be fluffy? This elegant dress is tailored indeed! Piping accents the triangular front panels on both the skirt and bodice. The double-piped collar, sash, and sleeves with piping on both sides echo the effect. Decorative buttons are the focal point on the design.

This dress calls for linen, broadcloth, or heavier silk linen. White linen with navy blue or marine blue piping would capture a crisp nautical style. Self-covered buttons would be my first choice, but pearl buttons would be suitable.

A simple beginning for a classic dress adequately describes this late 19th century skirt. Just repeat the skirt design on the bodice of the dress, and you have 90 percent of the tailored garment. Double-scalloped collars, trimmed with piping, complete the design.

Antique Skirt Pattern Used For Designing "Buttons And Piping Dress"

5568 Three Piece Skirt, 22-30 Waist.

Zigzag Ruffle Dress

Warm up your gathering foot. You'll need it to gather yards of edging for this Zigzag Ruffle Dress. A triple row of netting ruffles zigzag round the bottom of the dress, and gathered edging trims three rows of insertions on the bodice. The three-tiered angel sleeve can be softly gathered by hand. Lace at the edge of the puffed sleeves appears to be gathered with elastic.

A white-on-white version of this design would be the obvious choice since netting is mostly made in white. This is another design to reserve for a special occasion as the trim alone would be worth a small fortune.

Antique Dress Pattern Used For Designing "Zigzag Ruffle Dress"

1710 An Elaborate Afternoon Dress
32-40 Bust 22-30 Waist

Despite excess trim, this dress was designed as an afternoon costume. The double frill-caps fluff out over the two-seam sleeves, which end in several rows of baby puffing and a lace ruffle. A wrinkled ribbon belt is finished with a small bow at the back.

The skirt is composed of seven gores and fits smoothly over the hips. It is gathered and falls in soft folds in back. A bustle or any style of skirt extender would have been worn to achieve the popular S-shape silhouette. Four, lace-edged ruffles of the material form an elaborate decoration at the hem. The lowest ruffle is put on straight; the other three are arranged in a zigzag fashion.

Surah, taffeta, and China and India silk, nun's vailing, plain or dotted Swiss, plain or embroidered nainsook, dimity, and lawn are some of the materials suggested in the catalog description.

Pretty Peplum Dress

This dress is almost puritan in its design due to the large, split-bertha collar, trimmed with Swiss handloom and entredeux. The same insertion/edging treatment defines the edges of the sleeves, skirt, and peplum. The controlled peplum follows the curves of the skirt. The fabric ruffle extension at the hem of the dress would be a perfect way to lengthen any French dress that ends in straight, gathered edging.

This timeless dressing gown would be a best seller in today's lingerie departments. Notice the split-bertha collar that inspired Angela's dress. On this version, wide lace falls from the edge of the sleeve to cover the hand, a typical design element found in antique lingerie.

Antique Pattern Used For Designing
"Pretty Peplum Dress"

5361 Dressing Gown

103

Antique Middy Dress

Chapter Three

Pick and choose
from antique middy
designs to make your
creative version.

The descriptions of middy dresses I've found in antique pattern books have been such a pleasure to read, I've decided to share a few with you:

"The association of nainsook, fancy tucking, ribbon-run beading and edging is charming in the little frock depicted here."

"Originality of design distinguishes the frock of dahlia-red albatross and applique band and black velvet ribbon produce pleasing contrast." "Even when elaborately trimmed, white-wash dresses have an air of simplicity that is eminently appropriate for children. No material is better adapted to these charming little frocks than fine India lawn."

Using the antique middy dress as our foundation, Angela Cataldo and I designed 12 new dresses, and Cynthia Handy put pen to pad, interpreting the designs for you to see. Two of the patterns, which come with this book, are copies of actual middy dresses from my antique collection. One has a lowered, square neckline; the other has a rounded neckline. Notice that waistbands on antique middy dresses were not placed at the hipline; instead, a band of fabric was sewn between the waist and hips. If you prefer a lowered hip band on your pattern, simply add 2 or 3 inches to the length of the bodice pieces.

One of the joys of writing this book has been the time I've spent pouring over heirloom garments, trying to incorporate some of the details into designs that could be worn today. Often the lines were outdated and inappropriate for a modern wardrobe, but most of my pieces had at least one element — a collar, or a cuff, or innovative lace work — that I could borrow. The final garments should be a joy to create. It wouldn't surprise me if your sewing machine lit up without your even touching the on-switch.

Enjoy the patterns included in this book, keeping in mind they're "new" designs made for you from "old" ones. Feel free to change the basic patterns and draft new collars or use the ones given. After you see how we have borrowed ideas from yesteryear, I feel sure that you will be inspired to do the same. It's fun and easy; we are pronouncing that you are the best designer of all.

Fold-Over Ribbon Collar Middy

Never before had I seen a ribbon collar until I unearthed this drawing from an 1892 book. The waistline on the antique dress is actually empire; we adapted it to a middy dress. I don't know about the availability of extremely wide ribbon, as shown on the antique dress; therefore, we designed our version with narrower ribbon. Play with this fold-over ribbon concept on a gathered fabric or lace collar. Use the high-neck version of the middy in this book for your dress pattern.

Ribbons And Rosettes Middy

This antique dress was featured in a 1905 pattern catalogue. Angled lace edging extends the all-over lace yoke out to the sleeves giving the appearance of a dropped-shoulder design. Gathered (rouched) ribbon, kissed with ribbon rosettes, echoes the yoke line at center bodice. Gathered ribbon also finishes the neckline. The 1-inch wide (or wider, if preferred) ribbon is gathered with a thread, run down the middle to gather. I always use the gathering foot on my sewing machine for ribbon gathering.

Diamond Tucked Skirt Middy

This antique illustration comes from a 1919 magazine advertisement for Queen Undermuslins' camisole and petticoat. Taking her cue from these gorgeous undergarments, Angela dreamed up a middy design. For the dropped-shoulder look, use either a dropped-shoulder pattern or a pointed bertha collar. The tucks and entredeux embellish lavishly the whole dress. The skirt treatment would glorify any garment for child or adult.

Large Split V Collar Middy

This gorgeous split V collar middy dress, which would mesmerize in eyelet or lace, is a 1905 design. The sharp double V gives this middy a more tailored appearance, despite the wide ruffled edging. Thus, it would be equally attractive in plaid wool, challis, or linen as in batiste or silk. Either of the middy patterns in this book could be adapted to this design.

Diamonds And Squares Collar Middy

I have seen a lot of French sewing, but never have I seen a collar quite like this squared-off, zigzag design from a 1905 catalog. This is a unique manipulation of lace edging. Although we've eliminated the high collar and lowered our waistband, our version is almost identical to the original dress. Wide puffing embellishes both skirts. Adapt the high yoke, middy pattern in the book to make this dress. Don't be afraid to draft collars. Use a basic, round bertha collar pattern, and trace off the squares and diamonds.

Deep V Pointed Collar Middy

This 1904 middy boasts two wonderful design elements. The first is a collar that dips to a dramatic V in the center front; the second is the creative use of tucks on both the body and skirt of the garment. Both or either one of these ideas would yield a magnificent middy. The collar, in particular, would be just as pretty on a to-the-waist dress.

1905 Flower Girl's Dress

I prefer to call this dress, "The Portrait Neckline, Pleated Collar Middy," for obvious reasons. Insertion curves around the neckline of the dress with the pleated collar attached below this curved insertion. On the skirt, more entredeux and gathered edging ("an entredeux and lace string") is zigzagged on for a lavish antique effect.

1906 Flower Girl Dress

The description on this dress from the May 1906 *Delineator* reads, "Little flower girls are dressed with fairy-tale daintiness." The words, alone, evoke a precious image. Using a high-necked, middy pattern, adapt this dress with its quietly-curved insertion in the neckline, tucks on the sleeves, and sailor collar, delicately trimmed with lace, entredeux, edging, and a rosette. "An entredeux and lace string" is how the pattern refers to the lace edging, gathered to entredeux and zigzagged to the top of the skirt.

Rosette And Puffing Middy

A collar and petticoat pattern inspired this particular middy. The collar divides into three wide sections in the front and back. Large ribbon rosettes or silk ribbon embroidery embellish each section as well as the waistband on the middy. On the antique petticoat, wide puffing gives the look of a wide band. This style would be just as attractive for an adult by substituting embroidery for ribbon rosettes and extending the skirt.

Puffing Pleated Collar Middy

The 1895 antique dress was originally designed for an older girl. It looks as if the heirloom design had tiny puffing strips circling the collar and skirt; however, the 1895 sketch is so fuzzy it is difficult to tell. I used my imagination. With the invention of a gathering foot, puffing doesn't take long to make. If, indeed this is puffing, it is stitched down on top of the pleated collar. Edging is gathered and stitched on top of the puffing on the skirt, eliminating the need for insertion.

1894 Fancy Middy

This design, adapted from the antique dress shown, features a straight yoke with a gathered section underneath. Try a high yoke pattern with a basic skirt, cut off and gathered for the dropped middy portion of the garment. Then add a traditional middy waistband and a gathered skirt. Stitch the gathered lace onto entredeux and zigzag onto the dress. Cut a 1/2 bertha collar. Gather fabric and laces around the neckline. Repeat the gathered lace treatments on the skirt, and you will have a dream of a dress following the ideas of 1894.

1830 Triple Collar Middy

Although, this dress came from an 1894 catalog, the description in the catalog reads "1830s collar," which I deemed appropriate for our purposes. To make a triple collar, simply add length to the original collar, and cut three of them. The entredeux, insertion, entredeux, wide puffing skirt is extremely elegant. Use the basic middy pattern in this book with the high neckline to serve as your guide pattern. Design and cut your own fancy collar.

Beautiful Blouses

Chapter Four

Adapting
May Minton
blouses to
today's fashion.

The popularity of vintage fashion has led to a shortage of antique clothing. Fortunately, I've been able to scavenge the antique shops in Australia and haunt the markets along England's famed Portobello Road. Here, in the United States, an antique dealer friend contacts me any time she gets in a new shipment of "white" clothing. Because of this, I have slowly built up a respectable collection of blouses.

Not everyone, however, has access to foreign markets, or a friend in the antique business. For this reason, I've devoted an entire chapter to antique blouse design. This alphabet of blouses, obviously 26 in all, is a French sewing by machine dream. The original designs were taken from the 1894 May Minton Glove Fitting Pattern Book and updated for you to reproduce. No design element is etched in stone. I encourage you to experiment, using the basic pattern found in this book.

General Construction Ideas
Adapting Antique Blouses To A Modern-Day Blouse
Using The Basic Blouse Pattern Included In This Book

Cutting Out The Blouse Pieces

1. You must trace the master pattern and cut a blouse pattern out of tissue paper, pattern trace, or lightweight interfacing (not fusible interfacing). This includes the backs, the sleeves, and the front of the blouse. Place the blouse front on the fold of your tissue paper or interfacing fabric and cut out a whole blouse front (Figs. 1 and 2).
2. To make these blouses, start with a large rectangle of fabric. Much decorative stitching will be done on this rectangle before the blouse front is ever cut out.
3. For many of these blouses, pintucks are on the bodice. Some begin at the shoulder. Others begin on the bodice. For most of the blouses the pintucks will be made from the top of the rectangle of fabric to a stopping point on the blouse.

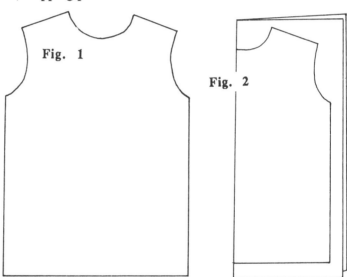

Fig. 1

Fig. 2

Designing And Drafting Your Version Of These Blouses

1. I would have needed to publish another book to include individually-drafted patterns and instructions for each of these 26 antique blouses. Thus, I'm letting you be the designer. With the help of the antique illustrations and updated drawings, you can create a blouse with an heirloom/antique feeling especially adapted to your tastes.
2. Now some of you are going to say, "I can't plan lace design for the front of a blouse." I say, "of course you can." That is where the real fun of designing comes in. If you are drawing scallops on the front of a blouse, for instance, fold the blouse pattern in half. Using a flexible curve (found at any art supply store) begin to trace, in pencil, some scallops. You can use the scallop template guide found in this book.
3. If the design you want is square or a V, mark the middle of your blouse pattern, and use your pencil to mark on your pattern. This way, you can make your V go as low or as high as you want.

Neckline Finishes For A Jewel Neckline Blouse

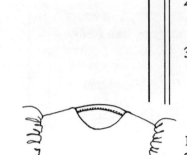

Entredeux, gathered lace neckline finish.

1. This is probably the most commonly-used jewel neckline (no collar) finish for heirloom clothing. Using the technique "Entredeux To Flat Fabric," stitch the entredeux to the neck curve.
2. Trim the entredeux seam allowance to the seam allowance that is allotted on your blouse pattern. In the case of this blouse pattern, the seam allowance is 5/8 inch for the whole blouse.
3. Trim away 1/8 inch of the neck edge. Then use the 1/2-inch seam allowance of the entredeux as your seam allowance for the blouse. Stitch in the ditch, trim to 1/8 inch, and zigzag. Or, use your serger/overlocker to complete the whole step in one operation.

Using a bias facing to finish the neck edge.

1. Trim away the whole seam allowance.
2. Cut a bias binding that measures 1-1/2 inches wide by the length of your blouse neck plus 1 inch.
3. Fold this bias binding in half. Right sides to right sides, raw edges to raw edges, stitch around the neckline with a 1/4-inch seam allowance.
4. Fold the finished bias binding into the neckline. This leaves a 1/4-inch seam in view at the neckline of the blouse when you whip the neck binding to the neckline of the blouse on the inside.

A BLOUSE A

This blouse features a deep V in the front of the blouse which can be filled with pintucks, laces butted together and zigzagged, or lace by the yard. The box pleats over the shoulders extend to the bottom of the blouse. Shadowwork embroidery can be stitched on the designs before the box pleats are sewn in.

Construction Units:

1. Cut the blouse pattern; front, back, and sleeve.
2. Trace blouse front onto a tissue paper pattern.

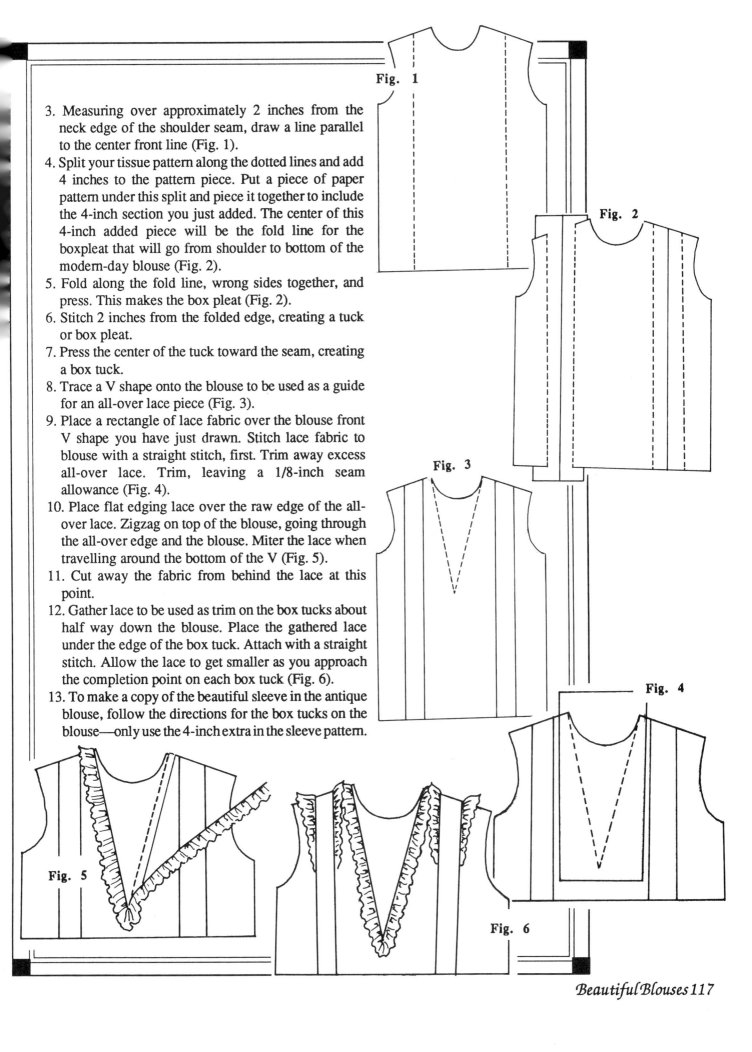

3. Measuring over approximately 2 inches from the neck edge of the shoulder seam, draw a line parallel to the center front line (Fig. 1).

4. Split your tissue pattern along the dotted lines and add 4 inches to the pattern piece. Put a piece of paper pattern under this split and piece it together to include the 4-inch section you just added. The center of this 4-inch added piece will be the fold line for the boxpleat that will go from shoulder to bottom of the modern-day blouse (Fig. 2).

5. Fold along the fold line, wrong sides together, and press. This makes the box pleat (Fig. 2).

6. Stitch 2 inches from the folded edge, creating a tuck or box pleat.

7. Press the center of the tuck toward the seam, creating a box tuck.

8. Trace a V shape onto the blouse to be used as a guide for an all-over lace piece (Fig. 3).

9. Place a rectangle of lace fabric over the blouse front V shape you have just drawn. Stitch lace fabric to blouse with a straight stitch, first. Trim away excess all-over lace. Trim, leaving a 1/8-inch seam allowance (Fig. 4).

10. Place flat edging lace over the raw edge of the all-over lace. Zigzag on top of the blouse, going through the all-over edge and the blouse. Miter the lace when travelling around the bottom of the V (Fig. 5).

11. Cut away the fabric from behind the lace at this point.

12. Gather lace to be used as trim on the box tucks about half way down the blouse. Place the gathered lace under the edge of the box tuck. Attach with a straight stitch. Allow the lace to get smaller as you approach the completion point on each box tuck (Fig. 6).

13. To make a copy of the beautiful sleeve in the antique blouse, follow the directions for the box tucks on the blouse—only use the 4-inch extra in the sleeve pattern.

Fig. 1

Fig. 2

Fig. 3

Fig. 4

Fig. 5

Fig. 6

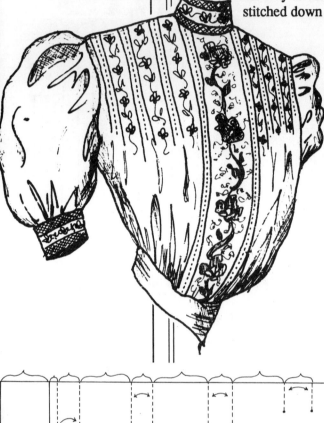

Blouse B

This blouse features embroidery down the front panel with embroidery in each of three sections on either side. Small box pleats run along either side of the front and on each side of the embroidery strips. The box pleats on the front piece are stitched down all the way to the bottom of the blouse. The ones on either side of the front are stitched down around 6 or 7 inches and then released.

Construction Units:

1. Cut out the blouse pattern pieces; front, back, and sleeves.
2. For this blouse, the fabric rectangle will be approximately 10 inches wider than the finished front blouse. Starting with a large piece of fabric, longer and wider than the finished blouse front, mark what will eventually be the center of the blouse. Fold in half and press in the usual way to mark the half point of anything.
3. Mark how wide the center embroidery section will be. We suggest about 4 inches wide.
4. Pin in two very small box pleats all the way to the bottom of the blouse. Tuck one inch all the way down. When you press this tucked inch flat and press so that the center of the tuck is laying on the seam; it will measure 1/2 inch (Fig. 1).
5. Mark the next three box pleat tucks which will only be stitched down 6 or 7 inches. Pin these box pleats in.
6. Place the pattern front over your work to be sure you have the proper widths for your size blouse front. Make adjustments as necessary.
7. Press in your box pleats. Mark the exact widths of embroidery space for the six small sections of embroidery.
8. Stitch in your box pleat tucks. Stitch the ones for the center section all the way to the bottom of your large square of fabric. Stitch the ones for each side section down as far as you want them to be. Press the tucks flat. Remember, each tuck, when it is pressed flat, will be no more than 1/2 inch wide (Fig. 2). Look at the antique picture. See the straight decorative stitching in the center of each tuck. Wouldn't it be pretty to feather stitch down each tuck rather than just straight stitch. You can do this either by hand or by machine. Places like this are wonderful to try out the decorative stitches on your new dream machine.
9. Now you have your exact sections onto which you will place embroidery. You still are working on a large piece of fabric. The blouse front has not been cut out yet. Trace the blouse front onto your large section of fabric.
10 Work your embroidery on all sections of the blouse.
11. After your embroidery has been completed, cut out your blouse.

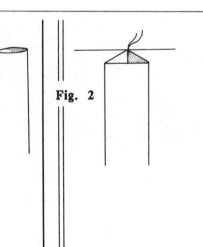

Fig. 1

Fig. 2

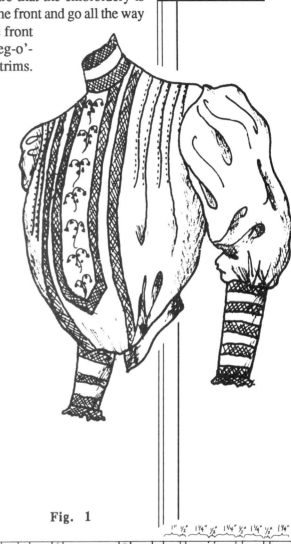

Blouse C

This blouse is almost like Blouse B. The main differences are that the embroidery is limited to the center section, and the lace trims form a long V in the front and go all the way to the bottom on either side. The tucks (five on each side of the front embellishment) have no embroidery in the center section. The leg-o'-mutton sleeves have alternating lace insertion and tucking trims. Gathered lace finishes the bottom of the blouse sleeve.

Construction Units:

1. Cut a large rectangular piece of fabric much wider and longer than your finished blouse will be. The fabric will be about 10 inches wider than the finished blouse front. This allows room for your tucking before you cut out your blouse. **NOTE:** If you want more than five tucks on each side of the blouse, allow a little more than 10 inches at this time on your large piece of fabric.

2. As always, cut out your paper pattern pieces for the blouse; front, back, and sleeves. Mark the center of the fabric. Trace off neckline and beginning shoulder seams on the fabric.

3. Shape your lace center section on the front. Draw in this lace section. Mark your lace strips beside this center section. At this point you have only drawn in the lace shaping on the front of the blouse. You have not stitched anything.

4. Place and stitch your five tucks on either side of this lace treatment. These tucks are approximately 1/4-inch tucks spaced about 3/4 inch apart (Fig. 1).

5. Draw your embroidery design. Embroider your design. Press.

6. Now you are ready to zigzag your laces into place.

7. After zigzagging your laces, cut out your blouse front (Fig. 2). If you would like a fancy treatment, use tucks on the back of the blouse, also.

Fig. 1

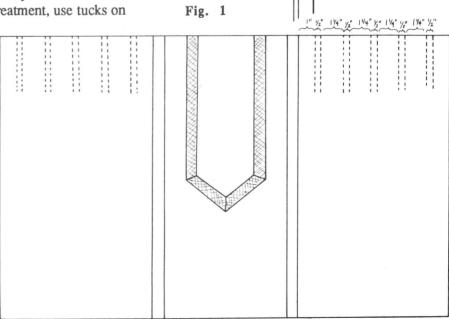

Fig. 2

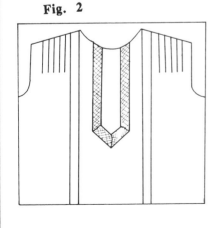

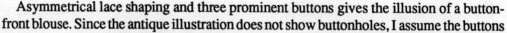

Blouse D

Asymmetrical lace shaping and three prominent buttons gives the illusion of a button-front blouse. Since the antique illustration does not show buttonholes, I assume the buttons are for decoration, not function. Two top-stitched tucks fit the blouse at the shoulders. Curved rows of insertion fill in the neckline V. Four rows of insertion embellish the extended cuffs of the leg-o'-mutton sleeves. This blouse would be a breeze to reproduce, using the directions below and the blouse pattern that comes with this book.

Construction Units:

1. Cut a large rectangular shape of fabric, wider and longer than the blouse pattern. Mark the center front of this piece of fabric.
2. Trace off the shoulder line.
3. Mark the center front of the fabric.
4. Decide how far down you want to place the center V of curved lace. Mark the V on the pattern.
5. Shape three pieces of lace insertion into the V. Pull a thread and curve. Pin these lace curves into place. Zigzag lace to the blouse, stitching from one edge of the V to the other edge of the V. Do not stitch the portions of the lace insertion that extend out onto the blouse. After stitching the curved V's to the blouse front, trim away the excess lace insertion (Fig. 1).
6. Mark the two tucks on the fabric. These appear to be about 1-inch tucks. Fold the tucks into place and press.
7. Stitch the tucks.
8. After stitching the tucks, draw the blouse front on the fabric, making sure the pattern is positioned correctly on tucks and V front.
9. Shape the straight piece of insertion, following the short side of the V. Zigzag the straight side of the V insertion to the blouse on both sides. Notice that this piece of insertion will cover the raw ends of the curved insertion, which you have already zigzagged to the blouse (Fig. 2).
10. Shape the long side of the curved V, which extends to the bottom of the blouse. Miter the corner (Fig. 2).
11. Zigzag the long side of the curved V and the straight piece down to the bottom of the blouse on both sides. This curved V insertion covers the other side of the raw edges of the curved short pieces of insertion, making a V design.

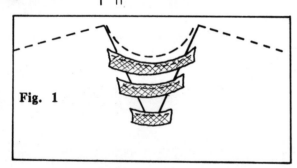

Fig. 1

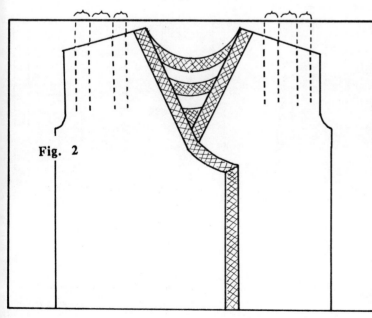

Fig. 2

Blouse E

This blouse features pintucks all the way across the blouse front and back. The laces are shaped in a diamond bottom with extended lace tabs. The tabs end in a V-shaped formation, which is made by folding back both sides of the lace end to a V.

Construction Units:

1. Cut a large rectangular shape of fabric, wider and longer than the blouse pattern you have cut out. Mark the center front of this piece of fabric.

2. Pintuck all the way across the fabric, gradually making the pintucks shorter. Measure with your blouse front pattern piece as you go along so that you will not have too much pintucking to waste after you cut out your blouse.

3. After you have more than enough pintucking, measure your blouse front again. Do you have enough for the whole blouse width? Trace your blouse front off on the pintucked fabric. In order to allow for the fullness of the pintucks at the bottom, place your gathered fabric up under the pattern. You might pin it onto a fabric board in order to get the side seams straight when you trace off your pattern.

4. Notice the V shape in the bottom of the lace (Fig. 1). In order to make this V, simply fold back into a V, each side of the cut end of the lace. Press. Place A and B lace pieces first. Pin. Place C and D pieces next. Pin. Place E and F pieces last. Pin. Zigzag around A and B first. Then, zigzag around C and D. Finally, zigzag around E and F.

5. Before you cut out your blouse, stay-stitch (straight stitch) all the way around the blouse arm holes, the shoulder seams, and the neckline. This will hold your laces into place while you cut out the blouse.

6. Cut out the blouse.

7. If you desire a fancy back, make one similar to this front.

8. For the sleeves of this blouse, make a fabric similar to the front. You can either have or not have pintucks. The lace shaping will be done in a similar manner to the front of the blouse. The sleeves consist of entredeux, two rows of insertion, entredeux, and gathered lace at the bottom.

9. The neckline can be finished with entredeux and gathered lace.

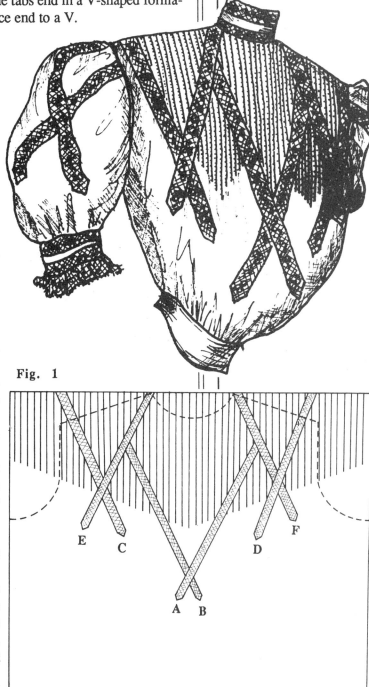

Fig. 1

Blouse F

What elegant simplicity. The antique version begins with pintucks all the way across the blouse front. Three strips of insertion are zigzagged on top of the pintucks. For the modern-day version, I suggest an entredeux and gathered neckline finish for the neckline. This is a great blouse for business wear underneath a suit. The sleeves on the antique blouse are insertions zigzagged together and stitched in a V shape. You can use our plain long sleeve, our short sleeve, or a sleeve of your choice from another pattern.

Construction Units:

1. This blouse is terribly simple to construct using our basic pattern. Pintuck across the front of the rectangular piece of fabric. Your fabric should be approximately 10 inches wider than your finished blouse front.
2. Trace your blouse front onto your pintucked piece of fabric.
3. Finding the center of the blouse, zigzag one piece of lace down the middle and two on either side of your blouse front. You have the option of trimming away the fabric from behind the insertion or leaving the fabric. Both would be pretty.
4. Cut out the blouse and follow the instructions in the pattern envelope.

Blouse G

This gorgeous blouse is very similar to Blouse F. The main difference is the width of the laces and where the laces stop. The pointed stopping point of the laces is easy to do. The short, puffed sleeves have one row of insertion; I would place entredeux at the top and bottom of this insertion. Gathered lace trim finishes the sleeve.

Construction Units:

1. Pintuck across the front of a rectangular piece of fabric. Be sure that the rectangle is at least 10 inches wider than the finished blouse front. Mark the center of your pintucked fabric. Continually measure the pintucks as you add them; you don't want to pintuck any further than necessary.
2. Trace the front of your blouse onto the pintucked fabric.
3. To make the pointed lace shapes, fold back the insertion to make a point of lace. Press. Zigzag the pointed, lace insertion strips to the blouse. You have the option of leaving the fabric behind the lace insertion or cutting it away. Both are acceptable.
4. Cut out the blouse front and follow the instructions in the pattern envelope.

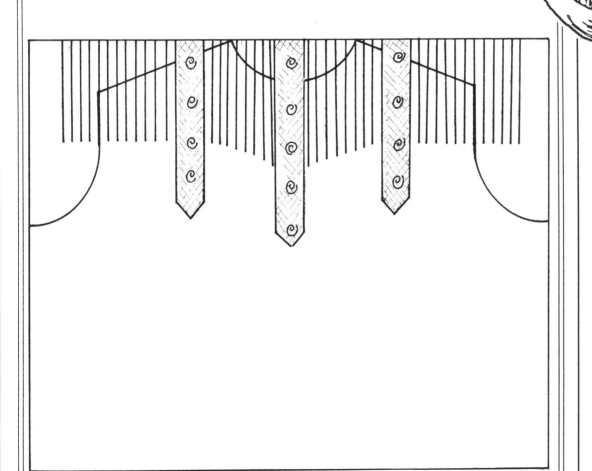

Blouse H

This very unusual blouse features tucks across the bodice front. It is quite tailored with lace only on the leg-o'-mutton sleeves in the antique version. The steps are very unusual for making this blouse into a modern-day adaptation.

Construction Units:

1. Begin with your large rectangular piece of fabric. You will construct all of the decorative work on this blouse before cutting out the blouse.
2. Make six horizontal tucks all the way across the top of the fabric. These tucks are approximately 1/2-inch tucks, 1 inch apart. You may make the tucks any length and depth you want. I have given you a tucking guide to use if you so desire (Fig. 1).
3. Divide the large piece of fabric into thirds. Cut the fabric at these third lines (Fig. 2, points A and B).
4. Cut two 4-inch strips of fabric. These will be stitched between A1 and A2 and B1 and B2. Use a 1/4-inch seam allowance. Straight stitch and zigzag to finish the edges; or overlock (Fig.3).
5. Bring the pieces of fabric together and straight stitch on the same seam, making a box pleat all the way down to the bottom of the blouse (Fig. 4).
6. On the outside of the box pleat on the section where the tucks run across the bodice, make some decorative top-stitching.
7. **NOTE:** There is another box pleat at the shoulder seam of the antique blouse. If you want to add it, trim away the tucks and stitch another piece on. This complicates the construction.
8. For the sleeves, use the same tucking guide and add lace insertion at the top of the sleeve and lace insertion at the bottom. I would also add entredeux at the top of the sleeve.
9. As with all of these patterns, you are now ready to trace the blouse and cut it out.

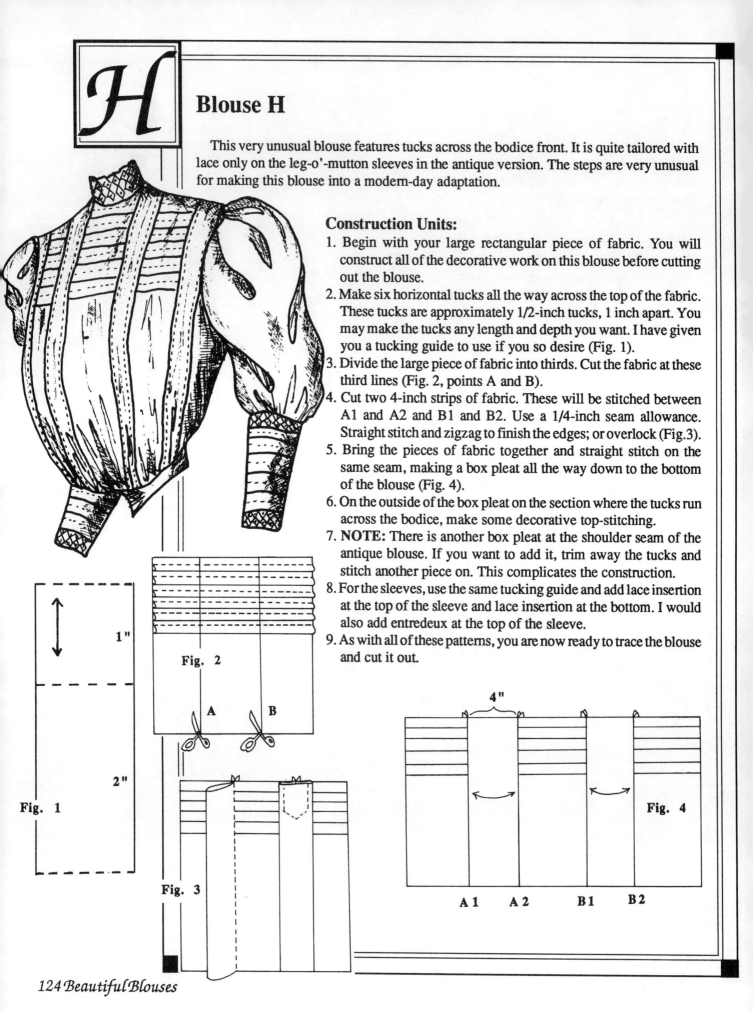

Fig. 1

Fig. 2

Fig. 3

Fig. 4

A 1   A 2   B 1   B 2

General Instructions For Blouses I, J, K, L, M, and N

The reason for giving a set of general instructions for blouses I - N is because the details of the basic garment drafting and construction are similar. Each of them works with a curved piece of fabric for the upper yoke and lace shaping for the bottom of this yoke. All have pintucks underneath the lace-shaped top bodice. Although the pintucks vary in number, type, and shape on the blouse, the idea is still the same.

The Fancy Yoke Top Portion Of These Blouses

1. Trace the pattern pieces onto tissue paper or pattern drafting interfacing. Trace the whole front of the blouse.
2. Trace the fancy yoke on a separate rectangular sheet of tissue paper.
3. Cut out a rectangular piece of lace the size of the rectangular piece of tissue pattern you just cut.
4. Using a straight stitch, stitch the lace to the paper pattern just inside the drawn portion of the paper pattern.
5. Place the lace/tissue piece you just made onto a fabric board.
6. Shape the lace to the lower drawn scallop, using the mitering and shaping techniques found in this book. Shape the curves and miter the tops of the scallops.
7. Zigzag the lace top edge into place, stitching through the overall lace fabric, the tissue paper, and of course the top edge of the lace. Spray starch and press several times. As a matter of fact, starch and press this section so stiff that it can get up and march away from your ironing board.
8. Trim away excess fabric from under the lace scallops.

The Pintucked Bottom Portion Of The Blouses

1. You can choose to pintuck in a point (Blouses J or M), in a curve (Blouses L or I) or a variation of a point (Blouses K or N).
2. The tucks can be equal distance apart, almost touching, unequal distance apart with space between the sets of tucks, or any other way you think would be pretty.
3. Begin with a rectangle of fabric, estimating the width that will be drawn up by the tucking. The general rule of thumb is to start off with 15 inches more fabric for the blouse front than the finished blouse. This is for the double needle pintucks made with your pintuck foot. If you desire to put in larger tucks, more fabric will be needed. If you have more fabric than you think you will need in this rectangular piece of fabric, you don't have to tuck the whole thing; however, if you need more, it will be there for you.
4. With a fabric marker, you will mark the center front of this piece of fabric.
5. You will draw the basic shape of the place where your tucks will end. Look at the antique blouses to determine this approximate line of tucking.
6. Tuck the piece of fabric, checking against your pattern piece for the fancy top for these blouses so that you won't waste time tucking in areas that would be cut away after you begin to assemble your blouse.
7. When using double needle pintucks, start at the top of the fabric. Stitch to the drawn line in Step 5 above, stop, and leave long threads (at least 6 inches long) before you cut your threads.
8. Start at the top again and stitch to the line. Repeat until you have your pintucked pattern completed.
9. After you have finished tucking your piece, pull all of these threads to the back and tie them off. You can make two back stitches at the end of each tuck line, but it is not pretty. Press the tucks however you see fit. It does not matter which direction you press them. This is personal preference.

Attaching The Fancy Yoke To The Pintucked Bottom Portion

1. Place the yoke on the top of the pintucked fabric, overlapping by 1/4 inch to 1/2 inch. Baste into place with a straight stitch very closely to the bottom of the insertion. In fact, you are actually on the heading of the lace for this straight stitch.
2. Check and rearrange any tucks that might have flipped to the wrong direction.
3. Zigzag the lace insertion bottom edge on top of the pintucked fabric right on the basting line. This stitch will go over the heading of the lace and off of the heading on the pintucked fabric side. Trim away the excess pintucked fabric from behind the bodice of the blouse.
4. Now it is time to cut out your blouse front using your original pattern.

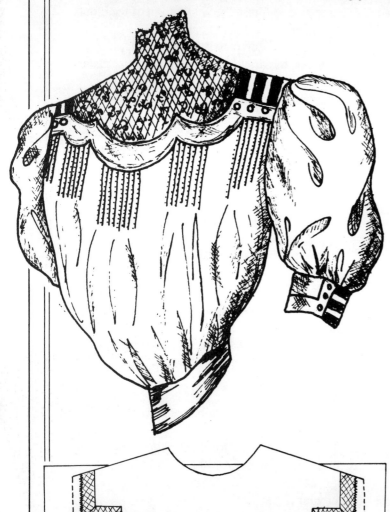

Blouse I

This delicate blouse is a fantasy of tucks, scallops, and all-over lace. The blouse front and back feature large center-placed scallops and two scallops that depart from the center scallops, ending in a flat piece of lace. The scallops are made of wide lace. Use the technique "Mitering Lace" and "Shaping A Dramatic Curve" to make the curved points. Five sets of six pintucks embellish the front of the blouse. The short sleeves have a side cuff that is 3/4-length. It is finished by lace insertion circling the bottom of the cuff and travelling up to form the buttonholes. Tulle, organdy, lightweight brocade, or a created piece of French-sewn fabric (that you have zigzagged together) would be just as lovely as all-over lace for the bodice fancy section of this blouse. Batiste, silk, handkerchief linen, taffeta or any lightweight fabric might be used for the rest of the blouse.

Construction Units;

1. Follow the general directions given for blouses I-N.

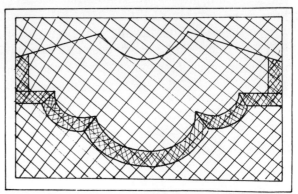

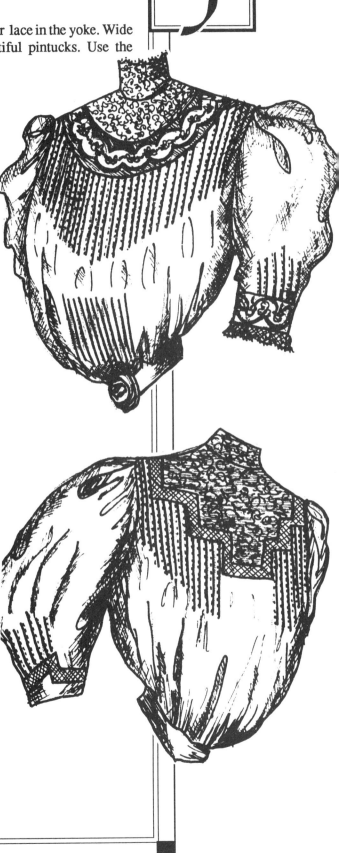

Blouse J

This beautiful antique blouse features a round yoke with all-over lace in the yoke. Wide lace insertion trims the circular yoke, below which are beautiful pintucks. Use the technique "Loops of Lace" for shaping the circular lace for the neckline. Notice the elegant curve of the pintucks. The same wide lace trim that encircled the neckline is repeated at the bottom of the cuff. Gathered lace edging finishes the sleeve. To make this sleeve for today's blouse, I suggest putting a row of entredeux at the bottom of the sleeve, using the technique "Entredeux To Flat Fabric." Since you have gathered the fullness into the tucks, the fabric will be flat at the bottom of the sleeve. Then, using the technique "Entredeux To Flat Lace," attach the lace insertion and one more row of entredeux. Using the technique "Entredeux to Gathered Lace," attach the gathered lace edging to the bottom of the sleeve. For a modern-day neckline to this blouse, using the pattern in this book, attach entredeux to the neckline using the technique "Entredeux to Flat Fabric" and attach gathered lace to the trimmed entredeux using the technique "Entredeux To Gathered Lace."

Blouse K

This stair-step lace blouse is truly different. The lace insertion makes stair steps down the blouse front and lands in the center front. Elegant tucks come from beneath each step of the lace. All-over lace is inserted in the bodice area. The sleeves end with tucks to hold in the fullness. The little cuff has a stair step also; notice the cuff finish. To finish this cuff for a modern-day blouse, I would make the little jut-up cuff, attach it to the bottom of the sleeve, and then turn it up. The lace is put on flat in the antique blouse; it would be easier to attach gathered lace when going around the curve on the stair step of the cuff. To attach gathered lace to a finished edge, simply butt the two together and zigzag. I suggest an entredeux, gathered lace neckline finish for this blouse for a more modern version than this antique. You can also put a fabric bias binding around the neckline of the all-over lace bodice, or finish with a bias facing.

Construction Units:
1. To construct this blouse, use the general directions for blouses I-N.
2. To miter the laces around the stair steps, refer to the "Mitering Lace" technique found on page of this book.

Blouse L

This blouse uses two lace shaping techniques. The loops of lace and the shaped scallops enhance the bodice. A little piece of lace edging is gathered at the bottom of the scalloped edge where the blouse bodice joins the pintucked blouse portion. This blouse bodice is very similar to the Martha Pullen pattern "Loops of Lace." The pattern includes a leg-o'-mutton sleeve design.

Construction Units:
1. To construct this blouse, use the basic instructions for blouses I-N.
2. For more specific instructions for loops and for scallops above and below the loops, refer to "Loops of Lace."

Blouse M

This tucked blouse features zigzagged insertions graduating to a point on the bodice. The wider lace insertion, which encases the narrower lace insertions on the bodice, is mitered in the center front of the blouse. The sleeves have an elegantly tucked band to take in the fullness. Entredeux, insertion, entredeux, and lace edging finish the sleeve. For a more modern-day version of this blouse, I would only change the neckline from the high one to an entredeux/gathered lace finish or a bias binding.

Construction Units:
1. Use the basic construction techniques for blouses I-N.
2. For the lace insertion bodice, use the technique "Lace Flat Edge To Lace Flat Edge."
3. For the curved insertion, which encases the bodice, use the techniques "Mitering Lace" and "Loops of Lace."

Blouse N

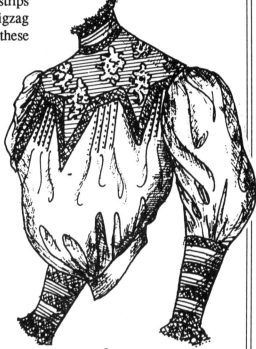

Beautiful sunburst shapes make this an unusual tucked design. The technique "Mitering Laces" will be used for the points of the blouse and for the gradual points connecting the dramatic points. The sleeves have four rows of insertions with tucked strips between the insertions. The easiest way to make this sleeve is to zigzag insertions onto solid fabric at certain points and then pintuck between these insertions. Gathered lace finishes the bottom of the cuffs.

Construction Units:
1. Follow the basic instructions for blouses I-N.
2. Use the techniques "Making Diamonds" for making the points.

General Instructions for Blouses O, P, Q, and R

The Fancy Yoke Top Portion Of These Blouses

1. Trace the basic pattern pieces (the pattern in your envelope with this book) onto tissue paper or pattern drafting interfacing. Trace the whole front of the blouse.
2. Trace the fancy yoke on a rectangular piece of tissue paper. You will have to freehand trace the dropped yoke portion of Blouse O or the rounded yoke version of Blouse P. Of course you will use the blouse pattern as your basic guide.
3. **BLOUSES O AND P** - Pintuck a piece of fabric wider and longer than the yoke pattern piece. The yokes in blouses O and P both have vertical tucks, which mean the tucks will be placed in the yoke, going from side to side instead of up and down. This brings us to the age-old question, "Are vertical tucks made from selvage to selvage (cross grain), or are they made parallel to the selvage (with the grain)?" I have found that double-needle pintucks behave when sewn parallel to the selvage. These tucks can then be placed in the garment in any direction, up and down, across, or diagonally. If you prefer to make real tucks (rather than machine pintucks), placing these either cross grain or with the grain will work beautifully.
   BLOUSES Q AND R - The fancy yokes on Blouses Q and R are simply solid lace with shaped lace over the solid lace.
4. Starch and press the pintucked fabric several times.
5. Trace the yoke pattern on the pintucked piece. Also trace all lace lines.
6. Place pintucked fabric on a fabric board to complete all lace shaping.
7. Zigzag shaped lace to the pintucked fabric **except** for the outside or lower edge. This edge will be stitched to the lower blouse in step to complete the blouse front. Spray starch and press several times.
8. Trim away excess fabric from under the lace scallop.

The Gathered Bottom Portion Of The Blouses

You will be stitching several gathering rows in the lower fabric. The yoke will be placed on top of these gathers and stitched in place. Any excess gathering threads will be pulled out, leaving beautiful gathers under the yoke. This method can be used any time shaped lace meets gathered fabric.

1. Begin with a rectangle of fabric, estimating the width that will be drawn up by the gathering. The amount of fullness will depend on you and the fabric you choose. You may choose a lightweight fabric that could have fullness without adding bulk or a heavier weight fabric that would not need to be gathered much at all.
2. Determine the length of the rectangle by measuring the length of the gathered fabric on blouse. The gathers in Blouse O start in the upper points under the yoke and this fabric extends to the bottom of the blouse. The gathered fabric in Blouses P and Q starts at the shoulders and extends to the bottom of the blouse.
3. Determining where to place the gathering rows depends on the design. Gathering rows should be run about 1/2 inch to 1 inch apart.

Attaching The Fancy Top Portion To The Gathered Bottom Of The Blouse

1. Place the yoke on the top of the gathered fabric, overlapping by 1/4 inch to 1/2 inch. Baste into place with a straight stitch very close to the bottom of the insertion. In fact, you are actually on the heading of the lace for this straight stitch.
2. Check and rearrange any gathers that might be out of place.
3. Zigzag the lace insertion bottom edge on top of the gathered fabric right on the basting line. This stitch will go over the heading of the lace and off of the heading on the gathered fabric side. Trim away the excess gathered fabric from behind the bodice of the blouse.
4. Now it is time to cut out your blouse front using your original pattern. Push the gathered fabric underneath the blouse front pattern so that the sides of the blouse run on the straight of the grain.

Blouse O

This blouse features the lace fan design on the pintucked yoke. The gathered fabric under the yoke also has a fan design that extends to the side of the blouse. The fan design appears once again on the sleeve. The fancy band for the sleeve has three layers of insertion with two layers of very narrow puffing. A gathered ruffle of fabric finishes the sleeve. In a modern-day version of this blouse, use an entredeux/gathered lace finish for a jewel neckline.

Construction Units:
1. Follow the basic construction directions given for Blouse O and Blouse P.
2. The fan shape for the sleeve is drawn onto the sleeve. The insertion is zigzagged onto the sleeve and the fabric cut away from behind the sleeve.
3. The fan on the gathered lower bodice of the blouse must be made before the gathering is completed. The choice is yours concerning whether or not the fabric will be cut away from behind the fan. I would suggest making the sleeve and the lower fan match.

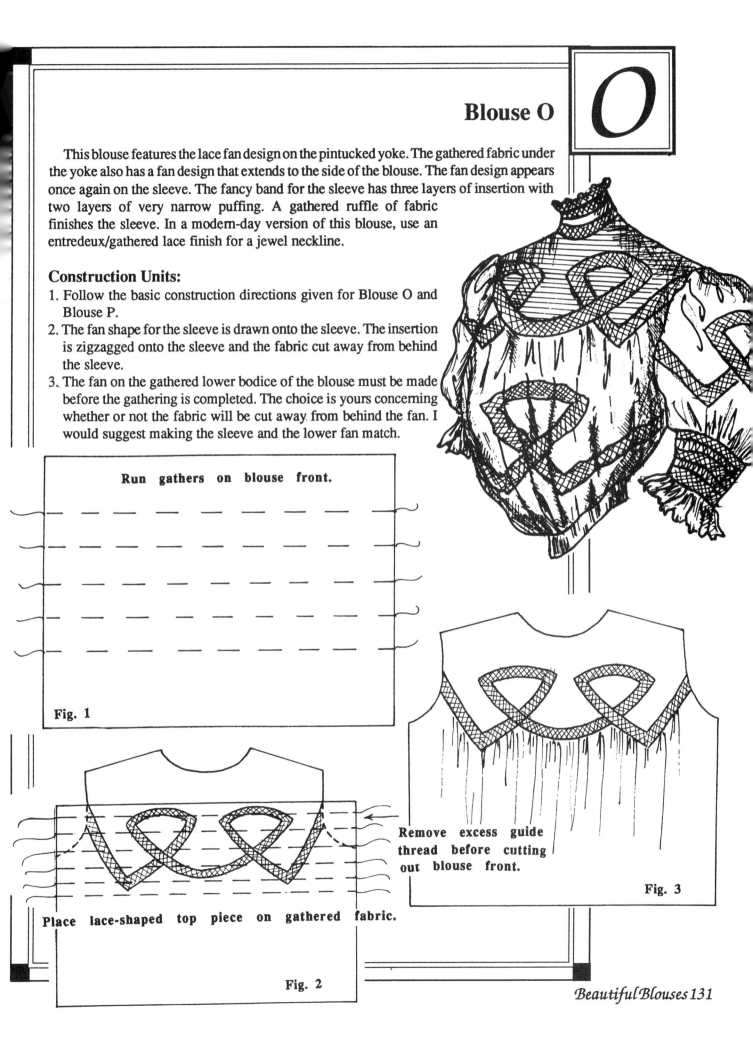

Run gathers on blouse front.

Fig. 1

Place lace-shaped top piece on gathered fabric.

Fig. 2

Remove excess guide thread before cutting out blouse front.

Fig. 3

Blouse P

The horizontal tucking, round bodice is elegant in this blouse. Wide lace insertion curves around this tucking piece. Wide lace edging curves around this insertion. The sleeves have entredeux, insertion, entredeux for the basic sleeve. Gathered lace is attached to the bottom of the entredeux.

Construction Units:

1. The basic blouse directions are found in the directions for Blouse O and Blouse P.
2. The gathers on this blouse go all the way to the shoulder; when you are measuring for your gathered piece of fabric, it will be the length of the blouse pattern front and the width you want to make it. This will depend on how many gathers you want and how much fullness you like.

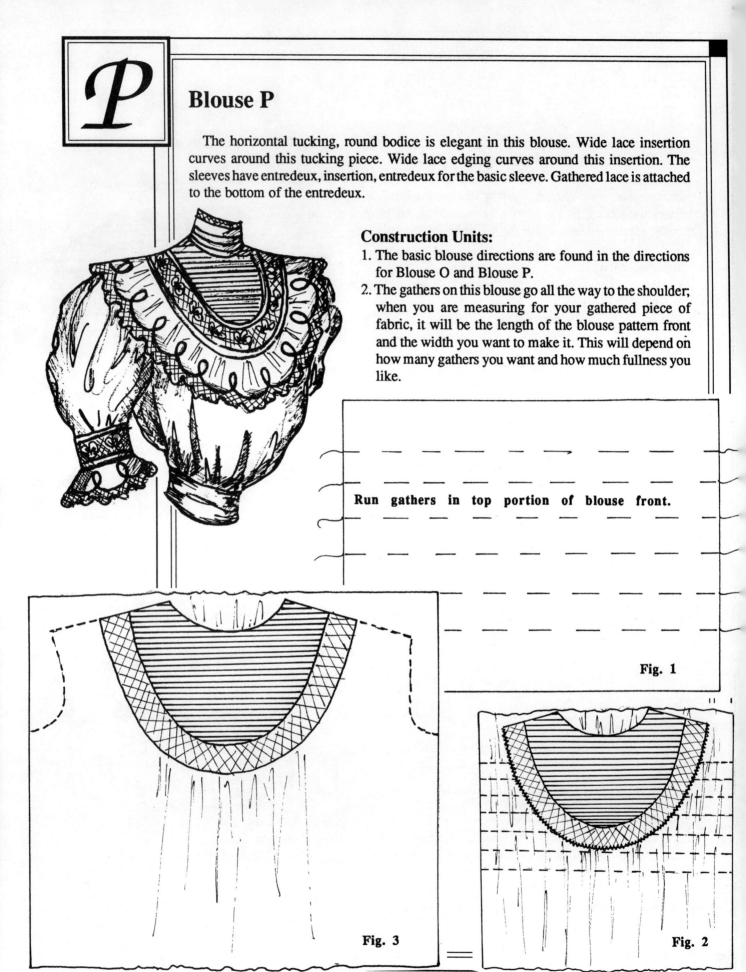

Run gathers in top portion of blouse front.

Fig. 1

Fig. 3

Fig. 2

Blouse Q

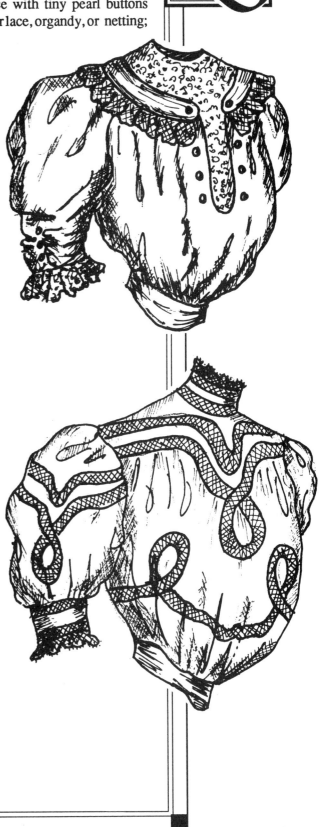

Dainty and school girlish, this blouse features shaped lace with tiny pearl buttons trimming the fancy V down the front. The neck section is all-over lace, organdy, or netting; the sleeves have a pretty shirring with pearl buttons for trim.

Construction Units:

1. This blouse has basic construction directions similar to blouses O, P, and R.

Blouse R

Looped, curved, and straight lace embellish the sleeves. The neckline laces follow the same lines and extend from shoulder to shoulder. The fancy band on the sleeve consists of entredeux, lace insertion, embroidery, lace insertion, entredeux, and gathered lace.

Construction Units:

1. The basic construction instructions are similar as for blouses O, P and Q.

Blouse S

Tailoring on this blouse includes one set of six tucks in the middle and one set of three on each shoulder. The fancy V shape in the middle is outlined by lace insertion. The sleeves have three layers of lace insertion.

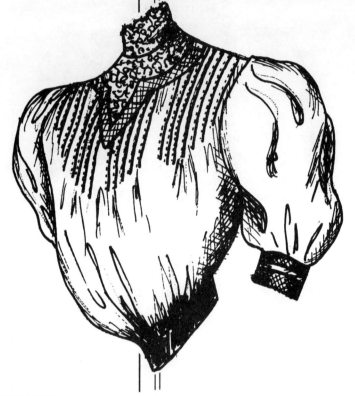

Construction Units:

1. Cut out the blouse pattern; front, sleeves, and back.
2. Make a complete front pattern on tissue paper.
3. Cut a rectangular piece of fabric 10 inches wider than the finished blouse front.
4. Make a fold in the center of this fabric.
5. Stitch six tucks in the center; three on each side of center front. Make the tucks from the top of the blouse front to the finish line below the center V. This upper portion of tucking will be cut away later after the fancy work is added (Fig. 1).
6. Skip over about 2 or 3 inches and make three more tucks (Fig. 1).
7. Lay your blouse pattern on your tucked fabric to see if your placement is correct.
8. Trace your blouse pattern onto your tucked fabric with a magic blue marker. Remember to squish the fullness in so that the straight line on the sides of the blouse will indeed follow the grain line correctly.
9. Estimate where the fancy V will be drawn onto the center of the blouse. Draw the V onto the blouse front (Fig. 1).
10. Trace onto a piece of tissue paper the fancy V yoke that you have just drawn on your tucked fabric. You can refer back to directions for Blouses I-N for the next section of your stitching.
11. Place a square of all-over lace fabric, organdy, netting or whatever you choose to use for the neckline fabric over the tissue pattern. The fabric will be on top of your tissue paper pattern. Transfer the markings onto your square of fabric. Baste the fabric onto this tissue paper. You will be sewing through the tissue paper when you place your lace V (Fig. 2).

Fig. 1

Fig. 2

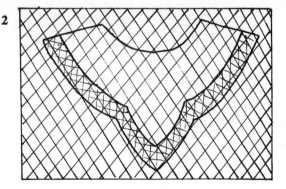

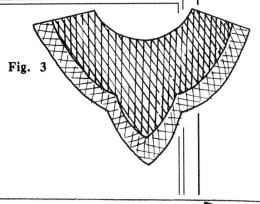

Fig. 3

12. Shape the lace insertion V to match the pattern. Using the technique "Mitering Lace," miter the points of the V.

13. Stitch the inside edge of the lace V to the fabric. Leave the bottom of the lace unstitched. Trim away all excess fabric and tissue paper pattern at this time. Spray starch and press very stiff (Fig. 3).

14. Place the fancy yoke onto your tucked piece of fabric. Straight stitch the bottom of the yoke (bottom heading of the lace) onto the tucked fabric. Zigzag over that straight stitching encompassing the whole heading of the lace and going off onto the fabric, slightly (Fig. 4).

15. Trim away fabric and cut out the rest of the blouse front.

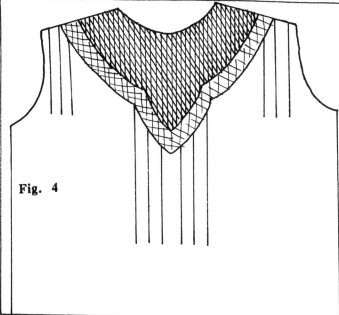

Fig. 4

Blouse T

Long strips of lace decorate the front of this blouse. A set of eight tucks trim the shoulders. Tucks pull in the fullness of the sleeve. Gathered lace, entredeux, insertion, and entredeux finish the sleeve.

Construction Units:

1. Follow the basic construction unit planning of Blouse Q. The main difference is that the front blouse piece runs the full length of the center front of the blouse.

Blouse U

This unusual blouse is pretty with its shirring on each shoulder. This particular treatment is a little different from most of the blouses of the era. The trim overlaps to go from the shoulder down to the bottom of the blouse.

Construction Units:
1. The construction units of this blouse are similar to Blouses Q and R. The main difference is shirring or gathering takes the place of tucking on the shoulder section.
2. Actually you could plan smocking over this shoulder section of the blouse. If you choose to smock, you will need to run your pleating across the complete top of the blouse. Then pull your threads out for the center section.
3. Gather and tie off the needed fullness for smocking on each side of the shoulder.
4. Proceed with the same instructions as Blouses Q and R.

Blouse V

This very tailored and elegant blouse consists of strips of lace running the whole front of the blouse, pintucks in varying lengths, and one short strip on the sleeves of the blouse. The description on the antique pattern simply reads "tucked blouse."

Construction Units:
1. Follow the same basic strip construction of blouse V.
2. The method for making the lace point is to fold the cut end of the lace into a point and zigzag around that point.

136 Beautiful Blouses

Blouse W

Perhaps the most delicate blouse in this whole section is Blouse V. What a stunning combination of tucking, V strips, and embroidery. Swiss insertions could be substituted for the embroidery of this handmade blouse. There is delicate embroidery between each V-shaped strip and a matching embroidery on the front strips and on the sleeves.

Construction Units:

1. I think the simplest instructions for this blouse are to plan the strips.
2. Cut the blouse pattern pieces; front, back, and sleeves.
3. Plan the width of your strips according to the size of your blouse. Using basic French sewing by machine techniques, make your strips and join them.

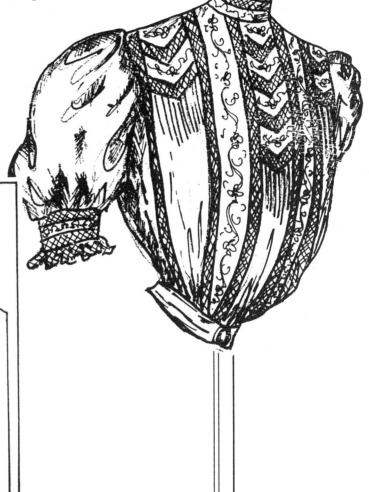

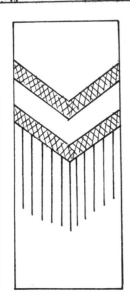

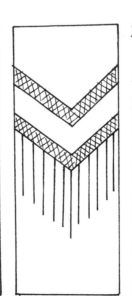

fabric

fabric

137

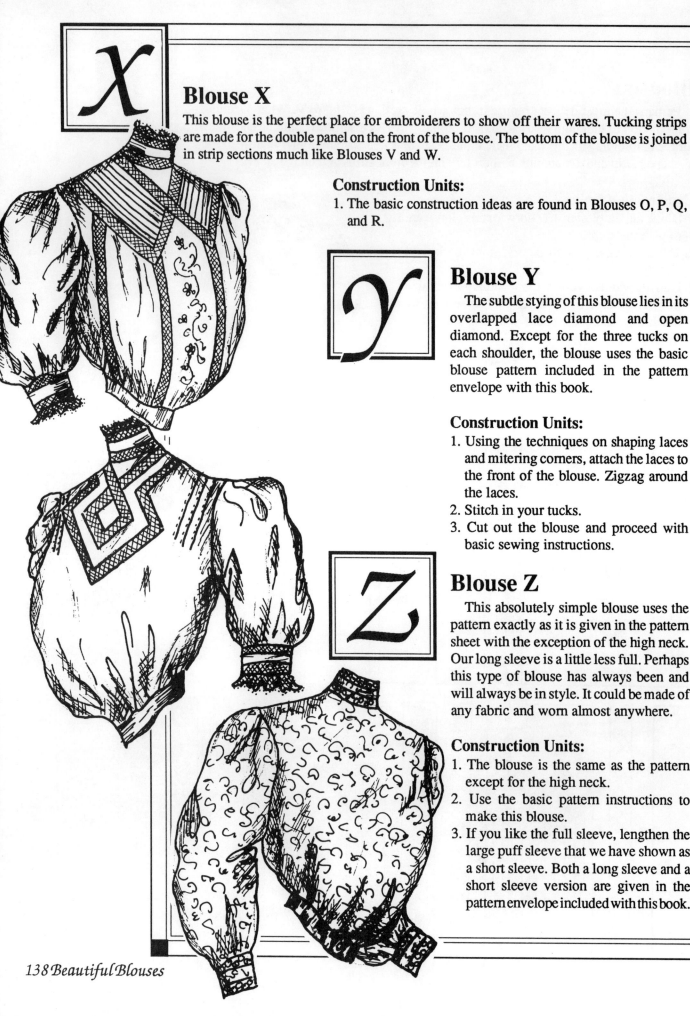

Blouse X

This blouse is the perfect place for embroiderers to show off their wares. Tucking strips are made for the double panel on the front of the blouse. The bottom of the blouse is joined in strip sections much like Blouses V and W.

Construction Units:

1. The basic construction ideas are found in Blouses O, P, Q, and R.

Blouse Y

The subtle styling of this blouse lies in its overlapped lace diamond and open diamond. Except for the three tucks on each shoulder, the blouse uses the basic blouse pattern included in the pattern envelope with this book.

Construction Units:

1. Using the techniques on shaping laces and mitering corners, attach the laces to the front of the blouse. Zigzag around the laces.
2. Stitch in your tucks.
3. Cut out the blouse and proceed with basic sewing instructions.

Blouse Z

This absolutely simple blouse uses the pattern exactly as it is given in the pattern sheet with the exception of the high neck. Our long sleeve is a little less full. Perhaps this type of blouse has always been and will always be in style. It could be made of any fabric and worn almost anywhere.

Construction Units:

1. The blouse is the same as the pattern except for the high neck.
2. Use the basic pattern instructions to make this blouse.
3. If you like the full sleeve, lengthen the large puff sleeve that we have shown as a short sleeve. Both a long sleeve and a short sleeve version are given in the pattern envelope included with this book.

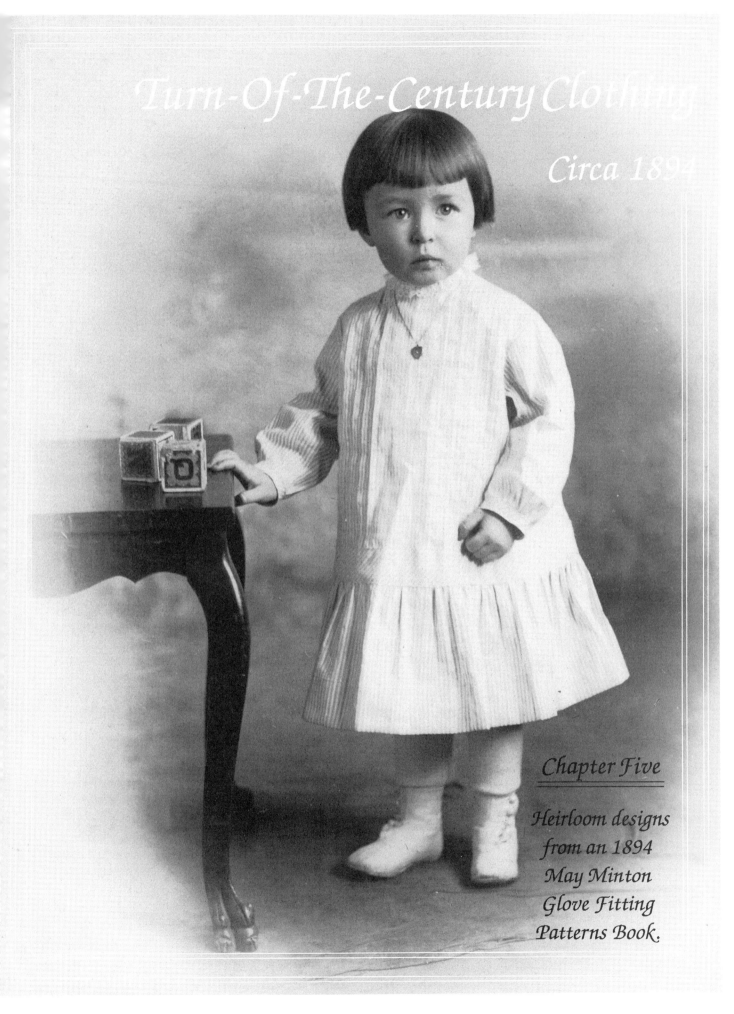

Turn-Of-The-Century Clothing

Circa 1894

Chapter Five

Heirloom designs
from an 1894
May Minton
Glove Fitting
Patterns Book.

I was like a child on Christmas morning when Billie Manning, my friend in the antique clothing business, presented me with a 1894 May Minton Glove Fitting Patterns Book. I had searched so long for patterns published just before the turn of the century, and here was an entire book of popular styles for me to pour over. I didn't open it immediately. Instead, I rubbed my hands over the worn cover, wondering if my excitement paralleled the feelings the original owner must have had so many years ago.

When I finally started to flip through the yellowed pages, all I could think about was how to share this treasure of lace shaping and heirloom designs with my readers. What better, than to copy, exactly, some of my favorites and include them in this book — giving credit to May Minton, of course.

These children's garments were traced from the catalog by Diane Zinser. Where the printing was too dark or blurred, she added her own special touches. My only regret is that we don't have patterns available for each design. It will take a little imagination, but you might try reproducing some of the middy designs, by adapting the antique middy pattern in this book.

If you are interested in making one of the antique coats, consult the pattern books at your local fabric store and choose a pattern that looks most like the antique design. If the coat you like is pleated in front, you you might use the techniques suggested in the blouse section of this book to pleat your fabric before cutting out the pattern pieces.

I hope you cherish these designs as much as Diane and I enjoyed bringing them to you.

Classic Coats

Mama and I used to have so much fun shopping for winter coats when my children were little. I have to confess that even though I made most all my children's clothing for church, I never attempted a coat. Joanna's prettiest coat was pastel blue wool challis, smocked at the yoke in pink, blue, and green. I always seemed to waver between navy, dusty blue, and pale blue when it came to the children's coats. With the variety of coat patterns out now, I hope to make at least one coat for a grandchild, when I am fortunate enough to have one!

Challis And Silk Coat

The cape coat was particularly popular around the turn of the century. This ruffle-trimmed version accommodates either lightweight or heavy weight fabrics, making it ideal for any season. I picture it made in rose challis or cashmere, trimmed with matching silk. A white pique with Swiss embroidered edging would be lovely for breezy summer days. The buttons are concealed, so there is no need to cover them.

Double-breasted Coat

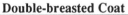

This tailored design with shawl collar, French-look cuff, and double-button front is reminiscent of puritan apparel. A winter wonder, it merits camel wool trimmed with navy velveteen or hunter green trimmed in black. Off-white velveteen with black or navy trim would be just the thing for a special holiday look. Since the buttons are particularly important to the design, they should be relatively large and covered in fabric. Wide piping, which trims the collar, the 3-inch cuffs, the overlap, and the hem of the coat, opens this coat up to a variety of trim options.

Lap-over Coat

Technically, this is a double-breasted coat with only one row of buttons, thus, I've dubbed it a lap-over coat. Despite the ruffled edging at the collar and hem, the French cuffs and double-breasted line give this design a tailored flavor.

If making a winter version of this coat in wool, for example a solid buff or plaid fabric, I would make the ruffle out of that same wool, rather than using the Swiss trim shown in the sketch.

Since this coat is dated 1894, I imagine it teamed with one of those pleated chiffon hats ornately trimmed in lace and ribbon bows at the crown — not something you would see today.

Sailor Coat

Classic sailor tailoring has been a strong influence in children's wear since who knows when. Most anyone you ask, parents, grandparents, great grandparents, can recollect wearing at least one outfit with navy piping and a sailor collar.

One of the more popular and comfortable sailor styles was the short jacket worn over an open-necked blouse, coat, and breeches. In the 1860s, sailor suits and caps for boys, as well as sailor blouses with skirts for girls were a favored fashion. Pattern makers coined the term, "Middy Suit" or "Middy Dress" during this era.

Not surprisingly, coats were just as apt to get the nautical treatment. The piping around the cuffs and collar of this tuck-front coat demands a combination of blue and white. I suggest a royal blue wool coat with a navy velveteen collar and cuffs, trimmed in white velveteen ribbon.

The obvious choice of hats would be a felt or straw boater with a ribbon around the crown and ribbons streaming down the back.

Swiss Eyelet Coat

Looking for the perfect spring coat to complement all those delicate French dresses? You've found it. This airy cover-up is a wealth of Swiss eyelet. The body of the coat, the turned-back cuffs, and the double-collar are Swiss eyelet. The elaborate collar treatment is actually a short collar further enhanced by a detachable shawl collar. The full, gathered coat is buttoned by three, presumably pearl, buttons.

An exact reproduction of the sketched design calls for white or ecru Swiss eyelet. Or, opt for a less-fancy version in linen, using Swiss eyelet for the cuffs and collar.

Pleated Coat

Despite the off-center buttons and shoulder pleats, this coat remains pleasingly simple. And simple lines call for simple fabrics. The plain-Jane styling has a timeless quality that would be as classic in a Scotch plaid as in a solid camel wool; with either, the collar and cuffs should be velveteen. This is the coat that will pass down from child to child with little chance of its going out of style.

Leggins

World War II brought about many restrictions in dress. Trims and embroideries were forbidden, the number of pockets was restricted, as were pleated skirts, turned up trousers, and extravagant use of buttons. Granted, most children stopped wearing leggins by the early '30s. But, if the leg coverings hadn't fallen out of fashion favor, they would have eventually landed a spot on the restricted list due to an excess use of buttons.

This particular pattern for leggins calls for buttons, running the entire length of the child's leg. However, it appears mothers could select a leggin according to the length of a child's coat. Ideally, buttons fastened around the leg tightly enough to hold up the leggins; they didn't have elastic in the top.

I'm not insinuating '90s mothers stitch up a pair of leggins. Today's comfort-conscious kids would sooner eat spinach then wear such a restrictive accessory. But since they were such an integral part of the outdoor wardrobe at the turn of the century, I felt a brief description was worth including in this section.

Challis Or Pique Inverness (Cape) Coat

My mother remembers having a coat in the early '20s that was similar to this design. This particular style was introduced in pattern books around 1890. It is comparable to the men's Inverness rain coat of the 1880s. It is one of those classic designs that never goes out of style for children. I picture it made in peach challis with ecru laces or white pique with Swiss trims. The sleeve has a 1-1/2-inch cuff trimmed with gathered lace. Your child will be set for church when you add a French organdy bonnet. The cape could be made detachable for occasions that call for a more tailored version.

The design suits children ages 12 months to 8 years. However, after giving careful consideration, I would make the coat in gray flannel trimmed with black velvet ribbon and heavy black English lace for an older child. If black lace isn't available, dye some with Rit dye. The black velvet ribbon would be of particular interest if trimmed every inch or so with a French knot of gray silk ribbon. A Christmas coat in this design could be made of burgundy or electric blue velveteen trimmed in black.

Little Red Riding Hood Cape

This turn-of-the-century cape begs to be reproduced in solid red wool — *Little Red Riding Hood* style — or in a rich Scottish plaid. A warm-weather reproduction calls for challis or heavy silk in fresh spring colors. Pique is another option for small children.

Capes are a functional favorite of mine. Because they aren't fitted, they can be worn for several years.

Classic Dresses

Lace And Challis Dress

This child's dress is decidedly non-fussy with its A-line styling and restrained use of lace. The simple lace border at the hem and extended V yoke balance the trim, thus drawing attention to the whole dress rather than one detail. Wide pleats at center front control the fullness. I picture this timeless design reproduced in challis or navy velveteen with heavy ecru lace

Bolero-Look High-Yoke Dress

Lace shaping at the shoulders of this dress create a bolero effect. Peaking out from under the faux bolero is a V-shaped lace insert, which appears to be part of a separate underdress. The fancy band at the bottom parallels the elaborate lace work at the yoke. The heavy use of detail calls for quiet colors.

Girl's Sailor Costume

This is the stuff from which classics are made — sailor tailoring at its best. I wouldn't be surprised to find a copy of this exact design in a children's store today. The styling is ageless. Wide tucks run the length of the bodice to mid skirt, creating a fan of pleats. The sailor collar dips to a sharp V; a neckerchief runs underneath the collar and ties at center front. White poplin with red or navy trims would be the ideal choice of fabrics.

Oval Lace Middy Dress

This dress, circa 1894, is proof positive oval lace shaping goes back a long way. The simplest of middys, this design could be adapted from the middy patterns in this book. A pink linen reproduction with winding trails of white French lace on the collar would be the epitome of sugar and spice.

Tucked Blouse And Pleated Skirt

The tucked-front blouse and quilt-look skirt must have been the quintessential back-to-school look at the turn of the century. Actually, it's quite like modern-day school uniforms worn in Australia. Fabric on the collar, blouse front, and cuffs, complements the window-pane print of the skirt.

Peasant Dress

Eyelet goes ethnic in this decked-out peasant dress. Wide Swiss eyelet trims the neckline and the bottom the skirt. The waistline and the top edge of the collar appear to be smocked. The beauty of this pattern is that it can be dressed up in lace for special occasions or dressed down with rickrack and ruffles for play.

143

Square-Neck Dress

This sheath dress with its high, square yoke reminds me of the airy gowns worn in France in the early 1800s. A splendid summer dress, the free-falling body and open neckline make for cool comfort. Mitered Swiss handloom trims the neckline. The handloom repeats around the puffed sleeves and skirt bottom.

Eyelet V Yoke Dress

This is just one more middy dress for you to admire or reproduce, using the patterns in this book. Here, wide, gathered-eyelet edging trims the collar. The ruffle-framed yoke begs for fancy embroidery.

Diamond Spoke Collar Dress

A series of embroidered handkerchiefs would fit perfectly within the spokes of the collar on this middy dress. Or, if you love to embroider, here's your chance. The bottom of the skirt could be left plain or tucked as shown. Adapt your design, using the middy patterns in this book.

Round T-Panel Dress

The T-panel that curves around the neckline and down the front of this pleated dress is the ideal place to plant a garden of embroidery. Stitch up this design in gingham or dotted Swiss and add bloomers for a sporty summer look, or opt for Nelona and shadow embroidery for special Sunday attire.

Triple V Collar Dress

Yards and yards of lace reserve this dress for special occasions. The zigzag shaping not only fashions the collar and marches around the skirt, it reverses to form diamonds on the gathered sleeve. The V's are mitered or flip-flopped; the choice is yours. Lace insertion trims the angel sleeves and outlines the puffing on the fancy band. The collar is actually a very short collar with one row of insertion and one row of gathered edging, making it just long enough to touch the top of a high-yoke dress.

Double-Suspender Jumper

"Back-to-school" and "jumpers" are practically synonymous. This double-suspender style with a deep-V front offers a new, or rather, revised look in a season when jumpers are all the rage. It's a middy version with rickrack trim. In an era prone to primarily solids, this printed blouse would have been a nice change. Corduroy with a calico blouse as well as gray, navy, red, or camel wool would suit this design.

Scooped-neck Pinafore

Years ago I purchased an eyelet pinafore for Joanna with a yellow gingham dress underneath. I am constantly amazed at how fashion cycles, even for children. Remember, pinafores give you extra mileage, as they can be worn without an underdress in the summer.

Jumper And Blouse

When I was a child we used to call the dark plaids and dark cotton fabrics "transitional cottons." Transitional cotton always signaled back-to-school clothes. In certain parts of the country, Alabama included, the weather simply doesn't warrant wool until late December or January. So, it's almost impractical to buy them. This plain T-front jumper could be cut in a dark plaid or lightweight washable wool. A Christmas jumper in burgundy or forest green velveteen is another option.

Plain Apron Dress

Originally, the term "apron" was used to describe the dress that was worn over a fancy garment to protect it from soiling. Later, I suppose, the style was so sweet on little girls, "apron" took on a whole new meaning when the functional garment became of style all its own. Today, a Battenberg collar could be attached underneath the Peter Pan collar for dress up.

Button-on Apron Dress

This is the original idea of an apron dress; it covered up the "better" dress, which could then be worn several times without laundering.

Ruffle Pinafore Dress

Once again the pinafore is used to cover up a plain dress. This time it has an angled ruffle from the waistline over the shoulder. A sash peeks out from the side view, indicating this pinafore ties in a bow at the back. Wide lace insertion trims the square neckline, the front panels and the waistline of the pinafore.

V-Neck Fancy Eyelet Pinafore

Bordered eyelet was probably the fabric used for this pinafore; however, it may be eyelet embroidery. I have seen handmade eyelet embroidery on antique garments of this era. It appears that five rows of lace insertion form the long cuff on the leg-o-mutton sleeve. Again, it is hard to tell from the sketch; it may have been a netting dress. The pinafore also features entredeux at the high yoke and a ruffled angel sleeves.

Puffing Middy

Random use of baby puffing is what makes this dress one of my favorites. Two puffing rows crown the portrait collar. Another row tunnels around the middle of the skirt and is sandwiched between two rows of tucking. Double ribbons at the waist are repeated on the fancy sleeve. The collar appears to be cut on the bias and hangs in folds. The possibilities are endless when it comes to reproducing this dress. You might try the high-yoke middy pattern in this book.

Plain Military Dress

This design has a strong military look, empha-sized by the star and bar motif. You might use a plain middy pattern embellished with grosgrain ribbon, embroidered military patches, and brass buttons to achieve the same effect. Poplin, wool, corduroy, or Scottish plaid would suit this design.

Plain Spoke Collar Dress With Tucks

The open panels in the spoke-collar dress could be embroidered or left plain. The double tucks, which form a front panel, are emphasized through the use of heavy top-stitching. Lace insertion forms a layer over the simple cuff.

Bertha Collar Embroidered Dress

We have seen a revival of peplum skirts; this double-tiered skirt is one version of that style. Simple circles of hand embroidery edge the bertha collar and the double skirt. A reproduction might call for more elaborate embroidery on the open collar.

Split-Ruffle Sleeve Dress

Split collars, which extend off the shoulders, were somewhat common around the turn of the century. This particular design borrowed that technique for a sleeve treatment. The square neckline is drawn down visually by the extended tucks. The dress has two sets of three buttons on one side only.

146

Classic Little Girls Lingerie

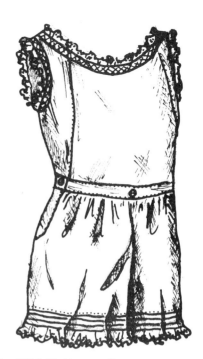

Middy Slip

This waisted slip could be made using one of the middy dress pattern included in this book. Simply scoop the neck somewhat and design it to button on the shoulders rather than down the back. The original has three tucks and an eyelet ruffle; however, a plain slip would be just as functional.

Chemise With Button-on Drawers

This was the traditional underwear worn by little girls at the turn of the century. The chemise, in this particular undergarment, attaches to the drawers with buttons. It is tucked and trimmed with lace.

Classic Little Boy Suits

Double-breasted Military With Bow Tie

The jacket on this double-breasted knicker suit rides almost to the bottom of the knickers, which was traditional in boys suits of this era. Three brass buttons and the military insignia trim the front of the coat. A bow tie sets off the band collar. Knicker suits were worn by young boys to about age 10.

Double-breasted Plain Suit

This simple suit has nothing but symmetrical buttons and a belt for trim. Pleated sleeves characterize all of the boys suits in this catalog. I've not seen this fitted sleeve on boys suits of a later vintage.

Classic Sailor Jacket Suit

Instead of having a middy-style top, common to so many of the boy's sailor suits, this one features a sailor jacket. The jacket drops to the bottom of the knickers and closes with the cross-over button belt.

Middy Sailor Suit

When I think of turn-of-the-century sailor suits, this is the image that comes to mind — a double-button panel, a scarf tied at the front. It could be reproduced in a variety of classic colors and fabrics.

Double-breasted Band Collar Suit

Although quite plain, this double-breasted suit is typical of an 1894 boy's suit. Notice that the belt on it has a buckle and, again, the sleeves are fitted at the bottom with the tucks.

Asymmetrical Breast-Pocked Suit

This suit, fashioned with buttons up one side, a Peter Pan collar, a bow tie, and a breast pocket, strays from the norm. The jacket is even shorter than the others in this series. Despite its unique styling, it would be much simpler to reproduce than the double-button varieties.

148

The Bin Dress

A Costume from the Collection of the Bethnal Green Museum of Childhood

Excerpted from Sew Beautiful magazine (Summer 1988) and Bethnal Green Museum of Childhood Guidebook

"Oh, look at this one," shout the children.

"Ah yes, that reminds me of a dress I had as a child," reply their parents.

London's Bethnal Green Museum of Childhood is a branch of the famed Victoria and Albert Museum, one of the world's great museums of art, craft, and design. The Victoria and Albert Museum is concerned with beautiful things man had made for his own use. Its Bethnal Green branch is concerned with what man has made for his children — toys, dolls, doll houses, games, puppets, books, and priceless, antique children's apparel.

The guidebook reads:

"What happens to us as children, influences us for the rest of our lives, So we all have good reason to preserve memories of our own childhood. The Bethnal Green Museum tries to preserve something of everybody's childhood, and it is a museum that should appeal to everybody for there is no-one who was not once a child. Our happiest memory of childhood, probably, is of playing. The wonderful experiences of "messing about" and "fooling around" cannot be put in a museum; but playthings can. So the brightest and most attractive feature of the museum is the collection of playthings.

"On the top floor of the museum are two more galleries, and here, gradually, a third section of the museum is taking shape. This is devoted to the social history of childhood. The core of it is the collection of children's dress, from the eighteenth century to the present. Do the collections always remain silent and motionless behind glass? Or, when the front door has closed in the evening behind the last visitor, do the showcases fly open, and toys scramble out to play? Visitors, unfortunately, will never know."

When Martha Pullen was invited to the museum, her main interest, of course, was the children's costume collection. The costumes are arranged so that changes of style and fabric can be followed clearly. Adult costumes have been included to show the similarities and differences between clothing worn by parents and children, and also to give a more complete picture of family life.

Outstanding among the early exhibits are two outfits of silk woven in Spitalfields, one for a girl (1741-2) and one for a boy (c.1780), and a girl's dress of Chinese embroidered silk (c.1760). Much more 19th century costume survives, including boy's suits of the "Little Lord Fauntleroy" type; a group of sailor suits, all different; and (the star exhibit) a complete wardrobe worn by a child named Henrietta Byron in 1840.

One garment of particular interest to Martha is "The Bin Dress," thusly named because it was rescued from a garbage bin and brought to the museum, covered in black soot. Hidden by filth was a wonderland of lace work and pintucks. It is thought to be an early 20th century piece. The bodice features diamonds woven into a base of pintucks, embroidered insertions, and lace insertions. On the skirt, lace insertion is mitered to form V's on a pintucked panel. Follow instructions on the next three pages for reproducing "The Bin Dress."

Illustrations by Tina McEwen, Instructions by Kathy McMakin, Photography by Di Lewis for Bethnal Green Museum of Childhood Special thanks to Noreen Marshall, curator of children's costume, for extending an invitation to view the archives of clothing and feature items from the collection in this book.

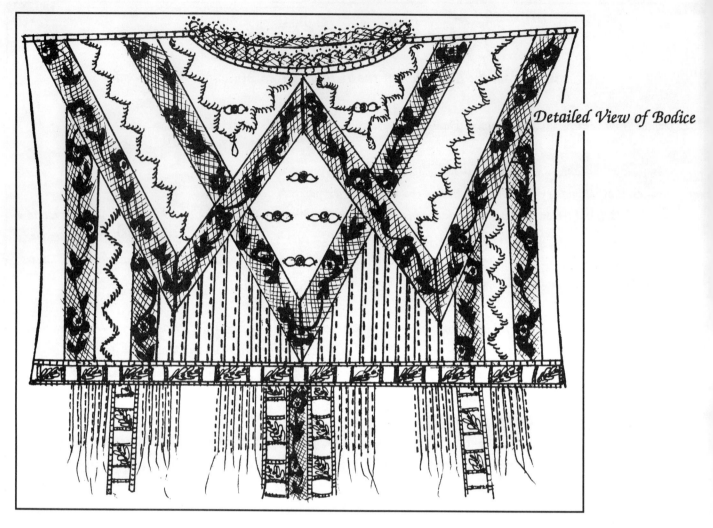

Detailed View of Bodice

How to Miter Lace

Fig. 1

Fig. 2

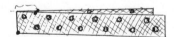

Fig. 3

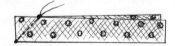

Fig. 4

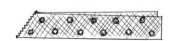

Fig. 5

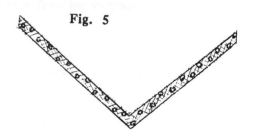

Directions:

1. Using 1/2-inch lace, cut six pieces 10 inches long.
2. Fold each piece of lace in half and dot the lower heading (Fig. 1).
3. Measure 1/2 inch (the width of the lace) from the fold and mark the upper headings (Fig. 2).
4. Right sides together, stitch from upper to lower dot (Fig. 3). Zigzag and trim (Fig. 4). Press into the angle formed (Fig. 5).

Applying Mitered Lace V

Directions:

1. Place laces on top of the tucked fabric, allowing 3-1/4 inch of fabric between the laces as shown (Fig. 1). Pin.
2. Zigzag the lace to the fabric along the top and bottom edge of the lace as shown.

NOTE: On the top lace piece, the zigzag is on the bottom edge only (Fig. 2).

3. Trim the excess fabric from the top piece of lace, starting above the zigzag. Be very careful not to cut the lace (Fig. 3).
4. Place this created fabric of tucks and lace on a second strip of fabric that fits between the yoke and the lace/tucked fabric. Zigzag the lace top edge to this second piece of fabric. Trim the excess fabric from the back. This completes one of the lace/tucked panels.
5. Repeat steps 1 through 4 for the second panel.

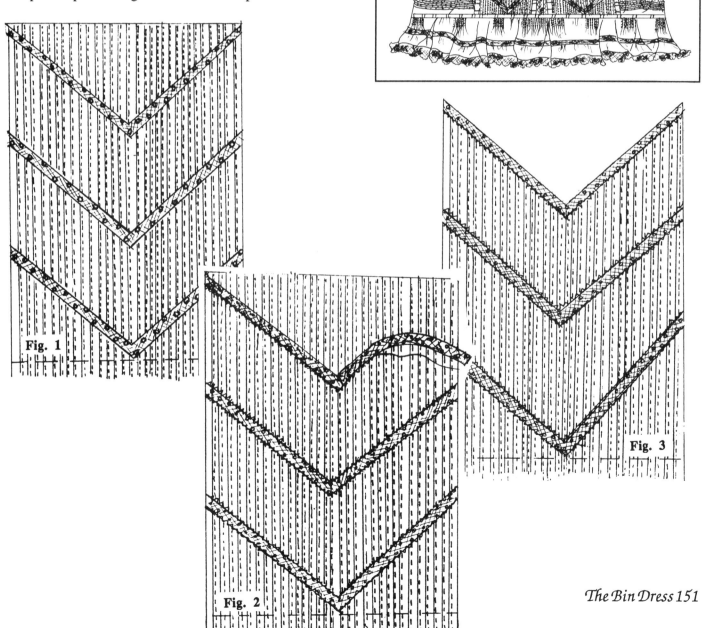

Fig. 1

Fig. 2

Fig. 3

How to Tuck Fabric

Tucking fabric can be done two ways: (1.) Using a double needle and a pintuck foot, or (2.) Pulling a thread in the fabric, folding the fabric on the pulled thread line, and stitching a small seam in the folded fabric.

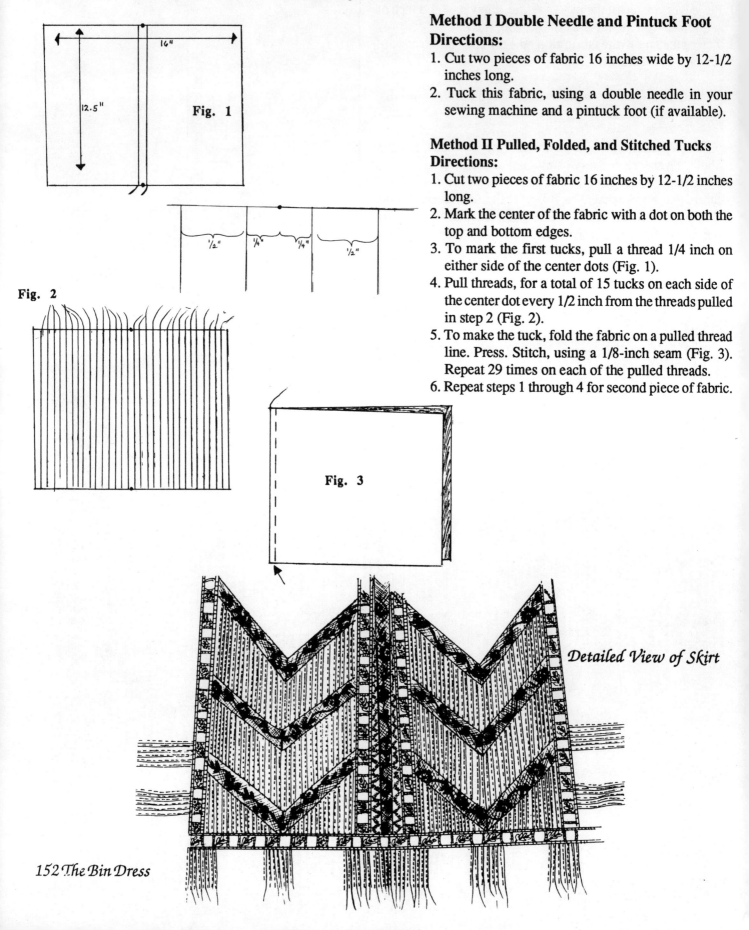

Method I Double Needle and Pintuck Foot Directions:

1. Cut two pieces of fabric 16 inches wide by 12-1/2 inches long.
2. Tuck this fabric, using a double needle in your sewing machine and a pintuck foot (if available).

Method II Pulled, Folded, and Stitched Tucks Directions:

1. Cut two pieces of fabric 16 inches by 12-1/2 inches long.
2. Mark the center of the fabric with a dot on both the top and bottom edges.
3. To mark the first tucks, pull a thread 1/4 inch on either side of the center dots (Fig. 1).
4. Pull threads, for a total of 15 tucks on each side of the center dot every 1/2 inch from the threads pulled in step 2 (Fig. 2).
5. To make the tuck, fold the fabric on a pulled thread line. Press. Stitch, using a 1/8-inch seam (Fig. 3). Repeat 29 times on each of the pulled threads.
6. Repeat steps 1 through 4 for second piece of fabric.

Fig. 1

Fig. 2

16"

12.5"

½" ¼" ¼" ½"

Fig. 3

Detailed View of Skirt

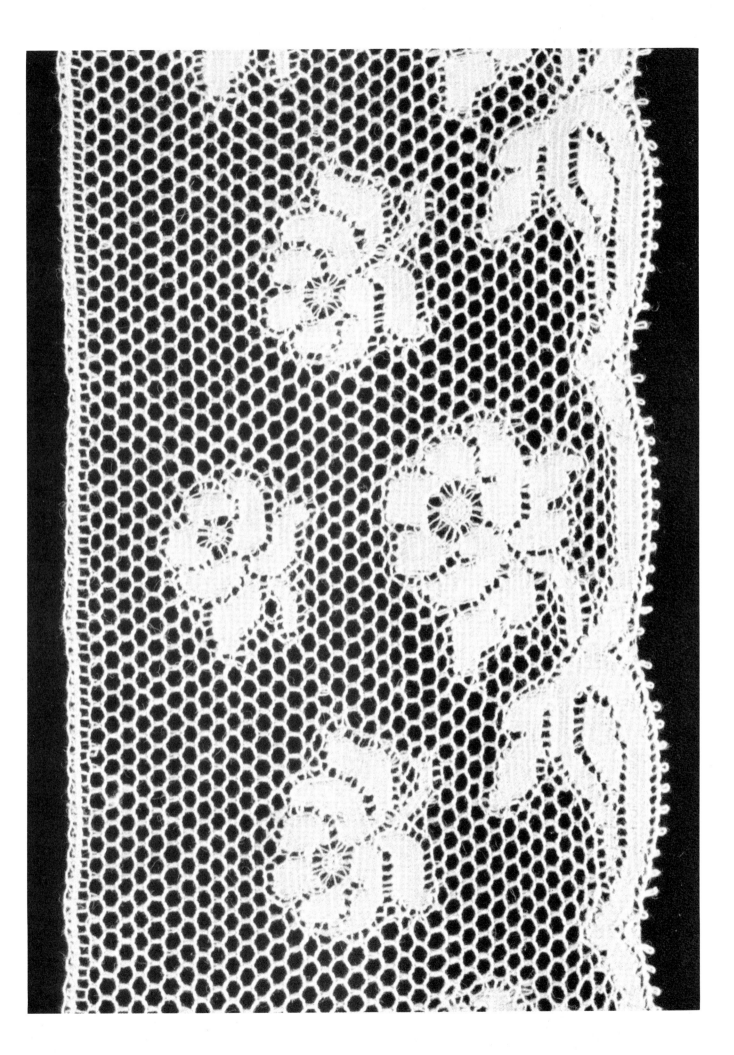

Questions and Answers

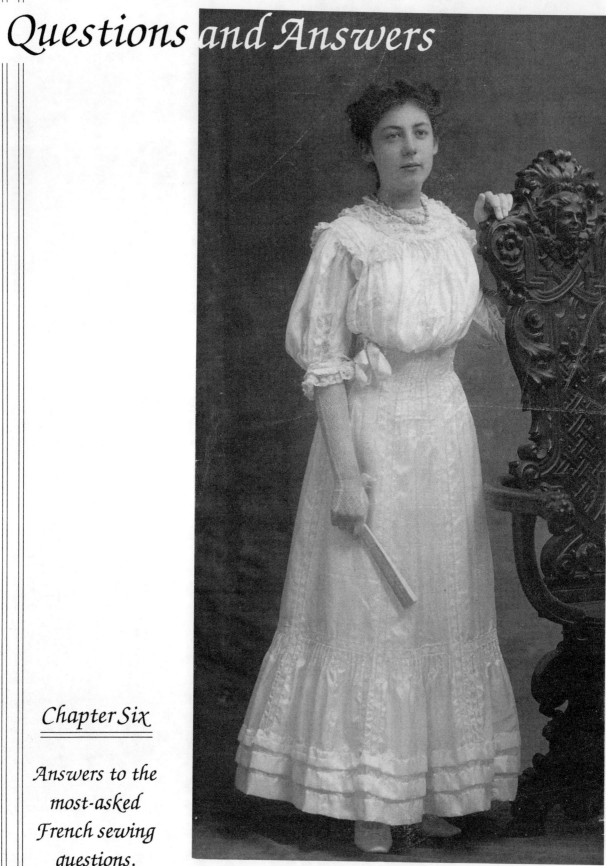

Chapter Six

Answers to the most-asked French sewing questions.

French and English Laces and Swiss Embroideries

Trims to use for French sewing by machine.

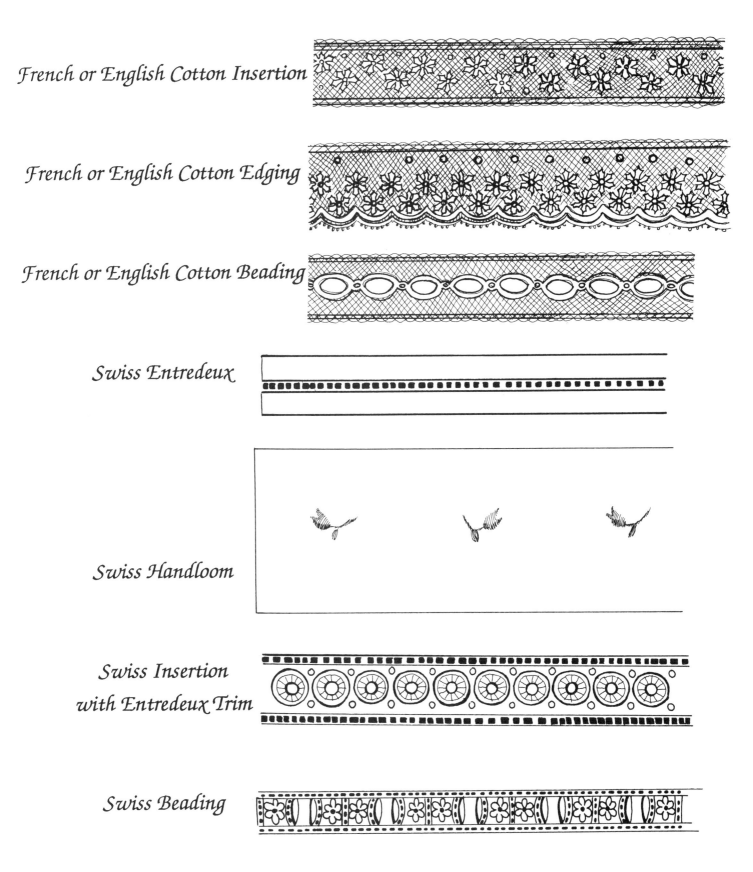

French or English Cotton Insertion

French or English Cotton Edging

French or English Cotton Beading

Swiss Entredeux

Swiss Handloom

Swiss Insertion
with Entredeux Trim

Swiss Beading

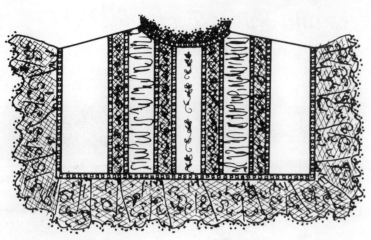

Q. What is French sewing by machine?

A. French sewing by machine is another term for heirloom sewing. Heirloom is defined by Webster's as: "1. *A piece of property as a deed or character that is viewed by law or special custom or will or s ettlement as an inseparable part of an inheritance and is so inherited with the inheritance. 2. Something having special monetary or sentimental value or significance that is handed on either by or apart from formal inheritance from one generation to another.*"
I would call French sewing by machine "sewing machine constructed, delicate clothing, using primarily batiste and silk fabrics, cotton laces, and Swiss embroideries."

Q. What fabrics are best for French sewing by machine?

A. I prefer Swiss batiste, particularly Swiss batiste from the Nelo company in Switzerland, for most all my French sewing. It's the fabric I've been recommending for nearly 10 years. There are three weights of Swiss batiste: 1. Very thin, shiny, and delicate (Finella and Oriunda); 2. Thicker, non-shiny batiste (Finissima); 3. Nelona, which is a cross between the Finella and Finissima. My favorite Swiss batiste is Nelona, and nearly every dress that my daughter, Joanna, and my niece, Anna, have worn to church since their birth has been made of Nelona. It is a cross between the thinnest, or "tissue," batiste and the thicker batiste. Nelona is available in white, bridal white, pale pink, pale blue, pale peach, pale lemon yellow, pale robin's egg blue (turquoise), real robin's egg blue, lavender, pale peach, and dusty rose.

Silk is absolutely beautiful for French sewing by machine. However, silk does not last as long as cotton and requires more care. Silk does wash, yet most sources do not recommend washing. Cotton laces should be washed, not dry cleaned, although dry cleaning should not damage them.

Q. Where would you use the three types of Swiss batiste?

A. The thinnest batiste is lovely when you want to put several different slips under the dress for different looks and seasons. Colored slips show through the sheer dress. Make a white dress of Finella. Run red ribbons through the beading for Christmas, and use a white slip. For spring, run pink, blue, or peach ribbons and make a slip of a matching color. Choose pale green or dusty rose ribbons for fall, and make a matching slip of green or rose.

When I use the heaviest batiste, I prefer Swiss embroideries for the trim. Try heavy batiste with a Swiss smocked collar or unsmocked collar gathered around the neckline, Swiss trims in the fancy band of the skirt, and Swiss beading for the sleeves. Heavier batiste works well for ladies blouses and nightgowns, as well.

Nelona is the best batiste for sewing machine enthusiasts. Don't let the sheer, delicate finish fool you. This is a strong batiste that doesn't tear easily and is perfect for machine sewing. My guess would be that it will hold up through the years quite well. Time will tell. Any 100 percent cotton should last, as long as it is washed before it is stored.

Q. What fabric should you use if you hate to iron?

A. Try Imperial batiste. There are several other brands you might want to consider also. Domestic batiste is a blend of 65 percent polyester and 35 percent cotton, permanent pressed. The colors are absolutely gorgeous. You can use these polyester/cotton blends anywhere you would use 100 percent cotton Swiss batiste.

Q. What laces and other trims do you use for French sewing by machine?

A. Always use 100 percent cotton laces and embroideries. Actually, few laces are true 100 percent cotton today. Even in France and England, where the best laces are made, the laces are 90 percent cotton and 10 percent nylon. This formula is still considered 100 percent cotton. Antique laces are 100 percent cotton.

Laces of 100 percent cotton come in a variety of widths and designs. Basically, French sewing calls for lace insertion, lace edging, and beading — refered to as "ribbon slot" in Europe. Insertion has two straight sides and is used between two other things. Edging usually is used on the edge of a garment for the final trim since is has one straight side and one scalloped or fancy finished side. Beading or "ribbon slot" is used where you want to run ribbon for trim or function; is has two straight sides.

Swiss, 100 percent cotton embroideries are used for heirloom sewing. Entredeux is an essential ingredient for strength and beauty. It means "between the two." Swiss insertions come either with entredeux on both sides or with an unfinished fabric finish on both sides. Swiss beading always comes with entredeux on both sides. Swiss edgings have an unfinished fabric side on one side and an embroidered finish on the other side. Swiss edgings range from very narrow to very wide; one common use of Swiss edgings is for a collar, smocked or gathered.

Swiss handlooms are one of the most beautiful additions to a child's or adult's garment. The delicate pinks, peaches, and blues offer a kiss of color; the white-on-white Swiss handlooms or ecru-on-ecru present a more subtle embellishment. One of my greatest pleasures in making children's garments is in choosing a Swiss handloom. I often repeat that color in ribbon at the sleeves.

Although you can get away with a polyester blend fabric for heirloom sewing, NEVER use polyester or nylon lace. They just won't do at all for French sewn garments. The sides of nylon lace aren't even, which detracts from the garment. I do not like any embroidered trims that aren't Swiss either; however, if the trim isn't Swiss, it still isn't quite as bad as nylon lace. Please use French or English laces and Swiss trims; and cut corners elsewhere if you have to.

Q. I have read that the royal Christening robe of England is made of silk. Would you ever use silk in French hand sewing by machine?

A. Indeed, many christening robes or dresses are made of silk. There are some new washable silks on the market coming in from Japan, which are fabulous.

All silk is washable; however, I never wash silks that have a "dry clean only" tag in the neck. Most of the newer silks are called "washable silk." Ask your fabric store about these delicate washable silks. Some people love China silk for heirloom sewing; I think it is a little hard to work with. I prefer a heavier weight silk. I have located a gorgeous silk in Hong Kong to begin importing for French sewing by machine.

Q. What kind of sewing machine do I need?

A. Your machine must make straight and zigzag stitches.There is all the difference in the world between old machines and the marvelous new computer machines. The tension on a computer machine is superior; the stitch capabilities seems endless. The creativity that can be obtained with these new machines is certainly something you will enjoy forever.

Try this. Explain to your husband, "Martha Pullen gave me permission to invest in a new sewing machine." See if he buys that line, but don't give him my phone number unless he thinks it is a good idea. Point out to your husband that a new automobile costs from $10,000-$25,000. Automobiles usually last three to five years before they start wearing down. Add to that the outrageous cost of insurance and upkeep. The best sewing machines cost anywhere from $1,500 to $2,500, and should last for 15 to 30 years without much repair.

If that doesn't work, try financing a new machine over several years. Sew for other people to earn extra money. Some of my friends have called everyone who is in the position to give them a present for the year and asked them to contribute toward a new machine. You might use up several birthday and Christmas gifts, but, believe me, it will be worth it.

Sometimes we mothers buy everything the family is in need of and wants and put our needs on the back burner. In this one case, don't do that. Your time is your most valuable asset. If you sew, you need a fine machine — for your pleasure and mainly for conserving your precious time.

Q. *Which sewing machine should I buy, if I decide to buy a new machine?*

A. There are a number of fine sewing machines on the market. All of them are manufactured outside of the United States. Please visit your sewing machine dealers — all of them — and take your laces and batiste with you. First ask the dealer for a demonstration. Then ask if you can sew on the machine, using your materials. Get the dealer to explain the proper adjustments for your fabrics and laces. One of the best tests of a sewing machine is to put two pieces of French lace under the presser foot and zigzag them together. Did they come through flat and pretty or did the machine gather it or eat it? Straight-stitch on Swiss batiste. Check the tension. Did you have to make a lot of adjustments, or did it come through nice and flat? Remember, time is your most precious commodity. You don't want to have to fool with a sewing machine to get nice stitches. Look at the embroidery stitches and the monograms. Do you think they are pretty?

One of the best ways to have fun on a sewing machine is to make your own Swiss handlooms. Ask the dealer to demonstrate pintucks with the double needles. Ask him to show you entredeux or hemstitching with double/wing-tip needles. Do you like this dealer? Ask about lessons on using the machine. Do these lessons come with the machine? One former dealer, who is a friend of mine, gave 12 hours of lessons with the purchase of each machine. I am a former sewing machine dealer; we gave six hours of free lessons with the purchase of a machine. You must feel comfortable with your dealer and your machine. Shop around.

The consumer, who has owned a machine for several years, will give you the most unbiased report on a machine's pluses and minuses. Call 10 people you know who love to sew. Ask them what kind of machine they have. If you belong to a sewing association, contact members of that association to talk about sewing machines.

Q. *I am really fascinated by those alphabets on the newest top-of-the-line machines. Where would I ever use letters in French sewing by machine? Decorative stitches are beautiful also. Where would I embroider little flowers and leaves?*

A. I love those alphabets! Use them to sign your art work. Artwork? You say. Your French clothes, of course! Special occasion clothes should be permanently signed. Oh how I wish signatures were in these antique clothes in my collections. What a story they would tell. Please use the alphabets in the machine to put: 1. Name of child or person; 2. parents of child; 3. occasion for garment; 4. who made garment; 5. city in which person lives; 6. date of garment; 7. age of child. For example, "Joanna Emma Joyce Pullen, Christening Dress, First United Methodist Church, Huntsville, Alabama, September 13, 1976, Daughter of Dr. and Mrs. Joe Ross Pullen, Granddaughter of Mr. and Mrs. Paul Jones Campbell and Dr. and Mrs. Joyce Buren Pullen, Dress made by Martha Pullen." This information can be "stitched or signed" in the hem of the garment, on the ruffle, on the slip, on a "garment tag" to be stitched in the seam of the dress or suit. You can even do your stitching in the placket of the dress.

I would buy an "alphabet machine" for French sewing if only to do this one thing; sign my child's clothing. You could even take down a hem in a special-occasion dress that you purchased and put the information on this garment also. For smocked dresses, put the information on the hem before you hem the garment.

To answer the second question, "Where would I embroider little flowers and leaves?" these designs are lovely on a pleat down the front of a garment, on the collar, around the ruffle, or around the sleeves. My favorite for the lovely decorative stitches; however, is to make your own Swiss handlooms with your machine. Just think of the money that you will save and of the fun you will have designing your one-of-a-kind handloom.

On one of the Martha Pullen patterns, "French Daygown," there are eight tucks on the front. I use the decorative stitch on one of my machines to run a little green stem-like stitch down the center of each tuck. Then I make, by hand, little pink French knots down the center of my machine-stitched leaf/stem combination. It is so sweet and it certainly takes less time than doing it all by hand. I must hasten to add that those decorative stitches aren't all just flowers and leaves. My favorite decorative stitch is perhaps the scallop. I scallop the edges of bonnets, sleeves of smocked and French dresses and skirts of several types. Use some of your decorative stitches to stitch over 1/16-inch and 1/8-inch ribbon. You can actually run decorative stitching down the center of a ribbon.

On the newer machines, you can make hemstitching and pin stitching with the decorative stitches. Ask your sewing machine dealer to demonstrate all of these decorative stitches and edgings, and see for yourself what the newer machines will do.

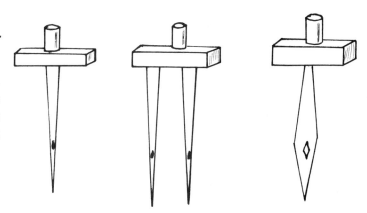

Q. What kind of machine needles do I need for French sewing?

A. For the basic zigzag and straight stitch, use a 60/8, 70/10, or 80/12. I prefer 60s or 70s. Double needles, wing needles, and other types of needles are all-important in French sewing for different stitches. You will learn more about them later.

Q. How often do I change my machine needles?

A. Change your sewing machine needle after four or five hours of sewing. Yes, even if it isn't broken, change it anyway. Needles become burred and may damage the batiste or delicate lace. Needles are inexpensive; don't ruin your sewing by using bad needles. I heard many stories while I was a sewing machine dealer about how a certain brand of needle lasted for several years. That is ridiculous. Throw those needles away. I dread to think what a 4-year-old needle would do for French sewing. Trust me! Put in new needles!

Q. What kind of threads must I use?

A. There are several kinds of thread I recommend. The most fabulous thread for French sewing by machine is Madeira 80 weight. It is also the most beautiful thread available. I began importing it about six months ago after discovering it in Australia. It is available in white, ecru, pale blue, pale pink, robin's egg blue, peach, gray, yellow, black, and lavender; we have had it dyed to go with the Nelona colors. The exact name of this thread is *Madeira Tanne 80;* 1,843 yards come on one spool. Another top thread is Coats and Clark. It is Dual Duty Plus-Extra Fine for Lightweight Fabrics and Machine Embroidery. It is cotton-covered polyester. D.M.C. 50 weight, Article 237 machine thread works as well. You can use 60 weight 100 percent cotton, but it is not my favorite. **Do not use polyester or nylon thread.** The only synthetic blend that will do is the Coats and Clark cotton-covered polyester mentioned above.

Q. How do I match my color thread to my dress color?

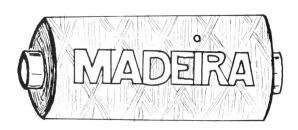

A. Until we had the Madeira threads dyed to go with our Nelona colors, this was almost an impossibility. Use the matching thread when you are sewing a batiste dress. When you are sewing the laces, the entredeux and the Swiss handlooms, use either white or ecru threads to match your chosen color of lace.

Q. Do I always match the patterns in my laces when I make a garment?

A. When you are French sewing you have complete control over what to put in your garment. When a mother is making her first few garments, she nearly always matches her laces. The more garments she makes, the more adventerous she becomes in selecting laces and trims. If you are copying antique dresses, you will often find three or four different lace designs in the dresses. My theory is that back then, a woman was forced to use what she had to make her clothing. Perhaps she had several yards of tatting, which her aunt made for her. Maybe she had several yards of French laces, which she took off of an old petticoat of Aunt Bernice's. Maybe she could get a little Swiss insertion and a little entredeux. She would then combine the materials in a masterpiece of handwork.

Experiment with your laces. Go to your fabric store and combine different designs. Be creative. Pull some laces you think wouldn't go at all and see if you find them pleasing after placing them side-by-side. This is the real design process.

Q. How do I dye white laces to ecru or cream? What about dyeing 100 percent cotton fabrics from white to ecru?

A. Ecru lace isn't always available in the patterns you want. But any white cotton lace can be successfully dyed:

- Step 1: Add two tablespoons a vinegar to one cup of coffee, warm or cold. If you are dyeing a large piece of fabric (100% cotton only) or a large amount of lace, you will want to make more than one cup of the mixture. Use the same proportions, just make more.
- Step 2: **NOTE:** Thoroughly wet your fabric with water before placing it into the coffee.
- Step 3: Leave the fabric in the coffee mixture for several minutes.
- Step 4: Remove the fabric and rinse with water until the the fabric or lace rinses clear.
- Step 5: Check your color. Do you want it darker? If so, repeat the procedure.
- Step 6: After getting the right color, let the laces or fabric dry before pressing it. When you press wet fabric, after dyeing it in this manner, you may get streaks.
- Step 7: Do not dry the fabric or laces in the dryer. Laces will tangle to the point of being ruined. Lay laces flat to dry, maybe on a towel. If you have one of those sweater stretcher dryers to lay over your tub, this is a good way to dry anything.
- Step 8: Do you want fabric which looks 100 years old? In this case, press it while it is still wet. It actually stains it in a very antique manner when pressed from a completely wet state. This technique does not work on laces, only fabrics. A very interesting effect can be obtained by coffee dyeing pastel-colored Swiss batiste. Try it.

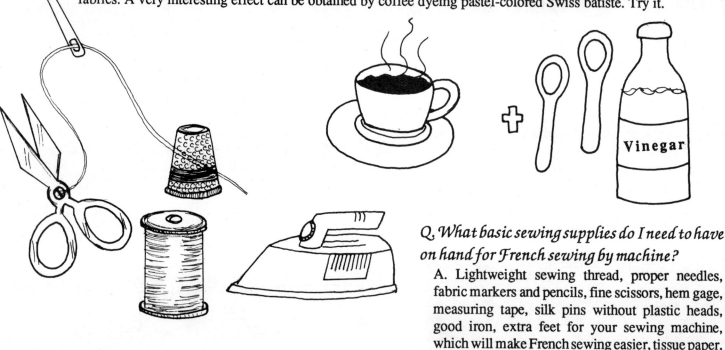

Q. What basic sewing supplies do I need to have on hand for French sewing by machine?

A. Lightweight sewing thread, proper needles, fabric markers and pencils, fine scissors, hem gage, measuring tape, silk pins without plastic heads, good iron, extra feet for your sewing machine, which will make French sewing easier, tissue paper, gimp cord or #8 pearl cotton, and hand sewing needles.

Q. How do I miter lace when I am going around a corner of a collar trimmed with entredeux?

A. This is very simple. First you zigzag the lace to the finished entredeux down to the corner. Then, extend the lace down the same measurement as it is wide. The illustration insertion is 1/2 inch wide; so extend it down 1/2 inch below the entredeux. Stitch from the corner to the outside corner. Then proceed to zigzag the lace on across the finished edge. Simple, isn't it?

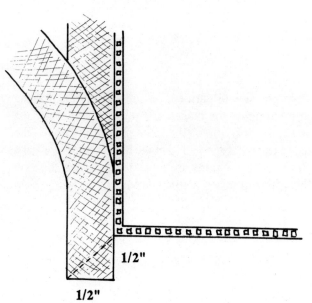

1/2"

1/2"

The Bin Dress
Photo by Di Lewis
for Bethnal Green
Museum of Childhood

Triple-layer net Christening dress worn by Renee Weller for her Christening at Shoreditch Parish Church on June 11, 1923. The dress was made by her mother, Elizabeth Charlotte Weller, who worked in the fashion industry as a sample-hand at blouses. The complete layette consists of a Christening cape, bonnet, petticoat, and gown; five day dresses of different designs, three petticoats, and four barracoats.
Photo by Di Lewis for Bethnal Green Museum of Childhood

Baby's long dress (not documented as Christening dress) of white cotton with a center panel of tucked fabric and machine-embroidered insertions. Its date is problematical because the original register entry says that it is about 1888; however, the original neckline has been filled in with additional fabric and topped with a lace frill, and a second pair of sleeves (long ones) have been stitched inside the earlier shorter ones.

The original dress is in the style of the 1860s or 1870s; alterations date from about 1888.
Photo by Di Lewis for Bethnal Green Museum of Childhood

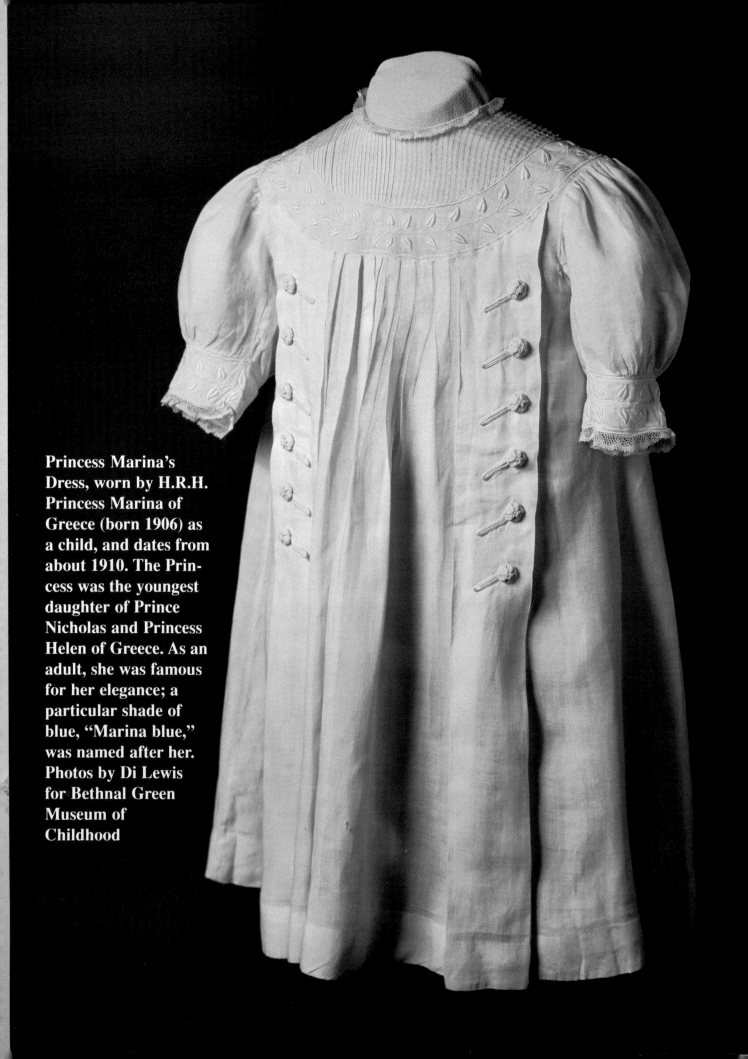

Princess Marina's Dress, worn by H.R.H. Princess Marina of Greece (born 1906) as a child, and dates from about 1910. The Princess was the youngest daughter of Prince Nicholas and Princess Helen of Greece. As an adult, she was famous for her elegance; a particular shade of blue, "Marina blue," was named after her. Photos by Di Lewis for Bethnal Green Museum of Childhood

Top: Dress trimmed with tatting and made of white lawn; worn by Frances Yates, the art historian. Frances was born in about 1900, and the dress dates from about 1903. It was made by her mother Mrs. Yates and elder sister Ruby

Bottom: Little girl's dress of white cotton, trimmed with machine-made lace in a medallion design, dating from 1910

Photos by Di Lewis for the Bethnal Green Museum of Childhood

**Bias Tubing,
Triangular Sleeve
Christening Dress,
circa 1900-1930**

Top left: Bias Tubing, Triangular Sleeve
Christening Dress bodice detail

Top right: Hem detail

Bottom left: Sleeve detail

Bottom right: Back closing

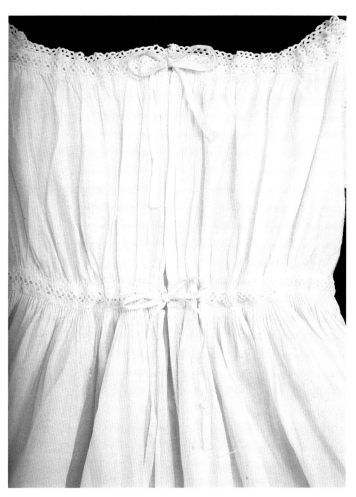

Top left: Shoulder Puffing Christening Dress, circa 1890

Bottom left: Antique vertical lace middy dress, circa 1885

Right: Embellished hem of the Tucked-to-the-Shoulder dress, circa 1900

Top right: Rouching Baby Dress, circa 1860-1870

Left: Sleeve detail

Bottom right: Angled Swiss Insertion Dress, circa 1900

Antique camisole, top petticoat, and bottom petticoat,
circa 1900

Antique apron,
circa 1900,
over linen dress

(Left to right) Silk Charmeuse
Button-On Boy's Suit,
circa 1920; linen dress with collar
of net overlay with lace diamond
shaping, clipped lace medallion,
and a high bone neckline, taken
from woman's antique dress,
circa 1900; silk antique middy
dress with tucks and lace insertion, circa 1900

Antique child's dress, circa 1900 (right), used to create "Victoria" pattern (left) for Matha Pullen Company

Antique Diamond Blouse,
circa 1885, and Ladies
Diamond Puffing Skirt,
circa 1885

**Tucks and Swiss Dress,
circa 1900 (left)
and antique eyelet
Christening gown, circa 1870**

Top: Susan York original

Bottom: *Sew Beautiful* pattern, Christmas 1989 (left); "Pollyanna Dress" by Gooseberry Hill Country Craft Patterns

Top: Shadow Diamond technique used on French dress by Patty Smith

Bottom: Antique Tucked and Shadow Diamond Skirt, circa 1890-1910

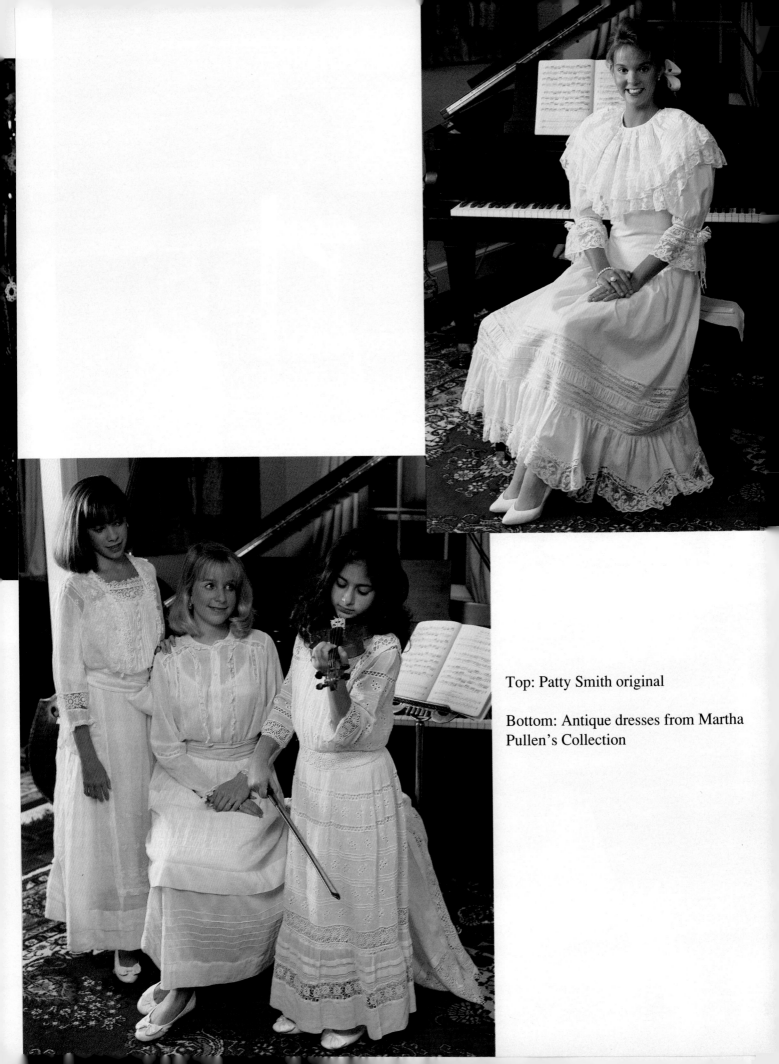

Top: Patty Smith original

Bottom: Antique dresses from Martha Pullen's Collection

Top: Antique drawers

Bottom: (Left to right) Smocked Puffing Christening
Dress, circa 1890 ; antique batiste dress with Swiss
insertion, circa 1910; Broadcloth/Eyelet Christening
Dress or Daygown, circa 1850-1880

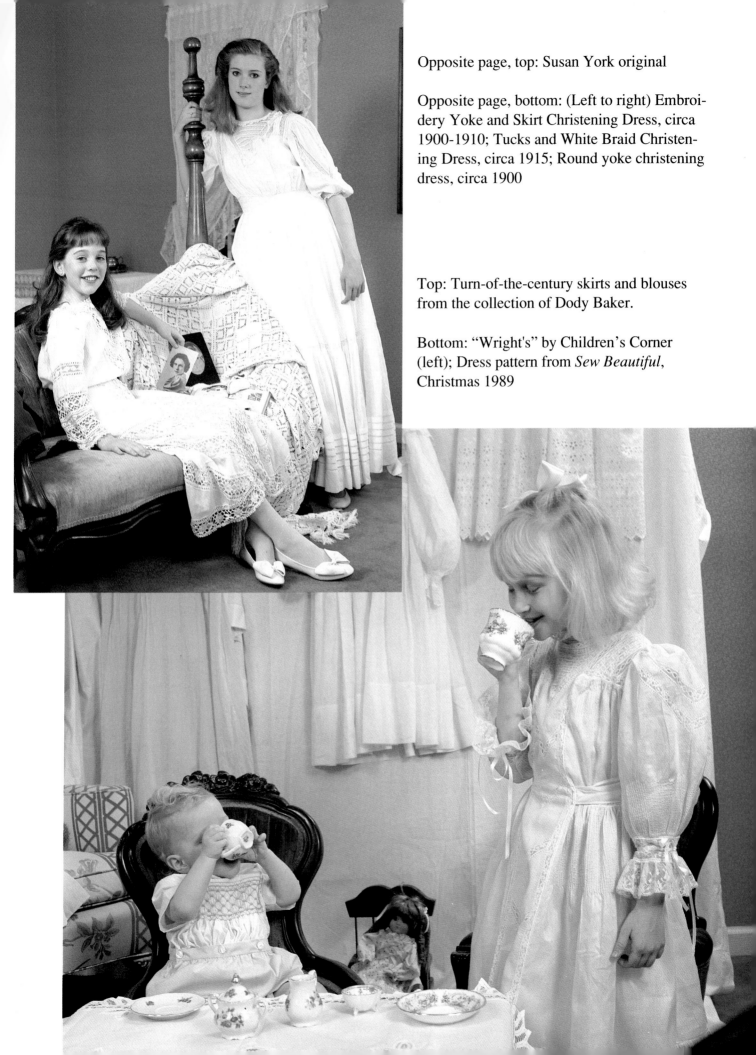

Opposite page, top: Susan York original

Opposite page, bottom: (Left to right) Embroidery Yoke and Skirt Christening Dress, circa 1900-1910; Tucks and White Braid Christening Dress, circa 1915; Round yoke christening dress, circa 1900

Top: Turn-of-the-century skirts and blouses from the collection of Dody Baker.

Bottom: "Wright's" by Children's Corner (left); Dress pattern from *Sew Beautiful*, Christmas 1989

Top: Handkerchief linen boy's suit with tatted insertion, a front panel of Swiss embroidery and tatting collar, design by Ninon Parker (left); handkerchief linen dress with square lace yoke with shirring below, lace backed, scalloped hem made with buttonhole stitch, circa 1920

Bottom: Susan York orginals

Top: Crossed Tucks Silk Dress, circa
1890 (left); "Foster's Sailor Suit" from
Deborah's Designs

Bottom: Round-Yoke Middy, circa 1910
(left); Middy Embroidered Dress with
Raglan Sleeves, circa 1890

Top: "Victoria" and "Rosemary" pattern adaptations by Patty Smith

Bottom: 1890s embroidered blouse and reproduction (left) made with Swiss embroidery motifs.

Top: Both dresses "Christian Elizabeth's Blue Ribbon Dress" from Ruffle Bunnies and Lace

Bottom: "Royal Babe" by Terry Jane Inc.

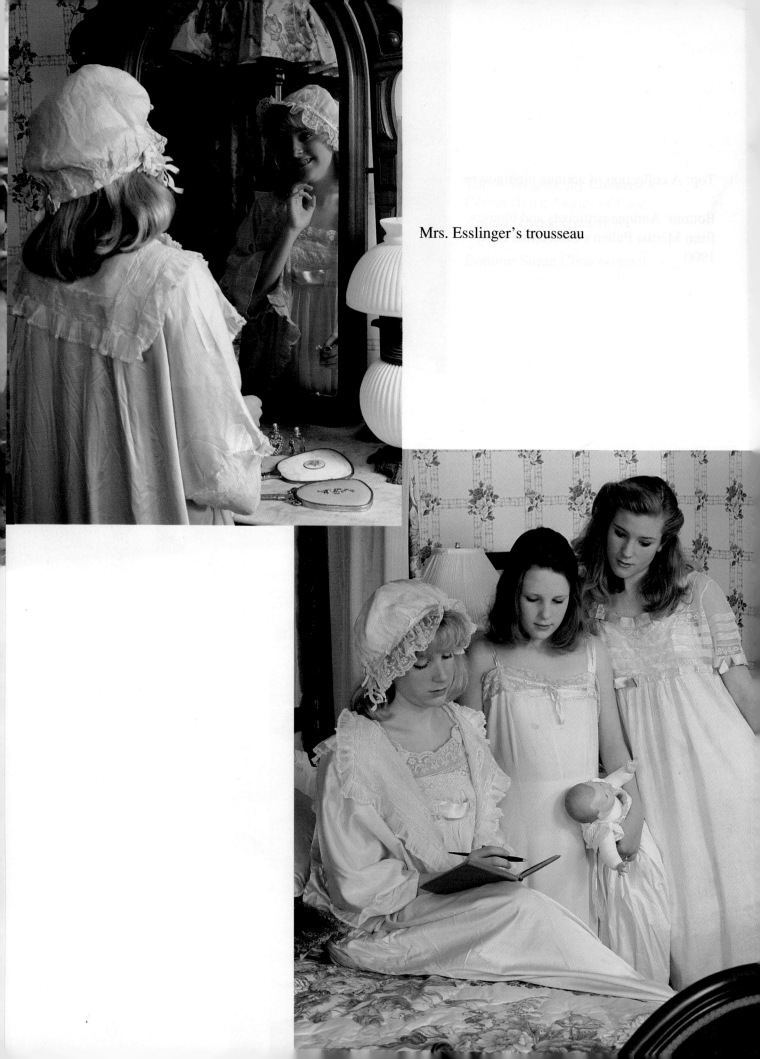

Mrs. Esslinger's trousseau

Top: A collection of antique nightgowns
Center 1910s, angora-trim caps
Bottom: Antique nightgowns and blouses
from Martha Pullen
1900
Bottom: Susan Close collection

Top: Eyelet Fabric Dress, circa 1930 (right); "Eton Ensemble" from Chery Williams

Bottom: Antique Swiss eyelet dress (left); "Little Lord Jeffery" from Deborah's Designs

Top: (Seated) "Wright's" by Children's Corner with French Shirt; "Victoria" adaptation by Patty Smith

Bottom: (Left to right) "Stick Horses" by Ellen McCarn, "Boy's Button-On Suit" by Chery Williams; "David" pattern with "Apple Blossom" plate by Children's Corner; "Boy's Button-On Suit" by Chery Williams with embroidered insertion by Capitol Imports; "David" pattern with "Candyland Express" plate by Children's Corner. (Seated) "Wright's" by Children's Corner with French shirt

Eyelet dress (right)
and split-sleeve day dress
circa 1895

Top: Antique engagement dress, circa 1915

Bottom: (Left to right) "Eton Ensemble" from Chery Williams, shirt from Sarah Howard Stone's *French Hand Sewing Volume I*; "Boy's Basic I" shirt and "Wright's" pants from Children's Corner; "Boy's Basic I" shirt and "Wright's" pants from Children's Corner; "David" suit from Martha Pullen Company with "Andrew's Pull Toys" plate by Terry Collins

Top: Susan Oliver original (left);
Susan York original blouse

Bottom: Susan Cline original

Top: (Left to right) Crocheted lace blouse and tucked skirt, circa 1900; Swiss eyelet wedding dress with extended peplum, circa 1900; Swiss Triple-Eyelet Dress, circa 1900

Bottom: Turn-of-the-century dress with Christmas tree embroidery (left); Double Puffing Netting Dress, circa 1900

Antique
netting dress,
circa 1900

Australian
Organdy Masterpiece,
circa 1900

Top: "Melissa" pattern by Kay Becraft for Ruffle Bunnies and Lace.

Bottom: "Katherine Lee" pattern from Ruffle Bunnies and Lace

Antique baby dress with square
yoke and Swiss insertion trim,
circa 1890 (left); Stripes and
Curves Middy, circa 1890

Q. How do you make those knotted rosettes or "froufrou's" as I have heard some people call them?

A. One of the most beautiful touches to a French dress is the addition of one or more rosettes. I love the knotted rosettes. Where did the tradition of ribbon flowers originate? My close friend, Margaret Boyles, told me that in the olden pictures the child who had on a rosette was the birthday girl! That sounds like a lovely thing to do for a birthday — to single-out the special child with a ribbon rosette! I used to put rosettes on almost all of Joanna's French dresses.

Making a rosette can become very habit forming. Since French sewing by machine can be used for pillows, doll clothes, and other lovely things, you might want to start adding rosettes to other items. A ribbon rosette would be pretty on a diaper holder bag, on each corner of a baby crib canopy, or even a canopy for a bed for you. Small rosette are pretty on doll clothes, bear clothes and on "Easter" purses.

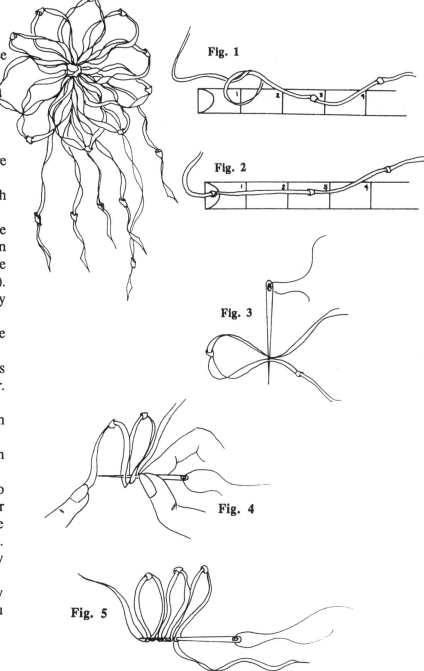

Materials Needed:

• 5 yards 1/16-inch, 1/8-inch, or 1/4-inch double-face satin ribbon
• Ruler or tape measure
• Needle and thread; thimble (optional)

Knotted Rosette Directions:

1. Leave 12 inches to 15 inches of ribbon before making your first knot.
2. Make one knot at either the 12-inch or the 15-inch point.
3. Tie another knot (Fig. 1). Before tightening the knot, lay the first knot on the 2-1/2-inch mark on your ruler. Carefully slip the other, new knot, where it tightens on the 0-inch mark on your ruler (Fig. 2).
4. Continue across the ribbon, making knots every 2-1/2 inches.
5. Stop when you are 12 inches to 15 inches from the end.
6. Tie a knot in the thread that is in your needle. It is best to use a double thread; this makes it stronger. You can also use quilting thread.
7. Your needle will go between the knots for each stitch (Fig. 3).
8. Keep your knots above the needle for each stitch (Fig. 4).
9. When you make loops all the way across (Fig. 5) to the other unknotted end, pull the loops up rather tightly and begin to stitch the rosette together at the bottom. Play with the rosette to distribute the loops. Finish stitching when you have it looking the way you want.
10. If you want more than two streamers, add as many streamers to the back of the finished rosette as you wish. You may want to knot the streamers.

Unknotted Rosette Directions:

1. Mark every 2 to 3 inches with a water-soluble marker.
2. Pick up your loops, going into the marks. Follow the other instructions for making the knotted rosette.
3. When you mark every 2 inches, you will have a small rosette, since your loops will only be 1 inch tall. This is great for christening dresses and for babies clothing.
4. When you mark 2-1/2 inches, the loops are a little larger. Three-inch markings mean that each loop will be 1-1/2 inches. Your personal choice should be the only factor in your decision concerning the size of your rosette.

Original French Sewing Techniques

Chapter Seven

A review of Martha Pullen's favorite French sewing techniques.

Applying Lace Straight Edge to Lace Straight Edge

Where would this technique be used?

a. Lace insertion to lace insertion

b. Lace insertion to lace beading

c. Lace insertion, lace beading to non-gathered straight edge of lace edging

d. Swiss embroidered trims with entredeux edgings

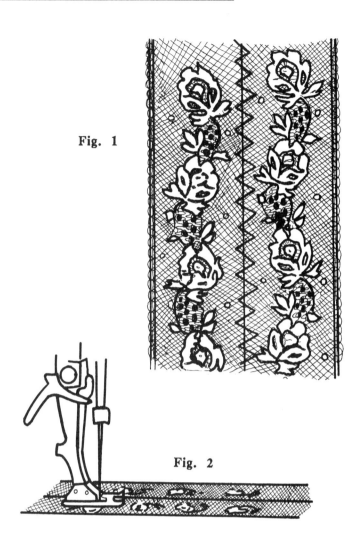

Fig. 1

Directions:

1. Spray starch and press each piece.
2. Place the two pieces, side-by-side, butting them together, but not overlapping. It is important to match patterns in the lace. If there are patterns, align them as you think they look prettiest (Fig. 1).
3. Begin 1/4 inch or 3/8 inch from the ends of the pieces to be joined. This keeps the ends from digging into the sewing machine (Fig. 2).
4. Zigzag the two edges together. If you miss some spaces, go back and zigzag again.
5. Stitch just widely enough to catch the two headings of the pieces of lace (or embroidery). Laces vary greatly in the widths of the headings. The stitch widths will vary according to the lace heading placement and your preference.
6. Stitch the length as tightly or as loosely as you wish. You don't want a satin-stitch; however, you don't want the dress to fall apart either. Work with your trims and your sewing machine to determine the length and width you want.
7. Suggested stitch width and length:

   Width=2 to 3 — I prefer 2-1/2

   Length=1 to 1/12 — I prefer 1

Fig. 2

Joining Lace Edging to Other Strips of Lace Edging

This technique is used when you need a wider piece of lace edging than is available. Using this method, you can make a double or triple lace edging.

Directions:

1. Spray starch and press the two edgings to be joined.
2. Lay one piece of edging on the table, right side up.
3. Lay the next piece of edging, right side up, on top of the first one.
4. Check to be sure that the scallops of the second piece overlap the heading of the straight side of the first piece by at least 1/8 inch.
5. Straight-stitch just inside the heading of the bottom straight edge (Fig. 1).
6. Suggested stitch length:

   Length=1-1/2 to 2-1/2

Fig. 1

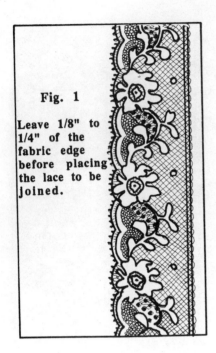

Fig. 1

Leave 1/8" to 1/4" of the fabric edge before placing the lace to be joined.

Where would this technique be used:

a. Lace edging to ruffle or skirt
b. Embroidered insertion to straight edge of lace
c. Lace edging to sleeve edge, as on smocked sleeve or bottom of sleeve with elastic casing
d. Swiss edging (with scallops trimmed) to a flat surface to fabric edge, as on ruffles, sleeves, or collars

Martha's Magic

Directions:

1. Spray starch and press both the lace and the fabric.
2. Place right sides to right sides.
3. **NOTE:** Leave 1/8 inch to 1/4 inch of fabric edge before placing the lace to be joined (Fig. 1).
4. Zigzag with a satin-stitch, going into the heading of the lace and all the way off the fabric edge (Fig. 2).
5. Suggested stitch width and length:
   Width=3-1/2 to 4
   Length=1/2 or as short as your machine will zigzag and not jam!

NOTE: 1/8 inch to 1/4 inch of the fabric is exposed before the lace flat edge is put into place. The fabric edge will completely fold into the stitch when you are finished.

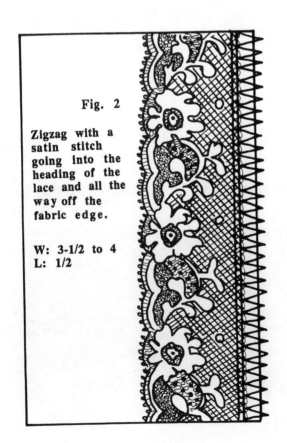

Fig. 2

Zigzag with a satin stitch going into the heading of the lace and all the way off the fabric edge.

W: 3-1/2 to 4
L: 1/2

6. Why shouldn't you just place the edge of the lace and the edges of the fabric together and zigzag? They will come apart. There is not enough strength in the edge of the fabric without the extra 1/8 inch or 1/4 inch folded into the zigzag.
7. Press the lace and fabric open.
8. My 600 pound gorilla story:
   After I tell my students to press the lace and the fabric open, the question, which inevitably follows, is "Martha, which way do I press this little roll?" I answer, "That is like asking where does the 600 pound gorilla sleep? Anywhere he wants to!" So the answer to that qu estion is "Just press that seam anywhere it wants to go! It will fold toward the lace naturally, which is fine, or you can iron all afternoon to make the lace go toward the fabric.

The Scotch Tape Stitch

Where would this technique be used?

1. When the section you have just stitched is to be gathered, as on the sleeve of a French or smocked dress
2. On the edge of a smocked bonnet, where pleating will be drawn up tightly
3. When you are using narrow baby lace on the edge — after baby lace edging is washed, it tends to not want to stay pressed open.

When is the Scotch tape stitch not necessary?

1. On the bottom of a dress ruffle where the gathers will not be drawn up too tightly
2. When you are using wide edging — 1 inch or wider
3. When you use the technique in a fancy band to stitch insertion and lace together

Directions:

1. Work from the right side, after the lace has been pressed open.
2. Zigzag on top of the little roll, which is on the back of the garment. Your width should be very narrow — just wide enough to go from one side of the little roll to the other side. It should not be too short. You want it to be as invisible as possible (Fig. 1).
3. This zigzag holds the lace down and gives added strength to the seam. Its main purpose, however, is to hold the lace down.
4. Suggested stitch width and lengths:
    Width=1/2 to 1-1/2
    Length=1 to 2

Fig. 1

Scotch Tape Stitch This top stitching is used to keep the lace from flipping toward the fabric when the fabric is gathered into a ruffle.

Directions:

1. Trim one batiste side of the entredeux.
2. Spray starch and press entredeux and lace.
3. Lay trimmed edge of entredeux beside the flat side of the lace. These should be right sides up. Butt them together; they should not overlap. In other words, zigzag, side-by-side, right sides up.
4. Zigzag them together, trying to make one stitch of the machine go into one hole of the entredeux and over, just catching the heading of the lace (Fig. 1).
5. Suggested stitch width and length:
    Width=2-1/2 to 3-1/2
    Length=2-1/2
6. **NOTE:** In machine stitching, it is not always possible for the needle to go into just one hole of the entredeux. Simply, set your machine to a stitch length and width that shows the best results.

Flat Lace Edge to Entredeux

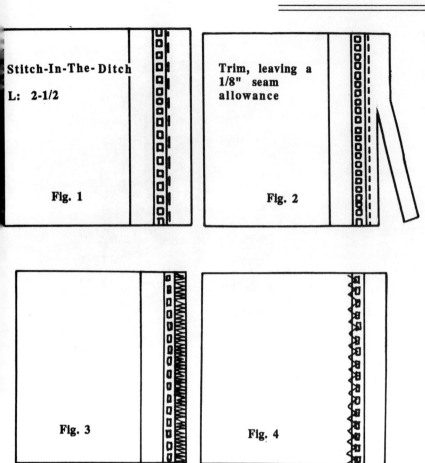

Stitch-In-The-Ditch

L: 2-1/2

Fig. 1

Trim, leaving a 1/8" seam allowance

Fig. 2

Fig. 3

Fig. 4

Method 1 - Stitch-In-The-Ditch Directions:

1. Do not trim entredeux.
2. Spray starch and press fabric and entredeux.
3. Place together batiste edge of untrimmed entredeux and edge of the fabric. (This is similar to the sewing of any two seams of a dress. Place the edges and sew the seam.)
4. Sew in straight, short stitches along the right-handside of the entredeux (the side of the entredeux that is next to the body of the sewing machine.) This is called "stitch-in-the-ditch" because it is just that — you stitch in the ditch of the entredeux (Length= 2-1/2) (Fig. 1).
5. Trim the seam, leaving about a 1/8-inch seam allowance (Fig. 2).
6. Zigzag a tight stitch (not a satin) to go over the stitch-in-the-ditch and all the way off the edge of the fabric edge. This zigzag will completely encase the fabric left on the entredeux and the straight-stitch you just made (Width=2-1/2 to 3, Length=1) Fig. 3.
7. Press the zigzagged seam toward the fabric. All of the holes of the entredeux should be showing perfectly.
8. This Scotch tape stitch step is not necessary if you are using entredeux to flat fabric; however, you may choose to make this stitching. When you make the Scotch tape stitch, zigzag on **top** of the fabric. As close as possible, zigzag into one hole of the entredeux and into the fabric. Barely catch the fabric in this top zigzag stitch. Adjust your machine length and width to fit each situation (Fig. 4).
9. My machine width and length:
   Width=1-1/2 to 2
   Length=2
10. You can choose to do Scotch taping from the back of the fabric. If you work from the back, you can hold the seam down and see a little better. On entredeux to flat fabric, the choice of Scotch taping from the top or from the bottom is yours.

Method 2 - Trimmed Entredeux Method Directions:

1. Trim one side of the entredeux (Fig. 1).
2. Spray starch and press both the entredeux and the fabric edge.
3. Run a straight row of short stitches as close to the edge of the fabric as is possible (Length=1-1/2 to 2) (Fig. 2).

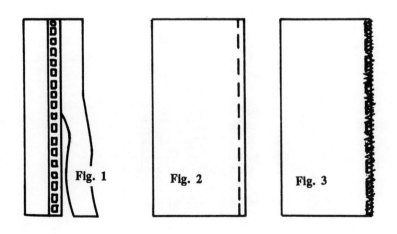

Fig. 1

Fig. 2

Fig. 3

4. Zigzag a tiny zigzag over this row of stitches. The zigzag should enclose the first row of stitching (Width=2-1/2, Length=1/2) (Fig. 3).
5. Place the trimmed entredeux edge into the ditch made by the previous two steps. The fabric and the entredeux are right sides to right sides (Fig. 4).
6. Zigzag off the edge of the fabric and into one hole of entredeux (Width=3, Length=1-1/2) Fig. 5. **Sew carefully.**
7. Press open.

Method 3 - Super Simple, Super Quick, Not-As-Strong Method
Directions:
1. Trim one side of the entredeux (Fig. 1).
2. Press and spray starch fabric edge and entredeux.
3. Lay trimmed edge of entredeux to fabric edge, right sides to right sides.
4. Leave 1/8 inch to 1/4 inch of fabric edge before placing the entredeux edge to be stitched on the fabric (Fig. 2).
5. Zigzag with a satin-stitch, going into one hole of the entredeux and off the fabric edge. This will be a short, wide zigzag (Width=3 to 4, Length=1 to 1-1/2) (Fig. 3).
6. The 1/8 inch to 1/4 inch of the fabric is exposed before the zigzag is sewn, attaching the entredeux. The fabric edge will roll into the entredeux completely when the zigzag stitches are completed.
7. Press open.

Method 4
Entredeux To Flat Fabric
Directions:
1. Do not trim border off entredeux.
2. Place edge of entredeux to edge of fabric.
3. Stitch in the ditch of the entredeux as close to the edge of the entredeux as possible (Length=2-1/2) (Fig. 1).
4. Trim the border of both the entredeux and the fabric down to a width of 1/8 inch (Fig. 2).
5. Zigzag, going all the way off of the fabric and into one hole. The batiste border will roll into the seam (Width=3-1/2, Length=1) (Fig. 3).
6. Press open.

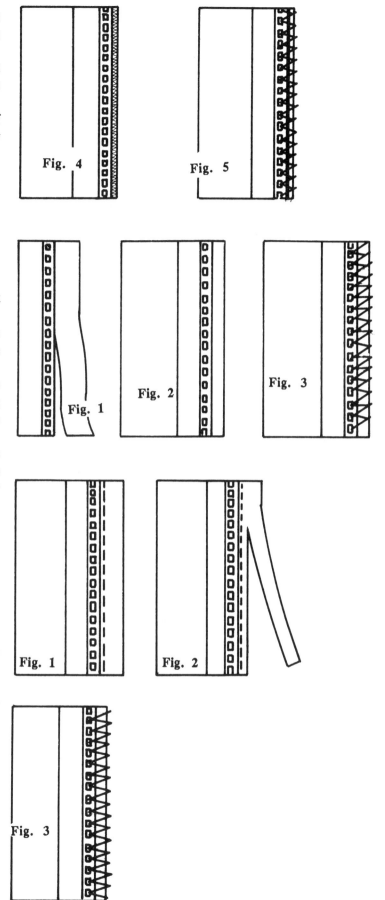

Entredeux To Gathered Fabric

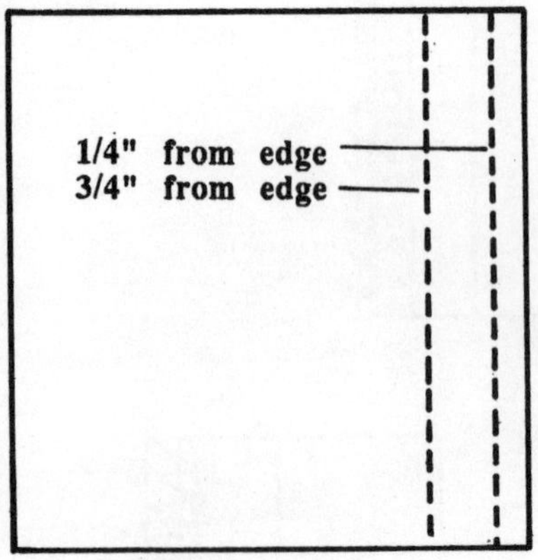

Directions:

Where would this technique be used?
a. Bottom edge of a sleeve
b. Top edge of a sleeve
c. Top edge of a ruffle attached to a skirt that has a fancy band
d. Bottom of a yoke to which gathered skirt is attached

Method 1
Directions:
1. Press, don't spray starch the fabric.
2. Do not cut off the edges of the entredeux.
3. Run two rows of long gathering stitches on the fabric (Length=4). There are two methods for running these gathering stitches. Try both methods. See which you prefer.
   a. Sew the first gathering row 1/4 inch from the edge of the fabric. Sew the second gathering row 3/4 inch from the edge of the fabric (Fig. 1).
   b. Sew the first gathering row 1/4 inch from the edge of the fabric. Sew the second gathering row 1/4 inch below the first row. This is the more traditional method of running two gathering rows (Fig. 2).
4. Gather by hand to adjust the gathers to fit the entredeux.
5. Lay right side of the entredeux to right side of the gathered fabric. This step reminds me of the days when we put waistbands on very full gathered skirts. This step is basic dressmaking.
   a. If you gathered by the first method (1/4-inch and 3/4-inch gathering rows), place the ditch of the entredeux below the first gathering line. This would mean that the ditch of the entredeux would be about 3/8 inch from the unfinished edge.
   b. If you used the second method (1/4-inch and 1/2-inch gathering rows), place the entredeux on or a little below the second gathering row.
6. Stitch in the ditch of the entredeux, using a short straight-stitch. This stitch is on the right side of the entredeux. This side is closest to the body of the sewing machine (Length=2) (Fig. 3).
7. Move over just a little and straight-stitch the second time (Fig. 4). This holds down the gathers under the entredeux.
8. Trim away both layers as close to the straight-stitch as you can trim (Fig. 5).

1/4" from edge
3/4" from edge

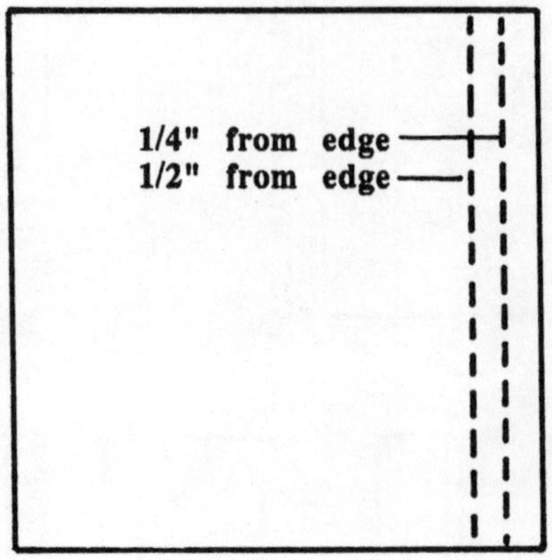

1/4" from edge
1/2" from edge

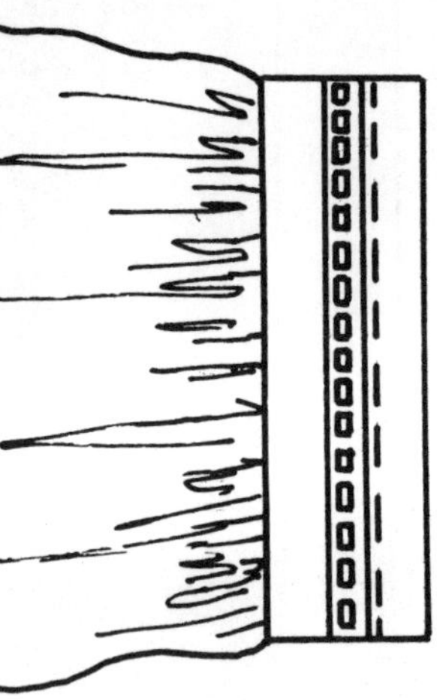

Fig. 1

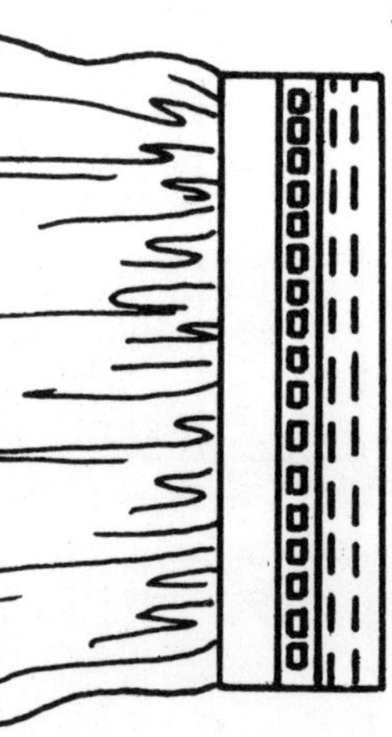

Fig. 2

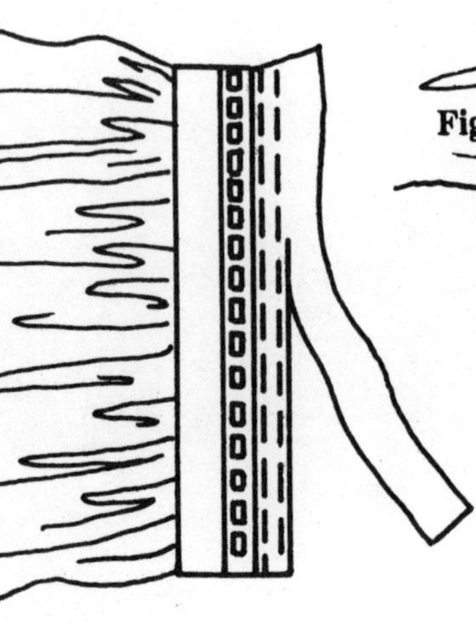

Fig. 3

9. Zigzag to finish the process. This zigzag is not a satin-stitch but close to a satin-stitch. This zigzag stitch encloses the stitch-in-the-ditch seam, the second seam and goes off the side to catch the raw edges (Width=3, Length=3/4 to 1) **Fig. 3**.

10. Press the satin-stitched roll toward the fabric.

11. Scotch tape stitch on the wrong side of the fabric. Zigzag into one hole of the entredeux and off into the zigzagged seam. This should be as narrow a seam a possible (Width=1-1/2 to 2-1/2, Length=2) **Fig. 4**.

12. This last step can be zigzagged from the top also. It is easier to zigzag it from the bottom if the step is "entredeux to gathered fabric" because of the bulk of the zigzagged seam. When zigzagging entredeux to flat edge (as given in the section just preceding this one) it seems easier to zigzag the final step from the top.

Method 2
Directions:

1. Follow steps 1 through 6 of Method I (Fig. 1).
2. Trim to within 1/8 inch of the stitch-in-the-ditch (Fig. 2).
3. Zigzag, going into one hole of the entredeux and all the way off of the edge of the fabric. This will roll the fabric/entredeux border right into the entredeux (Width=3 to 4, Length=1-1/2) Fig. 3.

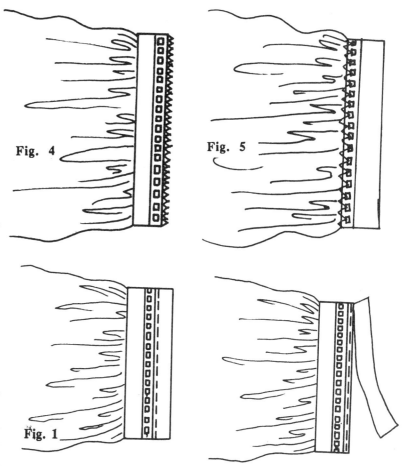

Fig. 4   Fig. 5

Fig. 1

Fig. 3

Serger Fever

Oh what a wonderful tool the serger is for French sewing by machine! I cannot say enough about how this machine has simplified the "Entredeux To Flat Fabric" technique and the "Entredeux To Gathered Fabric" technique. First of all, the serger does three things at once. It stitches in the ditch, zigzags, and trims. Secondly, the serger goes twice as fast as your conventional sewing machine. Probably you can eliminate two sewing steps and do that one step twice as fast. Kathy McMakin has written a how-to book, *French Sewing By Serger*. It gives complete instructions and settings on how to do these wonderful French sewing techniques by serger. It is available from Martha Pullen Company.

Another way to use the serger is for French seams. I always did hate those little things. Now, I serge my French seams. I serge in my sleeves! I serge the sleeves in my smocked bishops; you will not believe the improvement in getting bishops through the pleater! By the way, some people call this machine a serger! Some call it an overlock machine! Call it anything you like — just get one!

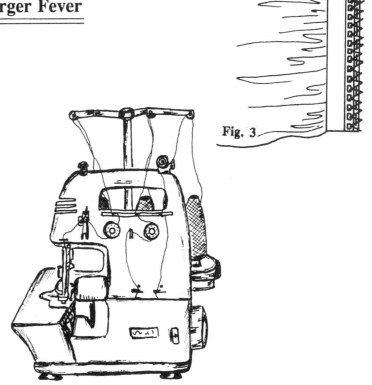

Holidays and Vacations

It's not uncommon to find a hole in the seam of laces, or between the laces and fabrics that have been joined. This occurs when both pieces of lace do not get sewn together in the zigzag or the laces do not get caught in the lace-to-fabric, zigzagged seam. This is not a mistake. I refer to this as a holiday or vacation. Sometimes we take long vacations (long holes) and sometimes we are only gone for a few hours (very tiny holes). These vacations and holidays are easily fixed by simply starting above the hole and zigzagging past the hole, being careful to catch both sides of lace or fabric to repair the opening. No back-stitching is necessary. Clip the excess threads and no one will ever know about your vacation.

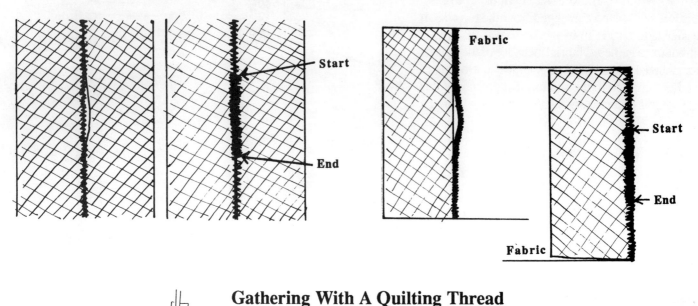

Gathering With A Quilting Thread

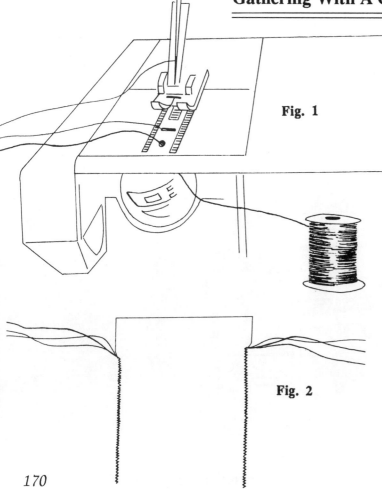

Fig. 1

Fig. 2

Directions:

1. Cut your ruffle strip at least two times the length of the finished puffing strip.
2. Run a quilting thread up through the hole in the bottom of your needle plate. You will not want any tension on this thread (Fig. 1).
3. Zigzag the edge of the fabric (Length=2-1/2 to 3-1/2, Length=1). Zig (the left stitch) going into the fabric and zag (the right stitch) going all the way off of the fabric. The fabric will roll into a seam as you zigzag. The quilting thread will be rolled into that seam (Fig. 2). Later, you will use the strong quilting thread to pull the gathers in your puffing (Fig. 3).
4. You can use this technique other places if you like this method of gathering. When you attach it to entredeux, just butt the trimmed entredeux to the gathered, rolled, and whipped edge and zigzag them together.

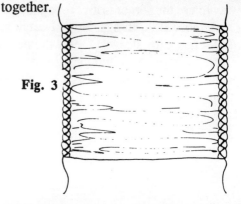

Fig. 3

Using The Gathering Foot For Ruffles

Directions:

1. I use the gathering foot for almost all of my ruffles.

2. Traditionally, ruffles on a French garment are a 2-1 fullness. This means, for example, that a child's garment, which is 45 inches in the front and 45 inches in the back, would have a 45 inch + 45 inch + 45 inch = 135-inch ruffle or three 45-inch strips gathered onto the bottom (Fig. 1).

3. How to adjust your gathering foot so that it gathers your 135-inch ruffle properly:

    a. Cut a 9-inch piece of fabric (Fig. 2).

    b. Adjust your stitch length to around 3 on your machine.

    c. Attach your gathering foot.

    d. Stitch the 9-inch piece of fabric. You want this piece of fabric to eventually end up measuring 6 inches gathered (Fig. 3).

    e. Your first stitiching line will probably not be correct. If you want your piece longer, make the stitch length shorter. If you want your 9-inch piece shorter, lengthen your stitch length.

    f. If your 9-inch piece did not become 6 inches, putt out the stitching you just did. Reset your stitch length. Stitch again. When your 9-inch piece becomes 6 inches, your stitch length is set correctly.

    g. It is now time to run your 135-inch ruffle under the gathering foot to gather your ruffle. Hopefully, your ruffle will be about 90 inches (45 inches + 45 inches) long when you finish! Some gathering feet are more accurate than others!

4. Do not put your fabric in the slot in the middle of most gathering feet! Just run your fabric under the gathering foot!

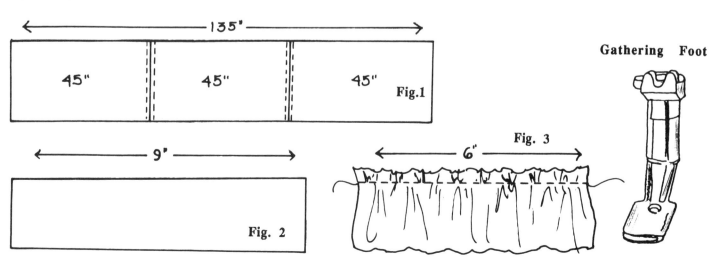

45"   45"   45"   **Fig.1**

Fig. 2

Fig. 3

Gathering Foot

How To Make Puffing

Puffing is defined as fabric that is shirred and made into puffs. It stems from the word "puff," which means a gathering of fabric, giving an inflated appearance.

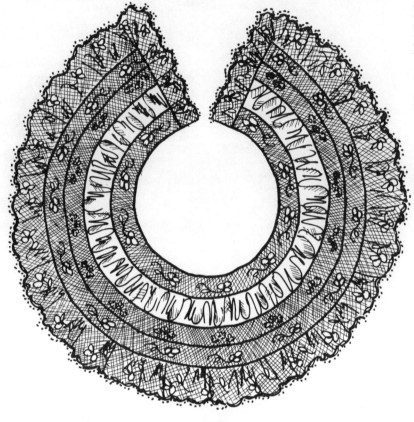

Puffing Strips With Entredeux On Both Sides
Directions:

1. Puffing is made just like "Entredeux To Gathered Fabric" except the fabric is gathered on on both sides.
2. A 2-1 fullness is desirable on puffing to make it full enough.
3. Cut the desired number of strips to make the 2-1 fullness. To make the strips, pull a thread and cut or tear your strips from selvage to selvage.
4. Seam the strips together. Cut off the selvage edges and make tiny French seams or use your **serger** to join.
5. Proceed with the same steps as if you were making "Entredeux To Gathered Fabric." Just gather both sides (Fig. 1) and apply entredeux to both sides.
6. Here is the perfect place to use your gathering foot. Run the strips under the bottom of the gathering foot. (First, work with a scrap piece of fabric to be sure that the length stitch you have chosen gathers the fabric to half of its original size.) Run both sides of your puffing strip under the gathering foot; attach entredeux to both sides.
7. If you want to make puffing without entredeux, follow the instructions for "Puffing Without Entredeux."

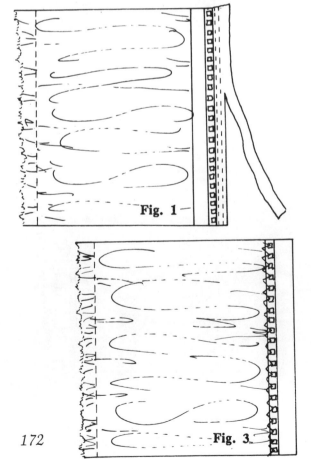

Fig. 1

Fig. 2

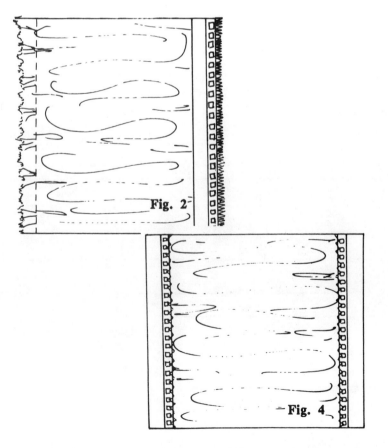

Fig. 3

Fig. 4

Using The Gathering Foot For Puffing

I think the easiest way to make puffing is by using the gathering foot. You will stitch, using between a 3 and 4 length. Here are some suggestions for machine puffing and a few tricks to enable you to make long strips of even puffing.

Long Strip Of Puffing
Directions:

1. Serge or French seam together three 45-inch strips.
2. Using a fabric marker, make vertical lines at the half points and quarter points of each 45-inch piece (Fig. 1).
3. These marker lines are to ensure that your gathering foot is gathering straight on the second line of stitching.
4. If your gathering foot's, second line of stitching is similar to Figure 2, you must make some adjustments to straighten up those lines. You can adjust the second line of stitching while you are sewing, by either pushing a little more fabric up under the foot or by pulling fabric so that it doesn't go under the foot as quickly.
5. If you want to finish the whole piece and you still have crooked lines, pull the bobbin thread and adjust the second side to the point where it is correct.

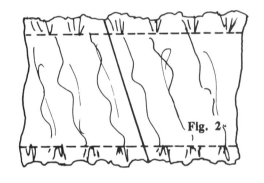

Fig. 2

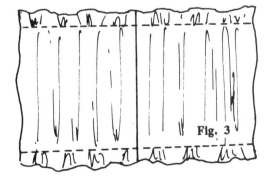

Fig. 3

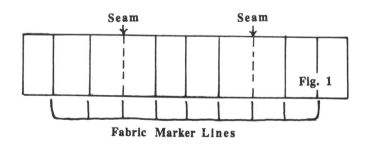

Seam   Seam

Fig. 1

Fabric Marker Lines

Making Puffing With A Gathering Foot and Attaching It To Lace Flat Edge

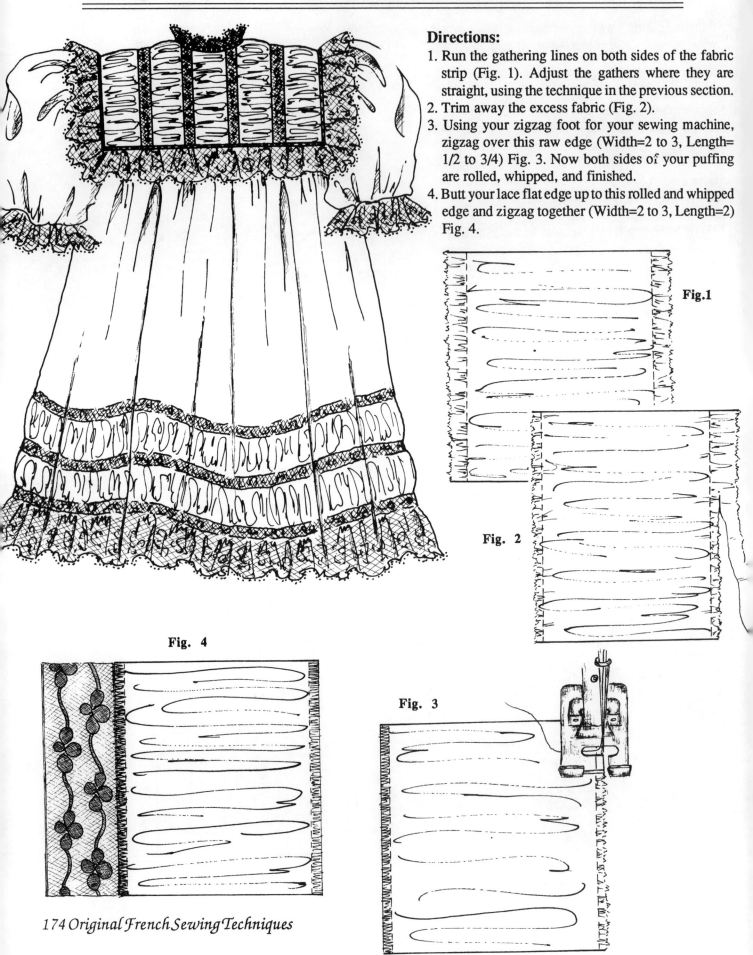

Directions:

1. Run the gathering lines on both sides of the fabric strip (Fig. 1). Adjust the gathers where they are straight, using the technique in the previous section.
2. Trim away the excess fabric (Fig. 2).
3. Using your zigzag foot for your sewing machine, zigzag over this raw edge (Width=2 to 3, Length= 1/2 to 3/4) Fig. 3. Now both sides of your puffing are rolled, whipped, and finished.
4. Butt your lace flat edge up to this rolled and whipped edge and zigzag together (Width=2 to 3, Length=2) Fig. 4.

Fig.1

Fig. 2

Fig. 4

Fig. 3

Lace Insertion Placket

Directions:

1. Cut a slit in the garment the desired length of the placket opening. Cut a piece of 1/2-inch insertion or edging twice this measurement.
2. Pull the skirt apart so that the fabric slit is in a V-shape (Fig. 1).
3. Place the right side of the lace to the right side of the V, allowing 1/8 inch of the fabric to extend past the lace.(Fig. 2).
4. Zigzag the lace to the fabric, using the method "Lace to Fabric" (Fig. 3).
5. Press the seam allowance to the fabric.
6. Pull lace to the inside at the point of the V. Sew a dart, starting 1/2 inch from the fold in the lace and stitching to the point (Fig. 4). Optional: Zigzag over the stitching line and trim away excess lace (Fig. 5).
7. Turn back the side of the placket that will be on top when overlapped (Fig. 6)

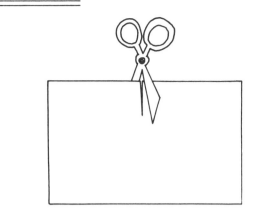

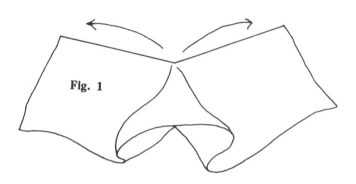

Fig. 1

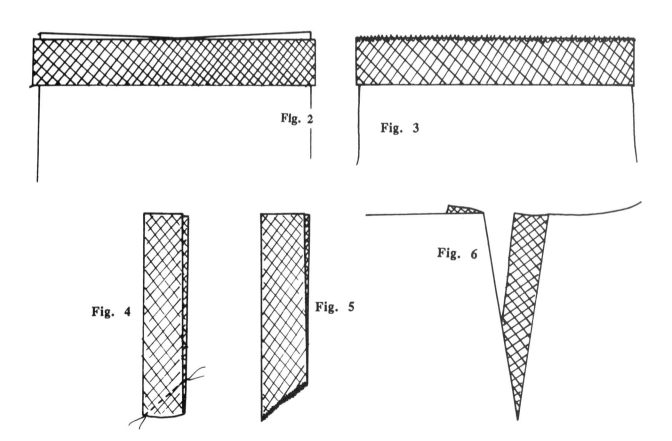

Fig. 2

Fig. 3

Fig. 4

Fig. 5

Fig. 6

Continuous Lap Placket — The Easy Way

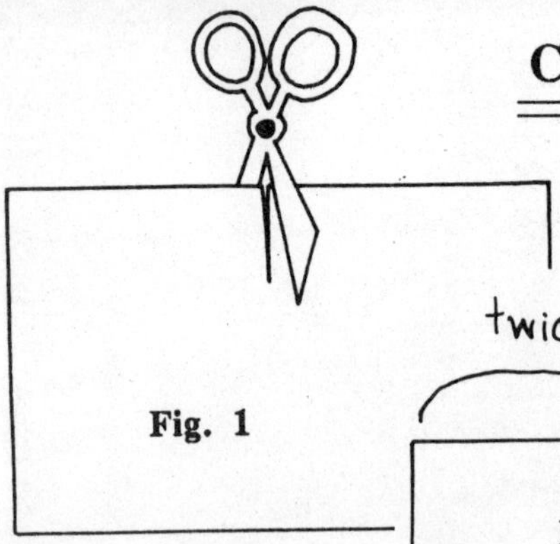

Fig. 1

twice length of slip + ½"

Fig. 2

selvage

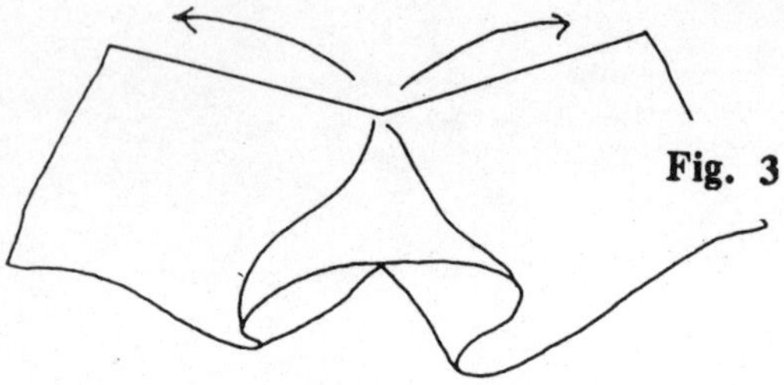

Fig. 3

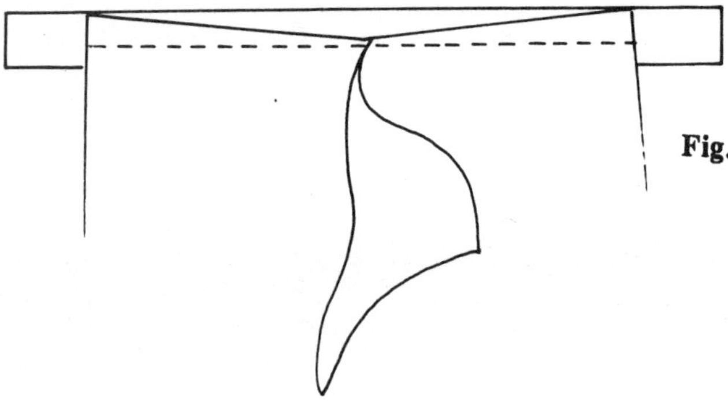

Fig. 4

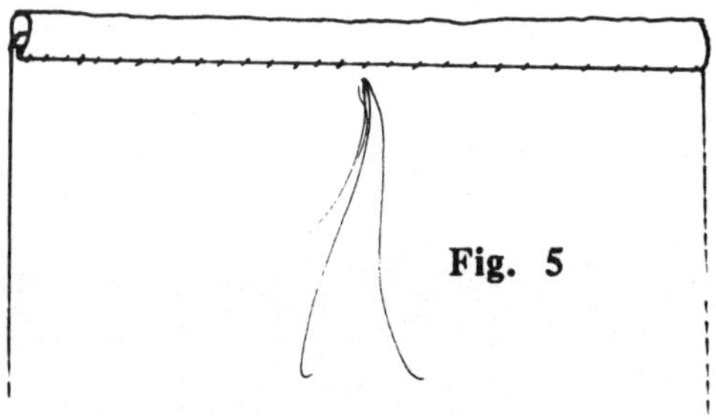

Fig. 5

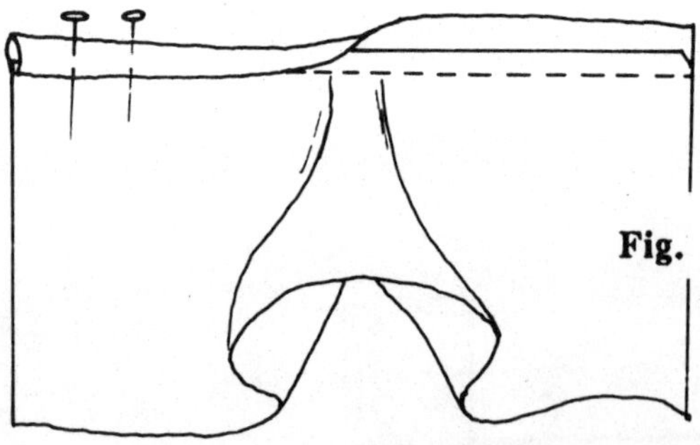

Fig. 6

Fig. 7

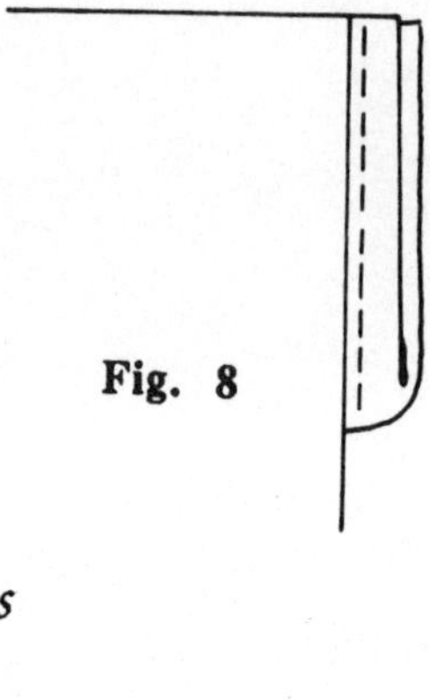

Fig. 8

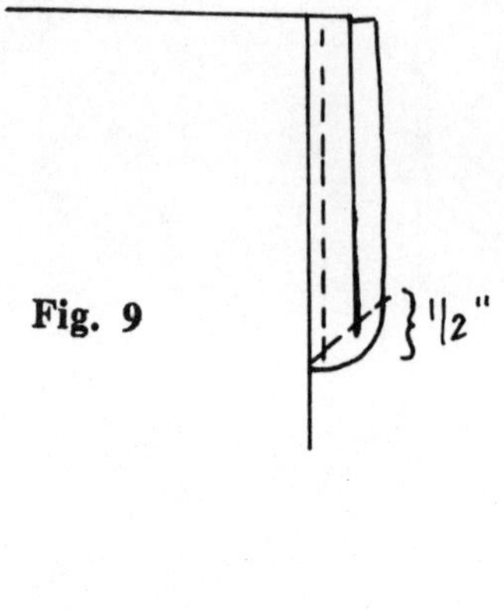

Fig. 9

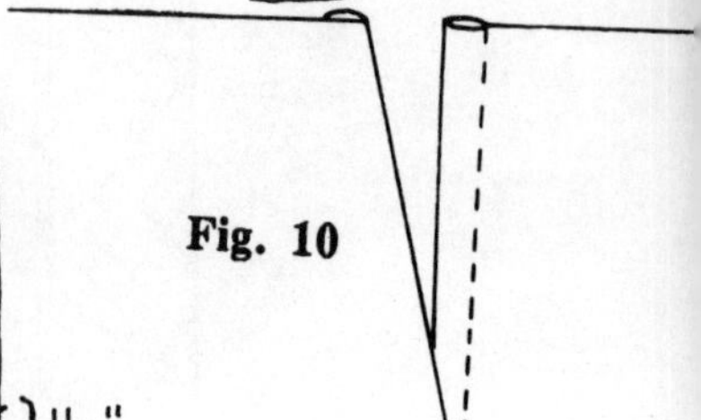

Fig. 10

} ½"

Directions:

1. Cut a slit in the garment piece the length needed for the placket (Fig. 1). Cut a placket strip from the fabric along the selvage 3/4 inch wide and 1/2 inch longer than twice the length of the slit (Fig. 2). Make the placket, using the following directions.

2. Pull the slit apart in a V-shape (Fig. 3).

3. Place the placket to the slit, right sides together. The slit is on the top and the placket is on the bottom. Note that the raw edge of the placket meets the V in the slit.

4. Stitch, using a 1/4-inch seam allowance only catching a few fibers at the point. The placket strip will be straight. The skirt will form a V (Fig. 4).

5. Press the seam toward the selvage edge of the placket strip. Fold the selvage edge to the inside (Fig. 5). Whip by hand (Fig. 6) or finish by machine, using the following directions.

6. Pin placket in place. From the right side of the fabric, top-stitch ON THE PLACKET 1/16 inch away from the original seam (Fig. 7).

7. Pulling the placket to the inside of the garment, fold the placket in half, allowing the top edges of the garment to meet (Fig. 8). Sew a dart, starting 1/2 inch up from the outside bottom edge of the placket to the seam (Fig. 9).

8. Turn back the side of the placket that will be on top when overlapped (Fig. 10).

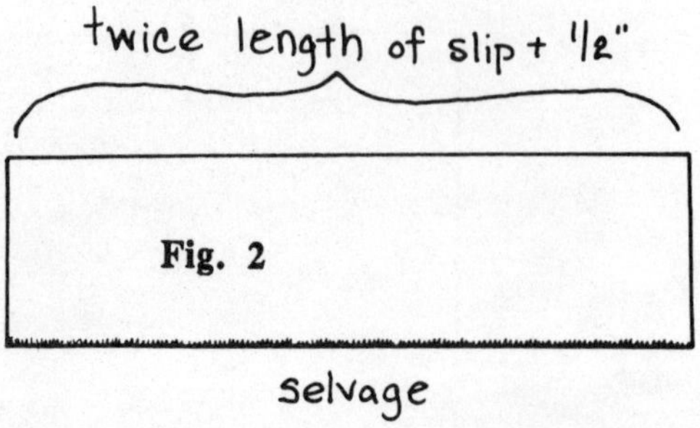

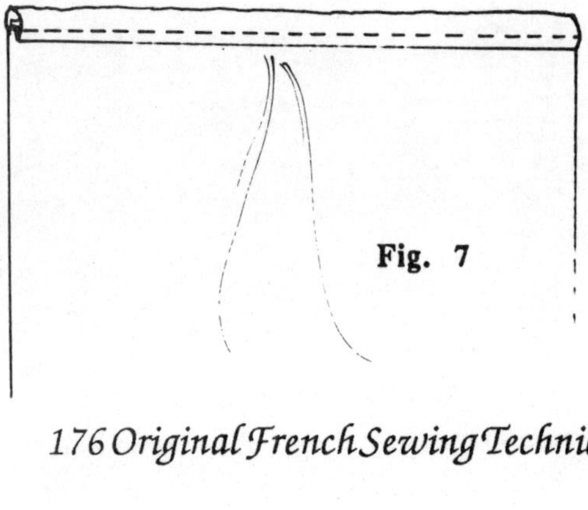

Lace Shaping in French Sewing

Chapter Eight

*Learn to stitch
scalloped skirts
and shapes
(hearts, diamonds,
and flip-flopped
lace bows)
with ease.*

Thinking back, I vividly remember the reaction I had to seeing my first round portrait collar, "How did anybody make those laces curve around a collar?" Puzzled, I thought, "If laces are straight, how did the seamstress get them to curve? Logically, it seemed to me, there should have been tucks or pleats or something to create those flawless curves." Many years after making my first French dress, I have become adept at shaping lace. I made a promise to myself that I wouldn't start writing another book until I untangled the skills for portrait collars, lace bows, lace hearts, and lace diamonds. Since this book is now in your hands, I can assure you that I have spent several years researching these lace-shaping skills. The techniques presented here are simple and easy to understand.

I am not a first grade teacher; however, because I like everything terribly simple and explained completely, that is what I have tried to do in this chapter. For two months, I worked on illustrations with artist Cynthia Handy, placing the exact step in front of her either through slides or actual work. I challenge you to let this section be the beginning of your imagination for stitching shapes. Don't be afraid of scalloped skirts, hearts, diamonds, or flipflopping lace bows. Before long, you'll be stitching shapes with ease.

Making a Fabric Board

Fabric boards have become a must for lace shaping or any kind of working-in-the-round in heirloom sewing. They double as portable ironing boards also. At my School of Art Fashion in Huntsville, we make these boards in the double-wide version for collar classes and in the single-wide version for single lace shaping of hearts, diamonds, ovals, loops, and other shapes. Instructions for the double board follow, since it is the most convenient to have.

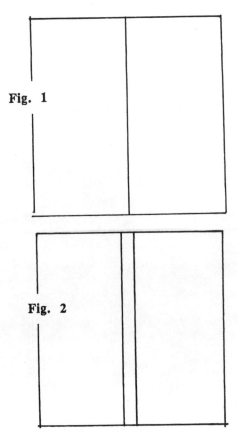

Fig. 1

Fig. 2

Materials Needed:
1. Two fabric rolling boards from the fabric store
2. Wide duct tape
3. Double thickness of fabric to cover the board

Directions:
1. Place two fabric boards (the kind on which is rolled Imperial batiste or broadcloth) side by side (Fig. 1).
2. Tape the boards together, lengthwise (Fig. 2).
3. Cover the board with a double thickness of fabric. This hides the tape and makes the board look nicer. Safety pin or staple the fabric to the back of the boards. Both methods work wonderfully.

Making A Scalloped Skirt, Martha's Way

Those of you who have been sewing with me for the past 10 years know that my philosophy is to make the prettiest dress possible with the least amount of frustration. I have played with, sewn, and re-played with the scalloped skirt. I think I have come up with the easiest method.

Tearing and Marking Your Skirt

Directions:

1. Pull thread and either tear or cut your skirt. I usually put two 44-inch widths in my skirt, one for the front and one for the back. Make the skirt length the proper one for your garment (Fig. 1).

2. Put in a French seam (or serge) one side seam only. You now have a flat skirt, which is approximately 88 inches wide (Fig. 1).

3. Fold the skirt in half at the seam line (Fig. 2). Press. Fold it again (Fig. 3). Press. Fold it again (Fig. 4). Press. Fold it again (Fig. 5). Press. When you open up your skirt, you have 16 equal sections (Fig. 6). This is your guideline for your scallops. Each section is 5-1/2 inches wide.

4. Draw your scallops between these creases (Fig. 7). The bottom of the scallop (Line A to B) is 1-1/2 inches from the bottom of the skirt fabric. The top of the scallop (Line C to B) is approximately 3-1/2 inches from the bottom of the skirt fabric.

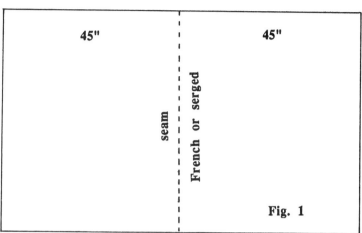

Fig. 1

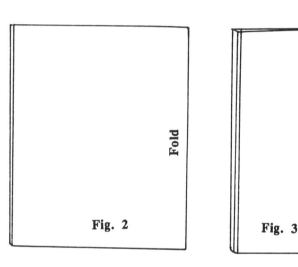

Fig. 2

Fig. 3

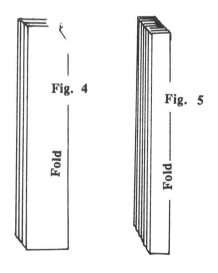

Fig. 4

Fig. 5

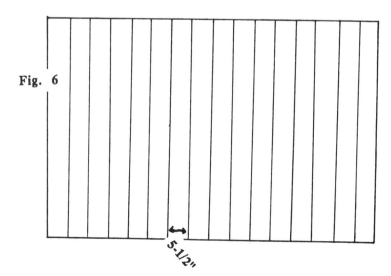

Fig. 6

Preparing the Skirt For Lace Shaping

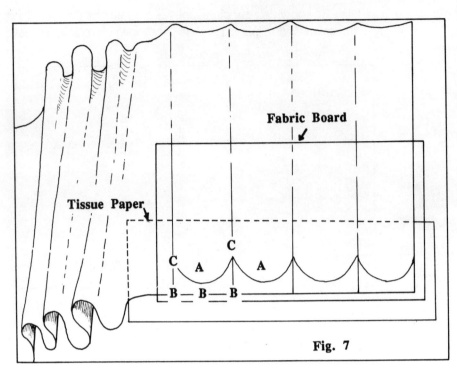

Fabric Board

Tissue Paper

C
C A A
B — B — B

Fig. 7

Directions:
1. Get a fabric board. This board is approximately 23 inches, which will allow you to work effectively with four scallops at one time.
2. Place a piece of tissue paper about 25 inches long by 7 inches wide. The purpose of this tissue paper is to have a stabilizer on which to work, after you cut away the bottom of the fabric. When shaping lace directally on fabric you do not have to use tissue paper. It is strictly optional.
3. Working from the right side of your skirt, place the skirt right side on the fabric board (Fig. 7).

Pinning The Lace Insertion To The Skirt Portion On The Fabric Board

Directions:
1. Cut enough lace to go around all of the scallops on the skirt. Allow at least 16 inches more than you measured. You can later use the excess lace insertion in another area of the dress.
2. Pin the lace insertion to the skirt (four scallops at a time only) by poking pins all the way into the fabric board, through the bottom lace heading, the fabric of the skirt, and the tissue paper. Notice on Figure 8 that the bottom of the lace is straight with the pins poked into the board. The top of the lace at this point is wavy and a little floppy (Fig. 8).
3. When you use any guideline for lace scalloping, pin the heading of the lace to the drawn design.
4. You will need to miter the lace at the point of the scallop. As you come up to the top of the scallop, pin the upper point. Fold the excess lace at the bottom to one side and pin through the two layers of the lace (Fig. 8). Later, the excess lace will be pulled to the back and stitched.
5. Place the pins at an angle away from the lace. That makes it easier to starch and press later (Fig. 8).

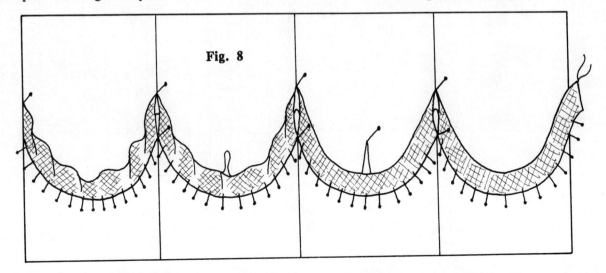

Fig. 8

Mitering The Scalloped Laces

Directions:

1. After you have pinned and starched and pressed four scallops, take the lace off of the fabric, and fold your miters to the back (Fig. 9).
2. Stitching from the one dot to the two dots, make a tiny zigzag (Width=1, Length=1) to make the miter. Repeat on the other three scallops with which you are presently working (Fig. 10). Trim the miters (Fig. 11).

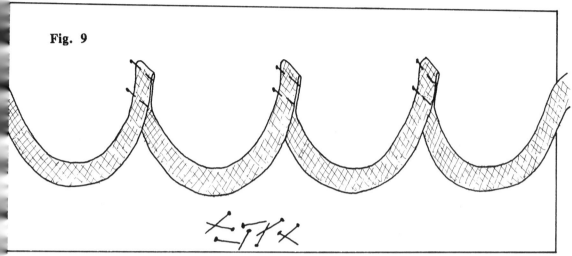

Fig. 9

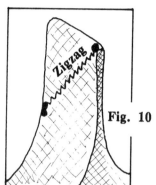

Fig. 10

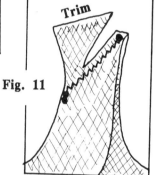

Fig. 11

3. You have four lace scallops ready to go back to the fabric board and the skirt. Re-pin them in place (Fig. 12). Press and starch again.
4. Pin the scallops through the lace, the fabric skirt, and the tissue paper. Remove from the fabric board.
5. Beginning about 1-1/2 inches in, from the top of the side scallop, zigzag the top of the scallop to the fabric, through the fabric and the tissue paper (Width=1-1/2, Length=1-1/2). Fig. 13.

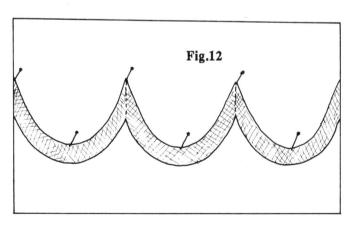

Fig.12

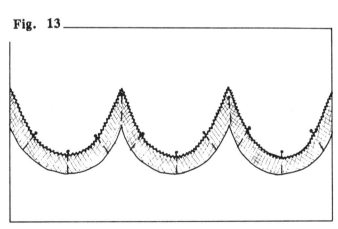

Fig. 13

Finishing The Under Side Of The Skirt Under The Scallops

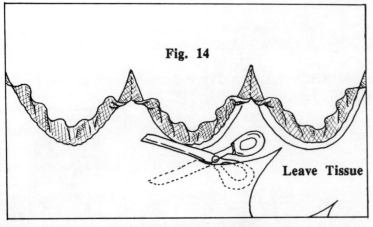

Fig. 14

Leave Tissue

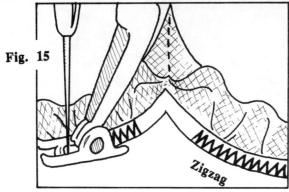

Fig. 15

Zigzag

Directions:

1. Lifting the lace insertion, trim away the fabric of the skirt ONLY! Trim it down to a 1/8-inch seam allowance. DO NOT TRIM AWAY THE TISSUE PAPER. You will stitch on it later (Fig. 14).

NOTE: This step is optional. I think it gives the dress a nicer finish to zigzag the seam allowance underneath the lace. You can leave a raw seam and it will be just fine. The choice is yours.

2. At the sewing machine, zigzag this 1/8-inch seam allowance to finish (Width=4, Length=1/2). Fig. 15.
3. You can't zigzag underneath the mitered lace pieces without tearing them up. Just leave them unstitched.

Shaping and Stitching The Entredeux To The Bottom Of The Scallops

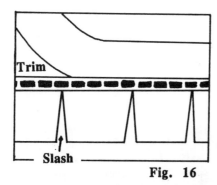

Trim

Slash

Fig. 16

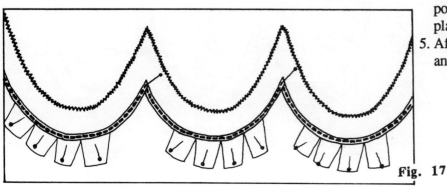

Fig. 17

Directions:

1. Trim off one side of the entredeux completely (Fig. 16).
2. Slash the other side of the entredeux (Fig. 16).
3. YOU MUST PIN, STARCH, AND PRESS THE ENTREDEUX BEFORE SEWING IT TO THE SCALLOPS. It won't hang right if you just begin to sew it into the scallops.
4. Here is a great trick. In order to pin the entredeux into the points of the scallops most effectively, trim entredeux about 1-1/2 inches on either side of the point. This allows you to see exactly where you are placing the entredeux (Fig. 17).
5. After pinning the entredeux into the points, starch, and press the entredeux into its shape.

6. Remove the pins from the skirt.
7. Zigzag the lace to the entredeux through the tissue paper, trying to go into one hole and off onto the lace. When I work with entredeux around curves, my preferred stitch settings are a width of 3 and a length of 1-1/2.
8. As you go into the points with the entredeux, simply "smush" the entredeux into the point, stitch over it, and turn the corner.
9. Optional method for sewing entredeux onto the scallops:
   a. Trim away both sides of the entredeux, making a skinny string.
   b. Starch and press this "skinny entredeux string" into the curved shape.
   c. Zigzag the skinny entredeux to the bottom of the lace scallop.

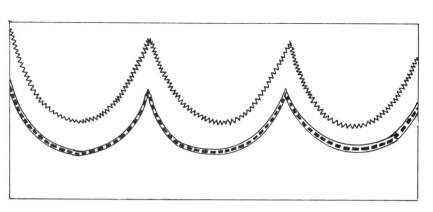

Adding Gathered Lace To The Entredeux At The Bottom Of The Scallops

Directions:

1. Measure around the scalloped skirt to get your measurement for the gathered lace edging you are going to attach to finish the skirt bottom. Double that measurement for a 2-1 fullness.
2. Cut your lace edging.
3. Using the technique "Sewing Hand-Gathered French Lace To Entredeux Edge" zigzag the gathered lace to the bottom of the entredeux.
4. You can also choose to use the method "Gathering French Lace By Machine, While Applying It To Trimmed Entredeux Edge" to attach this lace edging.

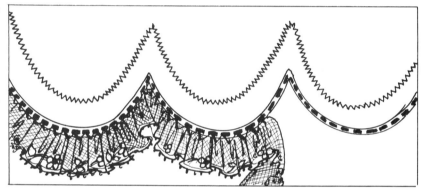

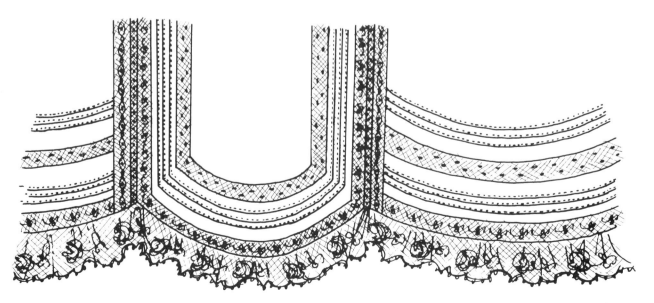

Gathering French Laces By Hand
Pull Thread In The Heading Of French Or English Laces

On the straight sides of French or English cotton laces are several threads called the "heading." These threads serve as pull thread for lace shaping. Some laces have better pull threads than others. Before you begin dramatically-curved lace shaping, check to be sure your chosen lace has a good pull thread. For lace shaping into diamonds or other non-curved shapes, the pull thread does not come into play, since lace is mitered for geometrical shaping.

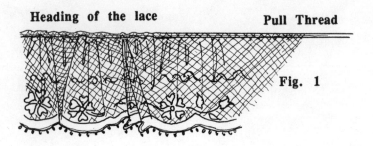

Heading of the lace   Pull Thread

Fig. 1

Directions:
1. Cut a length of lace 2-3 times the finished length in order to have enough fullness to make a pretty lace ruffle.
2. To gather the lace, pull one of the heavy threads that runs along the straight edge or heading of the lace (Fig. 1).
3. Adjust the gathers evenly before sewing the lace ruffle to the garment.

Sewing Hand-Gathered French Lace To Entredeux Edge

Directions:
1. Gather lace by hand.
2. Distribute gathers evenly.
3. Trim the side of the entredeux to which the gathered lace is to be attached.
4. Side by side, right sides up, zigzag the gathered lace to the trimmed entredeux (Width=1-1/2; Length=2) Fig. 1.
5. Use a pick or long pin of some sort to push the gathers evenly into the sewing machine.
6. If you are sewing a relatively long piece of lace to a relatively long piece of entredeux, it is a good idea to fold the lace and entredeux in half first, before you gather the lace, and mark the half-way point. Then, fold that piece in half once again, and mark the quarter points. You can then distribute the gathers accurately by matching the quarter points (Fig. 2).

Mark quarter points of the lace before gathering and the entredeux.

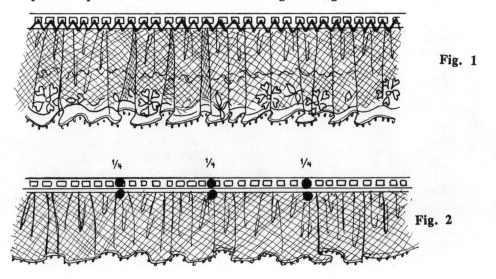

Fig. 1

¼   ¼   ¼

Fig. 2

Making Lace Diamonds

Mitering Lace

Lace diamonds can be used almost anywhere on heirloom garments. They are especially pretty at the point of a collar, on the skirt of a dress, at angles on the bodice of a garment, or all the way around a collar. The easiest way to make lace diamonds is to work on a fabric board with a diamond guide. You can make your diamonds as large or as small as you desire. Here is a wonderful trick. You only have to make one diamond on the board with all of the pins, etc. After you mark on one piece of lace, transfer those markings to as many pieces of lace as you will need diamonds. Stitch up each diamond and press onto your diamond guide before attaching to the garment.

Materials Needed:
1. Spray starch, iron, pins, fabric board, water-soluble pen or pencil
2. Lace insertion
3. Diamond guide

Directions:
1. Draw the diamond guide or template (Fig. 1).
2. The guide or template, which you have just drawn, will be the inside of the diamond (Fig. 2).
3. To shape the laces, work on the outside of this template (Fig. 3).
4. Make your diamonds on a fabric board. This way, you can stick pins into the board, for ease. After diamonds are marked, mitered, and finished, place them on the chosen garment to be zigzagged.

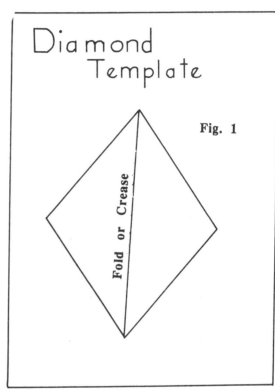

Diamond Template

Fig. 1

Fold or Crease

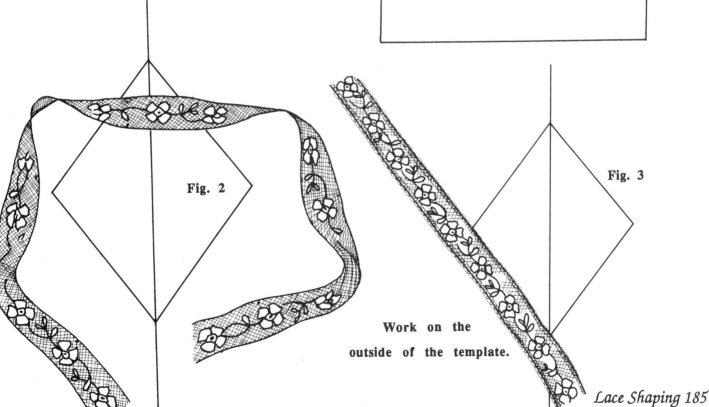

Fig. 2

Fig. 3

Work on the outside of the template.

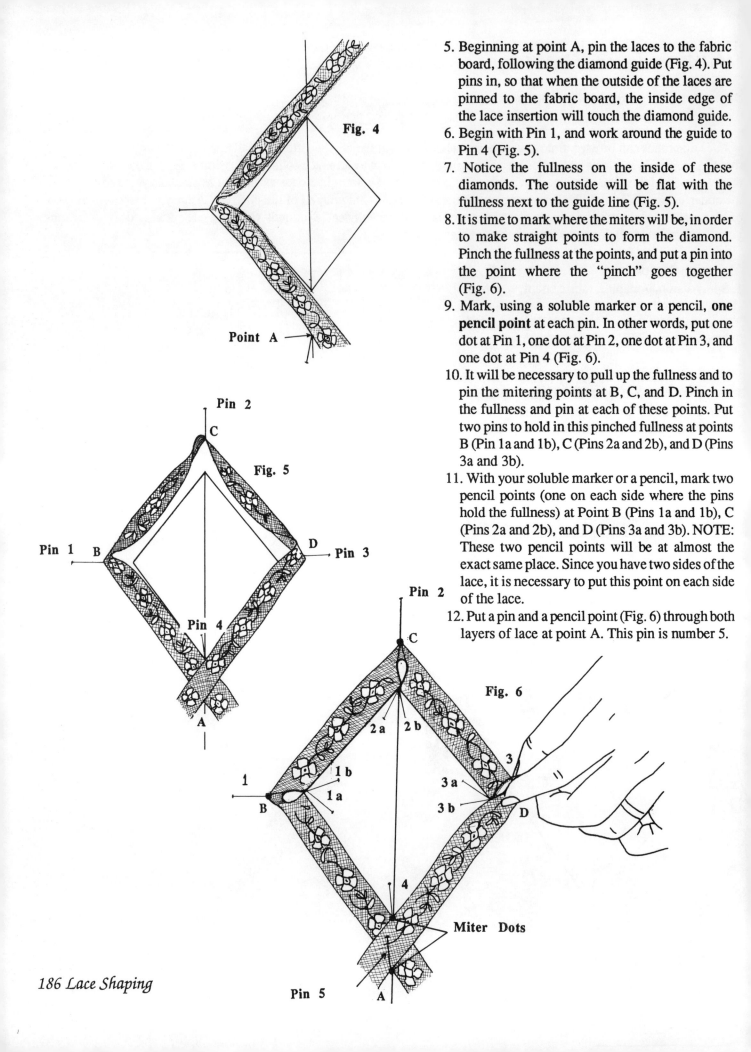

Fig. 4

Point A

Pin 2

C

Fig. 5

Pin 1   B

D → Pin 3

Pin 4

A

Pin 2

C

2 a   2 b

Fig. 6

1   1 b

1 a

B

3

3 a

3 b   D

4

Miter Dots

Pin 5   A

5. Beginning at point A, pin the laces to the fabric board, following the diamond guide (Fig. 4). Put pins in, so that when the outside of the laces are pinned to the fabric board, the inside edge of the lace insertion will touch the diamond guide.

6. Begin with Pin 1, and work around the guide to Pin 4 (Fig. 5).

7. Notice the fullness on the inside of these diamonds. The outside will be flat with the fullness next to the guide line (Fig. 5).

8. It is time to mark where the miters will be, in order to make straight points to form the diamond. Pinch the fullness at the points, and put a pin into the point where the "pinch" goes together (Fig. 6).

9. Mark, using a soluble marker or a pencil, **one pencil point** at each pin. In other words, put one dot at Pin 1, one dot at Pin 2, one dot at Pin 3, and one dot at Pin 4 (Fig. 6).

10. It will be necessary to pull up the fullness and to pin the mitering points at B, C, and D. Pinch in the fullness and pin at each of these points. Put two pins to hold in this pinched fullness at points B (Pin 1a and 1b), C (Pins 2a and 2b), and D (Pins 3a and 3b).

11. With your soluble marker or a pencil, mark two pencil points (one on each side where the pins hold the fullness) at Point B (Pins 1a and 1b), C (Pins 2a and 2b), and D (Pins 3a and 3b). NOTE: These two pencil points will be at almost the exact same place. Since you have two sides of the lace, it is necessary to put this point on each side of the lace.

12. Put a pin and a pencil point (Fig. 6) through both layers of lace at point A. This pin is number 5.

13. Now remove your lace from the diamond board. You will have pencil markings at Pin 1 (through two pieces of lace), at Pin 2, at Pin 3, at Pin 4, at Pin 5 (through two pieces of lace), at Pin 1a and 1b, at Pin 2a and 2b, and at Pin 3a and 3b (Fig. 7).

14. At this time, cut the number of pieces of lace to match the number of diamonds that you will need for your garment, and transfer the markings on each piece of lace. That way you will not have to reshape each diamond on the fabric board.

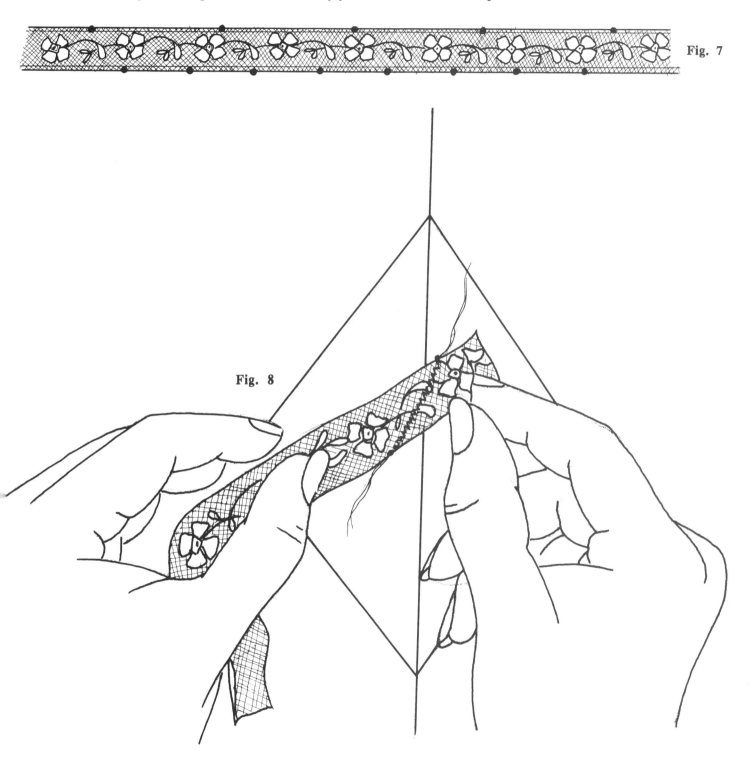

Fig. 7

Fig. 8

15. Stitch (Narrow zigzag: Width=1 to 1-1/2, Length= 1/2) to form a miter between Pin 1 and 1a and 1b (Fig. 8). Follow suit for the other two miters.

16. Overlap the cut ends and stitch between the two dots at Point A or Pin 5 and the two dots at Pin 4.

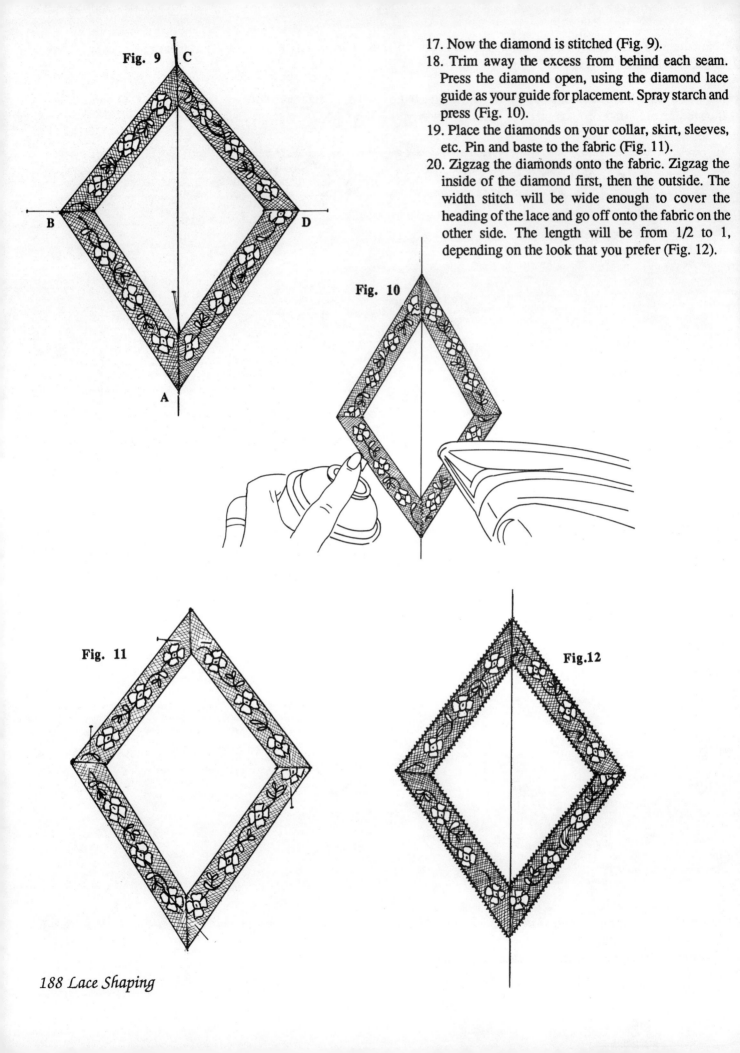

Fig. 9

C

B   D

A

17. Now the diamond is stitched (Fig. 9).
18. Trim away the excess from behind each seam. Press the diamond open, using the diamond lace guide as your guide for placement. Spray starch and press (Fig. 10).
19. Place the diamonds on your collar, skirt, sleeves, etc. Pin and baste to the fabric (Fig. 11).
20. Zigzag the diamonds onto the fabric. Zigzag the inside of the diamond first, then the outside. The width stitch will be wide enough to cover the heading of the lace and go off onto the fabric on the other side. The length will be from 1/2 to 1, depending on the look that you prefer (Fig. 12).

Fig. 10

Fig. 11

Fig.12

Lace Bows

Flip-Flopping Lace

I make lace bows using a technique called "flip-flopping" lace — a relatively unsophisticated name for such a lovely trim. I first saw this technique on an antique teddy I bought at a local antique store. It had the most elegant flip-flopped lace bow. Upon careful examination of the bow, I noticed the lace was simply folded over at the corners, then continued down forming the outline of the bow. The corners were somewhat square. Certainly it was easier than mitering or pulling a thread and curving. Using trial and error, I found it not only looked easier, it was easier.

Follow the instructions for making a flip-flopped bow, using a bow template. This technique works just as well for lace angles up and down on a skirt. As a matter of fact, you can flip-flop any angle that traditionally would be mitered. It can be used to go around a square collar, around diamonds, and around any shape with an angle rather than a curve.

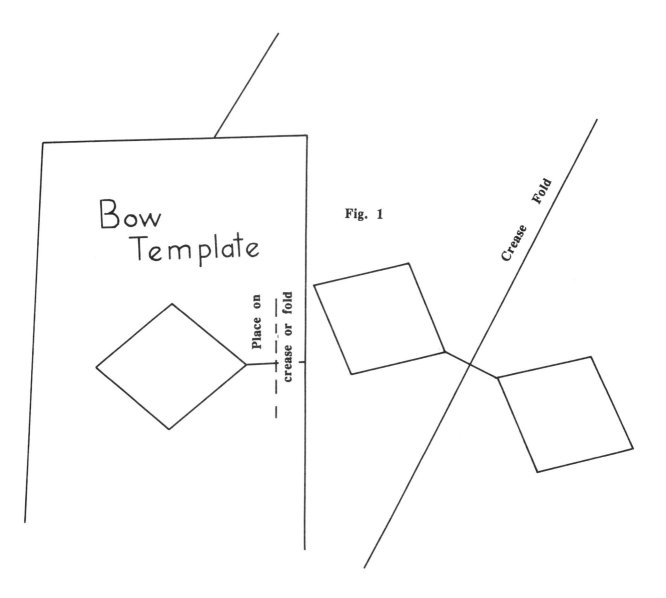

Fig. 1

Directions:

1. Trace the template where you want to place bows. Remember, the easy way to put bows around a skirt is to fold the fabric to make equal divisions of the skirt (Fig. 1).

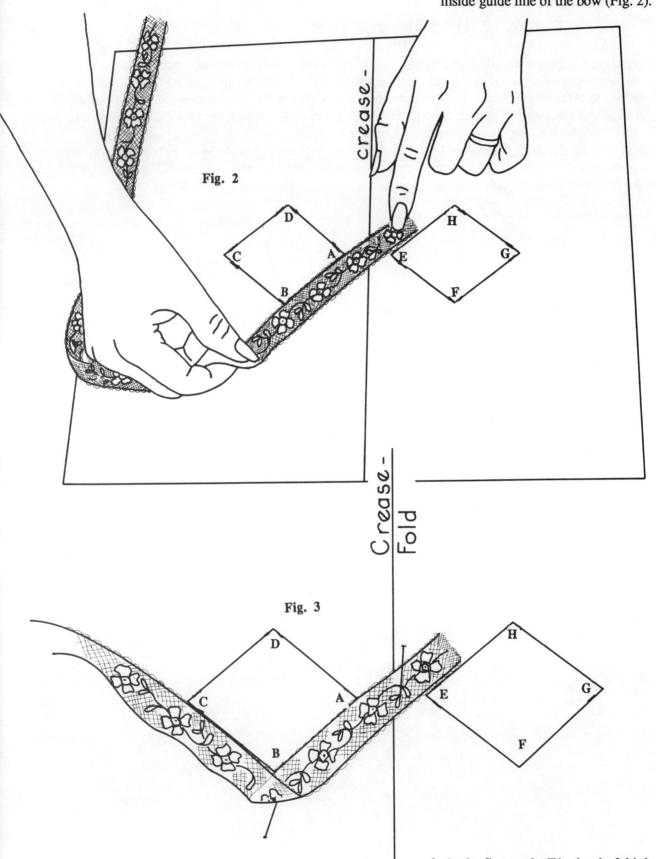

2. Beginning above the inside of one bow (above E), place the lace along the angle. The template is the inside guide line of the bow (Fig. 2).

Fig. 2

Crease -

Crease - Fold

Fig. 3

3. At the first angle (B), simply fold the lace where it will follow along the next line (B-C) (Fig. 3).

4. The lines go as follows: A-B, B-C, C-D, D-A, A-E, E-F, F-G, G-H, H-E. Tuck your lace end under E, which is also where the first raw edge will end (Fig. 4).

5. Cut a short bow tab of lace that is long enough to go around the whole tie area of the bow (Fig. 4).

6. Tuck in this lace tab to make the center of the bow (Fig. 5).

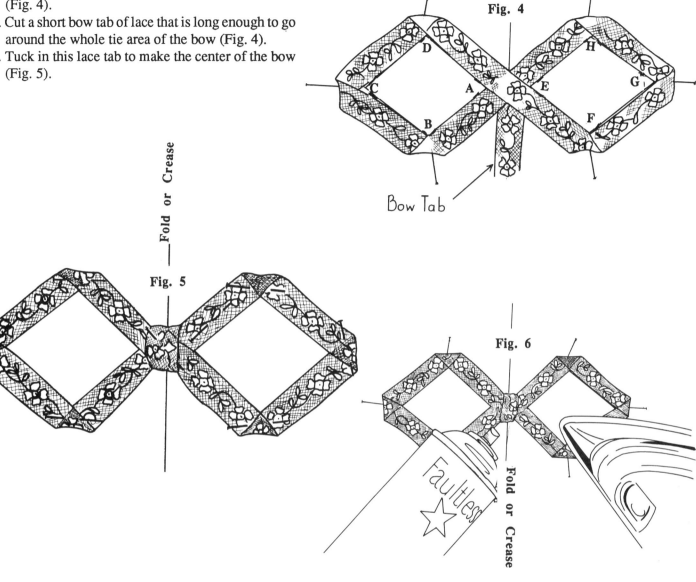

Fig. 4

Bow Tab

Fold or Crease

Fig. 5

Fig. 6

Fold or Crease

7. Spray starch and press the bow, that is shaped (Fig. 6).

8. This illustration gives you ideas for making a bow two ways. First, the "A" side of the bow has just the garment fabric peeking through the center of the bow. Second, the "B" side of the bow illustrates what the bow will look like if you put a pintucked strip in the center. Both are beautiful (Fig. 7).

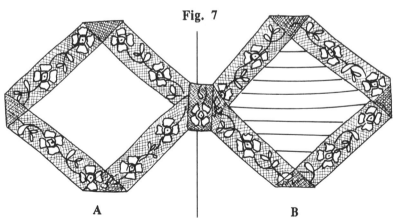

Fig. 7

A

B

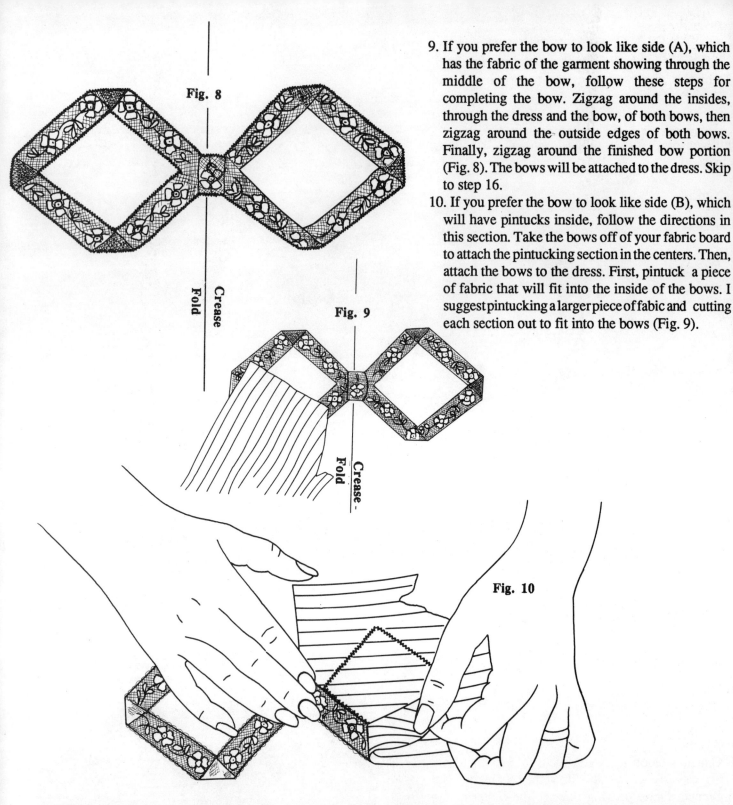

Fig. 8

Crease — Fold

Fig. 9

Crease - Fold

Fig. 10

9. If you prefer the bow to look like side (A), which has the fabric of the garment showing through the middle of the bow, follow these steps for completing the bow. Zigzag around the insides, through the dress and the bow, of both bows, then zigzag around the outside edges of both bows. Finally, zigzag around the finished bow portion (Fig. 8). The bows will be attached to the dress. Skip to step 16.

10. If you prefer the bow to look like side (B), which will have pintucks inside, follow the directions in this section. Take the bows off of your fabric board to attach the pintucking section in the centers. Then, attach the bows to the dress. First, pintuck a piece of fabric that will fit into the inside of the bows. I suggest pintucking a larger piece of fabic and cutting each section out to fit into the bows (Fig. 9).

11. Remove the shaped bows from the fabric board. Cut a pintucked piece a little larger than the center sections of your bow. Place a pintucked piece behind the center section of the bow.

12. Zigzag the center portions of the bow by stitching through the bow and the pintuck section.

13. Now place the bows back on the garment to which it is to be attached.

14. Zigzag the center section to the garment, stitching through the rows of stitching you just made, to attach the pintucked section.

15. Zigzag the outside of the bow to the garment.

16. (This step is for either bow version.) Now, very carefully cut away the fabric from behind the lace (Fig. 10). You do not have to cut away the fabric from behind the lace; however, I think it is prettier this way.

Hearts

Curving Lace

Since many heirloom sewers are also incurable romantics, it's no wonder hearts are a popular lace shape. Hearts are the ultimate design for a wedding dress, wedding attendants' clothing, or on a ring bearer's pillow. As with the other lace shaping discussed in this chapter, begin with a template when making hearts. Our template technique uses the template as the inside design. I work outside the template.

Directions:

1. Draw a template in the shape of a heart. Make this as large or as small as you want. If you want equal hearts around the bottom of a skirt, fold the skirt into equal sections, and design the heart template to fit into one section of the skirt when using your chosen width of lace insertion (Fig. 1). As always, when shaping lace, work on a fabric board.
2. Beginning at the bottom of the heart, pin the lace outside of the heart where the inside touches the shape when mashed down. Work around the heart (Fig. 2).
3. Finish pinning around, to the center of the heart only (Fig. 3).

Fig. 1

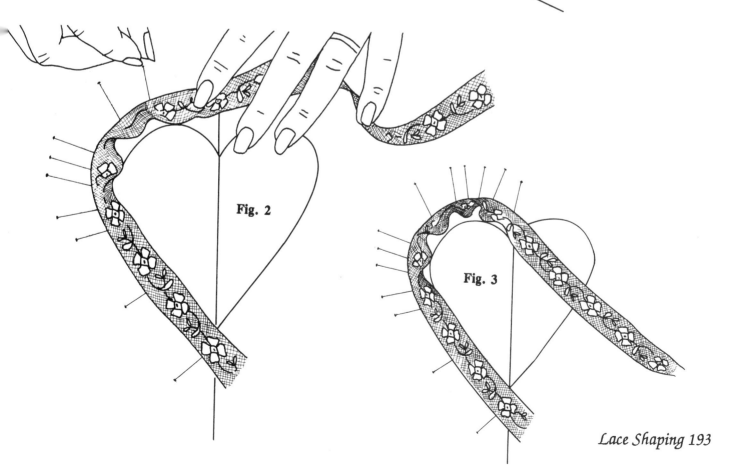

Fig. 2

Fig. 3

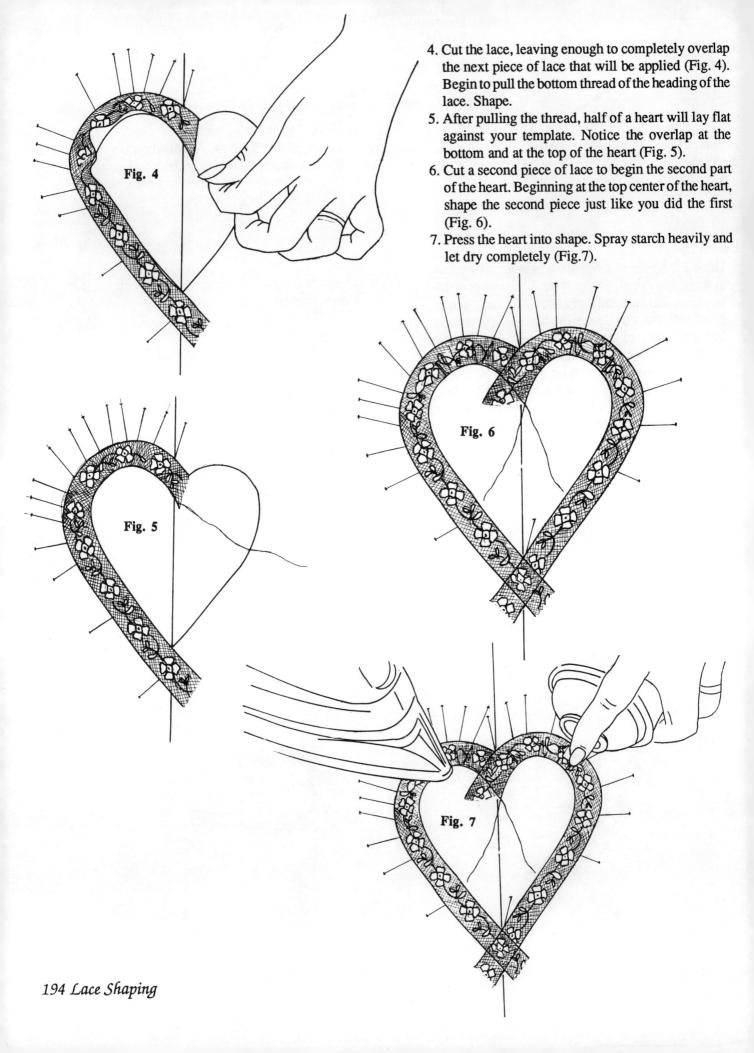

Fig. 4

Fig. 5

Fig. 6

Fig. 7

4. Cut the lace, leaving enough to completely overlap the next piece of lace that will be applied (Fig. 4). Begin to pull the bottom thread of the heading of the lace. Shape.

5. After pulling the thread, half of a heart will lay flat against your template. Notice the overlap at the bottom and at the top of the heart (Fig. 5).

6. Cut a second piece of lace to begin the second part of the heart. Beginning at the top center of the heart, shape the second piece just like you did the first (Fig. 6).

7. Press the heart into shape. Spray starch heavily and let dry completely (Fig.7).

194 Lace Shaping

8. It will be necessary to stitch the heart together at the top center as well as the bottom center. Mark the two exact center points on the top and bottom of the heart (Fig. 8).

9. Carefully remove the two pieces of heart from the fabric board. Matching the pencil points, stitch at both places (Fig. 9). You now have a heart.

10. Place the heart on the template and press into its final shape (Fig. 10).

11. You are now ready to place the heart (or hearts) onto the garment to zigzag into place. Zigzag the inside of the heart to the garment first, then the outside (Width=1-1/2, Length=3/4 to 1) Fig. 11. Actually, you should look at your particular pattern of lace to determine how wide the heading is to gauge the width of your zigzag. The given width and length are general suggestions. Some people use the 1/2-length setting for stitching on this lace. I personally think it is a little too heavy.

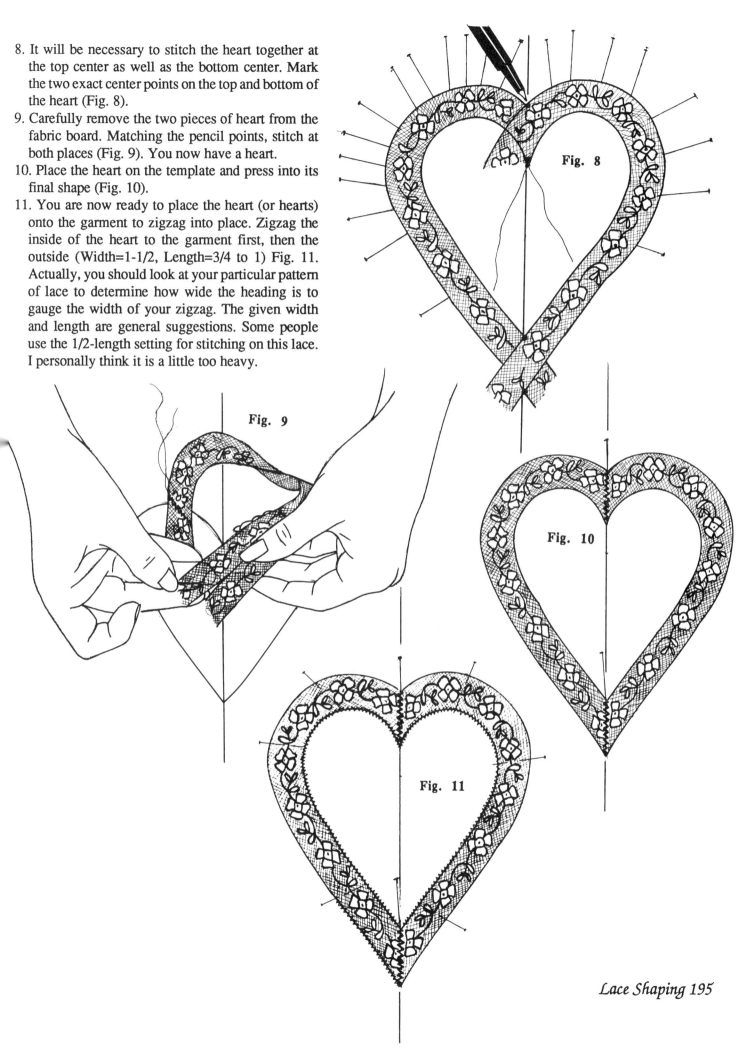

Fig. 8

Fig. 9

Fig. 10

Fig. 11

Making Fancy Square Lace Shapes

Geometric designs puzzled me until I began to experiment with them and discovered a surprisingly easy technique. Let me unravel the mystery of fancy squares, which are just as sweet on the bodice of a boy's suit as they are on a blouse or skirt! Start with a very long strip, and then cut it into little pieces. You can use embroidery, Swiss embroidered insertion, or pintucked fabrics for fancy squares. Let your imagination guide your journey!

Two sets of fancy square instructions follow. The first set is for Swiss insertion, which is bi-directional; that is, it can be used either horizontally or vertically. The second set is for embroidery, which can only be used in one direction. Both are easy!

Method I
Bi-Directional Swiss Insertion, A Fabric Strip Or A Tucking Strip

Directions:

1. To determine how long to make your "strip," measure how wide each piece of fancy square will be. Each Swiss embroidered (insertion) strip will be approximately 2 inches by 2 inches. In adding 2 inches of insertion, zigzagged together in between each 2-inch wide strip, you will need approximately 25 small sections (entredeux, embroidered square, entredeux, three pieces of lace insertion zigzagged together) to be sure you have enough to go around 90 inches of skirt. These little square sections will be approximately 4 inches wide. If you want to be much more careful and conservative in your measuring, make 23, and see if you have enough before going on to 25.

2. Using the technique "Entredeux To Flat Fabric," sew or serge the entredeux to both sides of the Swiss embroidered insertion. If you are using a tucking strip, do the same thing (Fig. 1). Trim the entredeux on both sides.

3. Zigzag three pieces of lace insertion together, using the technique "Lace Straight Edge To Lace Straight Edge." Make the strip the same length as the strip of embroidered insertion and entredeux that you made in step 2 (Fig. 2).

4. Butt the lace insertion to one side of the entredeux and zigzag together (Fig. 3).

5. Divide the strip up evenly; cut between the strips (Fig. 4). Directions continued on next page.

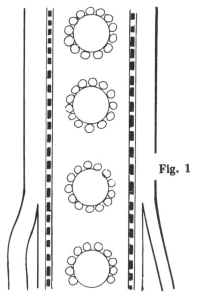

Fig. 1

Fig. 2

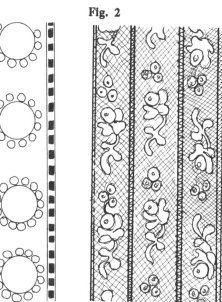

Fig. 3

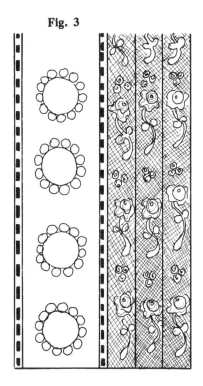

Fig. 4

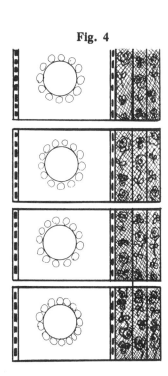

6. Butt the lace insertion edge to the trimmed entredeux edge and zigzag the pieces into one strip (Fig. 5).
7. Using the technique "Entredeux To Flat Fabric," sew or serge entredeux to both sides of the strip you just made. You now have a fancy band to go around the skirt (Fig. 6).
8. Look back at the dress in the illustration. You can see that another row of insertion plus another row of entredeux has been added before the fancy band was stitched into the dress. The same strips were repeated on the bodice of the dress.

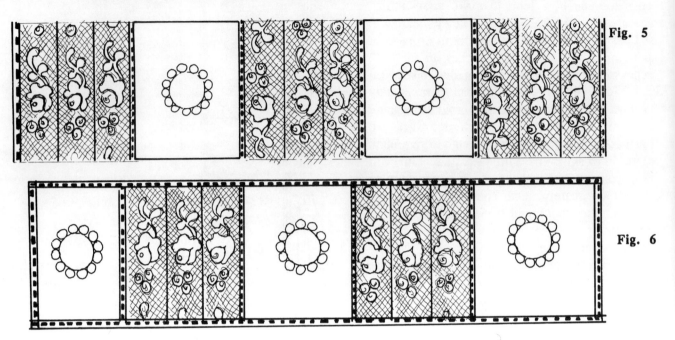

Fig. 5

Fig. 6

Method II
Swiss Insertion, Which Can Only Be Used In One Direction (Fig. 1)

Fig. 1

1. To determine how long to make your "strip," measure how wide each piece of fancy square will be. Each Swiss embroidered (insertion) strip will be approximately 2 inches by 2 inches. In adding 2 inches of insertion, zigzagged together in between each 2-inch wide strip, you will need approximately 25 small sections (entredeux, embroidered square, entredeux, three pieces of lace insertion zigzagged together) to be sure you have enough to go around 90 inches of skirt. These little square sections will be approximately 4 inches wide. If you want to be much more careful and conservative in your measuring, make 23, and see if you have enough before going on to 25.
2. Cut apart your designs, in this case a bird flying with flowers (Fig. 2).

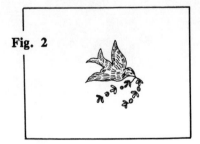

Fig. 2

3. Before applying the entredeux, it is a good idea to trim the seam allowance to 1/4 inch or 1/8 inch. The purpose for trimming the entredeux, is for the stitching of the entredeux to take off as little of the fabric square as possible. Using the technique "Entredeux To Flat Fabric," sew or serge the entredeux to both sides of the pieces of cut insertion. Trim away the seam allowance on both sides of the entredeux (Fig. 3).

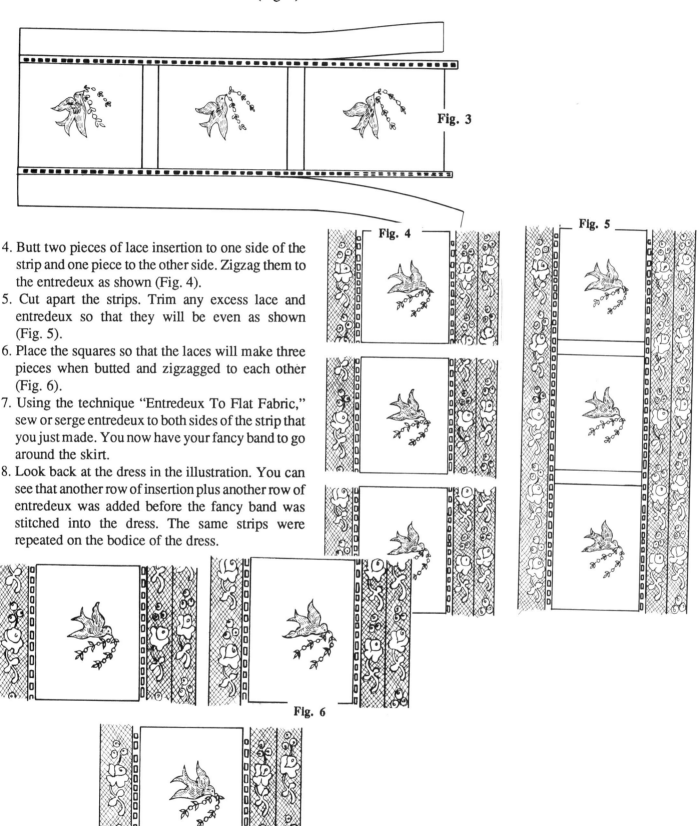

Fig. 3

Fig. 4

Fig. 5

4. Butt two pieces of lace insertion to one side of the strip and one piece to the other side. Zigzag them to the entredeux as shown (Fig. 4).

5. Cut apart the strips. Trim any excess lace and entredeux so that they will be even as shown (Fig. 5).

6. Place the squares so that the laces will make three pieces when butted and zigzagged to each other (Fig. 6).

7. Using the technique "Entredeux To Flat Fabric," sew or serge entredeux to both sides of the strip that you just made. You now have your fancy band to go around the skirt.

8. Look back at the dress in the illustration. You can see that another row of insertion plus another row of entredeux was added before the fancy band was stitched into the dress. The same strips were repeated on the bodice of the dress.

Fig. 6

Making A Round Lace Portrait Collar

Materials Needed:
- Sizes 4 and Under: 4 yards of 1/2-inch to 3/4-inch insertion; 2 yards of edging
- Sizes 5-12: 5 yards of 1/2-inch to 3/4-inch insertion; 2 yards of edging
- Adult: 6 or 7 yards of 1/2-inch to 3/4-inch insertion (This will depend on how wide you want to make your collar, of course.)
- 3 yards of edging

  NOTE: If you are using wider insertion, you need less yardage. If you are using narrow insertion, you need more yardage. You may want your collar wider than the shoulder/sleeve point. Get more lace. And vice versa. There is really no exact lace amount.

- Iris Super Fine Nickel-Plated Steel Pins. **NOTE:** Do not use plastic head pins. They will melt when you iron the curves!
- Iron
- Magic Sizing or Spray Starch.
- Make a double-wide fabric board using the directions given earlier in this chapter. You can ask your fabric store to save two for you.
- Threads to match your laces
- A large piece of tissue paper like you use to wrap gifts
- Scissors

200 Lace Shaping

Making Your Fabric Board

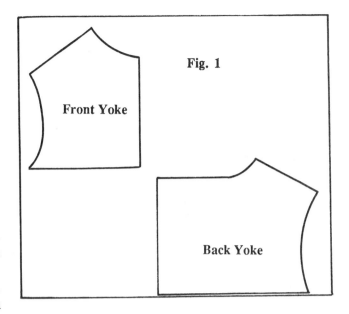

Fig. 1

Front Yoke

Back Yoke

Directions:
1. Use the directions found earlier in this chapter.

Preparing The Paper Guide

Directions:
1. Trace your collar guide onto a piece of tissue paper.
2. If your pattern doesn't have a collar guide, you can make one.
3. Cut out the front yoke and the back yoke (Fig. 1). Put the shoulder seams of your paper pattern together to form the neckline. Be sure to overlap the seam allowance to get a true seam line at the shoulder (Fig. 2). Subtract the seam allowance around the neckline. This is the neck guide to use for your paper pattern. Trace the neckline off. Mark the center-back lines, which will be evident from your pattern pieces (Fig. 3). As you look at Figure 3, you will see that a large circle is on the outside of this pattern piece. You can draw this large circle on if you want to; however, you only need the neckline shape and the center back. You must draw the center back the length of your collar.
4. Mark the fold-back line. To get your fold-back line, measure the width of the gathered lace that will be used around the bottom of the collar and up the center back on both sides. Take that measurement off of the center-back point and mark the fold-back line (Fig. 3).
5. You will probably notice that the neckline isn't really round, but oval shaped. That is the true neckline on any pattern, not an exact circle. Use that shaped neckline as your neckline guide.
6. This neckline guide and the center-back line on the pattern are the only lines that you need to shape the circular laces around the collar. You will use the fold-back line after the lace shaping is done to finish the back of the collar. You only use the neckline guide for the first piece of lace. After that, you use the previously-shaped piece of rounded lace as your guide.

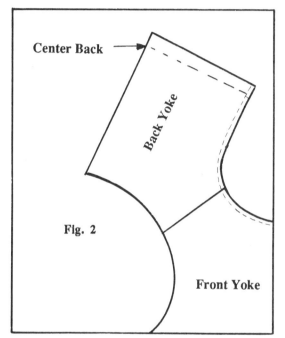

Center Back

Back Yoke

Fig. 2

Front Yoke

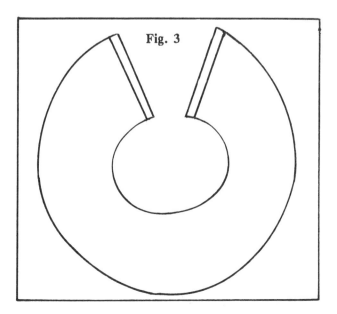

Fig. 3

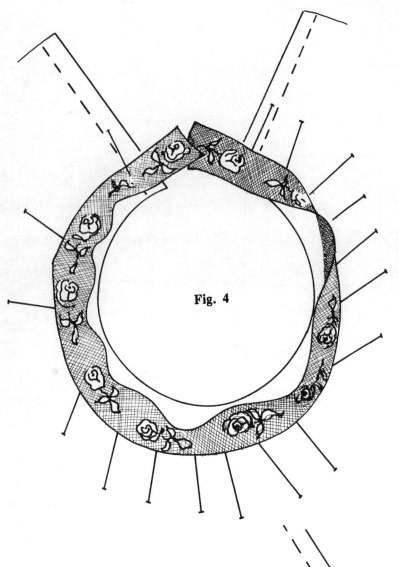

Fig. 4

Making The First Two Rows Of Insertion

1. Shape the neckline row first. Then work from the neckline downward to complete the collar width you want.
2. Cut your lace for the neckline or first row of your collar. **NOTE:** Cut extra. You will want to cut your laces longer than the center-back line of the collar you have marked. I suggest at least 3/4 inch to 1 inch longer than the exact center back.
3. Place the tissue paper guide on the fabric board.
4. Using your fabric board as your work base and your tissue paper collar guide, you are now ready to begin shaping your collar.
5. Pin the outside of the lace where the inside will touch the neck guide when it is pressed down. The outside lace will have the pins jabbing right into the fabric board. This outside line is not gathered at all. The inside will be wavy. At this point, the inside has no pins in it (Fig. 4).
6. After you have pinned the outside of the lace onto the fabric board, gently pull the gathering string in the heading of the INSIDE of the lace. The lace will pull flat (Fig. 5). Gently distribute the gathers by holding the lace down. Be certain that it is flat on the fabric board. You can pull your gathering rows from both ends. It is now time to put pins on the inside of the first row (Fig. 5). Jab them into the fabric board. Spray starch lightly and steam.

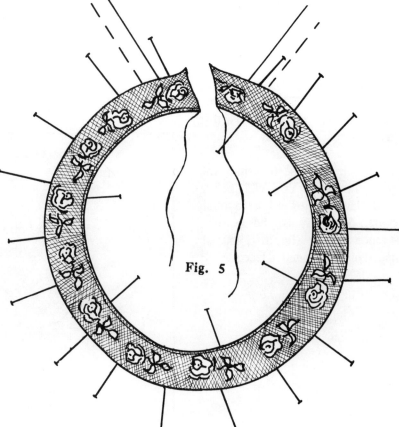

Fig. 5

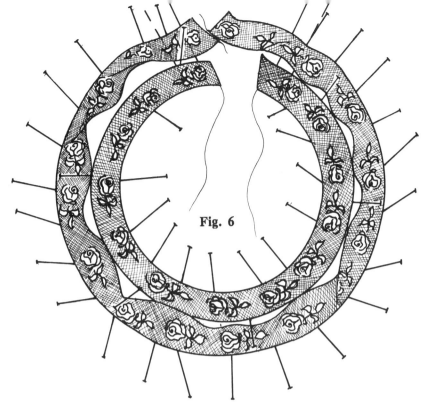

Fig. 6

7. Now that the first row is pretty and flat, you are ready to do the same thing with the second row. Pin the OUTSIDE edge to the board by jabbing the pins, just like you did on the first row. Be sure the inside of the lace touches the first row when you press it down with your fingers (Fig. 6). After you have gone all the way around with the second row of lace, pull from both ends to gather the inside row, just like you did the first row (Figs. 7 and 8).

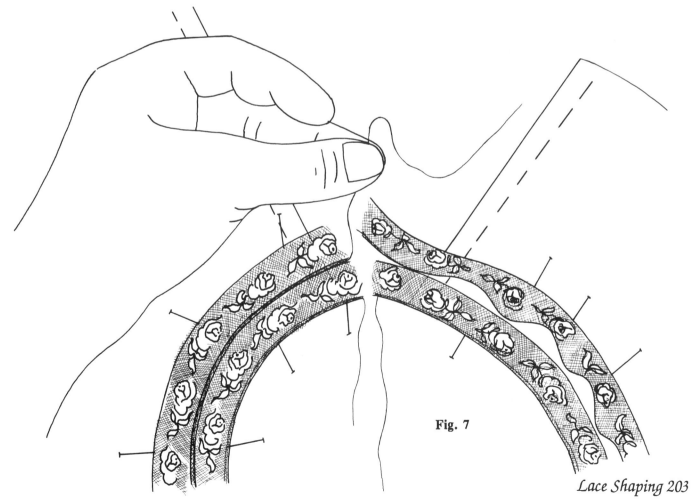

Fig. 7

Lace Shaping 203

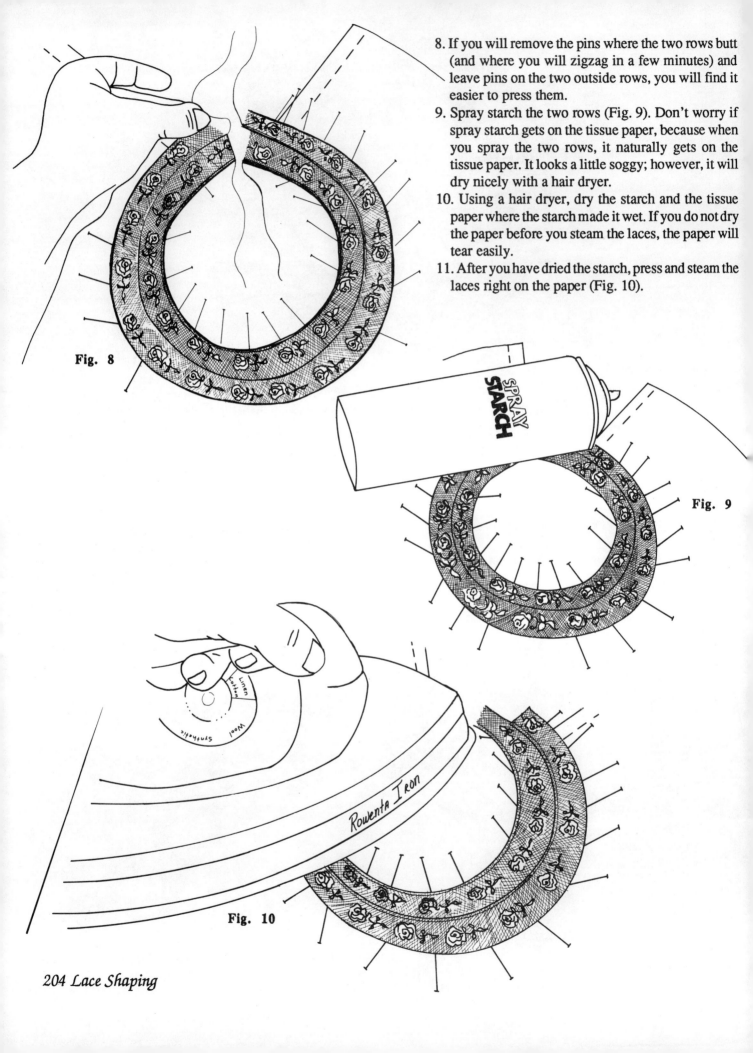

8. If you will remove the pins where the two rows butt (and where you will zigzag in a few minutes) and leave pins on the two outside rows, you will find it easier to press them.

9. Spray starch the two rows (Fig. 9). Don't worry if spray starch gets on the tissue paper, because when you spray the two rows, it naturally gets on the tissue paper. It looks a little soggy; however, it will dry nicely with a hair dryer.

10. Using a hair dryer, dry the starch and the tissue paper where the starch made it wet. If you do not dry the paper before you steam the laces, the paper will tear easily.

11. After you have dried the starch, press and steam the laces right on the paper (Fig. 10).

Fig. 8

SPRAY STARCH

Fig. 9

Linen
Cotton
Wool
Synthetic

Rowenta Iron

Fig. 10

12. Remove the jabbed pins, one at a time, and flat pin the lace to the paper on both rows. Pin with the points toward the neckline. This makes it a lot easier when you stitch your collar, because when the pins are in this position, you can pull them out as you zigzag. If they are pinned the other way, it is difficult to remove the pins as you stitch. Never sew over pins, please! It is easier to remove the pin than it is to replace the needle (Fig. 11).

13. (Stitch right through the tissue paper and the lace. Later, you will tear away the tissue paper.) Move to your sewing machine, and zigzag (Width=1-1/2 to 2, Length=1-1/2 to 2) Fig. 11. This width and length are just suggestions. Actually, the width and length will depend on the width of the laces in the heading of your particular lace. The length stitch will depend upon your preference. If you like a heavier, closer together look, make your stitch length shorter. If you like a looser, more delicate look, make your stitch length longer.

14. The first two rows should now be zigzagged together.

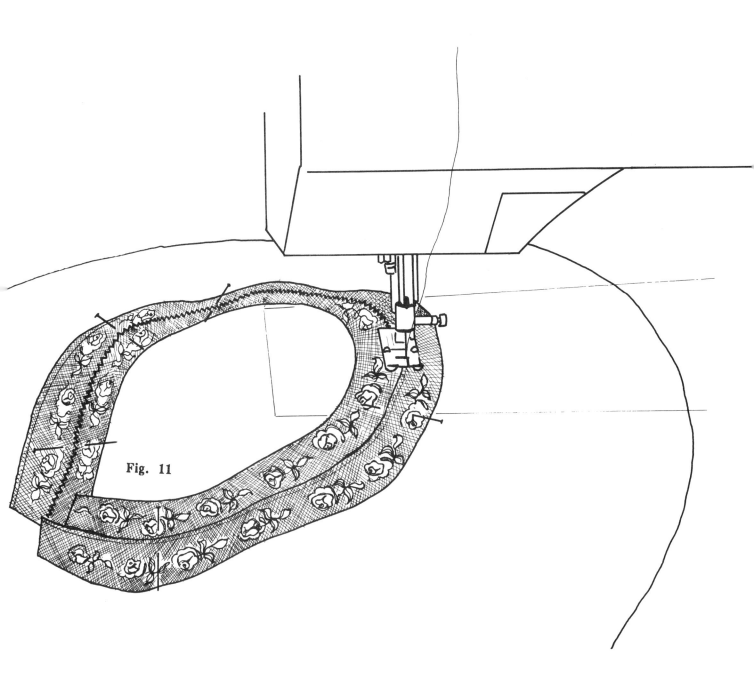

Fig. 11

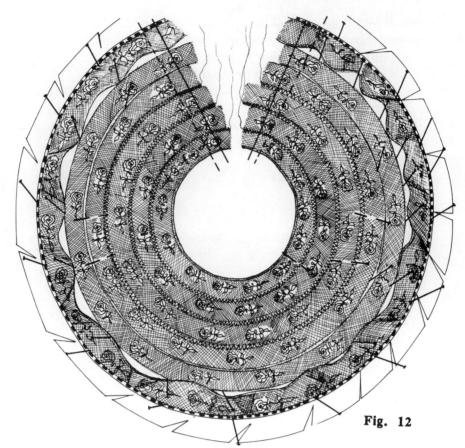

Fig. 12

Making The Rest Of The Rows Of Insertion

Directions:
1. Following the directions given for applying the second row, pin, and stitch the rest of the rows that you want to have on your collar. Make the collar as wide as you want it (Fig. 12).
2. Here is a little trick that I have learned through experience. After you have pinned, pressed, starched, pressed, **and zigzagged your first two rows together,** the remaining rows can be made on the paper pattern at the same time. You don't have to stitch each row of insertion right after shaping it. (Fig. 12).
3. Shape the laces on the rest of the collar by pinning, pressing, starching, pressing, and letting dry (Fig. 12).
4. After all the lace rows are shaped and the tissue paper is completely dry, pin them flat, remembering to place the pins with the points toward the neckline and the heads away from the neckline (Fig. 12).
5. Cut a piece of entredeux with enough length to go completely around the outside row of lace insertion, allowing for plenty of excess. You don't want to run out.
6. Trim off one side of the entredeux completely (Fig. 12).
7. Slash the other row so it will curve easily (Fig. 12).
8. Pin the entredeux around the outside row of lace, jabbing pins into the holes of the entredeux about every 2 inches or so. After the entredeux is all the way around the curved lace collar, press, starch, press again, and allow to dry. You can always dry it with a hair dryer if you want to begin stitching immediately (Fig. 12).
9. Pin the entredeux to the tissue paper at several places. You are now ready to begin stitching the first row of lace insertion that is not already stitched.
10. Stitch each row, starting with the unstitched one closest to the neckline. Move outward with each row for your stitching. Remove the pins, one at a time, as you are stitching.
11. With each successive row, carefully remove the pins, and be sure to butt the lace edges exactly as you stitch around the collar.
12. The entredeux to the last row of insertion may or may not be the last row that you will stitch, while the tissue paper is still on the collar. You will have to make a decision concerning whether you want to use Method I or Method II a little later on in the instructions.

Using The Center Back
Of The Collar
Check Your Fold-Back Line

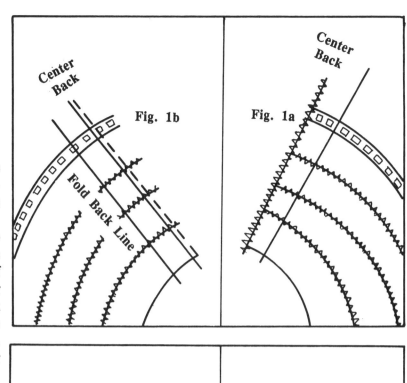

Directions:

. The center back of a garment is just that. Where the backs meet. This collar will not end at the center-back point unless you are not putting laces up the center back of the collar.

. You can choose to put no laces and no entredeux up the center back. In this case, you will work on the center-back line. The best way to finish the back of the collar, if you make this choice, is to serge or overlock the collar just **outside** of the center-back line (Fig. 1a). Then fold your serged seam to the back, and straight-stitch it to the collar (Fig. 1b). That leaves just a finished lace edge as the center back.

. If you are adding lace edging and entredeux up the back of the collar, you will have to use the fold-back line you made in the beginning on your pattern. Laces don't need to overlap at the center back, but meet instead. Check to be sure that your fold-back line is as wide as your lace edging is from the center-back line on your pattern.

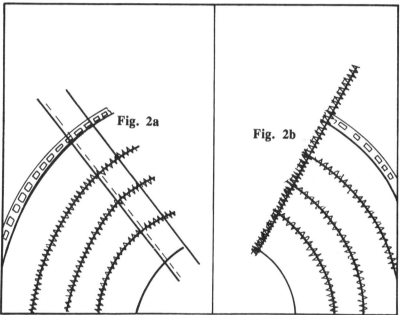

Method I For Adding Entredeux

Directions:

1. Make a straight row of stitching on the fold-back line. You are still stitching through the tissue paper.
2. Trim away the laces, leaving about 1/8 inch of raw lace edge (Fig. 2a).
3. Zigzag very tightly (Width=1-1/2, Length=1/2) to finish the lace edge (Fig. 2b).
4. Butt the entredeux to the finished edge (Fig. 3a) and zigzag, going into the holes of the entredeux and off (Fig. 3b).

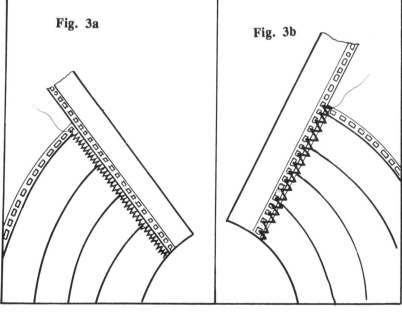

Method II For Adding Entredeux

Directions:

1. Using the technique "Entredeux To Flat Fabric," attach the entredeux to the back of the collar. Stitch in the ditch (Fig. 1), trim (Fig. 2), and zigzag (Fig. 3).
2. You have two options when finishing this straight line of stitching. Either serge or zigzag along this line. You will make the decision in the next section. For right now, don't trim away any laces along the fold-back line; just leave the collar like it is.
3. After you make your decisions, finish this back edge.

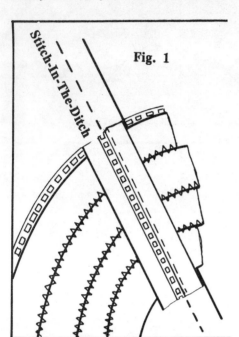
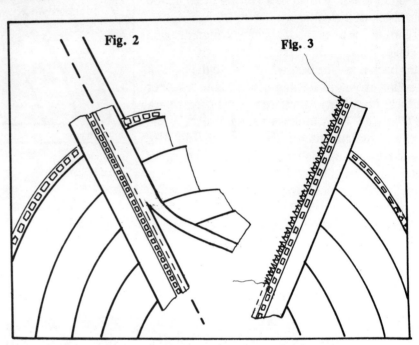

Method I For Attaching Gathered Lace To Entredeux Of The Collar

With Tissue Paper

Question: When would you use Method I?

Some people consider this method the easiest for distributing the lace evenly because you can put the quarter points exactly where you want them and control the fullness. If you have a machine, which isn't up to par, stitching laces on tissue paper is easier than working without it. So, for some people the method of stitching the gathered lace on while tissue paper is still attached is the easiest.

Directions:

1. Cut lace edging to be gathered around the bottom and up the back of the collar. You can use a 1-1/2 - 1 fullness or a 2 - 1 fullness. It really depends on how much lace you wish to use.
2. After cutting your lace, (allow about 2 inches to turn each back corner and about 10 inches to gather and go up each back of the collar) fold the rest of the lace in half, and mark the center of the lace. Fold once again, and mark the quarter points. This will allow you to distribute the fullness accurately.
3. Pull the gathering thread in the top of the edging. Pin the center of the lace to the center of the entredeux edge of the collar. Pin the quarter points of the lace to the approximate quarter points of the collar. You should have about 12 inches of lace on each end to go around the corner of the collar and to gather it up the back of the collar. After figuring out these measurements, begin to distribute and pin the gathered lace to the bottom of the collar entredeux. Distribute the gathers carefully so that they will be pretty. Pin all the way around.
4. Stitch the gathered lace (Width=1-1/2 to 2, Length=1/2) to the entredeux, still stitching through the tissue paper. You are only going to stitch around the bottom of the collar. Leave the laces unattached at this point, coming up the center back.

5. Carefully tear away the tissue paper from the collar.
6. If you are not going to use a serger, trim away the lace ends 1/4 inch away from the fold-back line of the collar where you have stay-stitched. This 1/4 inch gives you a seam allowance to zigzag to finish. If you plan to serge the outside of this line, you do not have to trim away the lace since the serger does this for you.
7. Zigzag tightly over this stay-stitched line (Width=1 to 2, Length=1/2).
8. If you have a serger, serge this seam rather than zigzagging over it.
9. If you serged this seam, fold back the serged edge, and straight-stitch it down.
10. If you zigzagged over this seam, use this rolled and whipped edge as the finished edge of this seam.

Finishing The Application Of Entredeux And The Gathered Lace Edging

Directions:
1. Now that your fold-back line is finished, you are ready to finish gathering the lace edging and zigzag it to the back of the collar.
3. Trim the other side of the entredeux up the back of the collar.
4. Put extra gathers in the lace edging when going around the corner. This will keep it from folding under.
5. After gathering the lace edging, butt the gathered laces to the trimmed entredeux and zigzag to the collar.
6. Fold down the top of the lace edging before completely zigzagging to the top of the collar. That way you have a finished lace edge on the top of the collar.

Method II For Attaching Gathered Lace To The Entredeux Of The Collar

Without Tissue Paper

Question: When would you use Method II?
If the tension is good on your sewing machine, use Method II. If you don't mind the laces not being exactly the same gathering all the way around, use Method II. By the way, the laces won't be distributed evenly using Method I either. I haven't found a way to perfectly distribute and gather laces and attach them using any method, including hand sewing! However, Method II is the easiest.

Directions:
1. Tear away the tissue paper from your collar.
2. Cut the lace edging, which will be gathered around the bottom of the collar and up the back of the collar. You can use a 1-1/2 - 1 fullness or a 2 - 1 fullness. It really depends on how much lace you wish to use.
3. Now that your fold-back line is finished, you are ready to finish gathering the lace edging and zigzag it to the back of the collar.
4. Trim the other side of the entredeux.
5. Using the techniques found in "Gathering French Lace By Machine, While Applying It To Trimmed Entredeux Edge," attach your lace to the bottom of the collar and up the back edges.

Gathering French Lace By Machine, While Applying It To Trimmed Entredeux Edge

NOTE: You must have a little extra lace when using this method. It may use more than the pattern requires. This method is easy and time saving. It can be used when attaching gathered lace around a collar that has entredeux at the bottom before the gathered lace. It is especially good when attaching gathered lace around a portrait collar. It is the only way to attach the gathered lace to an entredeux-trimmed neck edge. Actually, you can use this technique anytime you attach gathered lace to trimmed entredeux. It results in fairly even gathers, and saves you from having to pin, distribute, and straighten-out twisted lace.

Directions:
1. Trim off the edge of the entredeux.
2. Press both the entredeux and the lace.
3. Side by side, right sides up, begin to zigzag with lace still straight (Fig. 1).
4. About 6 inches out on the lace, pull one of the gathering threads. I find that using a little pick of some kind is effective. The same little pick that is used to pull a lace gathering thread, can also be used to push the gathers into the sewing machine. A pin will suffice if necessary (Fig. 2).
5. In order to get the gathers to move in the right direction (toward the foot of the sewing machine), you will need to pull on the side of the thread loop closest to the sewing machine. If you pull on the other side, the gathers will not go toward the sewing machine. Pull the thread, and push the gathers toward the sewing machine (Fig. 2).
6. Lift your pressure foot, and push a few gathers under it. Zigzag a few stitches (Width=3-1/2, Length=2). You may notice that the width is a little wider than usual for zigzagging lace to entredeux. I have found that with gathered lace, it is necessary to make the width wider in order to catch all of the heading of the gathered lace. As always, you should adjust the width and length, according to the width of your entredeux and your lace heading. They vary so much it is hard to give one exact width and length. Lift your pressure foot again, and push a few more gathers under it. Continue, until all of your gathers on that one section have been stitched in (Fig. 3).
7. Go out another 6 inches on your lace, and repeat the process. Continue, until all of the lace is gathered and stitched to the trimmed entredeux.

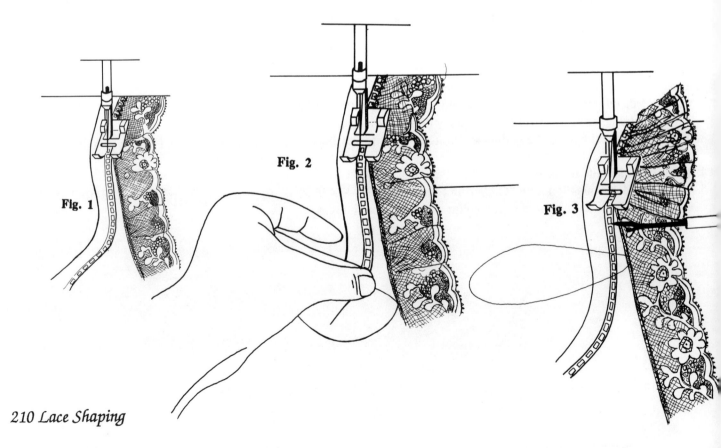

Fig. 1

Fig. 2

Fig. 3

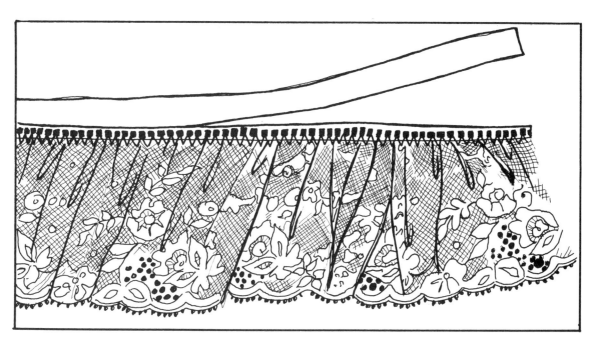

Making An Entredeux And Lace String

The method "Gathering French Lace By Machine, While Applying It To Trimmed Entredeux Edge" is the perfect way to make an entredeux/gathered lace trim for the yoke of a French dress. This is the easy way to trim your yoke with entredeux and gathered lace. The hard way would be to apply your entredeux in the seams of the yokes and the sleeves.

Directions:

1. Follow the techniques found in the technique "Gathering French Lace By Machine, While Applying It To Trimmed Entredeux Edge."
2. Make the entredeux and lace string as long as you need it to be to travel around the entire yoke (front and back) and over the shoulders of the dress. After making this long strip of entredeux and gathered lace, simply trim the other side of the entredeux. Pin into place, around the yoke edges, and zigzag the entredeux and lace string right onto the finished dress (Fig. 1).

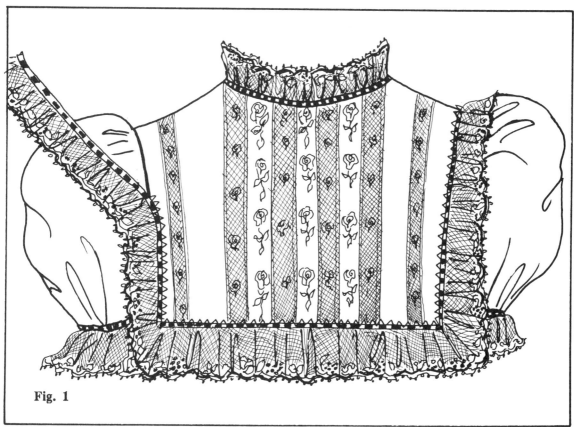

Fig. 1

211

Lace Shaping Plus Shadowwork Embroidery

While working on this chapter, I began to envision delicate shadowwork designs made specifically to go with certain lace shapes. Using my antique clothing collection, Cynthia Handy came up with some new ideas, combining lace shaping and embroidery. Our illustrations show the lace shapes stitched down with pin stitching on your sewing machine, rather than just a plain zigzag. To pin stitch lace shapes, first zigzag them to the fabric; then, following directions given by your brand of sewing machine, pin stitch, using the wing needle. It makes a beautiful finish to shaped laces.

Yoke Number One

This delicate yoke has tiny scallops plus shadow embroidered bows, flowers, and leaves. You can adjust the scallops, smaller or larger, to suit your pattern size. The Peter Pan collar has featherstitch for the trim and gathered lace to finish. Actually, this yoke is so pretty, it's all the trim you need for a precious child's dress.

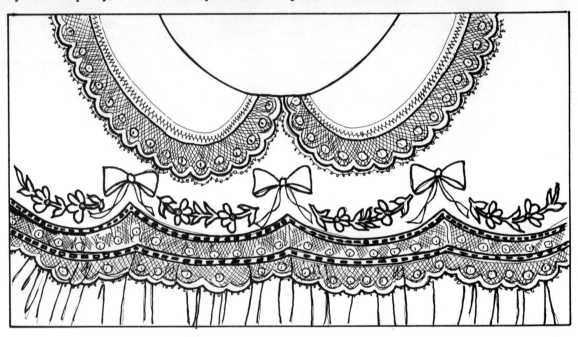

Yoke Number Two

This yoke is actually a square yoke with lace shaped in curves, giving the impression of a round yoke. The little bows and flowers would take almost no time to stitch, and with your wing needle and your pin stitch directions on your machine, this delicate beauty could be yours in no time flat.

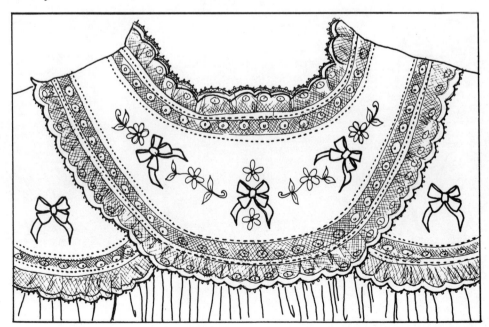

212

Skirt Number One

Curved lace, attached with a pin stitch makes a decorative trim for any baby or adult dress. You can make the curves wider apart and add more of the embroidery, or choose to let the embroidery stand alone.

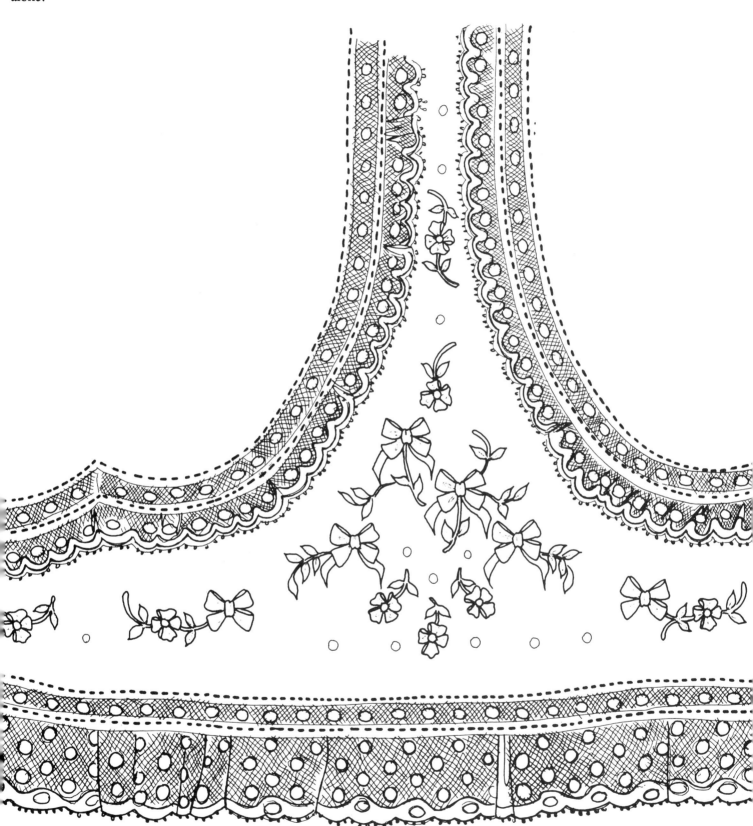

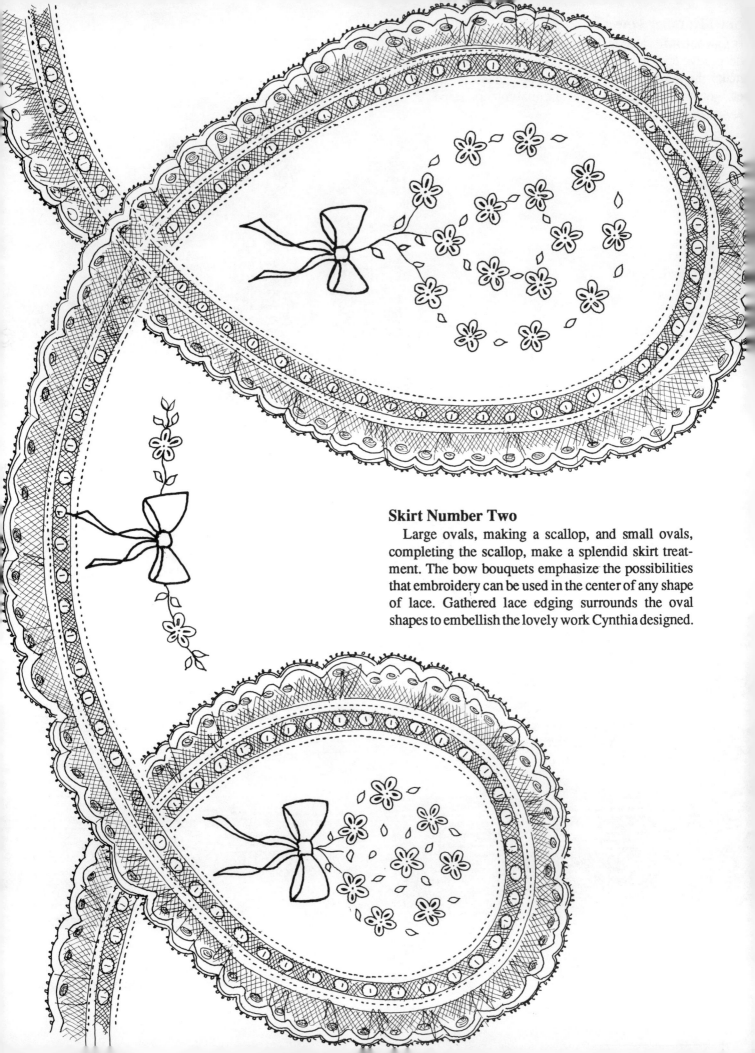

Skirt Number Two

Large ovals, making a scallop, and small ovals, completing the scallop, make a splendid skirt treatment. The bow bouquets emphasize the possibilities that embroidery can be used in the center of any shape of lace. Gathered lace edging surrounds the oval shapes to embellish the lovely work Cynthia designed.

Skirt Number Three

Designs as small as these tiny ovals are relatively new to the French sewing field. These ovals could go on the yoke of a dress or on the skirt; they could be scattered anywhere on a French dress; on a skirt, the bodice, the sleeves or a sash. Wouldn't two of the ovals plus a little embroidery be absolutely lovely on a sash?

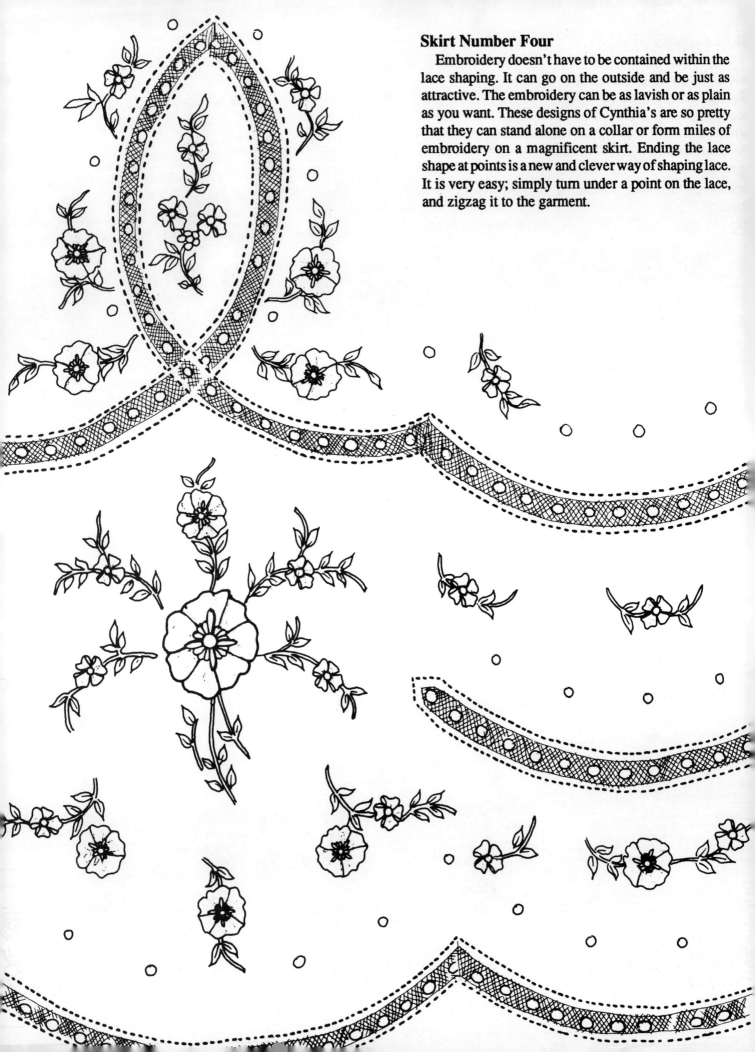

Skirt Number Four

Embroidery doesn't have to be contained within the lace shaping. It can go on the outside and be just as attractive. The embroidery can be as lavish or as plain as you want. These designs of Cynthia's are so pretty that they can stand alone on a collar or form miles of embroidery on a magnificent skirt. Ending the lace shape at points is a new and clever way of shaping lace. It is very easy; simply turn under a point on the lace, and zigzag it to the garment.

Skirt Number Five

Downward pointed columns with turned-under points are a delicate and fresh use of shaping. The V shaped embroidery designs with little circles connecting them match the circles in the lace. You could embroider the circles in shadowwork or make French knots or bullion rosebuds. Be sure you pin stitch or make machine hemstitching around the lace columns or any other lace shaping that you add to your garments. Take these embroidery designs to the collar, the sleeves, or to the sash for a splendid finish.

Ovals

I have a cute story to tell you about oval skirts. A few years ago, one of my Sew Beautiful *readers made her daughter a magnificent French dress with oval-shaped lace and delicate embroidery on the skirt. When she brought the dress to a photo shoot for the magazine, she asked her little girl to tell me what was on the skirt of her dress. "Miss Martha, I have footballs on my dress," she answered. If that weren't the cutest thing. Since then I have referred to lace ovals as footballs. Call them anything you want, they are lovely and quite easy to make.*

First you have to draw the oval shapes on your skirt. Margaret Taylor and I spent hours working on the easiest method to shape lace ovals or footballs. We tried everything and finally came back to my original thinking and the method I've always used. We align the outside edge of the lace to the drawn line, pin it, then pull the heading to shape the lace on the inside. The following technique is the one I recommend for shaping lace footballs.

45"   45"

Fig. 1

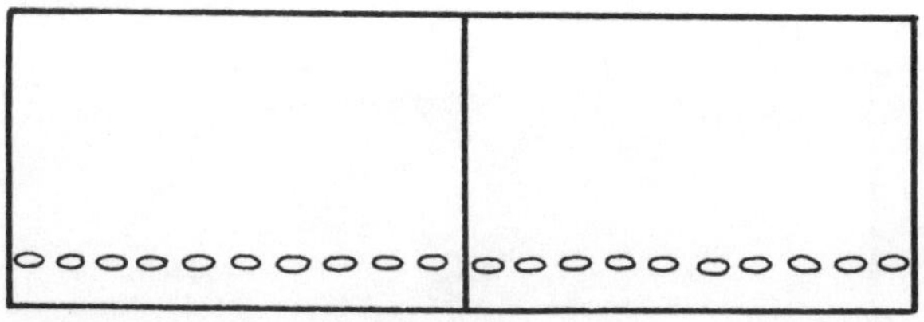

Fig. 2

Making Connecting Ovals or "Footballs"

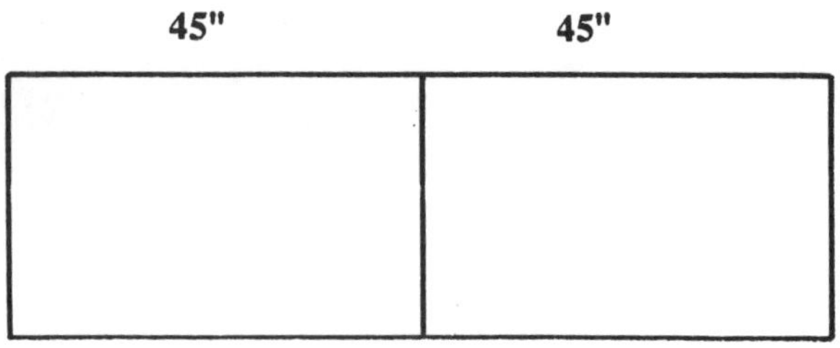

Directions:

1. Tear both of your skirt strips. I suggest a width of 45 inches; this makes the total fullness of the skirt 90 inches. Make a French seam or serge the two skirt strips together on one side. Leave the skirt flat (Fig. 1).

2. You are now ready to measure to see approximately how many ovals you will need for your skirt. For example, if you elect to make your ovals 4 inches across, and your lace is 1/2 inch wide, you will need 20 ovals (4 inches wide each) plus 1/2-inch space between each oval. The 1/2-inch space is for the laces to cross between the exact oval shape and not distort your 4-inch oval.

3. Pretend that you are using 1/2-inch insertion for this oval. Beginning from the seam you have just made, draw your ovals on the skirt leaving 1/2-inch space between each oval. If your lace is wider, say 3/4 inch, then, leave 3/4-inch space between each oval. Go ahead and draw on all of the ovals. If you have extra space left, you can quickly see that it is on the other side seam. You can just cut away any excess fabric before you put in the other side seam (Fig. 2).

4. You will need to work with two long pieces of lace insertion, long enough to go around either the top or bottom of your ovals around the whole skirt front and back. Measure around one oval and down to get the yardage you will need. Be sure to allow extra. Be sure you have two pieces of lace that are long enough. You could piece the lace by stitching it together (preferably at the overlap/mid point).

5. Get your fabric board, since you will be pinning your laces into the board. Pin the insertion on the outside where the edge touches your traced oval similar to the other lace-shaping instructions in this chapter. At the mid points where you have your 1/2-inch space, pin the lace on each side, touching the edges of the oval. Follow around, pinning enough ovals that fit on one fabric board (Fig. 3).

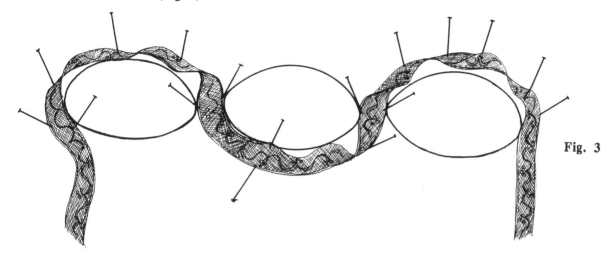

Fig. 3

6. Pull the threads in the center of the ovals to flatten the lace into the proper shape (Fig. 4).

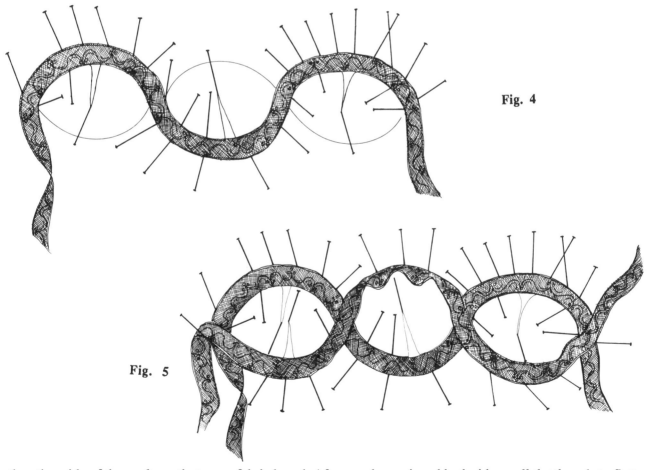

Fig. 4

Fig. 5

7. Pin the other side of the ovals on that same fabric board. After you have pinned both sides, pull the threads to flatten and shape the laces onto the board (Fig. 5).

8. Press. Spray starch. When I say spray starch, I mean **spray starch until the fabric and lace are glued together!** This helps hold the laces to the fabric while you shape the rest of the ovals.

9. One at a time, remove the jabbed pins from the fabric board. Pin the lace ovals flat to the fabric. This type of strong pinning is called pin basting. I very rarely baste anything (either by hand or machine); I do not think basting is necessary if you put in enough pins. If you want to baste by machine or baste by hand, feel free to do so. Remove from the fabric board and place another portion of the skirt on the board. Repeat the process until your whole skirt has been shaped. Remember to leave lots of pins in the skirt.

9. After the entire skirt is shaped, starched, pressed, and pinned, you are ready to start zigzagging the ovals into place.

10. Zigzag the top of each row of lace insertion. This first row of stitching will be in a scallop shape (Fig. 6). Notice that you do not stitch through the area where the laces cross each other.

Fig. 6

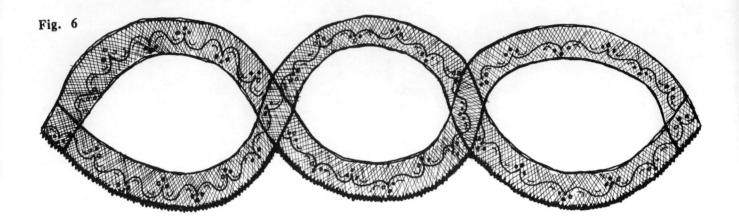

11. Zigzag around the inside of each oval shape (Fig.7). Do not stitch through the places where the laces cross each other. By not stitching through this area, cutting away the fabric from behind these areas will be easier. Later, if you want to, you can come back and zigzag over these pieces of lace. It is not necessary (Fig. 8). (If your oval shaping is not the bottom of a skirt but rather a decoration on the body of the skirt, it is now time to zigzag around the bottom part of the ovals.)

12. Cut away the excess fabric if you are putting these scallops on the bottom of a dress. Trim away the fabric from behind the lace. As you trim the fabric from the bottom piece of lace, a large overall piece of fabric will fall away, leaving the ovals for a scalloped skirt.

13. For a beautiful skirt bottom, trim away one side of a piece of entredeux. Slash the other side every 1 inch or so, so it will curve into the scalloped shapes. Go back to the fabric board and pin, starch, shape, and press this entredeux into the shape of the scallops. Let them dry stiff as a board. After your entredeux and lace skirt dry completely, zigzag the entredeux to the scalloped skirt edge by stitching into one hole and off on the lace.

14. Trim away the slashed edge of the entredeux. You are now ready to gather your lace edging and zigzag it to the trimmed entredeux edge of your garment.

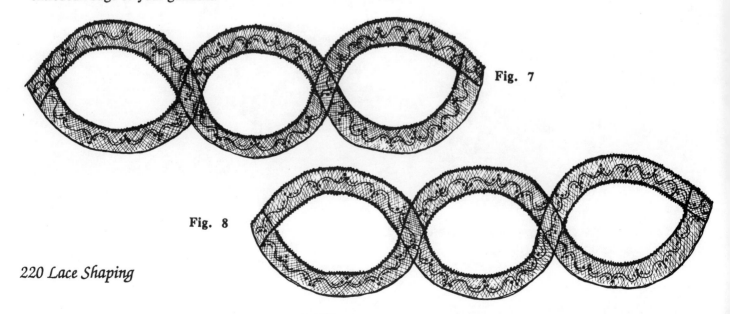

Fig. 7

Fig. 8

Loops Of Lace

Lace loops have been one of the most beloved skirt trims since I have been involved in the heirloom sewing industry and for many years prior. Turn-of-the-century garments, blouses, skirts, and dresses were filled with loops of lace. Loops can be as large or as small as you want them to be; or, you might try a combination of large and small loops. These directions will show you how to make a large loop and a small loop similar to those on Skirt #2.

Preparing The Skirt

1. Using the directions given for the skirt preparation for ovals, tear or cut two skirt pieces, stitch up one side of the skirt, and leave the whole skirt flat.
2. It is now time to divide your skirt into sections. Fold your skirt lengthwise until you have it folded into the size fold that you want your ovals to be. Press. Open up and you will have the lines on which to place your ovals. (Refer to "Making A Scalloped Skirt.")

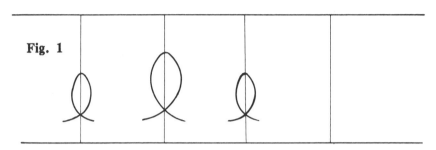

Fig. 1

3. After the skirt is folded and pressed into sections, make a loop guide (Fig. 1). You can use the ones given (Fig. 2), or make your own. Place the loop guide paper under the fold of the skirt. Measure up from the bottom to the place where the loop crosses. Be sure each loop is this distance from the bottom when you make your loops. Trace (using a #2 lead pencil or a Dixon pencil) the first loop, centering it on the fold in the fabric that you made when you pressed your fabric. Repeat for the other fold lines on your skirt front and back. Trace all of the scallops onto your fabric before you begin shaping the lace.
4. Place the fabric on the fabric board with as many of your drawn loops as possible on the board.

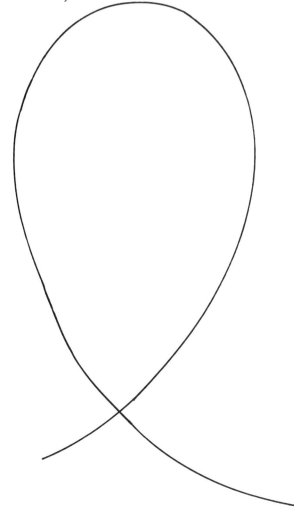

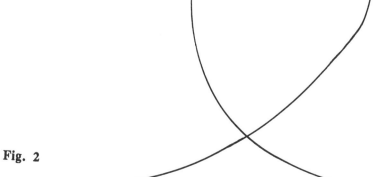

Fig. 2

221

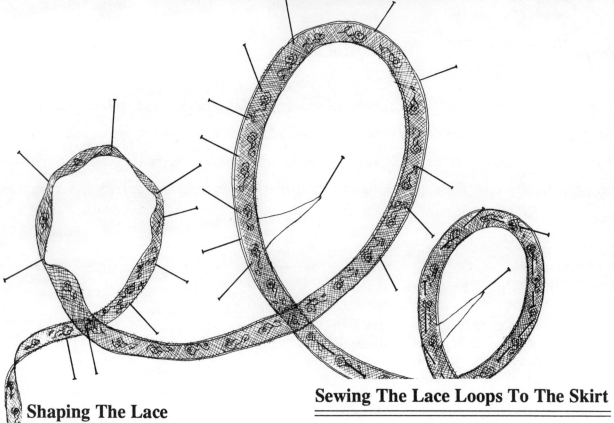

Shaping The Lace

1. Start the lace at one of the points of the loop bottom. Using the guide line you just drew as the inside point of the lace, poke pins and curve the lace around the loop. Press down the inside of the lace to be sure that when it is pulled and shaped it will touch the drawn guide on the skirt. Push your pins in at an angle, pinning the outside edge all the way around.
2. Complete the loop, and pin the lace along the bottom scallop, connecting the two loops. Continue this process until you completely run out of fabric board space to pin the laces.
3. After you have pinned as many loops onto the board as possible, it is time to pull the threads and finish these loops before travelling on to the next set of loops.
4. Pull a thread on the inside of one of the loops. Be sure that you pull the very top thread in the heading of the lace. Pull it tightly enough that you can draw up the slack and shape the lace in loops flat to the fabric. Hold this thread tightly by sticking a pin into the board to hold it after you get the lace pulled into shape.
5. Starch the laces. Press. Let them dry completely by using a hair dryer or by allowing time to dry naturally.
6. Pin baste the lace loop to the fabric by removing the pins that are poked into the board and placing them through the laces and the fabric of the skirt.
7. Remove this section of the looped lace from the board and move to the next section. Continue this process until the whole skirt has been shaped and pinned.
8. When you run short of lace, end the lace under the loop cross point to hide the patched lace.

Sewing The Lace Loops To The Skirt

1. After lace shaping has been made on the skirt, zigzag the laces to the skirt. Using a zigzag stitch (Width=1-1/2 to 2-1/2, length=1/2) stitch the top of the laces to the skirt. **NOTE:** Never cross an intersection of lace with the zigzag stitches. The top loops are zigzagged in one continuous zigzag all around the skirt.
2. Then, zigzag the loops in a circular shape to the skirt. Do not cross an intersection of the lace with the zigzag stitches.
3. If this is the bottom of a skirt, you will not stitch the bottom of the lace insertion to the skirt at all.
4. Trim away the fabric from behind the lace insertion. You will notice that the fabric falls away from the bottom of the skirt, leaving lace insertion shaped in a scallop for the bottom trim of the skirt.
5. You can finish this skirt in several ways. If you are putting these loops on the bottom of a dress, cut away the excess fabric. Trim away the fabric from behind the lace. As you trim the fabric from the bottom piece of lace, a large overall piece of fabric will fall away, leaving the loops for a scalloped skirt.
6. For a beautiful skirt bottom, trim away one side of a piece of entredeux. Slash the other side every 1 inch or so, so it will curve into the scalloped shapes. Go back to the fabric board and pin, starch, shape, and press this entredeux into the shape of the scallops. Let them dry stiff as a board. After your entredeux and lace skirt dry completely, zigzag the entredeux to the scalloped skirt edge by stitching into one hole and off on the lace.
7. Trim away the slashed edge of the entredeux. You are now ready to gather your lace edging and zigzag it to the trimmed entredeux edge of your garment.

Lace Shaping: The Bottom Line

Before delving into the chapters on entredeux techniques, pintucks, new French sewing techniques, and shadowwork, several questions remain concerning lace shaping. This question-and-answer section should clear up any confusion and give you the confidence to conquer a variety of lace shapes.

Q. How might I use these lace shapes on the new middy dress patterns included in the book?

A. Using the middy dress patterns, Cynthia created several designs to encourage you to come up with your own lace shaping ideas. *Scalloped Beauty* sports scallops, entredeux, and lace insertion around the bottom — a treatment which is echoed at the yoke and around the sleeves (Fig. 1). *Hearts And Scallops* features hearts and reverse scallops on the deep collar (Fig. 2), and again on the sleeves and around the skirt. *Geometric Delight* plays with the idea of combining shapes with a scalloped hem, entredeux, and gathered lace. At the bottom of the skirt, Cynthia has carried the "football" shaping through to form inverted V's, thus successfully blending two contrasting shapes (Fig. 3). The *Up And Down Bows* version is scalloped at the hem and treated with entredeux and gathered lace (Fig. 4). The dress looks to be tied up with bows like a Christmas package.

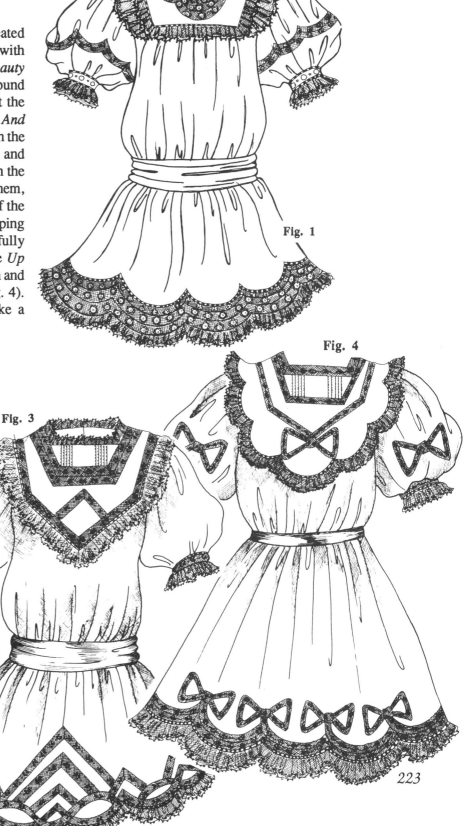

Fig. 1

Fig. 2

Fig. 3

Fig. 4

223

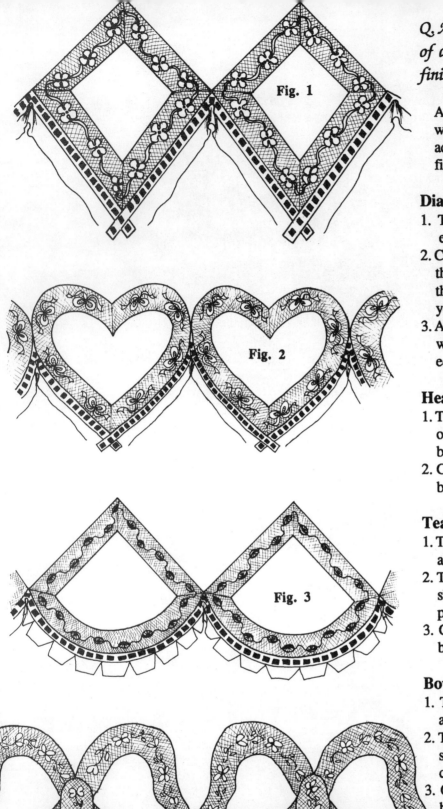

Fig. 1

Fig. 2

Fig. 3

Fig. 4

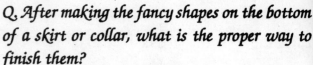

Q. *After making the fancy shapes on the bottom of a skirt or collar, what is the proper way to finish them?*

A. The line of the skirt or collar generally suggests what finish to use; however, here are my ideas for adding entredeux to the bottom of each of the figures:

Diamonds:

1. To outline diamonds with entredeux, shape the entredeux when going into the top angles.
2. Cut the entredeux and overlap it when going around the bottom points. Entredeux will shape just fine in the top points; however it will curve and buckle if you try to shape it around the bottom points.
3. After trimming off both seam allowances, cut points will join smoothly when you zigzag gathered lace edging around the bottom of the skirt (Fig. 1).

Hearts:

1. To add entredeux to heart shapes around the bottom of a skirt or collar, shape the entredeux when going between the hearts at the upper points.
2. Cut the entredeux and overlap the cut points on the bottom (Fig. 2).

Teardrops:

1. To add entredeux to the bottom of a teardrop, shape around the bottom of a skirt or collar.
2. Trim off one side of the entredeux completely and shape it around the teardrops in one continuous piece.
3. Clip the curves in the other side of the entredeux before you shape it around the teardrops (Fig. 3).

Bows:

1. To add entredeux to the bottom of a bow, shape around the bottom of a skirt or collar.
2. Trim off one side of the entredeux completely, and shape it around the bottom of the bow in one continuous piece.
3. Clip the curves in the other side of the entredeux before you shape it around the bows (Fig. 4).

Q. How do you finish the neckline on a French dress where it has an entredeux/gathered-lace finish?

A. So many times French dresses have an entredeux/gathered-lace neckline finish. Here is the technique I use:

1. Check the seam allowance on the neckline of your pattern. This is important.
2. Check the seam allowance on your entredeux. It is usually 1/2 inch; however, this is not always the case. Measure the seam allowance of your entredeux.
3. If the seam allowance at the neck of the pattern and the seam allowance of your entredeux do not match, **trim the seam allowance of the entredeux to match the seam allowance of the neckline of your garment.**
4. Using the techniques "Entredeux To Flat Fabric," attach the entredeux to the neckline of the garment.
5. Stitch in the ditch (Fig. 1). Trim, leaving a 1/8-inch to 1/4-inch seam allowance (Fig. 2).
6. Zigzag the seam allowance to finish (Fig. 3).
7. Trim the remaining clipped seam allowance. Press the seam toward the body of the dress.
8. Gather the lace edging. Butt it to the trimmed entredeux and zigzag (Fig. 4).

Q. How do you finish the edge of a square collar if you want to use an entredeux/gathered-lace edging?

A. Remember, entredeux buckles around square corners. But, because entredeux is embroidered so tightly, it does not ravel.

1. To shape entredeux around a corner, simply cut the entredeux, and begin with a new piece.
2. Overlap the corners (Fig. 1).
3. Zigzag the first row to one side of the fabric — this will attach the entredeux to the basic collar unit.
4. Gather the lace edging; butt it to the trimmed side of the entredeux.
5. When you travel around the corners of the collar, gather up a little more fullness to the edging so that it will not pull and cup under. As you can see, you will have to trim the overlap at the corners. When you zigzag your gathered lace around these corners, they will be permanently attached. If you try to turn corners without cutting the entredeux it will always look peculiar.

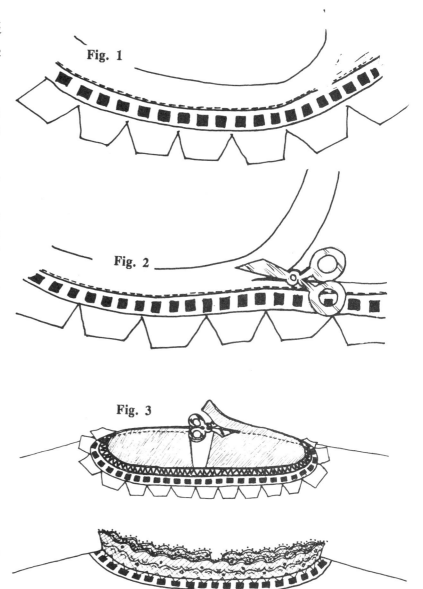

Fig. 1

Fig. 2

Fig. 3

Fig. 4

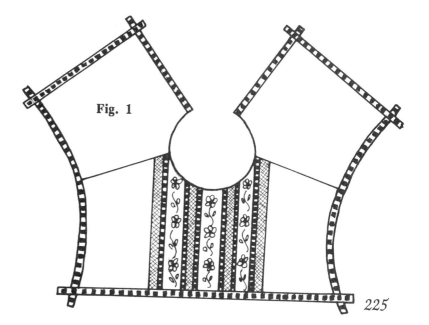

Fig. 1

225

Lace Shaping In Antique Garments

Just for fun, let's go to the antique garment section of our thinking and see how lace shaping was used in antique clothing. One of the lovely things about sewing is that beautifully-made garments have been treasured for centuries. Most "new" sewing techniques aren't new at all, but simply revised methods tried somewhere in our past. For more than a year, my real energies have been in planning and writing this book. A funny thing has happened. My love of old clothing has carried over to old movies — especially those made in the '30s and '40s and also those set in the late 1800s and early 1900s. I've become a real nostalgia buff and can't help but recall my own family's history.

In the 1920s, my father was transferred from Nashville to New York as the first national sales manager for Maxwell House Coffee. When I handle the delicate garments in my collection, I imagine New York ladies of my father's era dressed in such finery. My Nannie (grandmother) began teaching school in 1914. Fading photographs captured her in blouses like the antique ones I love so much today. My husband's mother, Emma, was named for her aunt Emma Kirby who was a coveted couturier to about 80 of Nashville's aristocratic families. A portrait of her in a white, lace creation hangs in our living room. Family stories tell of the annual Christmas visits to Nashville where Aunt Emma would have dresses made for her nieces, tempting food cooked, and exquisite decorations in her home. Oh, such nostalgia! I love it!

Since I was born in 1943, I am especially interested in the children's clothing of the 1940s. I have heard mother lovingly talk of taking the "Singer Sewing Course," and I am grateful to that company for being one of the first in the world to offer sewing education to the public. Years ago, women — often with names such as Miss Cotton or Mrs. Jones — headed up couturier shops in Southern communities, as surely as the President headed up the United States. Their mainstay, of course, was to design custom clothing, but many taught sewing courses on the side to proper young ladies. Our sewing machine dealers are doing such a good job today continuing this education, especially in heirloom sewing.

NOTE: The descriptions will be written exactly as they appeared in the 1904 Butterick Pattern Catalogue or in the 1894 May Minton Glove Fitting Pattern Book. Notice the unusual use of capital letters right in the middle of the description!

Curved V Lace Shaped Antique Dress

This design has been crafted with center tucks and a shaped lace collar. The sailor tie and tucked inside yoke give the dress a nautical flavor. The lace shaping on the cuffs echoes the V shape. The second version of the collar has three rows of lace, shaped and mitered. If these garments were, indeed, made like the illustrations, polka dot heavy faille, perhaps in forest green with black polka dots or deep red with black polka dots, would be an ideal choice of fabric. Look in the trim section of your favorite fabric store for a variety of heavy ribbon, trims. Use the same techniques for mitering the trims that you would for mitering laces. Just zigzag trims onto the garment, like you would zigzag the laces. In attaching laces to a collar, try using fancy stitches that look like pin stitching, entredeux, or faggotting. You will be amazed at what your wing needle can do.

The "simulated yoke" looks to be tucked. Just think, without the convenience of modern machinery, yesterday's woman had to spend hours making her tucks straight. With a double needle, or better still, the magic pintuck foot, we can make pintucks in a fraction of the time.

circa 1904

7182 Girls' Dress, with Scalloped or Plain Bertha, and with Attached Full Skirt having Tucks or a wide Hem at the Lower Edge. 10 Sizes: 3-12 Years. Price, 15 cents. 5-1/8 yards of material 27 inches wide, or 4 yards 36 inches wide, with 3/8 yard of tucking 18 inches wide for collar and simulating yoke, are required.

Diamond Skirt Antique Pattern

Lace shaping appears to ornament this gored skirt. My guess would be that velvet ribbon, not lace, was actually the recommended trim. However, if the skirt were made of spring or summer weight fabric, lace could have been used. Shaped diamonds with connecting lace running parallel to the floor, establish a tailored finish at the bottom of this skirt. Translated into today's French garments, these ideas would make a beautiful skirt with minimal frills. These diamonds, made smaller of course, would be just as pretty on the bodice or sleeves of a dress. A delicate Chinese handkerchief or a tucking strip, peeking from the center of each diamond, would be a sweet accent.

circa, 1894

5538 Nine Gored Skirt, 22-30 waist. 13-1/3 yards of material 27 inches wide, 6-1/4 yards of 44 inches wide.

Pointed V Antique Dress

The subtle styling on this design would see even the most finicky pre-teen through the winter months. This dress has deep, V-shaped lace at center front as well as on both sides of the collar. Laces are mitered in all of the V's. The laces are straight and embellish the sleeves and the high neckline. The separated V looks to be a distant cousin of the sailor collar. The large sleeves, so popular during the turn of the century, are trimmed at the cuff with three rows of straight lace. The same three rows of lace or braid grace the neckline. This design would delight in red and navy wool plaid from Scotland with red grosgrain ribbon for the trim. Opt for dusty rose velveteen with heavy burgundy braid for special occasion dressing.

To make one of these divided collars, simply draft your pattern for a large bertha. Then score the collar in the shape you desire; in this case the design is almost a square, which is taken out of the front of the collar. Experiment with collar drafting. It's quite easy and lots of fun. Who knows? You may be the next May Minton!

circa, 1894

7256 Girls' Dress with Attached Full Skirt. 9 Sizes: 4-12 Years. Price, 15 cents. 5-3/8 yards of material 27 inches wide, or 3-7/8 yards 36 inches wide, or 3-5/8 yards 44 inches wide, are required.

Misses' Curved V Lace Shaped Antique Dress

The skirt on this dress absolutely takes my breath away, yet it would be simple to recreate. The top layer of the ruffle is pointed: the bottom layer of the ruffle is straight. Shaped lace could be mitered or flip-flopped. The ruffle treatment at the skirt bottom could translate into a peplum/skirt combination.

The collar would suit a blouse or a high yoke dress, such as the "To-The-Waist" dress pattern contained in this book or the middy dresses. Here is an idea! Using the "To-The-Waist" pattern or the blouse pattern, curve the laces and entredeux around the neckline and zigzag right onto the bodice or blouse. Gather the collar and attach it. You could also make a separate collar using the directions for the round portrait collar found in this section.

The sleeves are longer in the back than in the front, hanging almost like a jabot when viewed from behind. Two pieces of insertion trim the neckline, the sleeves, the bottom of the skirt, and the bottom of the ruffle. Laces on this dress are curved, angular, and straight — it's the epitome of a shaped lace antique dress.

When I think of fabrics for French dresses, I rarely think of prints. However, this dress would delight in a prins. Darker color combinations would be appropriate for colder climates unlike pastels, which are only worn by babies during winter months.

circa, 1894

6703 Misses' Costume: consisting of a Waist, with High or Dutch Round Neck, and Full-Length or Elbow Fancy Sleeves; and a Five-Gored Flare Skirt, with an Inverted Box-Pleat or Gathers at the Back. The skirt measures about 3-1/2 yards at the lower edge in the middle sizes. Four Sizes 14-17 Years. Price, 25 cents. 11 yards of material 27 inches wide, or 9 yards 36 inches wide, are required.

What a collar! What a skirt! This curved V neckline is called a Pointed Dutch neckline! The closed-neck version uses the curved V neckline, which is the perfect complement to the curved V shapes on the rest of the collar. Knowing from history that white dresses were typically made for graduation ceremonies, I can just imagine this dress made for some lucky young lady's special day. The skirt employs the true V shaping; lace shapes travel into the gathers on the skirt. Two rows of straight insertion on the neckline, the sleeves, and the skirt complete this elegant dress.

6822 Misses' Costume: consisting of a Waist, with a High or Pointed Dutch or Low Neck and Full or Three-Quarter Length Sleeves; and a Five-Gored Flare Skirt, with an Inverted Box-Pleat or Gathers at the Back, and a Gathered Circular Flounce. The skirt measures about 3-1/4 yards at the lower edge in the middle sizes. 4 Sizes 14-17 Years. Price, 25 Cents. 8-1/2 yard of material 27 inches wide are required.

circa, 1894

Pyramids and Diamonds Antique Dress

Notice the pyramids or columns that gradually decrease in size on this garment. The all-over embroidery appears to have been cut and turned back to make this shape; however, any wide insertion could be used this way. The all-over embroidered fabric has been shaped and topstitched onto the blouse extending onto the sleeves. One of the first things I notice about this dress is the use of lace insertion diamonds embroidered in the center. Diamonds are staggered on the ruffle of the skirt and appear again on the sleeves of the dress. I don't believe I have ever seen insertion set into the the very bottom of a dress. If you need to add length to a garment, perhaps when you let out your hem, you could simply cover the raw edge with insertion. Since children grow so fast, I am constantly thinking of ways to get extra years of wear out of the garments.

circa, 1894

6748 Misses' Costume: consisting of a Yoke Waist, with High or Round Neck, and Full or Three-Quarter Length Sleeves or Cap Sleeves; and a Five-Gored Skirt, with a Gathered Flounce, and an Inverted Box-Pleat or Gathers at the Back. The skirt measures about 3-1/2 yards at the foot in the middle. Sizes 14-17 years. Price 25 cents.

9 yards of material 27 inches wide, or 7-1/8 yards 36 inches wide, with 1-1/8 yard of all-over embroidery 18 inches wide for yoke, caps, and wristbands, are required.

Lace Shaping 231

Double Lace Scalloped Collar Antique Dress

Scallops, dancing around the edge of a collar or hem, enhance any dress; this design is no exception. The scooped neckline, filled with curved laces, is a delightful companion. Straight insertion quietly finishes the skirt. I envision the short-sleeved dress in lavender Swiss batiste or pink dotted Swiss with generous use of French insertion and wide lace to match. The long-sleeved version calls for black taffeta or water-stained brocade, trimmed with ecru insertions and a wide edging. Notice the curved insertion around the neckline of the long-sleeved version.

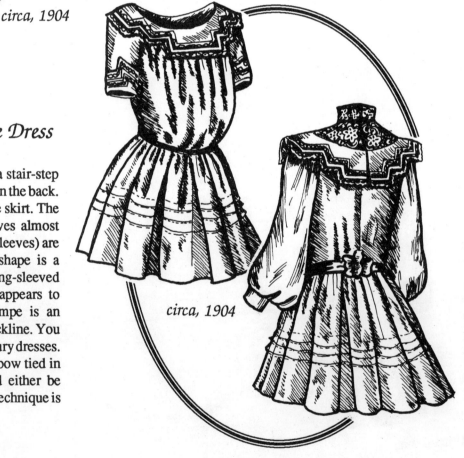

circa, 1904

6739 Girls' Dress with or without the Yoke and Body Lining, and with Full-Length or Elbow Bishop Sleeves and an Attached Five-Gored Skirt. 9 Sizes: 6-14 Years. Price 20 cents. 4-7/8 yards of material 27 inches wide, or 3-5/8 yards 36 inches wide, or 3 yards 44 inches wide, are required.

Tailored Square Lace Antique Dress

This dress has a square lace design, in a stair-step configuration up over the shoulder and down the back. The wide tucks are a simple addition to the skirt. The lace treatment on the short, straight sleeves almost forms a Z shape. The bishop sleeves (long sleeves) are free of embellishment, given that their shape is a strong design element in itself. In the long-sleeved version, an all-over embroidered fabric appears to have been used for the guimpe. A guimpe is an underblouse that peaks out of a lowered neckline. You will find guimpes in many turn-of-the-century dresses. Notice the smartly tailored, triple section bow tied in the back. The laces on this collar could either be mitered or flip-flopped, although the later technique is easier to do.

circa, 1904

6880 Girls' Dress, with Tucks or Gathers in the Top of the Front, with or without the Bertha, Body Lining, Cap Sleeves or Guimpe, and with Attached Full Skirt. 8 Sizes: 5-12 Years. Price 20 cents. For the dress, 3 yards of material 44 inches wide; for the guimpe, 1-1/2 yards of nainsook 36 inches wide, with 5/8 yard of all-over embroidery 18 inches wide for collar and simulating yoke, are required.

Reverse Scalloped Antique Dress

I had never seen a reverse scallop on a dress until I came across this dress pattern. I was curious also about the long sleeves with so much fullness in the back and less in the front, until reading the pattern description. They are now, and I suppose forever, called "Bishop Sleeves." Two rows of insertion are shaped and mitered, with the point at center front. Wide lace trims the sleeves and collar. If you do not have lace this wide, you could use a fabric ruffle with lace on the edge or several rows of insertion, butted together, with edging attached on the very edge. The dress appears to be made of a delicate batiste print; the wide silk sash completes the look.

circa, 1894

6951 Girls' Dress, with High or Round Neck and Bishop or Puff Sleeves, and with or without the Body Lining, and with an Attached Full Skirt. 10 Sizes: 3-12 Years. Price, 20 cents. 5-3/4 yards of material 27 inches wide, or 4-1/8 yard 36 inches wide, or 3-1/2 yards 4 inches wide, are required.

Round Yoke And Tucked Middy

This tailored garment's principle feature is the circular use of lace shaping on the yoke. The five little tucks on either side of the bodice are repeated in a section for the belt to ride through. The tucks are sweet underneath the short cap sleeve. Three more tucks trim the otherwise plain skirt. Round insertion trims the yoke as well as the bottom of the cap sleeve and the cuff of the dress. I envision this dress in navy wool, heavy ecru laces, and an ecru organdy sash. For warmer weather, this dress would be pretty in a print with delicate white or ecru laces. Medium weight antique green silk would lend itself beautifully to white laces and a darker green silk sash. Also lovely - ecru wool challis with heavy ecru laces tied with a peach silk sash.

circa, 1904

7517 Little Girls' Tucked Dress, Closed at the Back, with Body and Skirt in One, and Inverted Fullness Below the Belt at the Side and Centre-Back Seams, and, with or without the Yoke, Sleeve-Caps, Sash or French Waist-Line Tucks. Sizes 1-9 Years, Price, 15 Cents.

3 1/2 yards of material 27 inches wide, or 2 5/8 yards 36 inches wide; with 3/8 yard of tucking 18 inches wide for yoke, are required.

New Entredeux Techniques

Chapter Nine

Entredeux and its
functional and
decorative uses.

Entredeux, the ladder-shaped stabilizer of debatable pronunciation, is nothing new to heirloom sewing. It has been made in Switzerland since the mid 1800s. Quite of few of my antique garments have entredeux incorporated into the design, both functionally and decoratively. Hand attachment was the technique used through the beginning of this century, due to the newness and scarcity of the sewing machine.

As I took apart little sections of my antique garments, I uncovered several methods of attaching entredeux, some of which aren't practical today because of our advanced sewing equipment. Others, such as the "exposed seam allowance of the entredeux," were new ways to use entredeux as trim. I never considered leaving the seam allowance on the entredeux as part of the garment until I started research on this book. On my antique pieces it looks as if little ribbons were inserted between the holes of the entredeux and the next layer which was attached to the entredeux. This particular use of entredeux created what I refer to as an "exposed seam allowance;" this and other methods are described below.

In deciding which of these new methods you want to use in your next French sewing project, try out each one with scraps of fabric and entredeux. See what you like and don't like; then develop your own use. I have indicated which methods were the exact antique methods and which were adaptations.

Exposed Entredeux Seam Allowance Method-To Flat Lace

Several new entredeux methods are in evidence on the antique dresses I collected from three different parts of the world. The first one appears to be a tiny strip of fabric ribbon between the entredeux and the lace. Try this new technique on your next fancy band. Ours is an adaptation of an antique method, but looks almost identical when finished.

Directions:
1. Do not trim entredeux (Fig. 1).
2. Place the lace on top of the entredeux. Leave a tiny seam (about 1/8 inch) of entredeux seam allowance exposed (Fig. 2).
3. Using the technique "Lace Flat Edge To Fabric," zigzag the lace to the fabric seam allowance of the entredeux (Width=3, Length=1/2) Fig. 3.
4. When you finish you will have a narrow strip of fabric between the entredeux and the lace insertion (Fig. 4).

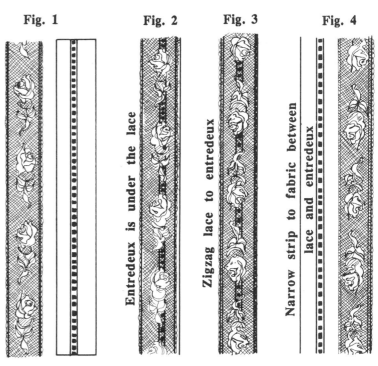

Fig. 1   Fig. 2   Fig. 3   Fig. 4

Entredeux is under the lace

Zigzag lace to entredeux

Narrow strip to fabric between lace and entredeux

Exposed Entredeux Seam Allowance Method-To Flat Fabric-Method I

This method allows a lot of precision since you first make a flat stitch before you zigzag to roll and whip the edge of the fabric. It takes a little longer; however, if you want that perfect look, you probably will want to use this method when adding entredeux to flat fabric. Try it. This method is an adaptation of an antique method.

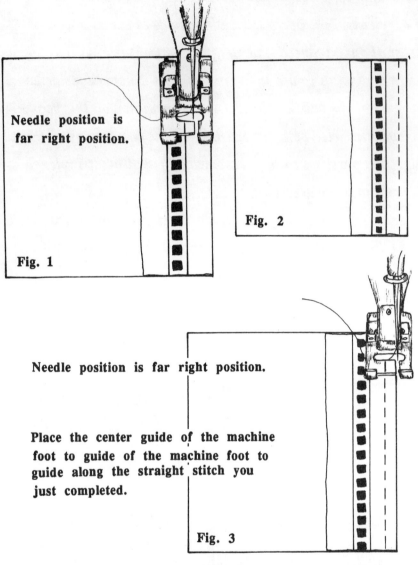

Needle position is far right position.

Fig. 1

Fig. 2

Needle position is far right position.

Place the center guide of the machine foot to guide of the machine foot to guide along the straight stitch you just completed.

Fig. 3

Directions:

1. Place the edge of the entredeux flush with the side of the fabric.
2. Make a straight-stitch by using the all-purpose foot to guide along the right-hand side of the fabric. In other words, place the right side of the foot even with the right side of the exposed fabric and entredeux edge. Put the needle position to FAR RIGHT (Fig. 1).
3. Straight-stitch (Length=2-1/2), making a straight-stitch along the strip (Fig. 2).
4. You are now ready to zigzag this raw edge (roll and whip). This next step is very important. Place the center guide-mark on your sewing machine foot where it will guide along the straight-stitch that you just made (Fig. 3). Place your needle in FAR RIGHT position. Set your zigzag width on 3 and your length on 1. (Width=3, Length=1) The reason for this is, with the needle in far right position and the center guide of your foot running down the straight-stitch that you just made, the zigzag will roll and whip the edge of the fabric and go over JUST BARELY to touch the straight-stitch. Zigzag the raw edge to finish (Fig. 4).
5. When you open the entredeux and the fabric, you will have a perfect finish and a little seam allowance of the entredeux will be there (Fig. 5).
6. I might add here that this technique can certainly be done faster and perfectly on your serger using the rolled hem foot.

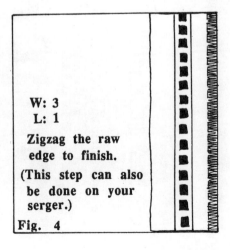

W: 3
L: 1
Zigzag the raw edge to finish.
(This step can also be done on your serger.)
Fig. 4

When you open your seam a tiny seam allowance of the entredeux will still be showing.

Fig. 5

Exposed Entredeux Seam Allowance Method-To Flat Fabric-Method II

This method leaves a tiny strip of the seam allowance of the entredeux exposed, adding length to your dress and leaving the entredeux clearly showing. This method is wonderful when you are adding entredeux to a handloom of Swiss embroidery; it takes practically no width off the expensive handloom. This method is an adaptation of an antique method.

Directions:

1. Place the entredeux to the fabric, right sides to right sides. Leave a 1/8-inch seam allowance of fabric (or Swiss handloom) exposed (Fig. 1).
2. Zigzag the seam allowance of the entredeux to the exposed edge of the fabric (Fig. 2).
3. When you open this up, you can see that a small seam allowance of the entredeux is showing (Fig. 3).
4. This method can be done quickly and perfectly on your serger using the rolled hem foot.

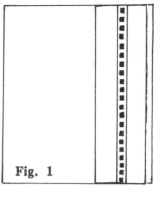

Fig. 1

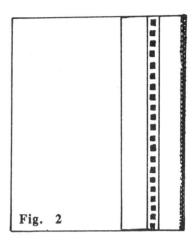

Fig. 2

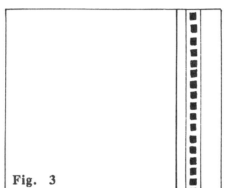

Fig. 3

Entredeux To Flat Lace — Fold And Sew Method (Double Straight-Stitch Finish)

This method is exactly like the method on some of the antique clothing. It has a little seam allowance showing underneath the lace. You fold the seam allowance of the entredeux back and press. Then using double needles or running a double stitch, stitch straight to the lace. This is an exact copy of the techniques used in the antique sewing method.

Directions:

1. You will need entredeux and lace insertion (Fig. 1).
2. Press back half of your seam allowance on the entredeux (Fig. 2). It has now gone from a 1/2-inch seam allowance to a 1/4-inch seam allowance.
3. Place the lace insertion on top of the right side of the seam allowance. Butt your lace insertion up to the holes on the entredeux. Your entredeux now has a right and wrong side since you pressed the seam allowance to the wrong side (Fig. 3).
4. Stitching from the front, make a straight-stitch very close to the ditch of the entredeux (Length=3) Fig. 3.
5. Moving your needle position to FAR RIGHT or simply guiding your needle, make another straight-stitch almost to the edge of the folded entredeux allowance (Fig. 3).

Fig. 1 Fig. 2 Fig. 3

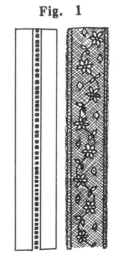

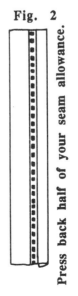

Press back half of your seam allowance.

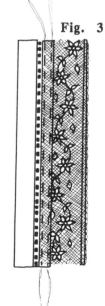

New Entredeux Techniques 237

Entredeux To Flat Lace-Fold And Sew Method (Zigzag Finish)

This method looks like you have a tiny binding or tiny ribbon between your entredeux and your lace flat edge. It is beautiful! It is different! This method is a copy of an antique method; although it can't be any older than the zigzag sewing machine.

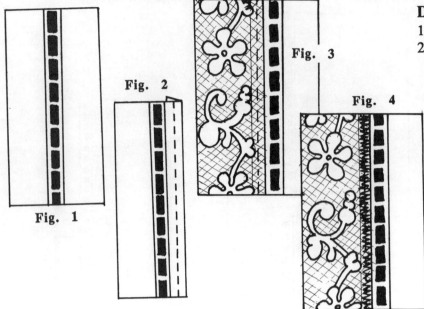

Fig. 1

Fig. 2

Fig. 3

Fig. 4

Directions:
1. Press entredeux flat (Fig. 1).
2. Fold half of the seam allowance of the entredeux down by finger-pressing as you stitch it with a straight-stitch on the machine (Fig. 2). Here is the easiest way to do this. Make a straight-stitch (Length =3) all the way down the folded seam allowance of your entredeux. I have tried this several ways including pressing before I make this straight-stitch. I believe it is easier to fold the 1/2-inch seam allowance in half (down to 1/4 inch), and stitch at the same time. I think to try to press it first is the hardest way. Let me rephrase this technique. As you finger-press half of the seam allowance back, make the straight-stitch (Length=3) Fig 2. When you have finished the strip of entredeux, it is half as wide as it originally was and has a straight seam down the middle of the seam allowance.
3. Place the lace insertion on top of the right side of the entredeux. Your entredeux now has a right and wrong side because the seam allowance has been stitched under to the wrong side. Place the heading of your lace all the way over to the ditch of the entredeux (Fig. 3).
4. Zigzag the lace insertion to the seam allowance you have just made (Width=1-1/2, Length=2) Fig. 4. You can play with the width and length of your stitch if you want to. Do not make the stitch so wide that it will roll in your seam allowance and your lace. You want them to stitch flat and straight.

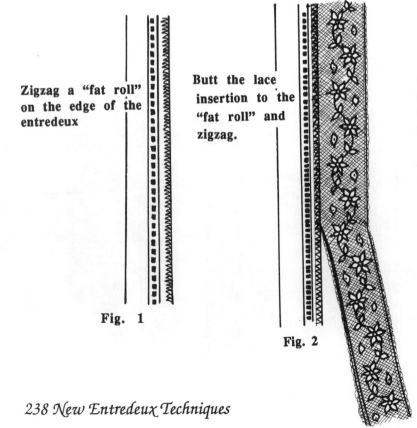

Zigzag a "fat roll" on the edge of the entredeux

Butt the lace insertion to the "fat roll" and zigzag.

Fig. 1

Fig. 2

Fat Roll Entredeux To Flat Lace

This method gives a very unusual effect. It looks almost like you have a ribbon running between the entredeux seam allowance and the edging. It adds texture and looks antique without the antique methods. This method is a copy of the antique method.

Directions:
1. Using the widest setting on your sewing machine (Width=5 or wider, Length=3/4), roll the outside edges of the entredeux. Be certain that this zigzagged edge comes only to approximately the half-way mark on your entredeux. Some of the entredeux seam allowance will still show after your "fat roll" is finished. This makes a "fat roll" finish on the very edge of the entredeux (Fig. 1).
2. Trim any bad fuzzies; don't worry about little fuzzies!
3. Butt your lace straight edge to the "fat roll" seam and zigzag the two together (Width=2-1/2, Length= 1-1/2) Fig. 2.

Antique Swiss Pique Coat Method of Entredeux Attachment To Flat Fabric

On the antique Swiss pique coat, the entredeux used on the edges of the Swiss embroidered white-on-white trim was attached in an unusual way. This method was used to attach entredeux to both flat and gathered fabric. Instead of cutting off the entredeux edge, it was folded back, leaving a 1/4-inch seam allowance. Then it was stitched down twice with double rows of stitching going directly onto the raw edge of the pique collar. Entredeux was mitered to go around the corners. For the gathered ruffle, the folded down batiste seam allowance (1/4 inch) of the Swiss trim was placed right on top of the raw edge of the gathered ruffle and stitched twice. Don't be shocked when the directions given below ask you to stitch on the raw fabric! It's O.K. when you are going to put this much stitching in it. The meticulous sewer may prefer to roll and whip the edges before placing the folded back Swiss trim down on the edge! But remember, this antique coat was made exactly like these directions imply! This technique is an exact copy of the methods used in the antique coat.

Directions:

1. Press down the seam allowance of your entredeux or Swiss trim. It should now measure 1/4 inch (Fig. 1).
2. Place the seam allowance of thre entredeux (or Swiss trim edged with entredeux) on the right side of the raw edge of the garment. If you prefer, you can finish the edge before you place this allowance on it (Fig. 2).
3. Stitch, using a very short stitch, as closely to the entredeux as you can. You are stitching from the right side of the garment (Length=2-1/2) Fig. 3.
4. Stitch again as closely to the outside folded edge of the entredeux as you can stitch without going off of the fabric (Length=2-1/2) Fig. 3.

Antique Swiss Pique Coat

1/4"

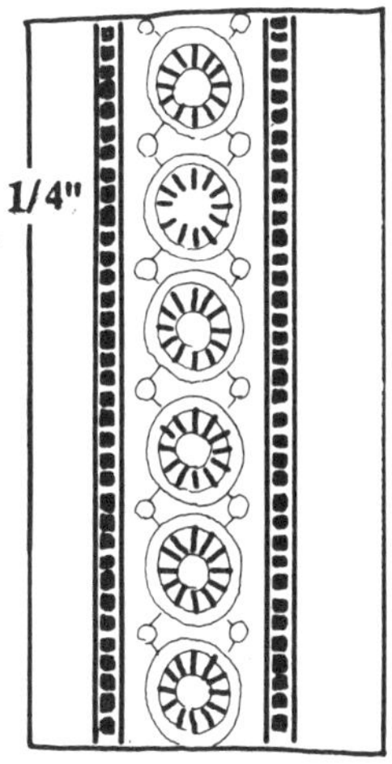

Press down
seam allowance.

Fig. 1

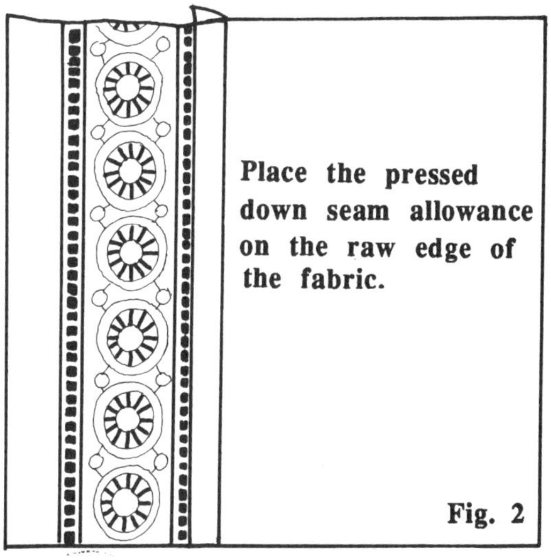

Place the pressed
down seam allowance
on the raw edge of
the fabric.

Fig. 2

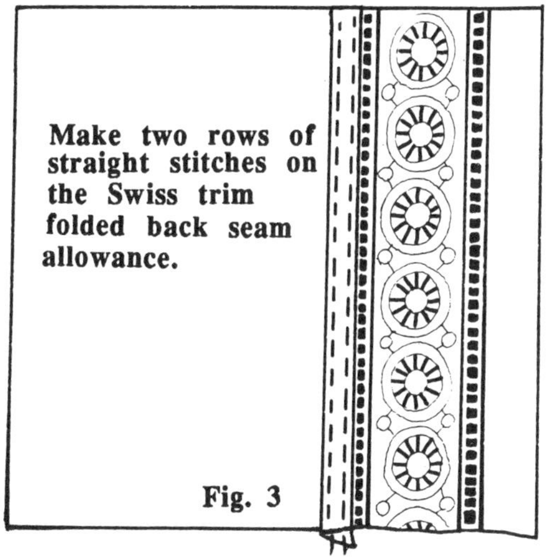

Make two rows of
straight stitches on
the Swiss trim
folded back seam
allowance.

Fig. 3

Antique Swiss Pique Coat Method of Entredeux Attachment To Gathered Fabric

This technique is the gathered version of the one just presented. The techniques given are exactly as they were used in the construction of the antique coat.

Directions:

1. Press down the seam allowance of the entredeux on the Swiss trim. It should now measure 1/4 inch, as illustrated in step 1 of "Antique Swiss Pique Coat Method of Entredeux Attachment to Flat Fabric" introduced on the previous page.
2. Gather the Swiss trim with two rows of gathering stitches placed as closely to the edge of the Swiss trim as you can place them (Fig. 1).
3. Place the folded-back seam allowance of your Swiss insertion on the right side of the gathered Swiss edging trim. The gathered Swiss edging trim will have a raw edge (Fig. 2).
4. Stitching from the right side of the garment, stitch one row of straight stitches using a short length (Length=1 to 1-1/2). This row will be close to the outside edge of the folded-back seam allowance of the Swiss trim, not close to the entredeux (Fig. 3).
5. Stitch again on the other side of the seam allowance as close to the ditch of the entredeux as you can stitch (Fig.3).
6. If there are fuzzies covering the holes of the entredeux, trim them VERY CAREFULLY!

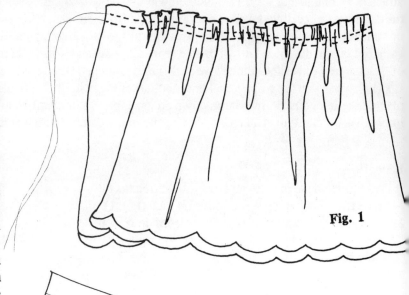

Fig. 1

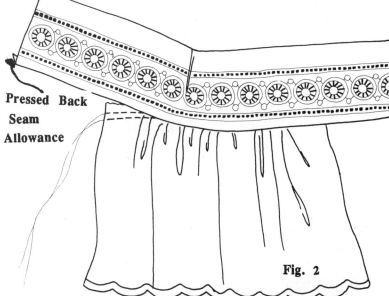

Pressed Back Seam Allowance

Fig. 2

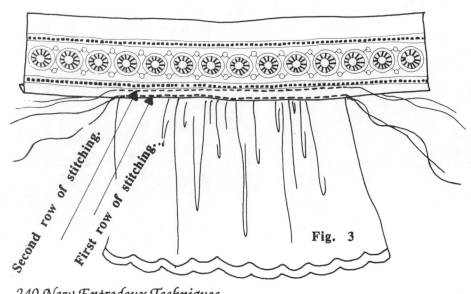

Second row of stitching.

First row of stitching.

Fig. 3

Gathering Foot To Attach Entredeux and Gather At The Same Time

I have experimented and experimented with the gathering foot to try to make gathering and attaching entredeux at the same time work. I think I have now perfected it enough to say that it will work perfectly if you use it for a ruffle. I have never made it work perfectly enough to use for the second side of puffing. It seems to gather more where the puffing comes out longer on one side. For ruffles, you may still need to practice a little; however, I have probably practiced enough for all of us to relate to you the techniques below. Please follow my instructions carefully because there are a few tricks.

Directions:

1. **Do not starch ruffle. Just press it.** Starching the ruffle fabric makes it too stiff and it does not gather well.
2. **Starch entredeux very stiff.** Starching the entredeux makes it easier to handle.
3. Set length on 3. If you want more fullness, set length on 4 or 5; however, I like a gathering length of 3.
4. Leave the tension on regular tension.
5. **Sew very slowly. This is not a time to speed up.** You are saving a whole step of sewing by using this gathering foot. You can speed up after you get comfortable with this technique; however, it is a little tricky when you sew fast or even at your regular sewing speed.
6. Place the fabric under the foot, lined up with the edge of the gathering foot.
7. Place the entredeux into the slot of the gathering foot.
8. Place the needle in FAR LEFT position. That will mean that you can leave the entredeux shoved all the way over into the slot of the foot; the needle stitches the entredeux right beside the holes of the entredeux.
9. Slowly begin to sew.
10. Look at the illustration. Using your left fingers, guide the fabric straight into the sewing machine, never letting it pull to the left or right. Keep the fabric edge in direct line with the right-hand side of the gathering foot. Watch this carefully.
11. Pull the entredeux over to the right with your right hand. Keep your eyes on two things: 1) The fabric's being guided straight, in line with the right-hand side of the gathering foot. 2) The needle's hitting the entredeux right next to the embroidered "railroad tracks" of the entredeux.

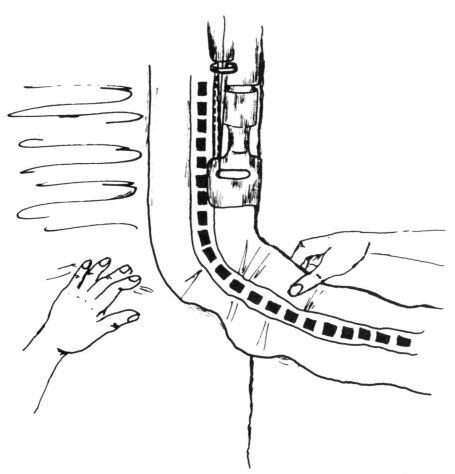

New French Sewing Techniques

Chapter Ten

Add these techniques to your French sewing library.

Quilted French Dress Skirt

An antique petticoat inspired the design for this French skirt. Since this is one of my English pieces, I imagine a London lady quilting her petticoat for warmth. Or perhaps she simply loved to quilt and wanted to embellish her undergarments. Whatever the reason, it is a clever use of quilting. This technique can be used on a skirt of a dress or high yoke, on a skirt, or on a petticoat.

Fabrics To Use:
1. Heavy Swiss batiste (Finissima — "Laura Ashley" batiste), Imperial batiste, or Imperial broadcloth
2. Swiss wide edging for the bottom ruffle
3. Baby quilt batting or other lightweight batting

Directions:
1. Cut two skirt or slip layers. One is the skirt (Fig. 1) and one is the lining (Fig. 2).
2. Cut a ruffle strip 1-1/2 times as long as the bottom of the finished skirt (Fig. 3). This is where you will use Swiss wide edging.
3. Run two rows of gathering threads in the top of the ruffle.
4. Gather and distribute the ruffle.
5. Stitch both side seams of the skirt and both side seams of the lining. Both of these are now circles. Stitch the ruffle into a circle also (Fig. 4).
6. Baste the ruffle onto the skirt with right sides together.
7. Place the right side of the lining to the right side of the skirt. (The ruffle will be between these two layers.) You will not be able to see the ruffle (Fig. 5).
8. Stitch the lining to the skirt/ruffle along the bottom edge (Fig. 5).
9. Allow the ruffle and the lining to fall below the skirt. In other words, open up the garment.
10. Baste the batting on the wrong side of the skirt along the upper and lower edge. I have chosen to place the batting just above the seam allowance (Fig. 6).
11. Pull the lining over the skirt to enclose the batting.
12. Stitch together (machine quilt) the lining, the skirt, and the batting. The design you stitch is up to you. The one on the antique skirt is in squares. You can stitch hearts, lines, squares, triangles — whatever your preference.
13. If your design does not stitch the top edge batting into place, you must stitch (quilt) the batting to the skirt, otherwise when the skirt is washed, the batting will slip and clump.
14. Baste the top edges of the lining and the skirt together.
15. To placket the back, simply cut down through both layers and treat as one layer of fabric.

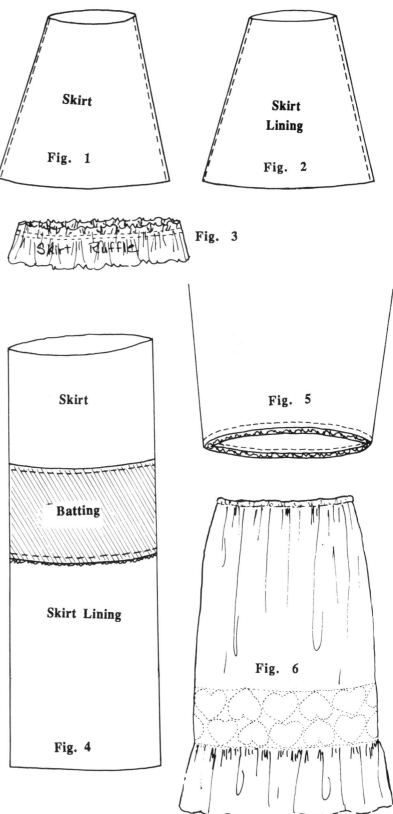

Skirt — Fig. 1

Skirt Lining — Fig. 2

Skirt Ruffle — Fig. 3

Skirt / Batting / Skirt Lining — Fig. 4

Fig. 5

Fig. 6

Cutting And Joining Bias Strips

A true bias is made when fabric strips are cut at 45 degree angles. Heirloom sewing calls for bias strips in bindings, piping, ruffles, and trims. Bias pipings, binds, and trims are absolutely beautiful in plaids or stripes. Any fabric that might need to be shaped into a curve, as in piping around a collar, looks best when the fabric is bias. The ideal bias is cut in one strip without a seam. However, sometimes the strip called for by the pattern is longer than can be cut from one piece of fabric. In this case, you will have to join bias strips.

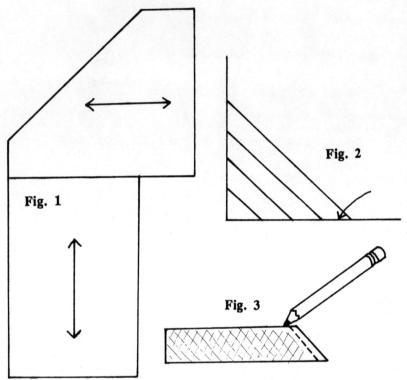

Fig. 1

Fig. 2

Fig. 3

Directions for Cutting Bias Strips:
1. Take a rectangular piece of fabric cut on the straight of grain. Fold it diagonally to find the true bias (Fig. 1).
2. Using the bias fold as a guide, mark your fabric with parallel lines in the width you desire for your ruffles or your bindings. A true bias is a 45 degree angle (Fig. 2). Take care to add fabric for seams if you are making bias ruffles.
3. Cut your bias strips (Fig. 2).

Directions for Joining Bias Strips:
1. The ends will appear to be diagonal.
2. Mark a seam line on these "diagonal ends," which is 1/4 inch from the edge (Fig. 3).
3. Match the lines, which you have just drawn, not the cut edges of the strip. Pin and stitch the pieces together (Fig. 4).
4. Open up your strip. Press (Fig. 5).
5. Trim away the overlapped edges (Fig. 6).

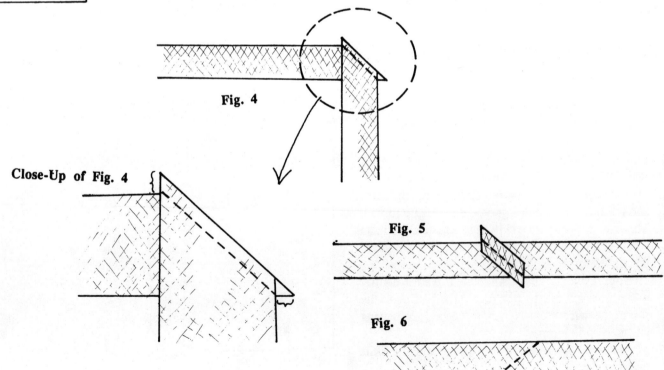

Fig. 4

Close-Up of Fig. 4

Fig. 5

Fig. 6

The Gorgeous Antique Triple Ruffle

The turn-of-the-century skirt from my antique collection called "Lady's Silk Triple Ruffle Skirt" inspired the following techniques. I've listed several ways to make the three-layer, bottom ruffle.

Directions for Technique I
Three Ruffles the Same Length

1. Finish the lower edge of the dress with a rolled-and-whipped edge. It will not show at all after the ruffle is attached. You can also turn up a double turn of 1/4 inch and stitch by machine to finish the bottom of the hidden skirt.

2. Cut three ruffles. Each ruffle will be 6 inches to 8 inches wide. Each ruffle will be two times the width of your skirt or dress skirt bottom. For example, if your dress is a high yoke "Heirloom Party Dress," you will probably have 45 inches in the front skirt and 45 inches in the back skirt. Your ruffle strips will be four strips of 45-inch fabric (6 inches or 8 inches wide), stitched or serged together. You will need three of these ruffle strips (Fig. 1).

3. Stitch your ruffle circles together by seaming, French seaming, or serging. You now have three circles 180 inches around. These are your three ruffles (Fig. 2).

4. To finish the bottom of each these ruffles, you have several options:
   a. Use the rolled hem foot or shirttail hem foot for your sewing machine. This is probably the easiest way.
   b. Turn up 1/4 inch and press. Turn it up again another 1/4 inch and press. Run a straight-stitch to hem.
   c. Turn up 1/4 inch and press. Turn up a 1-inch hem and hem, using your hemming foot to put in a traditional hem.
   d. Serge around the bottom and turn up the serged edge. Stitch in a straight hem on your sewing machine.

5. To finish the top of the ruffles:
   a. Use the rolled hem foot or shirttail hem foot on your sewing machine. This is probably the easiest way.
   b. Turn up 1/4 inch and press. Turn up again another 1/4 inch and press. Run a straight-stitch to hem.
   c. Serge around the bottom and turn up the serged edge. Stitch in a straight hem on your sewing machine.

6. Your ruffles are now hemmed, individually, on both the top and the bottom edges (Fig. 3).

7. These three ruffles are now going to be basted together to form one ruffle (Fig. 4). This attachment will be done with the first gathering row. This first gathering row will be 1/2 inch from the top edge of the ruffle. It is best to put quilting thread in the bobbin in order to assure that this triple-row gathering doesn't break when you are gathering and distributing the ruffles (Fig. 5).

8. Using a long basting stitch, run another row of gathering stitches. This second row will be 1/8 inch below the first row, which was 1/2 inch from the top of your ruffles.

Directions continued on next page.

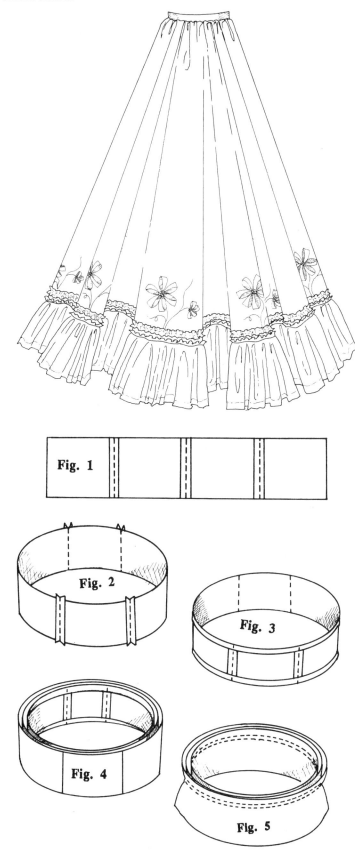

Fig. 1

Fig. 2

Fig. 3

Fig. 4

Fig. 5

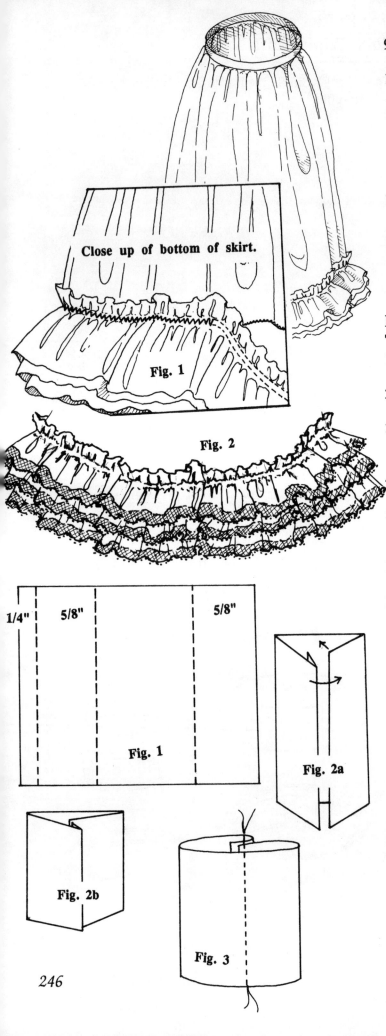

Close up of bottom of skirt.

Fig. 1

Fig. 2

1/4"   5/8"   5/8"

Fig. 1

Fig. 2a

Fig. 2b

Fig. 3

9. You now have three ruffle strips to gather and attach as if they were one row of ruffle.
10. Gather to fit the bottom of the skirt. Place the ruffle on top of the skirt, allowing the finished edge of the skirt to fall 1/4 inch below the two gathering rows in the ruffle. Pin. Remember, the wrong side of the inside ruffle will be laying on the right side of the skirt. The three gathered, finished edges of the top of this triple ruffle will be exposed on the outside of the skirt.
11. Stitch the ruffle to the skirt with a zigzag stitch (Length=2, Width=2). Fig. 1.
12. If you prefer, make two parallel straight stitches to hold on the ruffle. It will require a little width of the stitching (either zigzag or two rows of straight-stitching) to hold the three ruffles properly.

Directions for Technique II
Three-Tiered Variation With Lace Edging

1. Follow the techniques in Technique I, with the following exceptions.
2. Cut the ruffles three different lengths, according to the width of lace edging that will be put on the ruffle edge (Fig. 2).
3. For instance, if you are using 1-inch lace and you want a wide triple ruffle, cut one of your ruffles 8 inches, one 7 inches, and one 6 inches.
4. Using the technique "Attaching Lace Edging To Flat Fabric Edge," attach lace edging to the bottom of all three ruffles.
5. Finish the top edges and finish the ruffles exactly like Technique I, given just prior to this technique.

Directions for Bias Ruffle Above Triple Ruffle

This bias ruffle was situated above the triple ruffle on the lady's skirt. It is made of silk; however, Swiss or domestic batiste would work beautifully.

1. Cut 2-1/2-inch bias strips 1-1/2 times the desired length of your skirt or dress skirt. Join the individual bias strips with the technique given in "Cutting And Joining Bias Strips." If your skirt is 90 inches around, you will need a 135-inch piece of bias, 2-1/2 inches wide.
2. Press down 1/4 inch, **on one side only.** Press down again, this time (on this same side) 5/8 inch. In other words, on one side of this bias strip you press down 1/4 inch and then another 5/8 inch, which encompasses the 1/4 inch you first pressed down (Fig. 1).
3. Press down 5/8 inch on the other side of the bias strip (Figs. 2 and 2-b).
4. Stitching from the outside, run gathering stitches down the center of this strip (Fig. 3).
5. Gather to fit the skirt.
6. Stitch the gathered bias strip onto the skirt with a straight-stitch over the gathering stitches.

246

Making Cotton Netting Ruffles or Lace

On several of my antique dresses and on one of my bonnets, gathered double ruffles of netting were used instead of lace edging. One of the most beautiful garments I have ever seen, a high yoke organdy dress, was on a Simon and Halbig 119 Doll, dated 1880. The ruffle around the yoke was made of netting, edged with a narrow French lace. The ruffle around the three-quarter-length sleeves was netting, edged with the same French edging. Tucks and insertion embellished the bodice. The rest of the dress was plain organdy. The design would be just as elegant on a little girl as it was on the antique doll.

Directions:

1. For baby edging, which is finished to about a 5/8-inch width, cut 1-1/2-inch pieces of netting. This width of netting ruffle edging is used on an antique baby bonnet. Five of these strips embellish the crown.
2. Fold these strips in half. For fullness, you will need twice the length of netting that you want your finished pieces to be. You don't have to use exactly this much fullness; however, you don't want your netting pieces to run short. It is better to cut off and discard some than it is run out.
3. Cut strips of quilting thread longer than the lengths of netting. Use quilting thread the same color of the netting, which will probably be either white or ecru.
4. Lay the quilting thread in, 1/8 inch from the cut edges of this folded netting (Fig. 1).
5. Zigzag (Width=5, Length=4) to enclose the quilting thread in the zigzagged casing or overcasting of the raw edges of the netting (Fig. 2).
6. Pull the quilting thread to gather the netting to the fullness you want for your ruffle trim (Fig. 3).
7. To attach this netting ruffle or edging to your garment, straight-stitch as close to the rolled edge (between the rolled edge and the ruffle) as you can.
8. To make wider netting ruffles, follow the same technique, just cut wide pieces a little more than double the final width or your netting ruffle.

Lay the quilting thread in 1/8" from the cut edges of this folded netting.

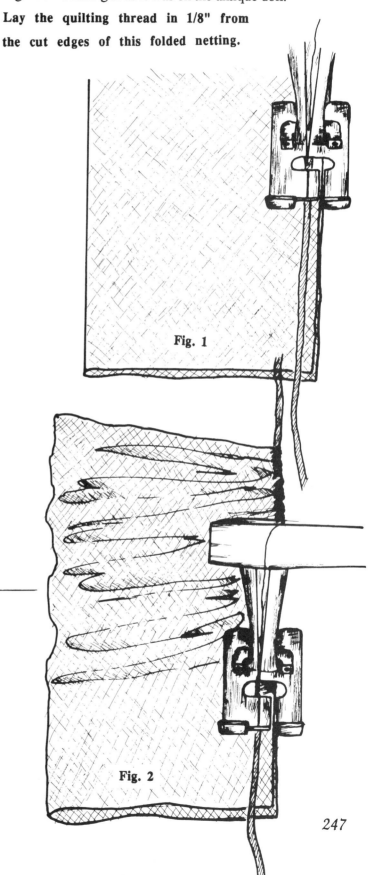

Fig. 1

Fig. 2

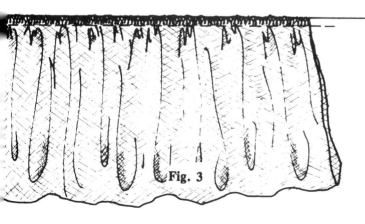

Fig. 3

247

Cutting Fabric Away From Behind Laces
That Have Been Shaped and Zigzagged To The Fabric

I recommend two pairs of Gingher scissors for cutting away fabric from behind stitched laces. One is the "Duck Bill" or applique scissors. The "Duck Bill" on the scissors allows you to hold the laces in safety while clipping the fabric from behind. For years, that was the only kind of scissor I recommended.

Now, Gingher has another pair suited for this task. They are called Pocket Scissors and look much like kindergarten scissors because of the blunt ends. But don't be fooled by appearances; the blades on Gingher Pocket Scissors cut fabric from behind lace with ease.

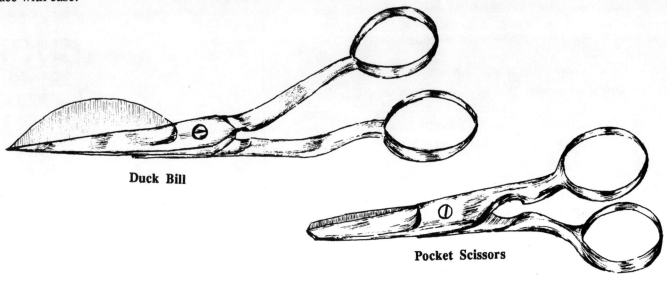

Duck Bill

Pocket Scissors

Patching Laces

Trimming fabric away from behind stitched-down lace can be difficult. It is not uncommon to slip and cut a hole in your lace work. How do you repair this lace with the least visible repair? It is really quite simple.

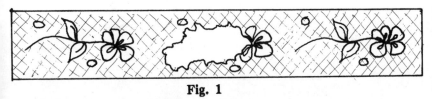

Fig. 1

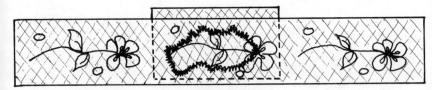

Fig. 2

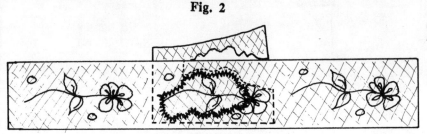

Fig. 3

Directions:

1. Look at the pattern in the lace where you have cut the hole. Is it in a flower, in a dot series, or in the netting part of the lace? (Fig. 1)
2. After you identify the pattern where the hole was cut, cut another piece of lace 1/4 inch longer than each side of the hole in the lace.
3. On the bottom side of the lace in the garment, place the lace patch (Fig. 2).
4. Match the design of the patch with the design of the lace around the hole where it was cut.
5. Zigzag around the cut edges of the lace hole, trying to catch the edges of the hole in your zigzag (Fig. 3).
6. Now, you have a patched and zigzagged pattern.
7. Trim away the leftover ends underneath the lace you have just patched (Fig. 3).
8. And don't worry about a piece of patched lace. My grandmother used to say, "Don't worry about that. You'll never notice it on a galloping horse."

Piecing Lace That Is Not Long Enough For Your Needs

From my sewing experience, sometimes you will need a longer piece of lace than you have. Perhaps you cut the lace incorrectly or bought less than you needed and had to go back for more. Whatever the reason, if you need to make a lace strip longer, it is easy to do.

Directions:

1. Match your pattern with two strips that will be joined later (Figs. 1 and 3).
2. Is your pattern a definite flower? Is it a definite diamond or some other pattern that is relatively large?
3. If you have a definite design in the pattern, you can join pieces by zigzagging around that design and then down through the heading of the lace (Fig. 3).
4. If your pattern is tiny, you can zigzag at an angle joining the two pieces (Fig. 2). Trim away excess laces close to the zigzagged seam.
5. Forget that you have patched laces and complete the dress.
6. If you discover that the lace is too short before you begin your stitching, you can plan where to place the zigzagged line that joins the pieces. You can choose the most inconspicuous place such as the off-center back shoulder area or back skirt area.
7. If you were already into making the garment when you discovered the short lace, simply join the laces and continue stitching as if nothing had happened

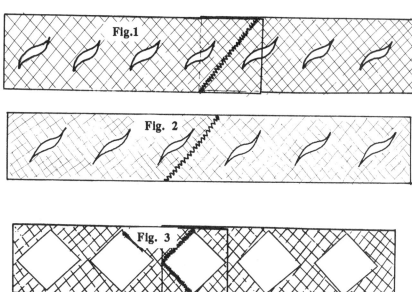

Stitching Fancy Bands From First One End and Then The Other

Sometimes fancy bands curve after you have sewn all of the laces and trims together. Usually, you can spray starch and iron the curve to straighten it out. According to Kathy McMakin, the way to stitch long pieces of laces together without resulting in a curve is to begin zigzagging your laces together at one end. To zigzag the next row, begin sewing from the end you just finished. In other words, bi-directional stitching of these laces will help tremendously in avoiding curved fancy bands. If you still end up with a slight curve in your fancy band, let the curved part face the ruffle.

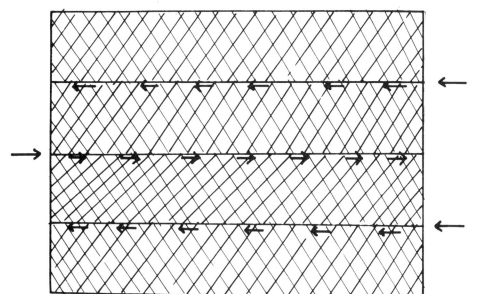

Matching Lace Patterns In French Sewing

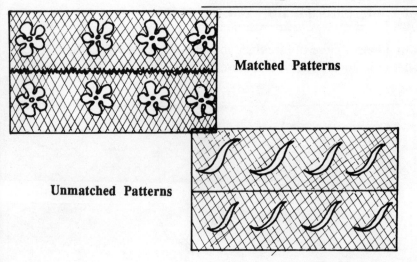

Matched Patterns

Unmatched Patterns

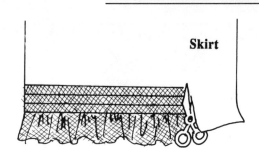

Do you match lace patterns as you stitch around your fancy band? For intricate patterns with small designs, the answer is "no." For very large patterns in round-thread laces, as in a huge flower every 1 inch or so, the answer is "yes." If you are stitching along on your fancy band and your pattern begins to fall out of design sequence, pull on the other side of the lace until the pattern matches again. Lace is a very forgiving textile which will allow itself to be pulled and pinched for various techniques. Pull it or pinch it until it lines back up. If you will do this as you sew, you won't have to be disappointed with the finished band.

If Your Fancy Band Is Too Short

Skirt

Not to worry; cut down the width of your skirt. Always make your skirt adapt to your lace shapes, not the lace shapes to your skirt.

Making Your Diamonds, Hearts, Teardrops, or Circles Fit Your Skirt Bottom

side seam

cut here

How do you make sure that you engineer your diamonds, hearts, teardrops, or circles to exactly fit the width skirt that you are planning? The good news is that you don't. Make your shapes any size that you want. Stitch them onto your skirt, front and back, and cut away the excess skirt width. Or, you can stitch up one side seam, and zigzag your shapes onto the skirt, and cut away the excess on the other side before you make your other side seam.

Planning The Width Of Your Skirt For A Fancy Shaped Bottom

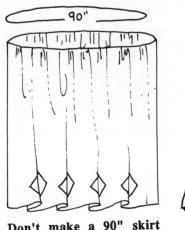

90"

Don't make a 90" skirt

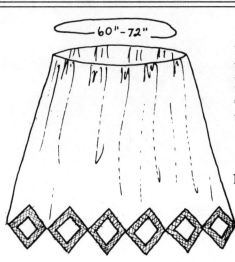

60"-72"

Please don't make a 90-inch skirt circumference when you are going to make intricate lace shapes on the bottom. The lace shapes will be lost in the fullness. I recommend a 60-inch to 72-inch total circumference; that's 30 inches to 36 inches of fullness in both the front and the back.

Make a 60"-70" skirt

Zigzag, Stair-Step Gathered Lace Trim (Ski-Slope Lace)

A very unusual method of attaching lace edging is to stitch it onto the bodice of a dress or a boy's shirt in a zigzag design. This is almost a ski-slope design for lace.

Directions:

1. Pull the thread in the heading of the lace edging to gather (Fig. 1).
2. Shape the first row of lace. Zigzag around the top edges and the center curve of the first row of lace to hold it in place (Fig. 2).
3. Shape the subsequent rows of lace, zigzagging on the curve of each row before moving on to the next.
4. The curved rows of zigzagged lace are hidden when the final ski-slope effect is accomplished (Fig. 4).

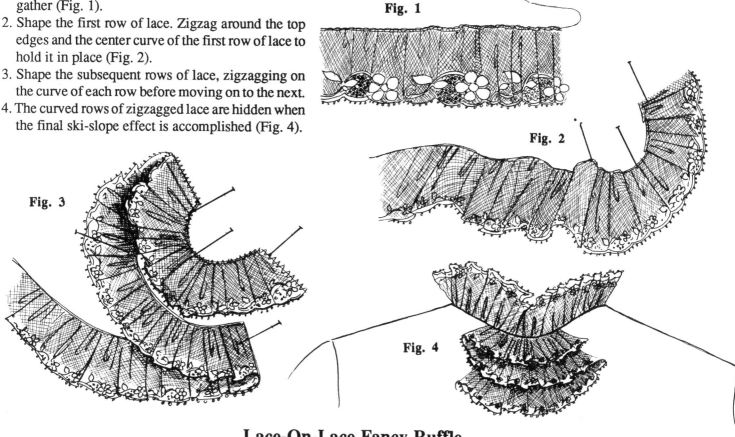

Fig. 1

Fig. 2

Fig. 3

Fig. 4

Lace-On-Lace Fancy Ruffle
(An elegant way to lengthen a dress)

On the "Ribbon and Lace Dress," from my antique collection, the bottom of the dress is wide edging, finished with a short ruffle. This would be a perfect way to lengthen a dress, and just may have been why the treatment was added to the original.

Directions:

1. Butt two rows of 1-inch insertion and zigzag (Fig. 1).
2. Cut two pieces of lace edging (1 inch wide). The length should be for 2-1 fullness; therefore cut your edging twice as long as the insertion you have just zigzagged together.
3. Gather the lace edging.
4. Butt one piece of the gathered edging to the bottom of the insertion and zigzag (Fig. 2).
5. Place the other gathered piece of edging right on top of the seam line that joins the two pieces of insertion (Fig. 3).
6. Stitching right on top of the gathered lace insertion, zigzag the insertion to the lace fancy band. This makes a three-dimensional fancy band.

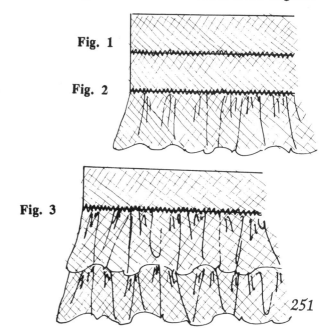

Fig. 1

Fig. 2

Fig. 3

251

Ribbon To Lace Insertion

This is tricky! Lace has give and ribbon doesn't. After much practice, I have decided that for long bands of lace to ribbon, as in a skirt, it is better to place the lace on top of the ribbon and straight-stitch (Length 2 to 2-1/2). For short strips of lace to ribbon, it is perfectly OK to butt together and zigzag.

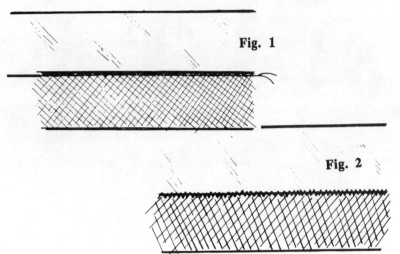

Fig. 1

Fig. 2

Directions for Straight-Stitch Attachment:
1. Press and starch your ribbon and lace.
2. Place the heading of the insertion just over the heading of the ribbon and straight-stitch (Length=2 to 2-1/2).

Directions for Zigzag-Stitch Attachment:
1. Press and starch your ribbon and lace.
2. Place the two side by side and zigzag (Width=1-1/2 to 2-1/2, Length 1-2).

Double-Lace Back Placket

One of the more unusual techniques found on the "Ribbon And Lace Dress" is the double-lace back placket. Since the fabric of the dress is composed of butted laces and ribbon zigzagged together, the center-back edge is raw. Thus, the seamstress made a strong back placket for buttonholes as follows.

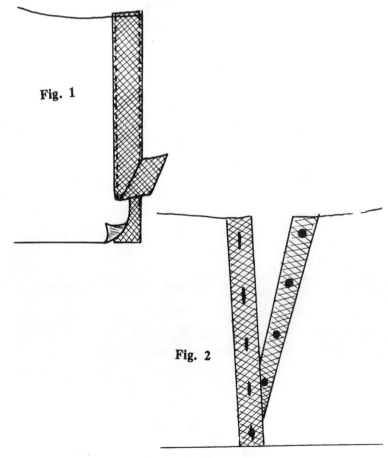

Fig. 1

Fig. 2

Directions:
1. Trim the center-back bodice, dress edge evenly. Trim away the fold backs.
2. Place a piece of lace insertion on both the front and the back of this raw, center-back edge (Fig. 1).
3. Stitch, using a tiny straight-stitch through both headings and the dress.
4. Fold both pieces of lace insertion over to the center-back edges. Press.
5. Stitch both pieces of lace insertion together (through the heading), using a straight-stitch at the center-back line.
6. Now, you have a back placket in which to make your buttonholes.

Fake Tiny Tuck and Lace Edging Finish

This finish is found on the "Tucking And White Braid Dress," circa 1915. What looks like a tuck with lace peeking out from under it, isn't really a tuck at all. The technique is used on the gathered collar and the sleeves of the dress. This technique can be used anywhere you traditionally put lace to fabric, as in ruffles on the bottom of a dress, lace edging on the bottom of a sleeve, or lace edging on the ruffle of a bonnet.

Directions:

1. Fold back your fabric once, 1/8 inch. Press (Fig. 1).
2. Fold back your fabric once more, 1/8 inch. Press (Fig. 2).
3. Place your lace heading on the wrong side of the ruffle. Line up the heading right under the folded side of the fold backs (Fig. 3).
4. Straight-stitch (Length 1-1/2 to 2) the lace edging to the fabric. Stitch from the back of the fabric (Fig. 3).
5. When you turn your fabric over, it appears that you have a tiny tuck with lace stitched into the tuck (Fig. 4).

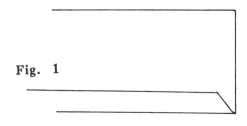

Fig. 1

Fig. 2

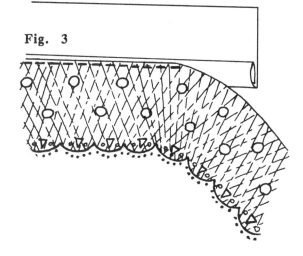

Fig. 4

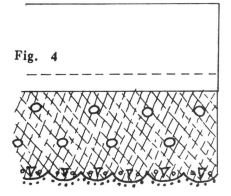

Fig. 3

Antique Tucking and Shadow Diamond Skirt

This skirt, which may have been a petticoat, is one of the most beautiful and yet one of the simplest of my antique garments. I purchased it from an antique dealer in Nashville. I believe its origin is America, circa 1890-1910.

The fabric is white Swiss batiste of a medium weight. It is tucked with 5/8-inch tucks placed 3/4 inch apart. A shadow of diamonds peeks through the hem. Every stitch of the 15 tucks and the 58 shadow diamonds was put in by hand. This skirt is a full 132 inches. The finished length is 36 inches. It is made with four skirt widths of 34 inches each.

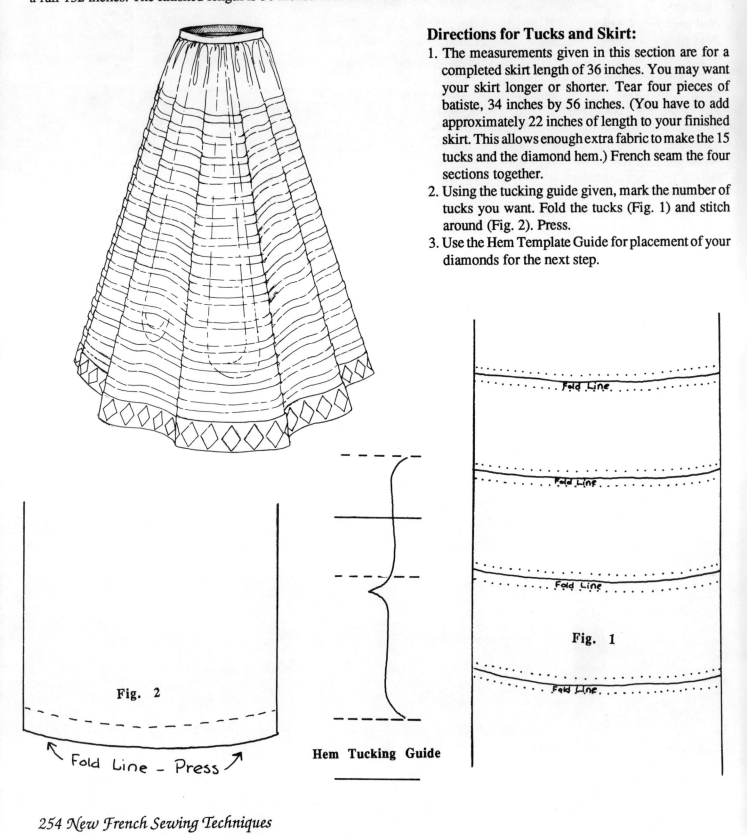

Directions for Tucks and Skirt:

1. The measurements given in this section are for a completed skirt length of 36 inches. You may want your skirt longer or shorter. Tear four pieces of batiste, 34 inches by 56 inches. (You have to add approximately 22 inches of length to your finished skirt. This allows enough extra fabric to make the 15 tucks and the diamond hem.) French seam the four sections together.

2. Using the tucking guide given, mark the number of tucks you want. Fold the tucks (Fig. 1) and stitch around (Fig. 2). Press.

3. Use the Hem Template Guide for placement of your diamonds for the next step.

Fig. 2

Fold Line - Press

Hem Tucking Guide

Fold Line

Fold Line

Fold Line

Fig. 1

Fold Line

Directions for Shadow Diamonds:

1. Your total finished hem is 2-1/2 inches.

2. One-half inch from the bottom of the skirt, draw your diamonds across the skirt (Fig. 3). Use the template given (Fig. 4). The diamonds are 1/4 inch apart. They measure 2 inches by 2 inches (Fig. 5).

3. Cut slits in the diamond on the dotted lines (Fig. 4-a). Cut all the way to the edge of the diamond. Do not cut any further and cut EXACTLY to the edge of the points of the diamonds.

4. Fold back each of the four sections you just made by this cut. Press (Fig. 6).

5. Fold up the shirttail hem of the skirt, 1/8 inch. Press.

6. Fold up your hem 2-1/2 inches. Press.

7. Slip-stitch your hem in place (Fig. 7).

8. Working from the back of the skirt, whip each diamond all the way around, stitching through the diamond and through the skirt.

9. Although on the antique skirt, the diamonds were hand slip stitched into place, this is the perfect place to use your sewing machine. You can straight stitch around the diamonds, zigzag around the diamonds, or use any one of your decorative stitches around the diamonds. Here is the place to use your pinstitch, hemstitch, daisy stitch, or other beautiful stitch.

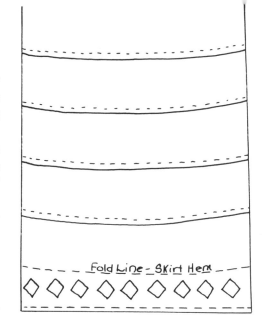

Fig. 3

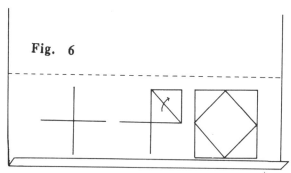

Fig. 6

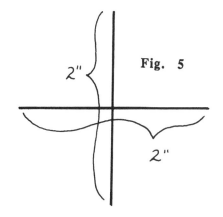

2"

Fig. 5

2"

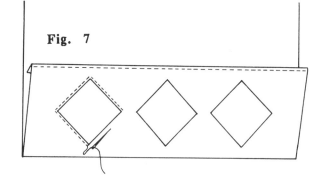

Fig. 7

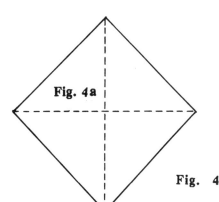

Fig. 4a

Fig. 4

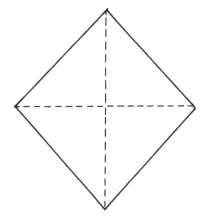

Be-ribboned Double Sleeve

Sometimes I fall in love with a particular detail so much I buy a garment just to examine one part of it! That is what happened with this dress, circa 1900-1910. The machine-made dress is pink Swiss batiste with off-white lace under-sleeves and insertion trims. It came from a New England estate and is actually faded and slightly torn in several places. I bought it to bring you the construction details of the sleeve. A color photograph in included in the middle of this book.

The under-sleeve comes almost to the elbow and is relatively straight and fitted. Upon first examination, I thought the top sleeve was fuller than the under-sleeve. Actually it is exactly the same sleeve, treated differently. The under-sleeve is an embroidered netting, lined in China silk. The over-sleeve has 1/4-inch tucks spaced 7/8 inch apart. The over-sleeve is not lined. The two sleeves were set into the armhole at the same time. The over-sleeve is finished on the edges with a 1-inch seam binding; the finished width of this binding is 1/2 inch. One-quarter inch seams are taken on both sides.

Silk ribbons are stitched in a crisscross pattern down the sleeves. The points where the ribbons attach to the sleeve were stitched by hand. Rosettes, at the bottom of the sleeve, complete the look. We sketched the front bodice of the dress in order for you to see the side view of the sleeve and the treatment the seamstress chose to complement her elaborate sleeve.

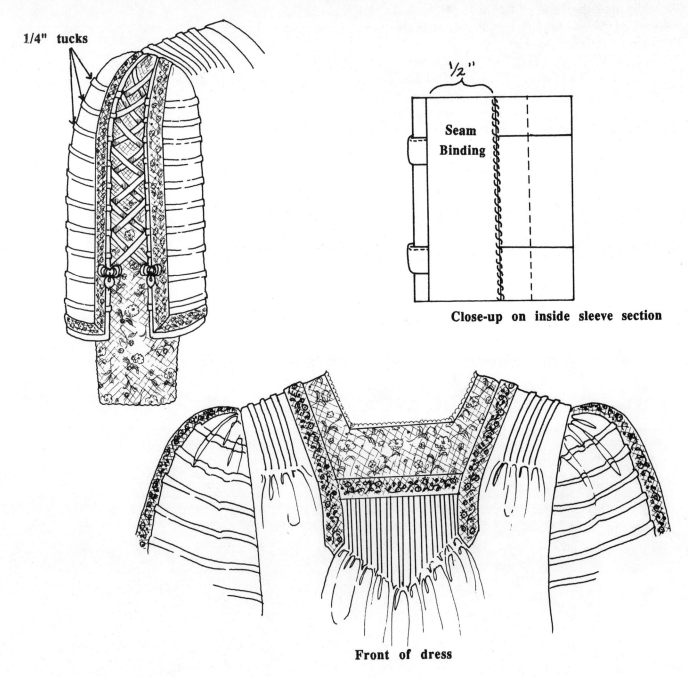

1/4" tucks

1/2"

Seam
Binding

Close-up on inside sleeve section

Front of dress

Fake Double Puffing

This technique, found on the "Netting Puffing Dress," appears to be a double row of puffing stitched together. Actually, it is a straight-stitch run through the netting before the gathering rows are placed at the top and bottom of the puffing strip. This center row is not gathered, just stitched in a regular stitch length (Length =1-1/2 to 2). The technique would be most effective on netting or sheer batiste.

Directions:

1. Tear or cut the puffing strips twice the length of the finished puffing row. This gives lots of fullness to the puffing.
2. The total finished measurement of the puffing strips on the antique dress is 2-1/2 inches wide. If you want your puffing this width, cut your strips 3-1/2 inches wide. This allows for a 1/2-inch seam allowance on either side of the puffing.
3. Run a straight-stitch through the middle of this strip. (Length=1-1/2 to 2) Do not gather this stitch. It is only to give the illusion of being another row of puffing.
4. Run your gathering rows on the top and the bottom of the puffing.
5. Gather them to fit your dress space or your entredeux (Fig. 1).
6. Attach to the garment or the entredeux. Press.
7. When you press this puffing, it will appear that you have two rows (Fig. 2).

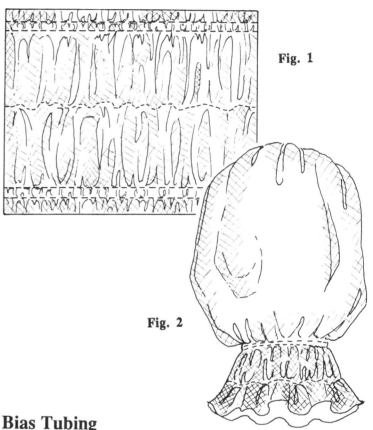

Fig. 1

Fig. 2

Making Bias Tubing

On the "Triangular Sleeved Christening Dress," the tiny bias tubing that covers the lace stitching lines is simple to make. The bias is cut and pressed to stretch slightly. The bias is then folded in half and stitched so that the turned loop or tube is thin, about 1/8 inch from the fold. One end should be stitched slightly wider than the other so that it may be more easily turned. The raw edges should be trimmed so that the seam is about the width of the stitching from the fold (Fig. 1). The bias is then turned inside-out so that the raw edges are concealed. A needle, threaded with a heavy twist, may facilitate the turning (Figs. 2 and 3). The tubing should then be pinned to the ironing board and steamed so that the loop is pressed.

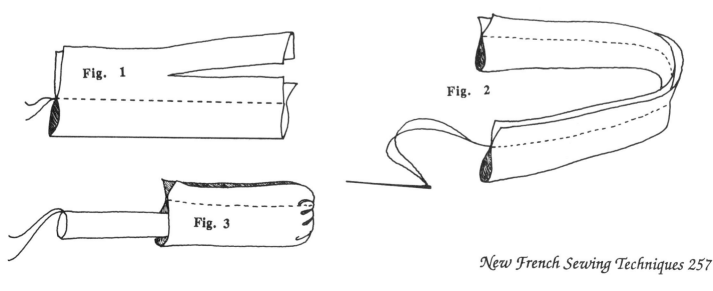

Fig. 1

Fig. 2

Fig. 3

Fold-Back Method For Attaching Gathered Fabric To Lace Insertion

This method is found on "Joanna's Blouse." It is used to attach the bottom of the sleeve to the lace ruffle. On the antique blouse, the gathering stitches were put in by hand; however, you can run gathering stitches on a sewing machine. Also, gathering stitches were left in the antique version. It is pretty to have the 1/8-inch row of gathering held in place by the gathering stitches that were not removed. You might want to see how you like it; leave them in or remove them according to your taste!

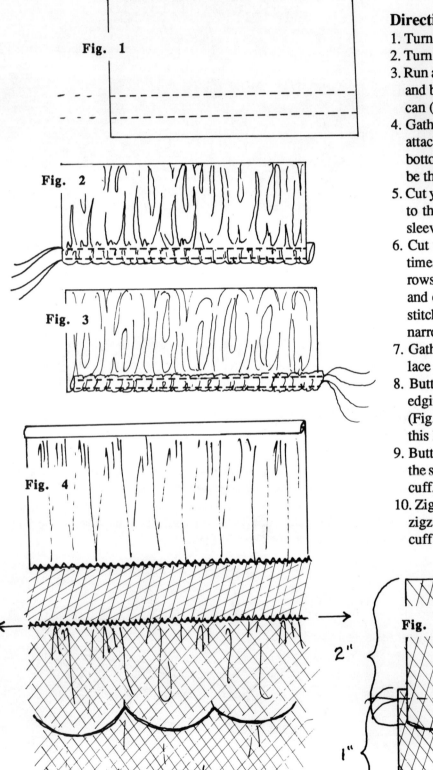

Fig. 1

Fig. 2

Fig. 3

Fig. 4

2"

1"

Directions:

1. Turn back 1/8 inch of fabric. Press.
2. Turn back another 1/8 inch of fabric. Press (Fig. 1).
3. Run a gathering row of stitches as closely to the top and bottom of this 1/8-inch seam allowance as you can (Fig. 2).
4. Gather the fabric to fit the lace to which it is to be attached. In this case, the measurement of the bottom of this fabric will be what would normally be the cuff of the sleeve (Fig. 3).
5. Cut your insertion for the top of the lace fancy band to the measurement that would be the cuff of the sleeve.
6. Cut two pieces of edging. These pieces are 1-1/2 times as long as the lace cuff. Stitch together two rows of edging; one is 1 inch wide (the bottom one) and one is 2 inches wide (the top one). To do this stitching, lap the wider piece of lace over the narrower one and straight-stitch (Fig. 4).
7. Gather this double piece of lace edging, to fit the lace cuff.
8. Butt together the heading of the middle piece of edging and the heading of the lace cuff of insertion (Fig. 5). Zigzag. French seam the underarm seam of this lace cuff.
9. Butt together this cuff and the gathered bottom of the sleeve. Adjust the gathers of the sleeve to fit this cuff.
10. Zigzag the two together, making the width of your zigzag just wide enough to catch the bottom of the cuff and go over the heading of the insertion.

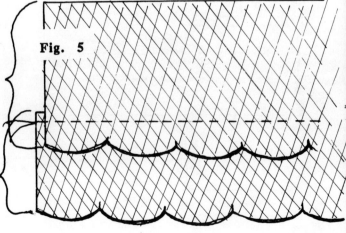

Fig. 5

Adding A Second Color Of Batiste To A Garment

In the "Pink Collar Long Baby Dress" the sweetest treatment is found on the collar, which uses a second color of batiste. A round collar, 2 inches wide, has a pie-shaped piece of pink batiste stitched on top of the center section. Two sets of three pintucks are found on each side of the pink fabric. It is stitched down to the collar, using a straight-stitch and leaving raw edges on the sides. Flat edging is then stitched down over the raw seam. This technique can be used on collars similar to the one on the baby dress, down the front of a skirt, on a fancy band, or on sleeves.

Directions:

1. Cut a round, white batiste collar.
2. Cut a square of pink batiste, 6 inches by 5 inches.
3. Stitch two sets of three pintucks on each side of this pink batiste.
4. Trace off a pie-shaped area on the center of the collar.
5. Cut out the pink batiste-tucked fabric to fit your shape.
6. Stitch the pink strip to the white collar, using a straight-stitch.
7. Stitch the lace edging over the stitch you just made, using a straight-stitch.
8. Finish the neckline with a bias strip, encasing both the white collar and the pink collar.
9. Press up a seam on the bottom of the collar all the way around. On the antique dress, the raw seam is left from the fold up. If raw seams bother you, serge around the bottom of the collar before turning it up. Or, turn up a double seam before you make the final finished seam.
10. Cut lace edging 1-1/2 times longer than the complete bottom edge of the round portrait collar.
11. Slightly gather the lace.
12. Place the slightly-gathered lace edging directly under the folded edge of the collar.
13. Straight-stitch around the collar in the color thread that you have used on the main part of the collar. Use white thread, even to stitch over the pink batiste, since white is the main color of the collar. This one row of straight-stitching hems the collar edge and attaches the lace.

New French Sewing Techniques 259

Dying Laces To Pastel Colors

Several of my antique pieces sport delicately-colored laces — shades of peach, pink, blue, yellow, and green. Since it is almost impossible to find pastel laces today, you can dye your laces with Rit dye. Mix the dye, according to the directions. Testing is absolutely necessary when you are custom dying to your specifications. Probably you will have to dilute the dye to make subtle colors. You can even dye laces ecru or bright white by diluting "Ecru Rit" to the right shade.

If your laces are almost all cotton, 90 percent they will dye beautifully. I have also dyed organdy and batiste. The most adventurous lace dying that I have ever done was for an evening gown bodice. I needed a pink evening gown with a re-embroidered lace, sequin, and pearl top which matched the pink satin and tulle I was using for the skirt. I used $200 per yard bridal, jewel-encrusted French lace. I tested my Rit dye, and when I got the right color, I put 1-1/2 yards of this expensive fabric right into my washing machine and washed it just like the directions suggested.

Be creative! Use some pastel laces on white or ecru batiste or organdy. If the women used this idea 90 years ago, why can't we try it?

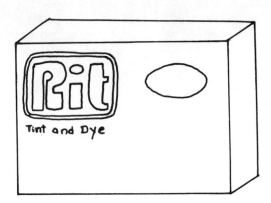

Directions:
1. Choose the nearest color of Rit fabric dye or other fabric dye available in craft stores.
2. Mix the dye according to the package directions.
3. Take some of the dye and dilute it with more water to make it softer in color.
4. Cut a sample piece of lace.
5. Dye the sample piece of lace. Rinse it. Let dry and press. Is it the right color? Is it still too dark? Is it too light? Evaluate the color and use stronger solution if necessary.

Smocked Puffing

On the "Smocked Puffing Christening Dress," the bodice and the skirt are one piece of fabric. The fullness of the bodice is gathered for smocking on the center section. A strip of Swiss insertion, which is finished on both sides, is stitched down at the bottom of the smocked section, and a sash is attached on either side.

The look of puffing is obtained by smocking only two rows of the 5-1/2 inches of the dress, which has pleating run through it. The two rows of smocking are about 1 inch apart.

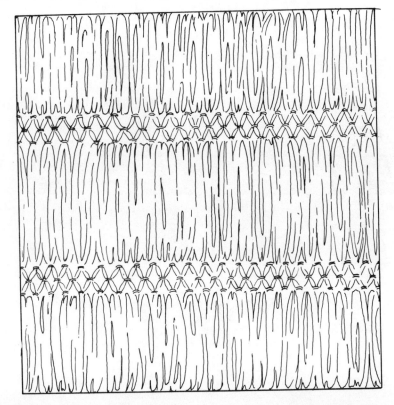

Directions:
1. Pleat the number of rows that you want the puffing to cover.
2. Smock only on the rows that divide the sections. On the antique dress, there were 5-1/2 inches pleated. Two rows of smocking were done; one 1-1/2 inches below the neckline of the dress; and one, 1-1/4 inches below that.
3. The smocking is a baby wave, reversed to form baby wave diamonds. Any smocking-stitch would do. Just leave rows unsmocked for the puffing look when the pleating threads are removed.

Lengthening An Eyelet Dress With A Batiste Hem

One of the most exciting ideas on the "Raglan Sleeve Border Eyelet Dress" is how the seamstress chose to lengthen the dress. Obviously, border eyelet cannot be lengthened. She added length by making an additional hem, straight-stitched underneath the hem.

Directions:

1. Cut a piece of fabric 6 inches wide by the circumference of the dress. You will need to piece it at least once. Using a French seam, seam the strip together at one point. Leave it flat.
2. Fold down 1/4 inch on either side of this strip. Press.
3. Fold the whole strip again, matching the folded edges. Press.
4. Your strip is now 2-3/4 inches wide.
5. Place your folded and pressed "hem" at the appropriate place in the eyelet. You can make this hem as wide or as narrow as you wish.
6. Straight-stitch your "hem" underneath the finished eyelet skirt. Do you see how much length you have added?

Adding Length To A Dress With A Fancy Band By Making An Extra Ruffle

You can use this technique to add length to a dress with a ruffle or a fancy bottom. When you first make the dress, make an additional ruffle exactly like the bottom ruffle, but 3 inches longer. Put the second ruffle away until the dress is too short. When it is needed, stitch it underneath the first ruffle at the same place the first ruffle is attached. You could roll and whip the second ruffle, gather and distribute it, and zigzag it to the dress (underneath the first ruffle) by going into the holes of the entredeux and off onto both ruffles.

Double Needle Pintucking

Heirloom sewing without pintucks would be like shortcake without the fruit; it's lovely by itself, but a little garnish makes it grand. Heirloom sewing fanatics use pintucks to decorate everything from daygowns to ladies blouses to the insides of fancy lace shapes. Nothing more than stitched folds of fabric, usually in rows of two or more, tucks have probably embellished clothing since the dawn of the needle. Portraits dating back to the 15th century indicate tucks were used on clothing at least as far back as the Italian Renaissance. Even doll clothes of yesteryear sported tucking. The Jules Nicholas Steiner (doll) Company, which was in operation for 1855 to 1891, used tucking extensively — primarily pintucking — on the sleeves, skirts, and yokes of the fancy doll dresses. These particular pintucks were so fine, they must have taken a seamstress days to complete.

The good news for today's seamstress is that the pintucks can be made quickly and easily on the modern sewing machine. Pintuck feet are available for nearly all models. Pintucks are made when two needle threads share one bobbin thread. The fabric between the needles is "pulled up" creating a tuck. If there isn't a pintuck foot available for your model, you may want to consider purchasing a new machine. Pintucks are one of the most elegant treatments in heirloom clothing, and unlike yards of lace, they don't factor into the cost of a garment.

Almost any fabric can be pintucked from Swiss batiste and delicate silk to wool and denim. For heirloom sewing, I suggest that you use Swiss batiste, American batiste, silk, or any lightweight fabric. Check with your sewing machine dealer about the pintuck feet and the corresponding needles that are available for your machine.

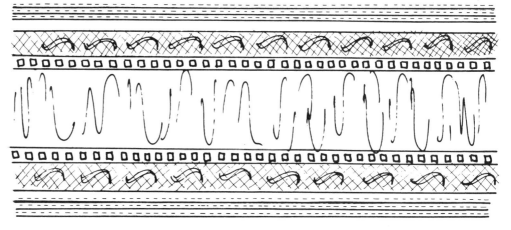

Double Needles For Machine Pintucking

Double needles come in different sizes. The first number on the double needle is the distance between the needles. The second number on the needle is the actual size of the needle. The chart below shows some of the double needle sizes. The size needle that you choose will depend on the weight of the fabric that you are pintucking.

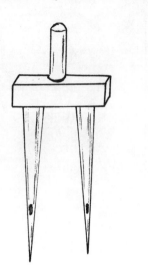 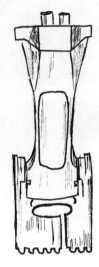

a. 1.6/70-Use with 9 groove pintuck foot
   Light Weight Fabric
b. 1.6/80-Use with 9 groove pintuck foot
   Light Weight Fabric
c. 2.0/80-Use with 7 groove pintuck foot
   Light Weight Fabric
d. 2.5/80-Use with 7 groove pintuck foot
   Light Weight Fabric
e. 3.0/90-Use with 5 groove pintuck foot
   Medium Weight Fabric
f. 4.0/100-Use with 3 groove pintuck foot
   Heavy Weight Fabric

Pintuck Feet
Bernina, Elna, New Home, Pfaff, Viking

Pintuck feet are easy to use and they shave hours off pintucking time. They enable you to space your pintucks perfectly. Pintuck feet correspond to the needle used with that pintuck foot; the needle used corresponds to the weight of fabric. The bottom of these feet have a certain number of grooves 3, 5, 7, or 9. The width of the groove matches the width between the two needles. The pintuck feet used in most French sewing are the 7 groove foot and the 9 groove foot. Check with your sewing machine dealer to insure that you choose the correct double needle and pintuck foot for your machine.

Preparing Your Fabric For Pintucking

Do I spray starch the fabric before I pintuck it? It depends. Always press all-cotton fabric. A polyester/cotton blend won't need to be pressed unless it is very wrinkled. Tucks tend to lay flatter if you stiffen fabric with spray starch first. Pintuck a small piece of your chosen fabric with starch and one without starch, then make your own decision?

Straight Pintucking With A Pintuck Foot

Directions:

1. Put in your double needle. Thread your machine with two spools of thread. Thread one spool at a time (including the needle). This will help keep the threads from becoming twisted while stitching the tucks. This would be a good time to look in the guide book, which came with your sewing machine, for directions on using pintuck feet and double needles. Some sewing machines have a special way of threading for use with double needles.

2. The first tuck must be straight. To make this first tuck straight, do one of two things: Pull a thread all the way across the fabric and follow along that pulled line; or, using a measuring stick or tape measure, mark a line along the fabric. Stitch on that line.

3. Place the fabric under the foot for the first tuck and stitch the desired length of pintuck. (Length=1 to 2-1/2; Needle position is center) Fig.1.

4. Place your first tuck into one of the grooves in your pintuck foot. The space between each pintuck depends on the placement of the first pintuck (Fig. 2).

5. Make as many pintucks as your heart (or pattern) desires. Continue pintucking by placing the last pintuck made into a groove in the foot.

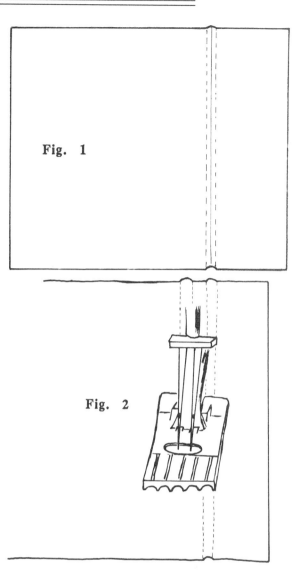

Fig. 1

Fig. 2

Pintucking If Your Machine Does Not Have A Pintuck Foot

Directions:

1. Use a double needle.
2. Thread your double needles as if you had a pintuck foot.
3. Draw the first line of pintucking. Stitch the line.
4. At this point you can either draw more lines for the pintuck lines or you can use the edge of your presser foot as a guide (Fig. 1).
5. You might find a "generic" pintuck foot for your particular brand of machine.

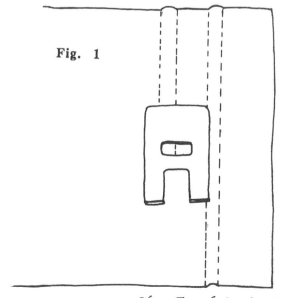

Fig. 1

Properly Tying Off Pintucks

Pintucks that are made on a piece of fabric, cut out and stitched into the garment, do not have to be tied off. Why? When you sew the seam of the garment, the pintucks will be secured within that seam. Released pintucks stop at a designated point in the fabric. They are not caught in a seam and, therefore, have to be tied off. To make the most beautiful pintuck possible, you must properly tie it off.

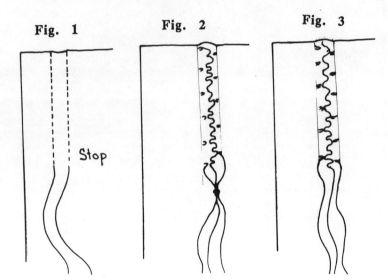

Fig. 1   Fig. 2   Fig. 3

Directions:
1. End your stitching at the designated stopping point (Fig. 1).
2. Pull a reasonable length of thread out before you go in the other direction for more pintucking.
3. Later these will be cut and pulled to the back (Fig. 2) to be tied off (Fig. 3).

I know that sounds like a lot of trouble and it is. It must be done this way if you want perfect pintucks. If you prefer not to go to all that trouble, end the pintuck, take one or two back-stitches, and cut your threads close to the stitching; however, the results will not be as pretty.

Bi-Directional Stitching Of Pintucks

The general consensus, when stitching pintucks, is to stitch down one side and back up the other side instead of stitching pintucks all in the same direction.

To prevent pintucks from being lopsided, stitch down the length of one pintuck, pull your threads, and stitch back up in the opposite direction.

Making Waffle Pintucks

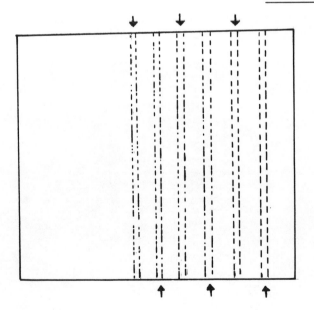

Directions:
1. Stitch pintucks all in the same direction to the width you desire.
2. Stitch pintucks in the opposite direction.

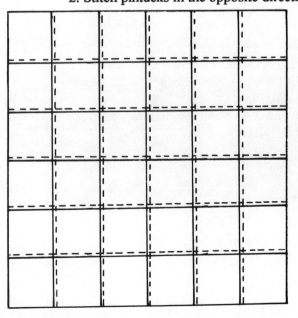

Cording Pintucks

Cords make pintucks more prominent. Use Mettler gimp or #8 pearl cotton. Cording comes in handy when pintucks are being shaped. When pintucking across a bias with a double needle, you may get some distortion. The cord acts as a filler and will keep the fabric from distorting.

Directions:
1. If your machine has a hole in the throat plate, run the cord up through that hole and it will be properly placed without another thought.
2. If your machine does not have a hole in the throat plate, put the gimp or pearl cotton underneath the fabric, lining it up with the pintuck groove. Once you get the cording lined up under the proper groove, it will follow along for the whole pintuck.

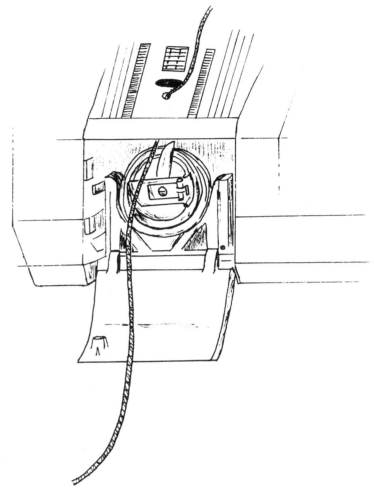

Shadow Pintucks

Shadow pintucks are pintucks with a touch of color showing through. To shadow pintuck, you must use sheer fabric — batiste, organdy, or pastel silk.

Directions:
1. Using the cording techniques, choose #8 pearl cotton in a color you would like to peek through the batiste or silk. I prefer a darker shade thread than what you will see from the front because the color will be less prominent when it is hidden within the pintuck.
2. Pintuck, using thread that matches your batiste in the regular sewing machine hook-up, and colored pearl cotton for the shadow.
3. I have seen pintucks with colored thread for the regular sewing machine thread and color for the cording.

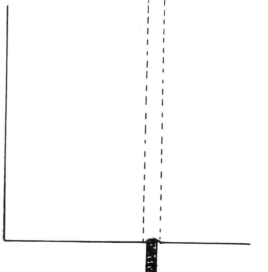

New French Sewing Techniques 267

Questions And Answers
Concerning Pintucking On The Sewing Machine

Q. What do I do about puckering when I pintuck fabric?

A. There are several things that you can try. Sewing machine pintucks tend to pucker slightly. You can shorten your stitch length. You can pull the fabric from the front and back as you sew. You can lightly starch your fabric before you pintuck. You can loosen your bobbin tension. If you do any or all of these things, you may prevent your fabric from puckering, but you will also change the look of the pintuck. Try various techniques on your particular sewing machine to see what happens. Actually, I don't mind the tiny puckers. They add texture to the garment and make the pintucks stand out.

Q. Would I ever want to use a cord enclosed in my pintucks?

A. Cords will keep the fabric from puckering so much. They also keep the pintuck from smashing flat when you press it. Some people absolutely love cords in their pintucks. In fact, all of the students I met while teaching in Australia use cords within their pintucks.

Cords are also used decoratively with a darker color of cord under white or ecru batiste. One of the dresses in the first *Sew Beautiful* Sweepstakes, had dark peach cording under ecru batiste pintucks; it was fabulous.

Q. Can pintucks be run any way on your fabric, or do they have to run vertically or parallel with the straight of grain?

A. Pintucks can be run in any direction. Consider scalloped pintucks. The ease or difficulty of making pintucks depends on the fabric you use. When making straight pintucks, I prefer to make them on the straight of the grain, parallel to the selvage.

Q. Are there any fabrics to completely avoid for pintucking?

A. Yes. Dotted Swiss is terrible. Printed fabrics, on which the design has been stamped, does not pintuck well. Resulting pintucks are uneven. Stiff fabrics do not machine pintuck well. You will end up with parallel stitching lines with no fabric pulled up between the stitching lines.

Q. What happens when I put a pintuck in the wrong place or my pintuck is crooked? Can I take it out?

A. Yes. Pintucks are easy to take out. Turn your fabric to the wrong side, and slide your seam ripper underneath the bobbin thread, which looks like a zigzag on the underside. The parallel top-stitching lines will just come right out after you slice the underside stitching.

Q. How do I press pintucks?

A. I prefer to spray starch a series of tucks before pressing it. Don't be afraid to starch and press pintucks. You might want to pin the edges of the pintucked fabric to the ironing board, stretching it out as far as you can. (This is nothing more than blocking your pintucked fabric.) Slide the iron in one direction to make all the pintucks lay in that one direction. Starch and press again. This will take out most of the puckers. Then, remove the pins from the ironing board. Flip over the pintucked piece you have just blocked and pressed, and press again. Not everyone prefers pintucks that lay in the same direction. For a less stringent appearance, lay your pintucked fabric piece face down on a terry cloth towel for the first and last pressing.

Curved Pintucks

Pintucks are inexpensive to make. They add texture and dimension without adding cost to the dress. They're rarely found on store-bought clothing. Follow pintucked shapes with lace insertion or decorative stitches on your machine for an enchanting finish. Simply use your template and pintuck, then use the insertion like you would use any Swiss handloom. For threads, use white-on-white, ecru-on-ecru, or any pastel color on white or ecru.

I would like to thank Gai Haviland and Lyn Herbert of Bernina of Australia for teaching me their way of curving pintucks when I was teaching at the Martha Pullen School of Art Fashion in Newcastle, New South Wales. We were talking about curved pintucks and she said, "Martha, I will show you the easy way to make these pintucks."

The big question here is, "What foot do I use for scalloped pintucks?" For straight pintucks, I use a pintuck foot with the grooves. That foot is fine for curved or scalloped pintucks also, but I prefer either the regular zigzag foot or the clear applique foot, which is plastic and allows easy "see through" of the turning points. Try your pintuck foot, your regular sewing foot, and your clear applique foot to see which one you like the best. Like all aspects of heirloom sewing, the "best" foot is really your personal preference.

Curved Pintucks

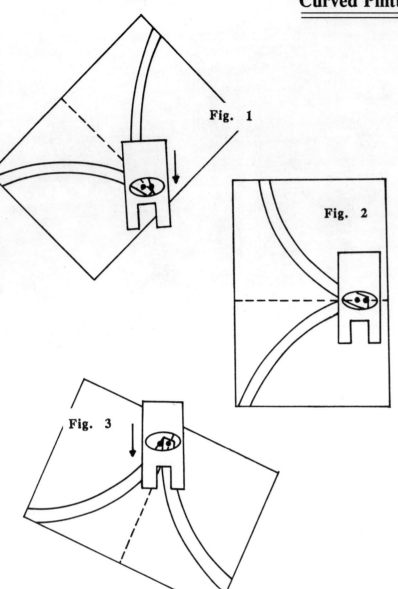

Fig. 1

Fig. 2

Fig. 3

Directions:
1. Draw the scallops.
2. I prefer the regular zigzag foot for curved pintucks. You can use a pintuck foot or a clear applique foot. Experiment for yourself.
3. Use a double needle (2.0/80) and a straight-stitch with the length of 1.5.
4. Stitch around the scallop up to the point (Fig. 1).
5. Lift the presser foot. **Leave the needles in the fabric.**
6. Turn your fabric 45 degrees.
   NOTE: Your needles are still in the fabric when you make your turn. (Fig. 2).
7. Lower the presser foot.
8. Using the hand wheel of your sewing machine, not the foot pedal, lift the needles out of the fabric and take one stitch (Fig. 2). When you use the hand wheel to take a stitch, it is called "walking the machine."
9. Raise the presser foot once again. Leave the needles in the fabric.
10. Turn your fabric another 45 degrees, leaving the needles just where they are in the fabric, lining up the next row of stitches with your presser foot (Fig. 3).
11. Lower the presser foot.
12. Begin sewing again along your template line to the bottom of the scallop and up to the next point.

Pointed Pintucks With Angles

Diamond, triangular, and square pintucks are made the same way as curved pintucks. Refer to our collection of pintuck templates for some ideas. Or better still, create some yourself!

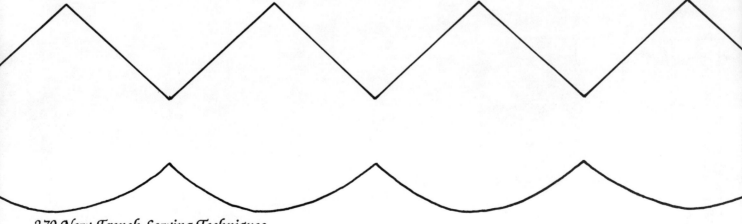

Sets of Curved Pintucks

To line up the tucks for a series of tucks on a skirt, draw on the template for the bottom tuck first. If you want curved pintucks about 1/2 inch apart, use the side of your regular sewing foot as your pintuck guide. If you want your pintucks further apart, you will need to draw on each line of pintucks. Several pintucks, 1/2 inch apart, can be made by lining up the pintuck above or below the next one with the edge of the sewing machine.

Marking A Skirt For Curved Pintuck Scallops Or Any Other Fancy Design

To divide any garment piece into equal parts, fold your skirt or bodice in half. This marks the half-way point. Continue to fold in halves until the piece is divided the way you want it. If you are to mark the bottom of a skirt, seam one side seam first so that you can work on the entire garment piece (Fig. 1).

Directions:

1. Take your skirt, sleeve, bodice, or pattern part and fold it in half. Press (Fig. 2).
2. Fold that in half again. Press. If you have a skirt with the front and back already stitched together on one side, you now have it folded in quarters. The seam will be on one side. Press on that seam line. Figure 3 shows what the skirt would look like if it were opened at this time.
3. Fold in half again. Press. Your piece is now divided into eighths (Fig. 4).
4. Repeat this process as many times as necessary for you to have the divisions that you want.
5. Open up your garment part. Use these fold lines as your measuring points and guide points.
6. Trace with a fabric marker the scallops between the fold lines (Fig. 5). Take care to assure that your template is equal distance from the bottom of your skirt. The easiest way to assure this straight marking for the bottom of the scallops is to mark however many inches from the bottom you want your scallops along every other fold point.
7. I think 2 inches from the bottom is sufficient.

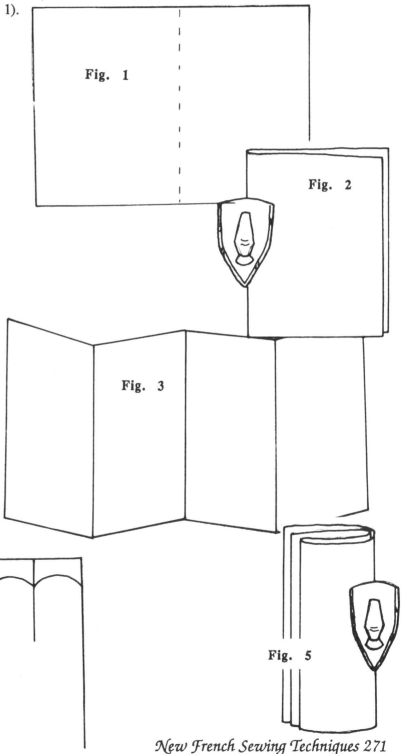

Fig. 1

Fig. 2

Fig. 3

Fig. 4

Fig. 5

Pintuck Templates

Included is collection of pintuck templates. Some of these can be curved-lace templates also. Feel free to experiment with our templates in order to draw your own. If you want to draw your own templates, use a dinner plate, a compass, a saucer, or a template from your local art supply store.

If you use a Flexicurve from the art store for your curves, make one scallop with this Flexicurve and transfer it to paper. Flexicurves are very flimsy and your shape could be distorted from one scallop to the next when traced directly onto fabric.

We have created some unusual pintuck shaping ideas for you to consider. How would you like diamonds connected with curves (Fig. 1)? Do three rows of connected scallops appeal to you (Fig. 2)? One design almost looks like short bananas (Fig. 3)! Waves from the ocean have inspired artists for centuries. Perhaps you could wave your pintucks (Fig. 4). Squares can be as fancy or as plain as you choose (Fig. 5).

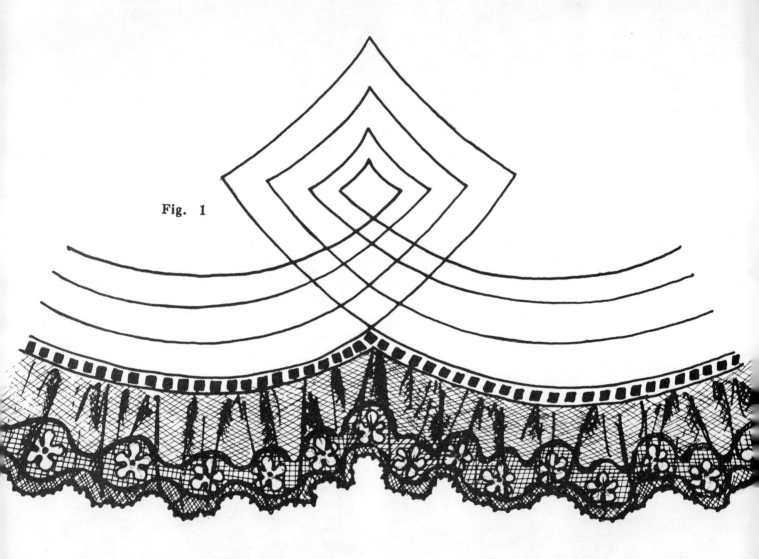

Fig. 1

Fig. 2

Fig. 3

Fig. 4

Fig. 5

Organdy and Ribbon Sandwiches

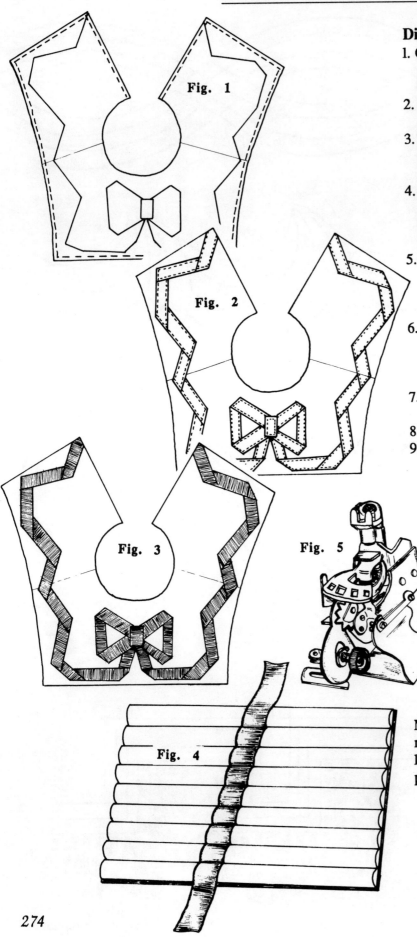

Fig. 1

Fig. 2

Fig. 3

Fig. 5

Fig. 4

Directions:

1. Cut outer collar from organdy or any sheer fabric. Cut collar lining from organdy, batiste, or dress fabric.
2. Stitch outer collar, right sides together, at shoulder seams. Repeat for lining.
3. The ribbon decoration will be done on the right side of the lining fabric. The wrong side of the lining fabric will be the underside of the collar.
4. Draw in the seam lines of the collar and ribbon design (Fig. 1). Shape ribbon in a flip-flop fashion. Flip-flopping is the only way to shape heavy-weight ribbon into a flat design.
5. Pin in place. Stitch the edges of the ribbon to the collar lining, using thread the color of the ribbon in the needle and thread the color of the lining in the bobbin (Fig. 2).
6. Place the collar lining to the collar, right side of the lining to the wrong side of the collar (the side without the ribbon). Stitch the lining to the collar along seam lines shown in Figure 1.
7. Turn through the neck, sandwiching the ribbon between the two layers of the collar (Fig. 3).
8. Press.
9. Attach ribbon to the outer edge using one of the following methods:
   a.) Clotilde's Perfect Pleater (Fig. 4):
      1.) Pleat ribbon using the Perfect Pleater. When using grosgrain ribbon, place ribbon in every third slot of the perfect pleater. Press pleats in place.
      2.) Place pleated ribbon 1/4 inch under collar edge.
      3.) Stitch into place with a top-stitch or blind-stitch.
   b.) Ruffler (Fig.5):
      1.) Pleat ribbon using the ruffler.
      2.) Refer to steps 2 and 3 in the Perfect Pleater instructions.

NOTE: If a round or curved collar is used, the pleated ribbon edge can be stitched between the two collar layers. If a square collar is used, it is easier to stitch the pleated ribbon to the edge of the finished collar.

Making Proper Slip-Stitch Hem By Hand

I am all in favor of doing everything by machine or by serger to insure speed and quality. The problem arises when you sacrifice quality for time. Machine hems, although almost everybody uses them, are always noticeable and they are not proper. You spend too much time smocking or French sewing to ruin the garment with a machine hem. The slip-stitch is my preferred hemming stitch.

The slip-stitch is almost invisible, the covering of the thread lessens the possibility of catching, and the use of a long stitch hastens the process. One technique I came across while flipping through an antique sewing book is to hold the hem with the open portion, on which you are actually doing the stitching, toward yourself. See Figure 1. I mistakenly held the garment with the open part away from me for my whole sewing career. Now I hem this way. Try it.

Directions:

1. Fold up a tiny hem, about 1/8 inch.
2. Fold up the final hem for your garment. Pin. Press.
3. Work the stitch from right to left.
4. Knot the thread. Bring it up in the fabric as illustrated (Fig. 2).
5. Take up a yarn or two of the fabric below (Fig. 3).
6. Bring the needle out, and insert it at the under side of the fold about 1/16 of an inch back of where it was last brought through (Fig. 4).
7. Slip the needle into the under side of the fold of the hem, just below the crease that holds the raw edge under, and bring it out on the same line about 1/2 inch ahead (Fig. 4).
8. This last step creates a figure eight that holds the hem. If the thread is broken at any time, the hem will not rip out.
9. Notice how the final stitch looks like a little cross stitch. Moving the needle back about 1/16 of an inch before travelling through the fold again, forms a lock stitch that anchors the hem.

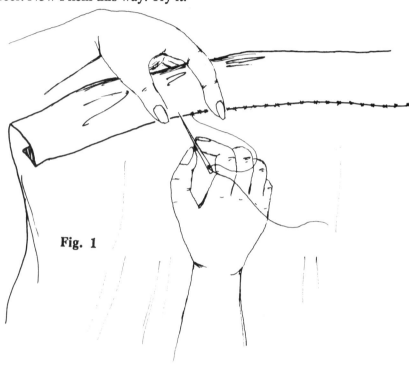

Fig. 1

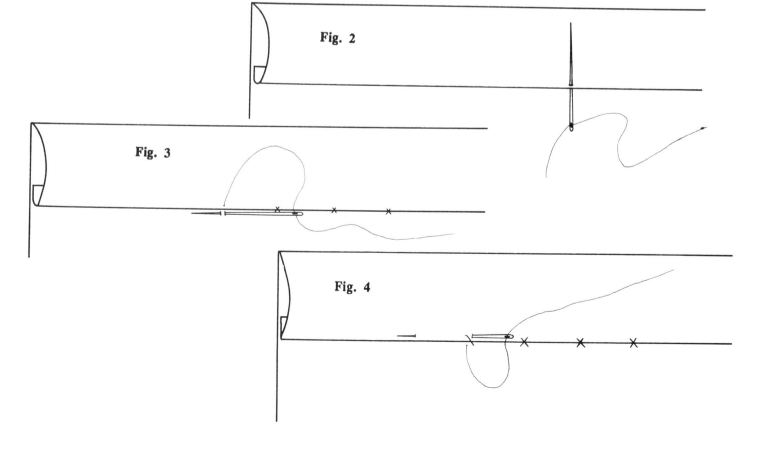

Fig. 2

Fig. 3

Fig. 4

Snaps

Snaps are used to fasten two parts of a garment together at points where there is little strain and where the closing must remain smooth and inconspicuous. Snaps come in various sizes. Number 4/0 snap size is for sheer fabrics; plastic snaps are good for heirloom sewing. A single, strong thread is used to sew on the snaps. This is one place where a synthetic thread might be better than cotton thread. The snaps should be concealed but placed near enough to the edge of the lap so that the edge does not roll back, and near enough together so the material will not gap.

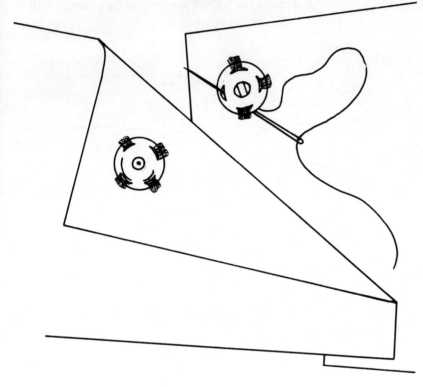

Directions:

1. A back stitch is taken in the center of the mark, and the needle is then placed through one of the holes in the snap.
2. The snap is sewn in place with buttonhole stitches in each of the four holes by sliding the needle from hole to hole underneath the strip.
3. Care should be taken that the stitches are not allowed to pass through the batiste or other heirloom material so that they show on the right side of the garment.
4. Sew on the ball part of the snap first.
5. To correctly locate the position for the socket portion of the snap, the ball part of the snap is placed over the under closing and the spot marked with a pin.
6. After finding the correct point, stitch the socket part on firmly.
7. To fasten the thread, two or three small stitches should be taken.

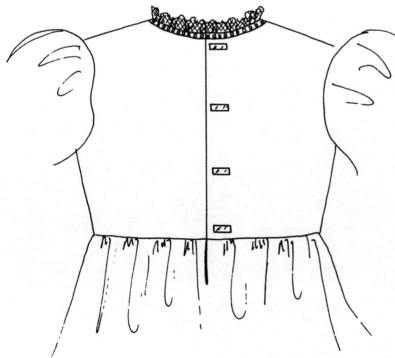

Beauty Pins

If you don't like to make buttonholes, beauty pins are the answer. These little bars (about 1/4 inch wide by 3/4 inch long) with pins attached to the back will act as a closure as well as an embellishment to the garment. Beauty pins are also used to decorate lapels and collars. They are sold separately or in pairs. Expensive 14 karat gold pins can be purchased at your local jewelry store. Most sewing shops carry the lesser-priced pins in various designs —plain gold, white background with pastel flowers, roses, kites, balloons, etc. Heirloom pins, similar in size, can be found at antique stores. Decorated pins can be purchased with one dress in mind; plain pins can be transferred from dress to dress.

Buttons, Buttons, Buttons

Buttons may be used for function or fashion. They may fasten with buttonholes or loops. The preferred button for heirloom sewing is pearl. Plastic is not acceptable for true heirloom sewing. There are two basic types of buttons: those with shanks and those with two or more holes (Fig. 1). When purchasing pearl buttons, check carefully for smoothness of finish and strong construction. Some antique pearl buttons might have cracks. These won't hold up well. Rough, sharp places anywhere on the button could tear up your buttonholes or the threads attaching the buttons. A weak shank could easily pull out, especially on a boy's button-on pants.

If buttons are used only as decoration, the location of each should be determined and marked by a water-soluble pen, a pencil, or straight pins. If buttons are to be used to fasten the garment, they should be sewed on after the buttonholes to determine proper placement. The opening of the garment should be lapped correctly, and the buttonhole position should be at the outer end of the buttonhole (Fig. 2). The position for all of the buttons should be marked before any of them are sewed on.

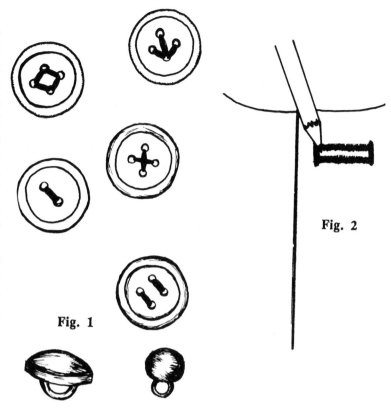

Fig. 2

Fig. 1

Sewing On Buttons

Directions for Button-Stitching Foot:

The method of sewing on buttons varies somewhat with the type of button. Sewing machines usually have a button stitching foot available, which will hold the button flat.
1. You will need to turn off your feed dogs if you are going to sew the button on with this foot.
2. Place a pin on top of the button to create a shank that will allow space for the overlapped layer of fabric to be buttoned (Fig. 3).
3. Carefully turn your zigzag width to the proper width to go in and out the two holes.
4. Turn the fabric slightly when you get ready to go in and out the other two holes — if it is a four-hole button.

To tie off a machine buttonhole, take several stitches in the same hole, after the button is stitched down. You will have to turn off the zigzag when you make this stitch. If you use Scotch tape to hold the button down while you are sewing it on, it won't slip.

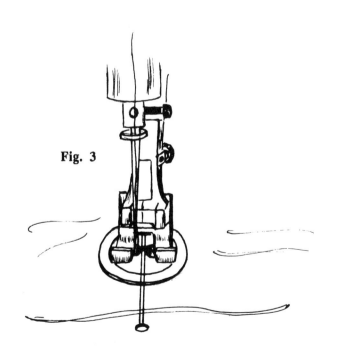

Fig. 3

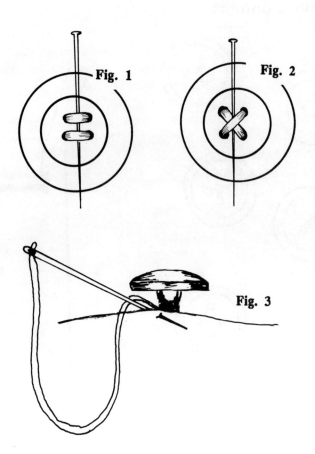

Fig. 1   Fig. 2

Fig. 3

Directions for Attaching Buttons by Hand:

The proper attachment of buttons by hand varies somewhat with the type of button. If the button is a flat button, a shank needs to be made. The shank must be added so that the buttonhole side of the garment may lie flat against the button side of the garment. A heavy single, medium double, or a heavy double thread is satisfactory for sewing on buttons.

1. A small stitch on the right side of the garment, which will be covered by the button, is used to fasten the thread.
2. The needle is passed up through a hole in the button and down through the other hole to the wrong side of the button. At this point a pin or a toothpick is slipped under the stitch.
3. If a two-hole button is used, stitches should be parallel with the buttonhole to prevent it from spreading.
4. The stitching is continued until the button is securely fastened.
5. Bring the needle out between the button and the fabric.
6. The pin is removed and the button pulled to the top of the loop.
7. The thread is then wound around the loose stitches to make a firm shank, and is fastened on the wrong side of the fabric with several small stitches.

Pin Stitching On Your Machine

Pin stitch, also called "Point De Paris," is a delicate, decorative stitch used to attach laces to fabric. With the invention of the computer machines you can make pin stitching in a flash. Ask your sewing machine dealer exactly how to use the wing needle and your sewing machine to make pin stitching. The pin stitch is one reason to consider investing in a top-of-the-line computer machine.

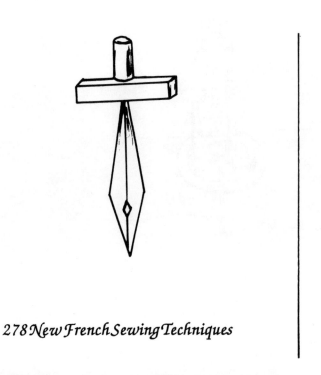

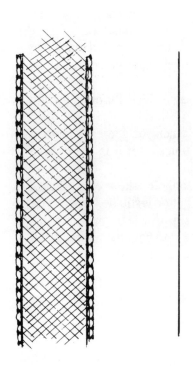

Making Entredeux (Or Hemstitching) On Your Sewing Machine

About eight years ago I was conned into purchasing a 1905 hemstitching machine for $1500. I was told that it made a perfect stitch and even had a sample stitch demonstrated to me by the travelling salesman who brought the machine to my store. I was so excited! I now had a hemstitch machine. Guess how long it lasted before it broke? About two weeks; after that, I had several mechanics work on it, but to no avail. It never sewed more than five yards of hemstitching.

The new computer machines do indeed make hemstitching, which looks much like old-time hemstitching. Instructions for making hemstitching vary according to the make and model of machine. If you are considering purchasing a computer machine, this is one technique you should ask your dealer to demonstrate.

Fabric must be stiffened with spray starch before you begin making machine entredeux. Hemstitching and entredeux work best on an all natural fiber — linen, cotton, silk, or cotton organdy. I don't advise hemstitching a fabric with a high polyester content. Polyester has a memory. If you punch a hole in polyester, it remembers the original positioning of the fibers, and the hole wants to close up.

Use all-cotton thread, 50, 60, or 80 weight. If you have a thread-breaking problem when making entredeux, change to a polyester thread. It doesn't break as easily.

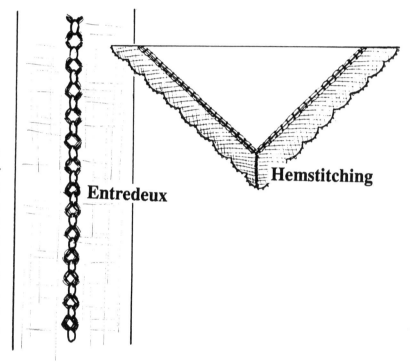

Entredeux

Hemstitching

Two Wonderful Needle Tricks On Machines

1. Needle Position — I could not sew without my needle positions. Your machine should have a center position and several positions to the left and several to the right. I flip the needle so that I don't have to re-guide my presser foot or whatever I am using to guide my fabric. When I am zigzagging entredeux onto lace straight edging, I move my needle position one place toward the entredeux because the bite into the entredeux is wider than the bite into the lace. Then I continue to guide my center mark between the two; the needle goes further left than right, making the needle position just right.

I always use the FAR RIGHT needle position when I am running two rows of gathering stitches at the bottom and top of a sleeve. One is 1/4 inch away from the edge and the other 1/8 inch away. Since my presser foot is exactly 1/4 inch, I guide on the edge of the presser foot. That gives me the inner gathering line. Then, I flip my needle position to FAR RIGHT and use the same presser foot edge to guide my second line of stitching.

2. Needle Down Position
The needle down position means that the needle will stop in the fabric rather than out of the fabric when you stop the sewing machine. Most of the time, when I am doing lace shaping, I use my needle down position. That way, if I have to lift the presser foot to look at my work, I don't have to lower the needle first.

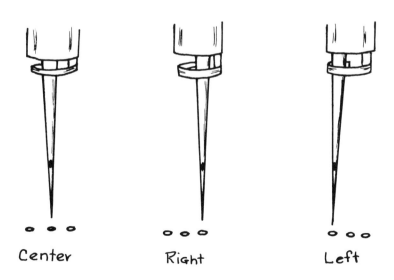

Center   Right   Left

Using Elastic in French Sewing

Elastic can be used in short or long sleeves, waist treatments of dresses, skirts or slips, and the legs of panties, bloomers, or knickers. It allow a better fitting garment while offering ease in movement.

Method I - Self-Fabric Casing

This method is most used in slip tops, bloomers, knicker legs, and panties. If this method is not called for in the pattern, simply extend the edge of the pattern piece about 3/4 inch for this self-fabric casing.

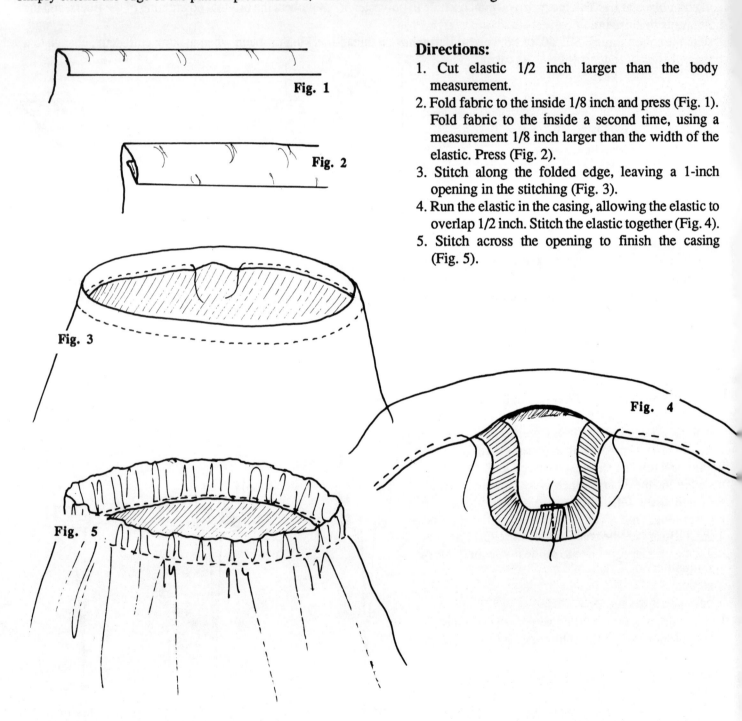

Fig. 1

Fig. 2

Fig. 3

Fig. 4

Fig. 5

Directions:

1. Cut elastic 1/2 inch larger than the body measurement.
2. Fold fabric to the inside 1/8 inch and press (Fig. 1). Fold fabric to the inside a second time, using a measurement 1/8 inch larger than the width of the elastic. Press (Fig. 2).
3. Stitch along the folded edge, leaving a 1-inch opening in the stitching (Fig. 3).
4. Run the elastic in the casing, allowing the elastic to overlap 1/2 inch. Stitch the elastic together (Fig. 4).
5. Stitch across the opening to finish the casing (Fig. 5).

Method II - Lace Insertion Elastic Casing

This method is used in sleeves and waists. I would not suggest using nylon lace for this method because nylon lace does itch, but the better laces that are 100 percent cotton or 90 percent cotton and 10 percent nylon will not itch.

Directions:

1. The length of the elastic should be 1/2 inch more than a loose body measurement.
2. Choose an insertion lace 1/4 inch larger than your elastic.
3. Mark the elastic placement in several places on the wrong side of the sleeve (Fig. 1).
4. If the sleeve has already been stitched into a circle, start the lace casing 1/4 inch from the underarm seam. If the sleeve is still flat, start the casing 1/8 inch from the seam allowance of the underarm seam.
5. Fold the cut edge of the lace to the inside 1/4 inch. Straight-stitch the insertion, along both sides of the headings, to the wrong side of the sleeve, centering the insertion on on the marks.
6. To finish the casing, turn the lace cut edge to the inside, allowing the laces to touch (Fig.2).
7. Run elastic through the casing. Stitch the elastic together allowing 1/2-inch overlap. Baste closed the opening in the casing (Fig. 3).

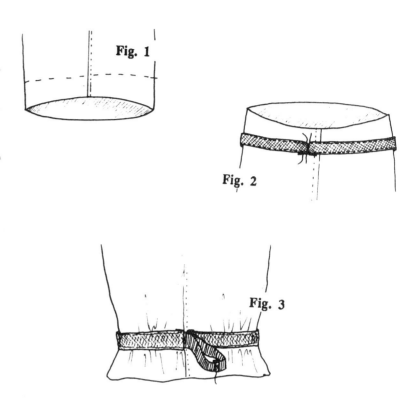

Fig. 1

Fig. 2

Fig. 3

Method III- Zigzagged Casing with Tied Elastic

This method is wonderful for those of you who do not have someone available to measure. It is also my preferred method for hand-me-down dresses. This elastic can be pulled tighter or released to fit each child who wears the garment.

Directions:

1. Cut a piece of 1/8-inch flat elastic, 4 inches larger than the body measurement or a length you know will fit plus 3-4 inches.
2. Mark the elastic placement on the wrong side of the sleeve in several places.
3. Machine setting: zigzag, widest width. Place the elastic on top of the marks. Starting 1/8 inch from the seam allowance, satin-stitch OVER the elastic about 10 stitches. Change the stitch length from satin-stitch to a length of 3 or 4. Continue stitching, stopping 1/8 inch from the seam allowance on the opposite side. Satin-stitch about 10 stitches (Fig.1).
4. Stitch the sleeve in a circle if not already stitched. Pull elastic tabs to fit and tie the ends in a square knot (Fig. 2).
5. Tack the ends of the elastic to the seam allowance (Fig. 3).

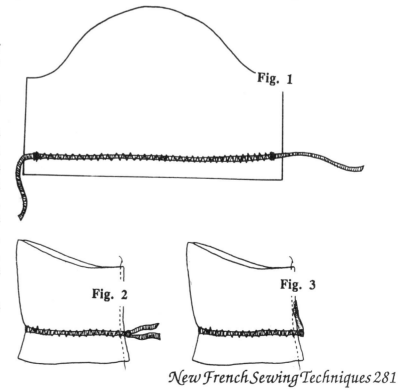

Fig. 1

Fig. 2

Fig. 3

Machine Scallops

Satin-stitch scallops are a standard on most zigzag machines with decorative stitch options. Machine scallops are used to embellish sleeves, collars, insertion pieces, cuffs, and ruffles. They can be used as finishing edges or for decorative embroidery. Scallops can be made to match the fabric, for instance a white scallop on a white christening gown. They can also add just a touch of color as seen on a white dress with a pastel pink scallop. When stitching any decorative satin-stitches I always place adding-machine tape, typing paper, or a water soluble stabilizer under the fabric. This will keep the fabric from puckering. This backing will easily tear away, leaving bits of paper in the scallop that wash out in the first washing.

Machine setting for scallops: The instruction booklet that comes with your machine will list the machine setting and options you have for making the scallops longer, wider, thinner, or fatter.

Single Satin-Stitch Scallops

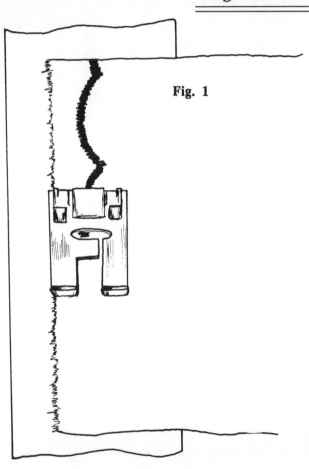

Fig. 1

Directions:
1. Place paper under fabric. Always allow fabric to extend 1/4 inch beyond the edge of the scallop. This will make trimming the scallop easier.
2. Stitch the scallop on the fabric, being careful not to pull or push the fabric under the needle. Let the machine work for you. Pushing and pulling will result in uneven scallops (Fig. 1).
3. Pull paper from the back.
4. Trim the fabric edge away from the scallop, if necessary, using pocket scissors or embroidery scissors (Fig. 2).

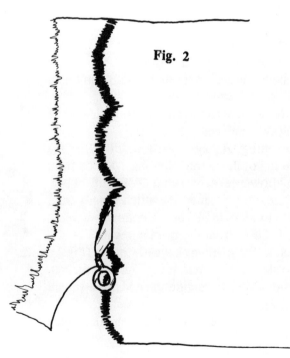

Fig. 2

Corded Machine Scallop

This scallop is perfect on the edges of ruffles and sleeves. Cording a scallop will raise and define the stitch.

Directions:

1. Place paper under fabric. Always allow fabric to extend 1/4 inch beyond the edge of the scallop. This will make trimming the scallop easier.
2. Place a cord or six strands of embroidery floss under the foot of the machine and thread the cord through the thread guide at the top of the needle, or hold the cord or floss by hand in front of the needle (Fig. 1).
3. Take a few stitches, allowing the cord or floss to be enclosed in the satin-stitches. Hold the cord or floss loosely, allowing it to feed into the scallop (Fig. 2). Let the machine work for you. Pushing and pulling will result in uneven scallops.
3. Pull paper from the back.
4. Trim the fabric edge away from the scallop, if necessary, using pocket scissors or embroidery scissors (Fig.3).

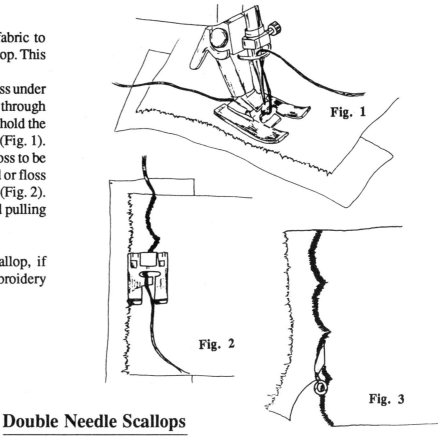

Fig. 1

Fig. 2

Fig. 3

Double Needle Scallops

This technique is used when a two-colored scallop is desired (Fig.1). I used this technique in two shades of pink or blue on baby clothes. I have also used this on Christmas dresses with red and green thread.

Directions:

1. Using a double needle and two spools of threads, thread your machine. Remember to reduce the width of the machine for use with a double needle. If the width is too wide, you will zig and break one needle and zag and break the other. On many of the newer computerized machines there is a double-needle button that when engaged will not exceed the safe width for using the double needle.
2. Follow the directions above for the single-needle scallop.

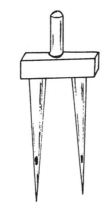

Shadowwork Basics

Chapter Eleven

*Martha's favorite
shadowwork
technique.*

Shadowwork Embroidery

This method, which is my favorite, makes the stitches from the wrong side of the fabric. When the fabric is loaded into the hoop, the wrong side of the garment will be facing out. The design is traced onto that side. The stitches are rather like "sewing" with a bite taken out of the top of the design and a bite taken out of the bottom. The stitch is a closed herringbone stitch. The reason that I personally like this method best is because it is the easiest, I think. Other people prefer working from the front of the finished piece. **Note:** One strand of embroidery floss is usually used in shadowwork embroidery. Needles you will use are #26 Tapestry or #10 Crewel.

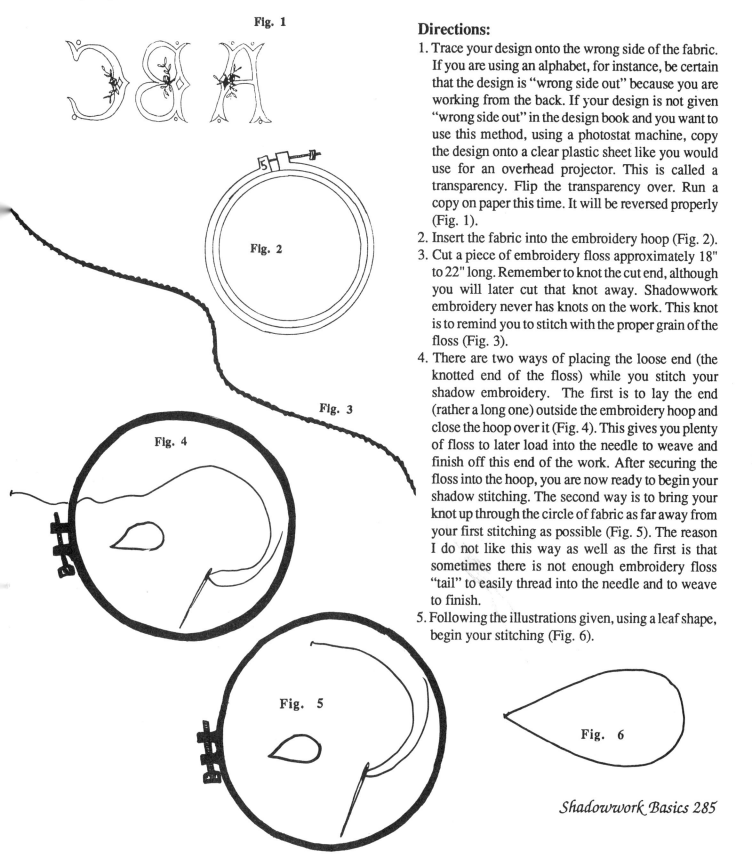

Fig. 1

Fig. 2

Fig. 3

Fig. 4

Fig. 5

Fig. 6

Directions:

1. Trace your design onto the wrong side of the fabric. If you are using an alphabet, for instance, be certain that the design is "wrong side out" because you are working from the back. If your design is not given "wrong side out" in the design book and you want to use this method, using a photostat machine, copy the design onto a clear plastic sheet like you would use for an overhead projector. This is called a transparency. Flip the transparency over. Run a copy on paper this time. It will be reversed properly (Fig. 1).

2. Insert the fabric into the embroidery hoop (Fig. 2).

3. Cut a piece of embroidery floss approximately 18" to 22" long. Remember to knot the cut end, although you will later cut that knot away. Shadowwork embroidery never has knots on the work. This knot is to remind you to stitch with the proper grain of the floss (Fig. 3).

4. There are two ways of placing the loose end (the knotted end of the floss) while you stitch your shadow embroidery. The first is to lay the end (rather a long one) outside the embroidery hoop and close the hoop over it (Fig. 4). This gives you plenty of floss to later load into the needle to weave and finish off this end of the work. After securing the floss into the hoop, you are now ready to begin your shadow stitching. The second way is to bring your knot up through the circle of fabric as far away from your first stitching as possible (Fig. 5). The reason I do not like this way as well as the first is that sometimes there is not enough embroidery floss "tail" to easily thread into the needle and to weave to finish.

5. Following the illustrations given, using a leaf shape, begin your stitching (Fig. 6).

6. With thread below the needle, (Fig. 7 and 8) bring your needle down at (A) and up at (B). Pull through.

7. Move down. Thread above the needle, put your needle down at (C) and up at (B) Fig. 9. Move into the exact same hole as your needle made on the first bite at (B).

8. Thread below the needle, bring your needle down at (D) and up at (A). Fig. 10.

9. Thread above the needle, bring your needle down at (E) and up at (C). Fig. 11.

10. When you come to a large curve, make your outside stitches (on the largest part of the curve) larger. Make the inside stitches closer together. You may sometimes find it necessary to go in one hole twice on the inside area (Fig. 12).

11. Keep turning your work so that the portion of stitching you are currently working on is horizontally in front of you and so that you are working left to right. This means that sometimes you will have the design upside down; however, just keep the section you are working on just like you would read the lines on a book. Horizontal and left to right (Fig. 13).

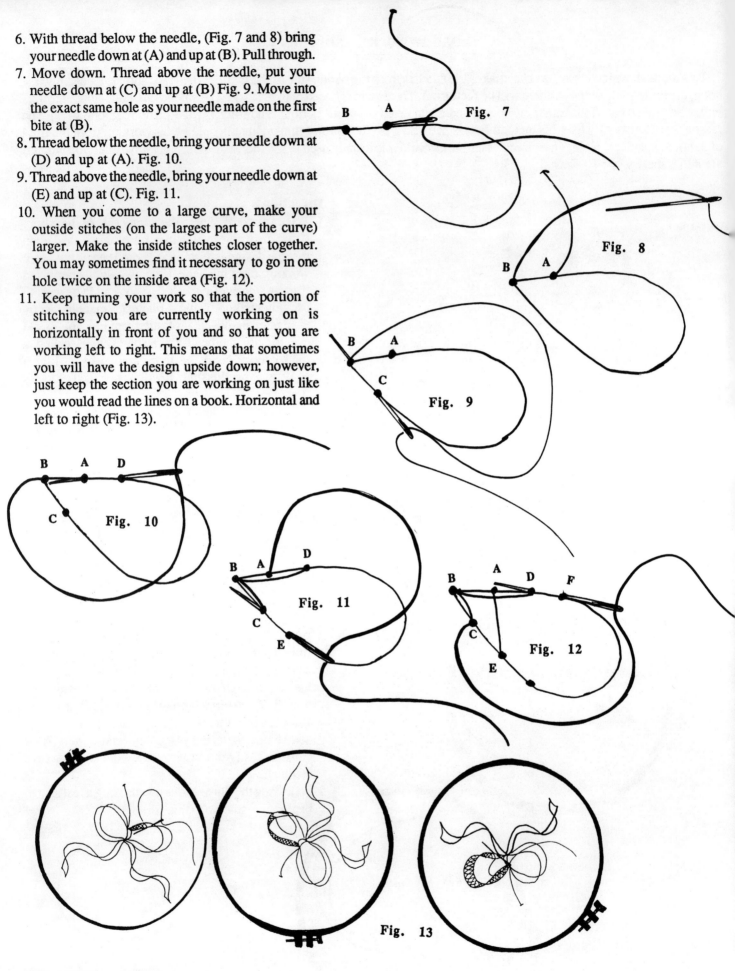

Fig. 7

Fig. 8

Fig. 9

Fig. 10

Fig. 11

Fig. 12

Fig. 13

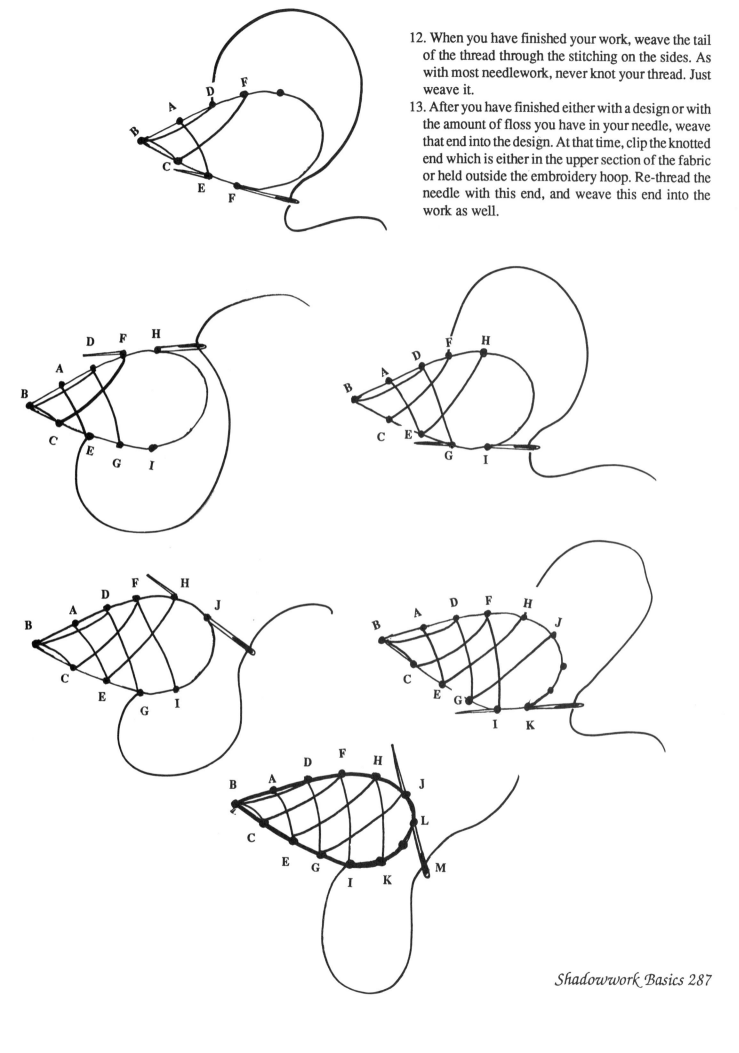

12. When you have finished your work, weave the tail of the thread through the stitching on the sides. As with most needlework, never knot your thread. Just weave it.

13. After you have finished either with a design or with the amount of floss you have in your needle, weave that end into the design. At that time, clip the knotted end which is either in the upper section of the fabric or held outside the embroidery hoop. Re-thread the needle with this end, and weave this end into the work as well.

Shadowwork Basics 287

Antique Adaptations Shadowwork Alphabets

How do you make an antique-looking shadowwork alphabet? This question was posed to Cynthia Handy and the research began. We wanted ribbons, a turn-of-the-century look and lily- of-the-valley. Her decision was to make three alphabets, which could be intertwined with each other for a Victorian look. You will notice that there is a tall alphabet and a shorter alphabet; use the letters together or separately. The lily-of-the-valley alphabet can be used with the shorter alphabet or by itself.

Angela Cataldo designed four flower combinations in shadowwork, which can be drafted to use in conjunction with Cynthia's alphabet. For the lovely white dress, pictured in the color section of this book, Margaret used two of the alphabets. She took sections of embroidery from the loops of lace designs and spaced the designs around the collar. Be creative with your shadowwork designing. Don't hesitate to cut a flower from one design, leaves from another, and curves from another.

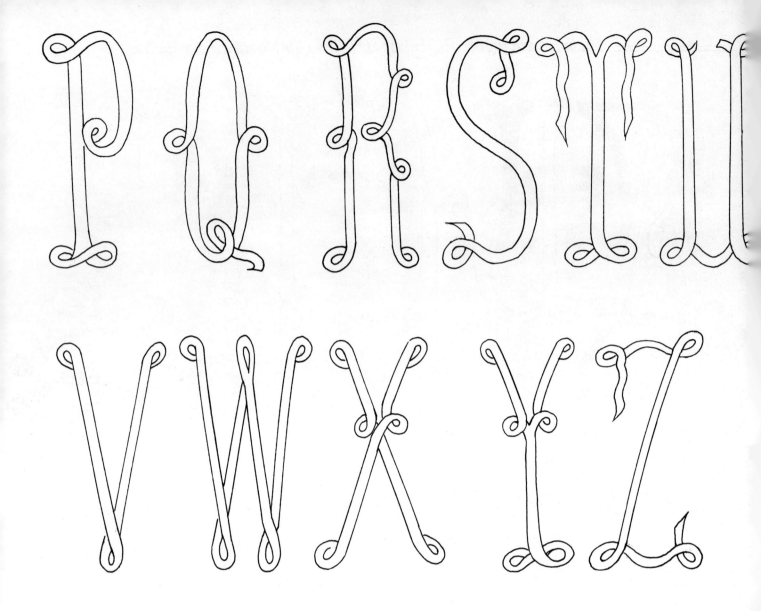

ABC

DEFG

HIJK

LMNO

P Q R S T U L W X Y Z

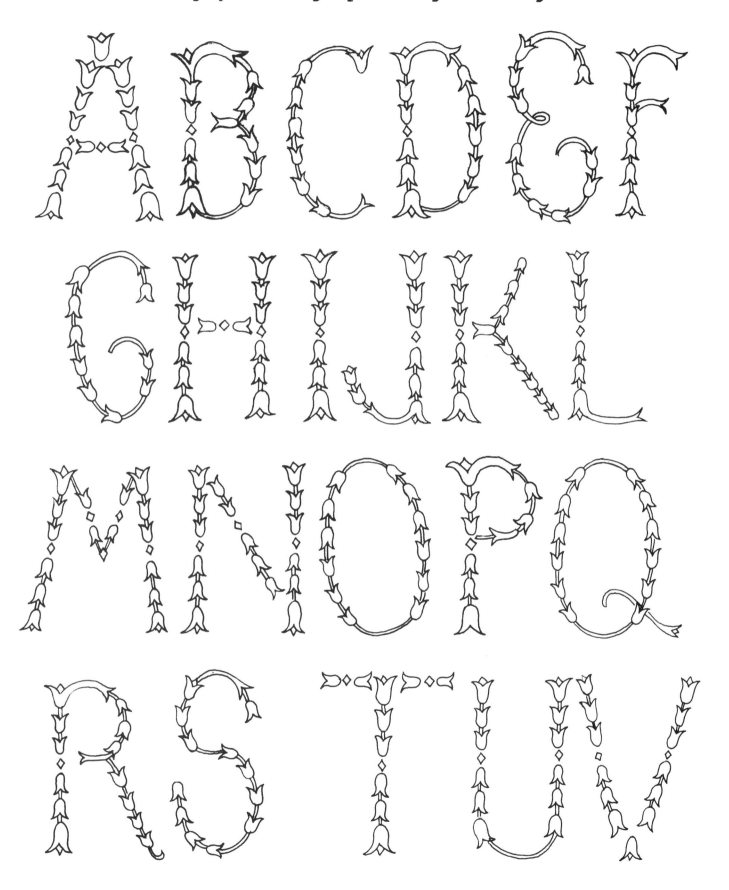

Index

About the Author

Martha Campbell Pullen, a native of Scottsboro, Alabama, is an internationally-known lecturer and author. After graduating with a degree in speech and English from the University of Alabama, she taught those subjects at almost every level of middle school and high school. Later, her studies led to receiving a Ph.D. in educational administration and management from the University of Alabama. She has served on the faculties of the University of Florida and Athens State College. She was director of development for the University of Alabama in Huntsville. She completed post doctoral studies at Vanderbilt University, the University of Alabama in Huntsville, and Alabama A and M University.

Her love of sewing and children's heirloom clothing encouraged the opening of Martha Pullen's Heirloom Shop in Huntsville, Alabama, August 1, 1981. Two months later, she opened Martha Pullen Co, the wholesale division. She has served on the board of directors of the Smocking Arts Guild of America and has presented workshops on French sewing by machine throughout the United States, Australia, and New Zealand. She imports laces from France and England; Swiss batiste and embroideries from Switzerland. She has written books: *French Hand Sewing By Machine: A Beginner's Guide, Heirloom Doll Clothes, Bearly Beginning Smocking, Shadow Work Embroidery, French Hand Sewing By Machine, The Second Book,* and *Antique Clothing: French Sewing By Machine.* She has designed and published many garment patterns.

She conducts the Martha Pullen School of Art Fashion twice a year in Huntsville, Alabama. People come from all over the world for a fabulous five days of sewing, fellowship, food, and fun. Once a year, she teaches this same school in Australia and in New Zealand. Classes are planned for students who know absolutely nothing about French sewing and smocking to those who are already experts and who want more mastery!

She is the founder and publisher of a best-selling magazine, *Sew Beautiful,* which is dedicated to heirloom sewing. The publication charms over 73,000 readers worldwide. She loves people so much and wishes, "that I could travel home with everybody who buys this book and get to know them personally. We could have so much fun talking about antique clothing, sewing, and our families."

She is the wife of Joseph Ross Pullen, an implant dentist. She is the mother of five of the most wonderful children in the world. She participates in many civic activities and is an active member of her church.

Notes

Notes